ZOFIA KULIK:
METHODOLOGY, MY LOVE

Kulik
KwieKulik
Foundation
Publication partner

BOOKS
N°17
The MUSEUM UNDER CONSTRUCTION book series
We are building a Museum of Modern Art in Warsaw
We are writing a new history of art

ZOFIA KULIK: METHODOLOGY, MY LOVE

EDITED BY
AGATA JAKUBOWSKA

MUSEUM OF MODERN ART
IN WARSAW 2019

BOOKS
N°17

Zofia Kulik says that she has a double artistic biography. Between 1970 and 1987 she formed a duo with Przemysław Kwiek called KwieKulik; after its collapse she began to develop her individual career intensively and successfully. While KwieKulik's activity is well documented and researched—an extensive monograph was issued in 2012[1]—Kulik's individual work has not to date been the subject of a comprehensive publication. Her work is by no means closed, so it is too early for a catalogue raisonné; however, it is high time to take a careful, in-depth look at this highly valued, but paradoxically little studied œuvre.

Kulik's words that appear in this book's title—"Methodology, My Love"—come from an interview that Hans Ulrich Obrist conducted with the artist during his visit to her home in Łomianki near Warsaw in 1999.[2] During their meeting, Kulik passionately explained to him different aspects of her complicated working methods, and concluded by admitting that: "I would like very much to make an exhibition entitled *Methodology, My Love*." Such a show has not yet been organized, but this book provides the opportunity to go beyond the attractive visuality of Kulik's works. They are spectacular designs that fascinate viewers, who often remain unaware of what lies behind them: the enormous image archive, collections of various things, storage items (sometimes specially designed), but also long-elaborated and still-developing practices of transforming the assembly of single images into complex visual structures. The essays gathered in this book offer insights, from different perspectives, into this dimension of Kulik's artistic practice.

This book also tries to capture and analyze the most significant stages in Zofia Kulik's rich artistic biography. One of its important subjects is therefore a woman artist's quest for emancipation, naturally intertwined with changes in her private life, but also with transformations of the social and political situation in Poland.

1 Łukasz Ronduda and Georg Schöllhammer, eds., *KwieKulik: Zofia Kulik & Przemysław Kwiek* (Warsaw: Museum of Modern Art in Warsaw and KwieKulik Archive; Wrocław: BWA Wrocław Galleries of Contemporary Art, Awangarda Gallery; Vienna: Kontakt: The Art Collection of Erste Group and ERSTE Foundation, 2012).

2 The transcript of the interview is in Kulik's archive.

These issues in particular are elaborated on by Angela Dimitrakaki and Wiktoria Szczupacka. Those authors obviously deal with Kulik's works created in the period after 1987, following the breakup of the KwieKulik duo, when her career flourished and her well-known pieces, such as *All the Missiles Are One Missile* (1993) and *From Siberia to Cyberia* (1998–2004), were produced. Yet they devote as much attention to works that have yet to attract the attention they deserve from art writers: pieces from the student years; from the time when Kulik was a member of KwieKulik (she also produced some solo works then); and from the later period of her artistic activities—the latter of which are the main subject of focus in the essays written by Anna Kałuża and by myself. What emerges from the texts published in this volume is a picture of artistic creativity in which we encounter great consistency and the continuity of certain problems (recurring images, themes, and schemas) taken up over the course of several decades. This is particularly visible in the texts that cover Kulik's artistic life as a whole and attempt to indicate specific, constant traits of her work, by Tomasz Załuski, Dorota Łuczak, and Katarzyna Ruchel-Stockmans.

Zofia Kulik's individual practice quickly attracted attention from both critics and curators. Since 1989 her works have been exhibited at numerous solo and group shows, both in Poland and abroad. The reception of her art became dominated by her ability to suggestively capture, in an attractive and vivid form, the experience of totalitarianism. We have decided to reprint two texts that first appeared in the 1990s—essays written by Ewa Lajer-Burcharth and Sarah C. Wilson—to recall the ways in which Kulik's art was framed in that decade. One of the aims of this book, however, is to enrich the image of Kulik's œuvre by offering a discussion of works and topics that are not directly related to the (post-)communist condition. For that reason the abovementioned texts are juxtaposed here with three essays—by Edit András, Suzana Milevska, and Michał Murawski—that present political aspects of her works from today's perspective and in relation to today's political tensions.

Kulik regularly prepares exhibitions of her individual work and of that undertaken by KwieKulik. KwieKulik's activity has not disappeared from the field of her artistic practice—for many years she has maintained the KwieKulik Archive, which was acquired by the Museum of Modern Art in Warsaw in 2011, and prepared its authorial presentations, which are explored in Luiza Nader's essay. At present she is working on its permanent exposition in the form of an installation that will open, along with the Museum's new building, in 2023.

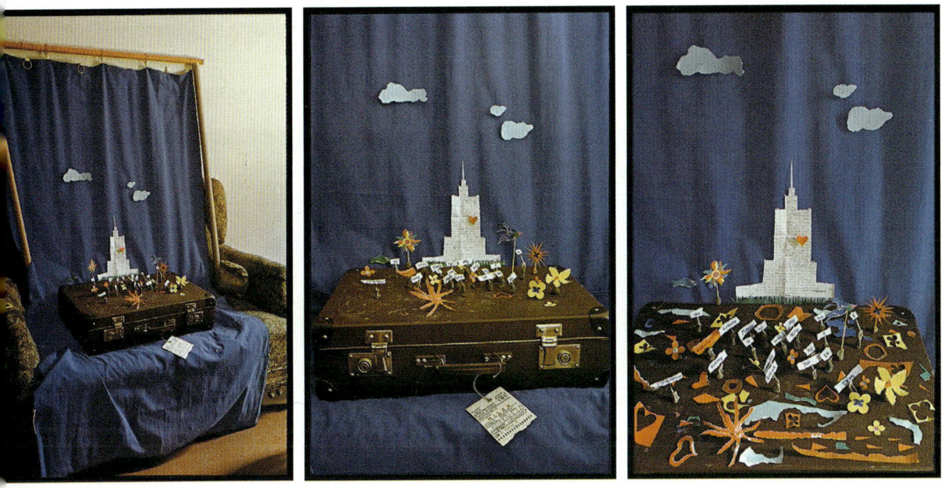

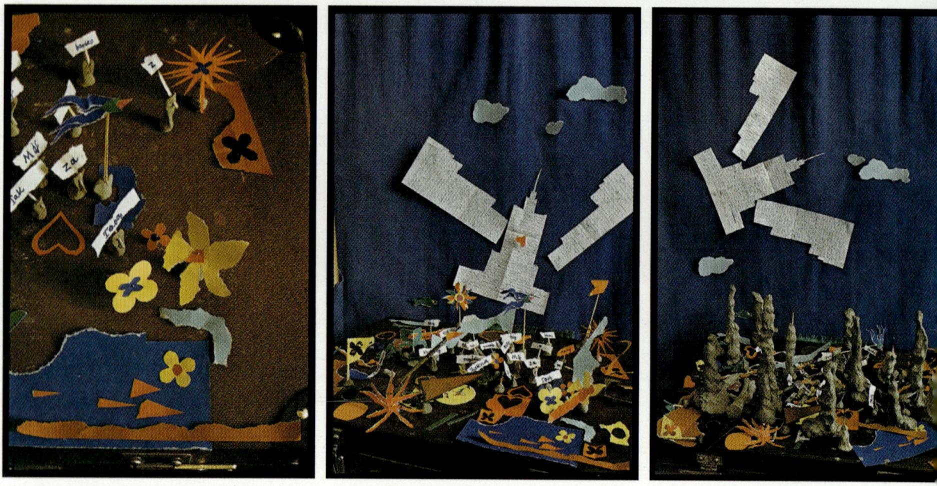

LETTER FROM MILAN (DETAILS), 1972

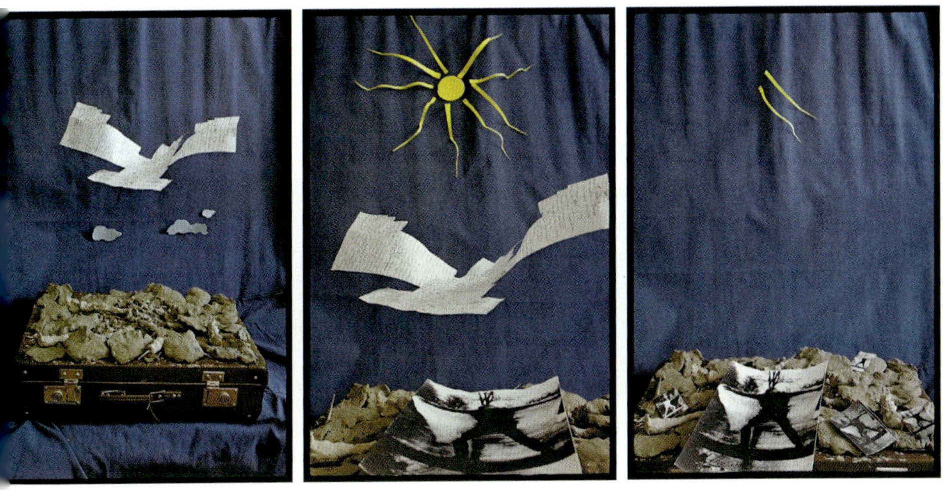

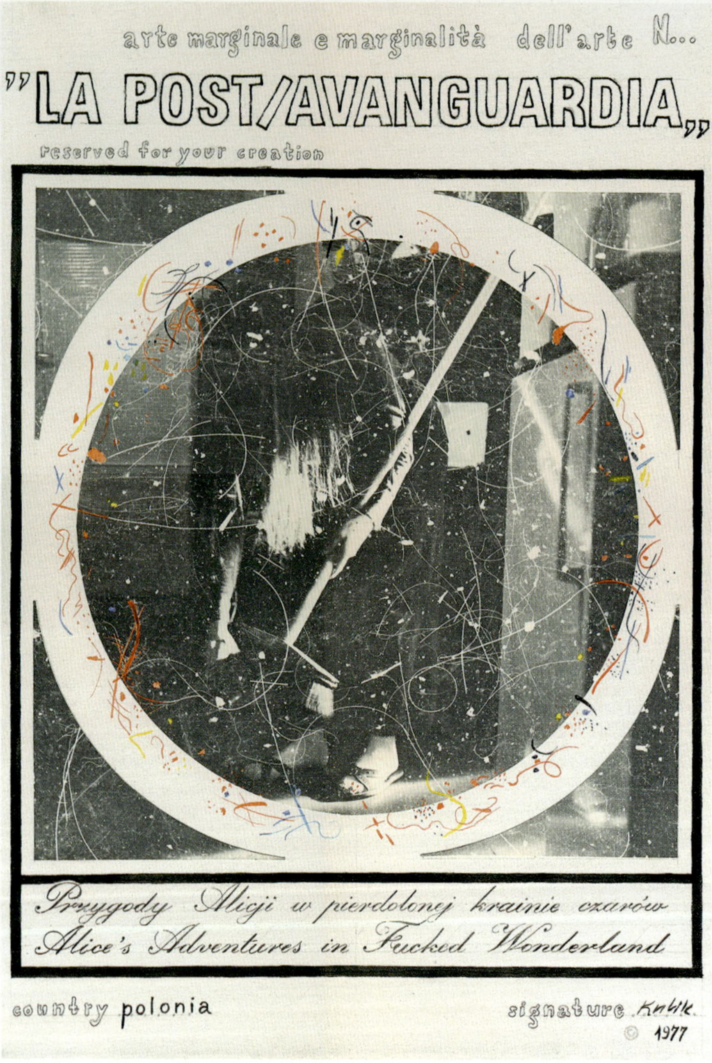
arte marginale e marginalità dell'arte N...
"LA POST/AVANGUARDIA"
reserved for your creation
Przygody Alicji w pierdolonej krainie czarów
Alice's Adventures in Fucked Wonderland
country polonia
signature Kulik
© 1977

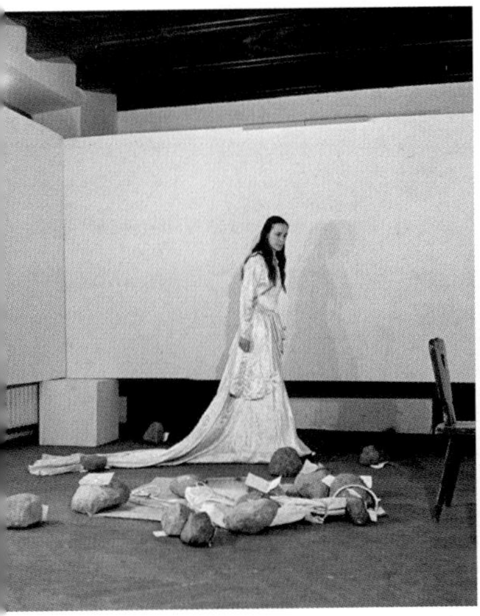

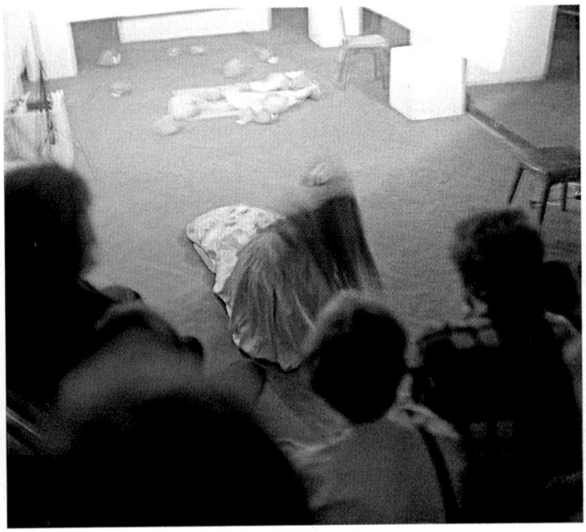

ARCHIVE OF GESTURES (DETAILS), 1987–91

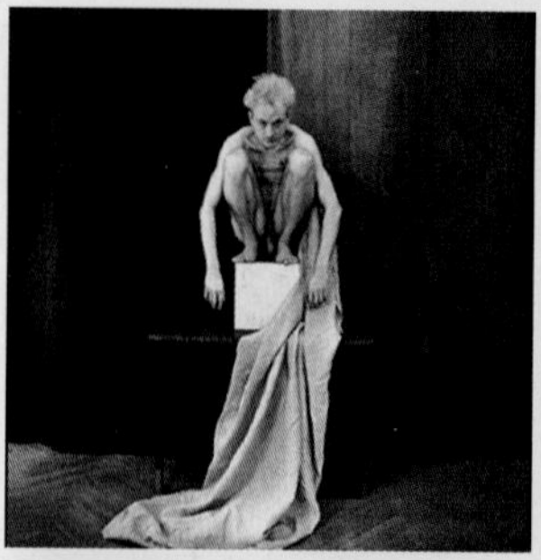
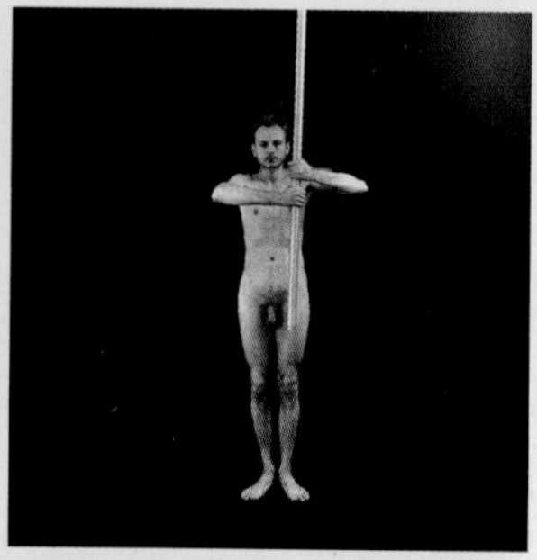
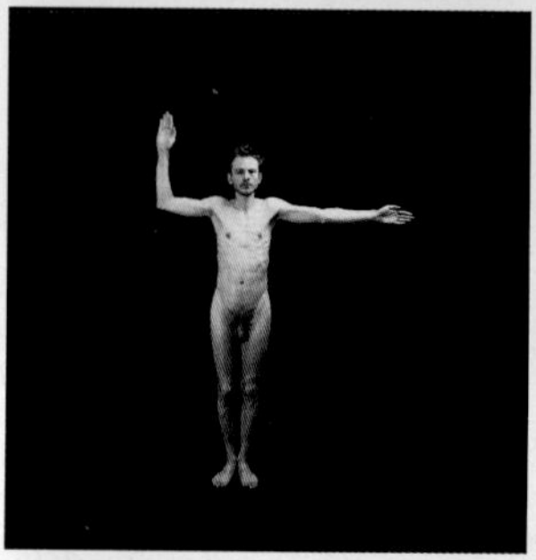
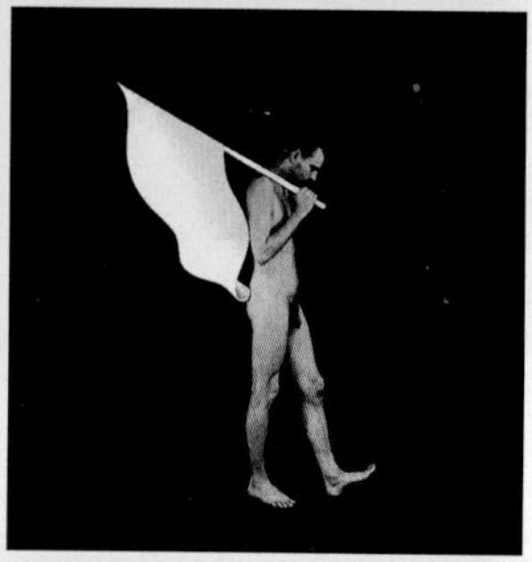
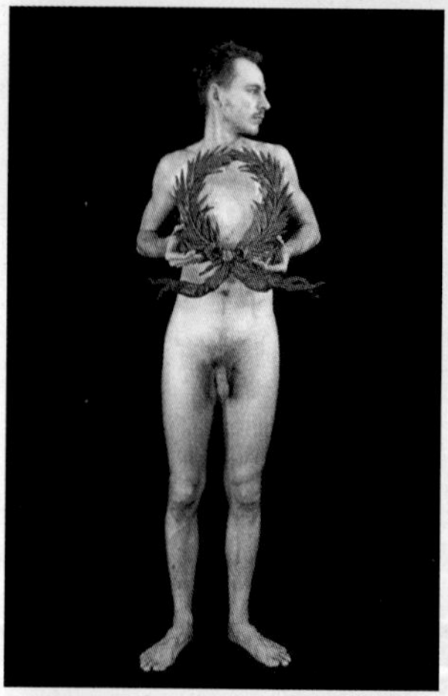
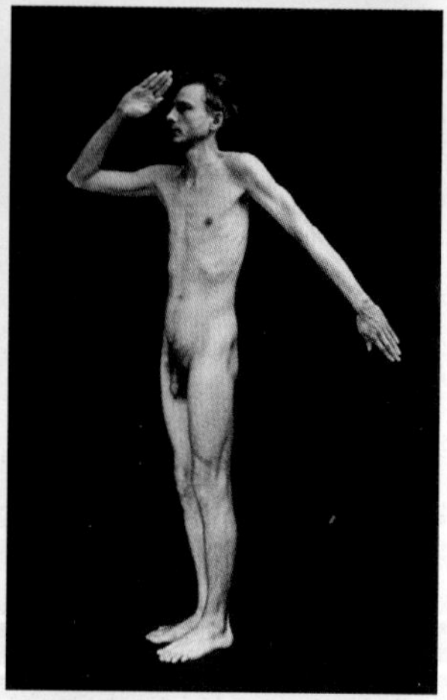
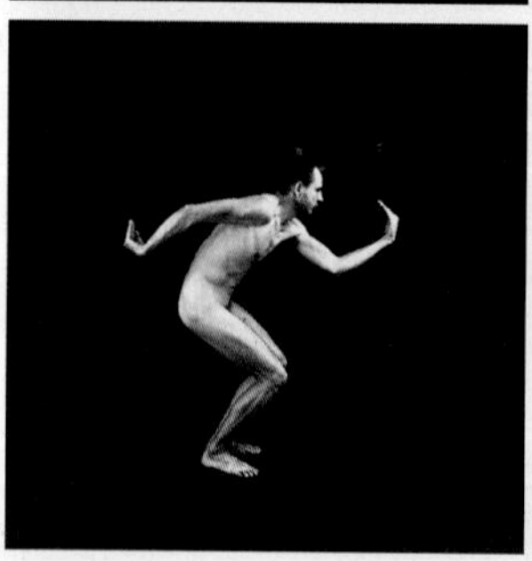
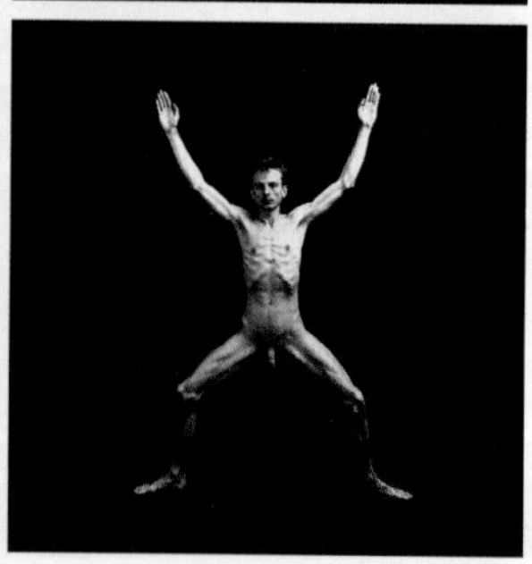

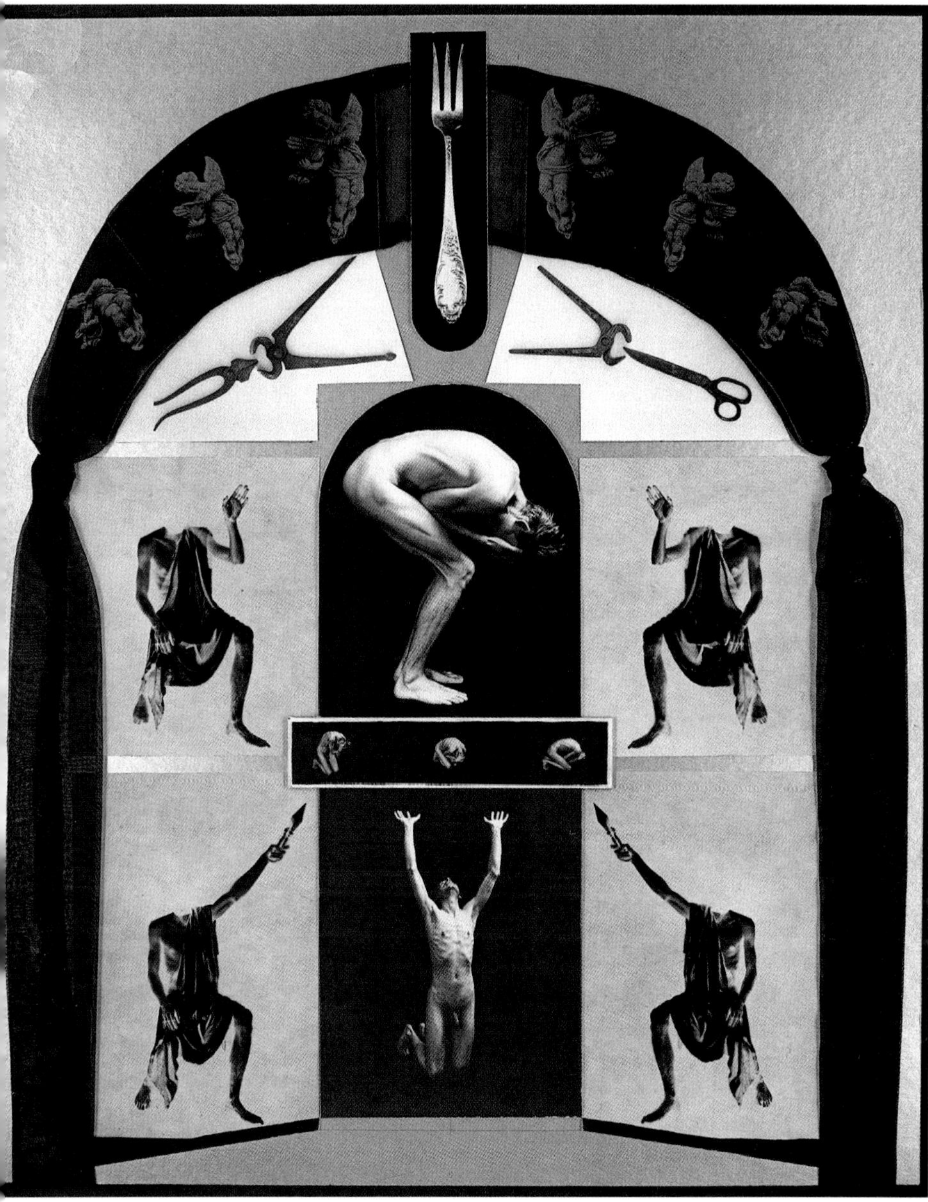

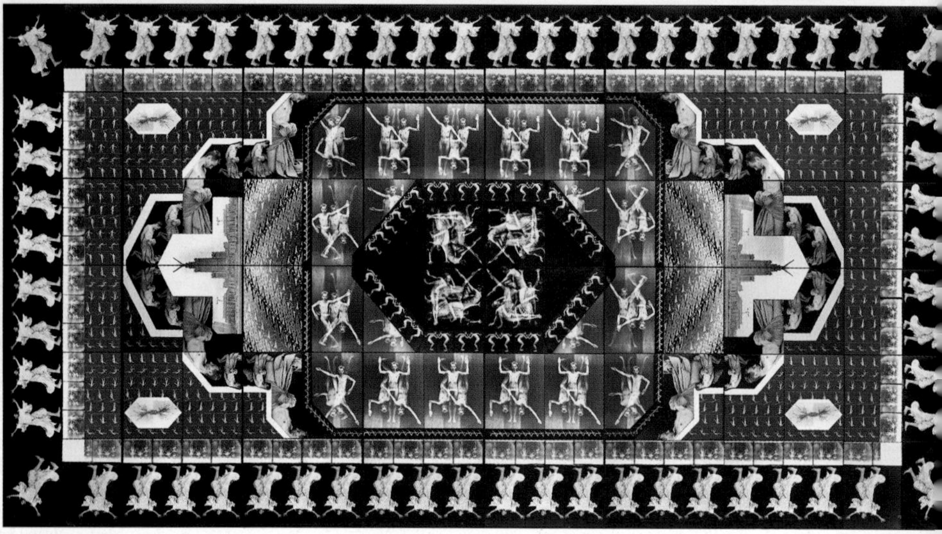

HUMAN MOTIF I (DETAIL), 1989

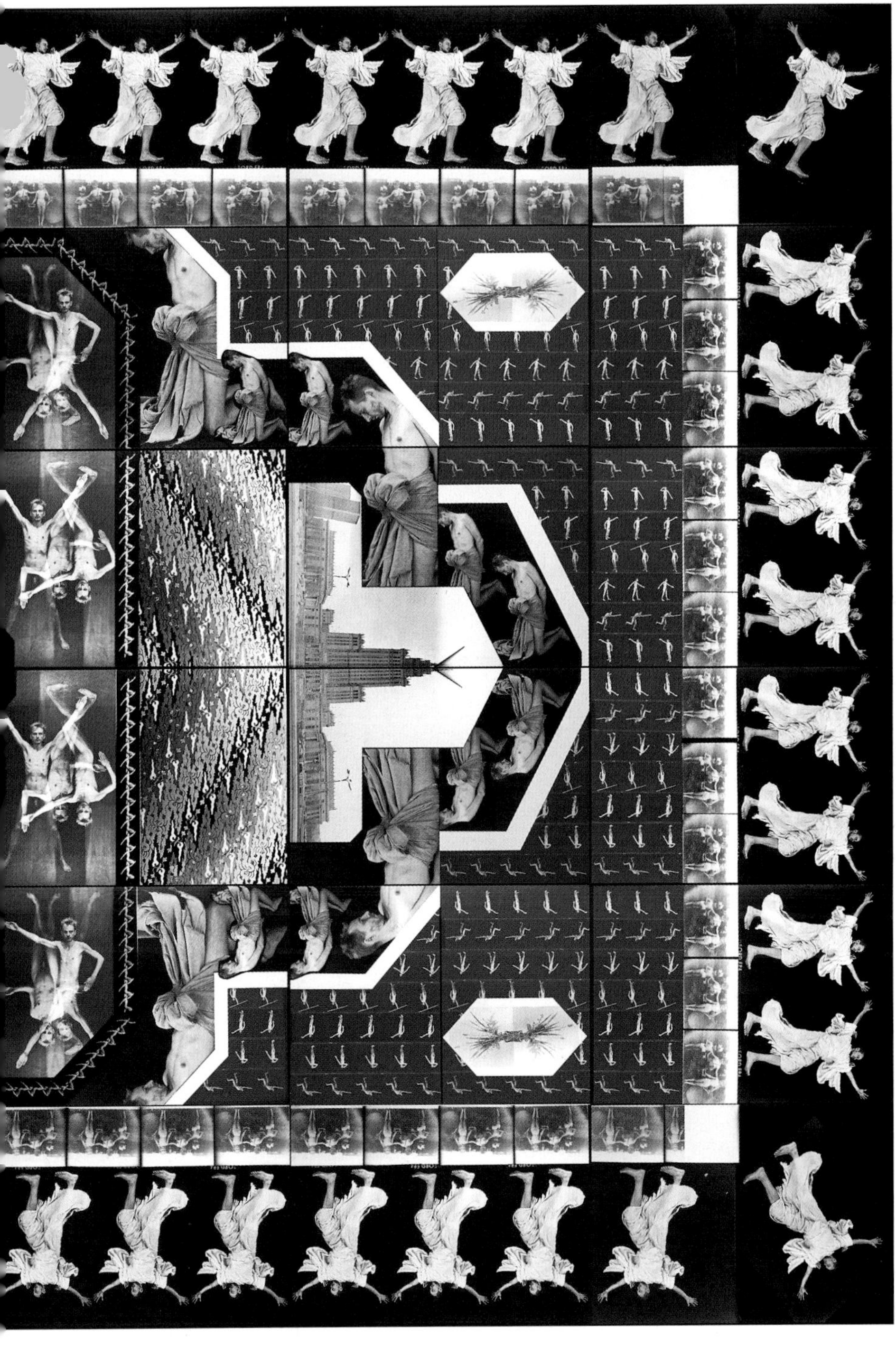

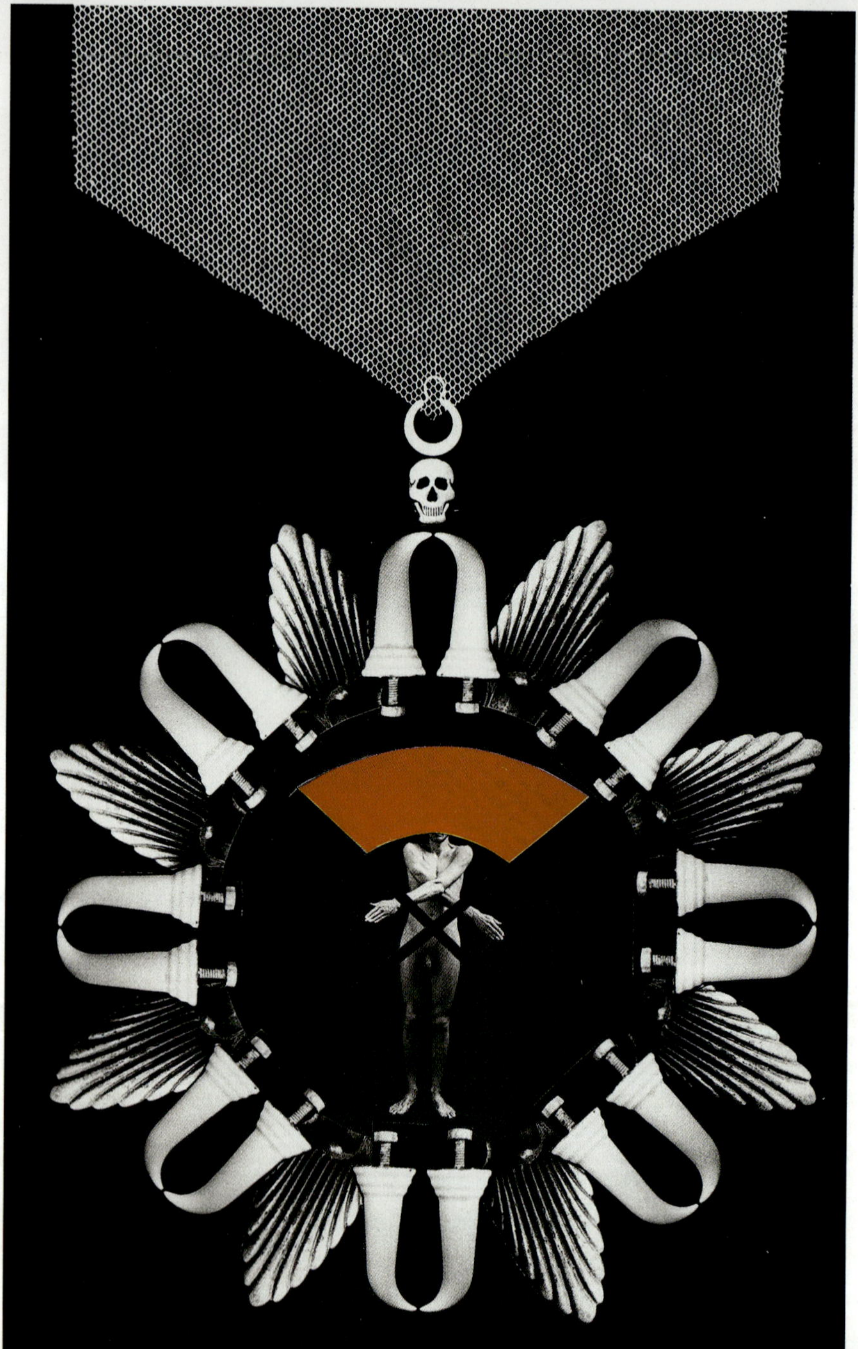

25 **MONUMENT I, 1989**

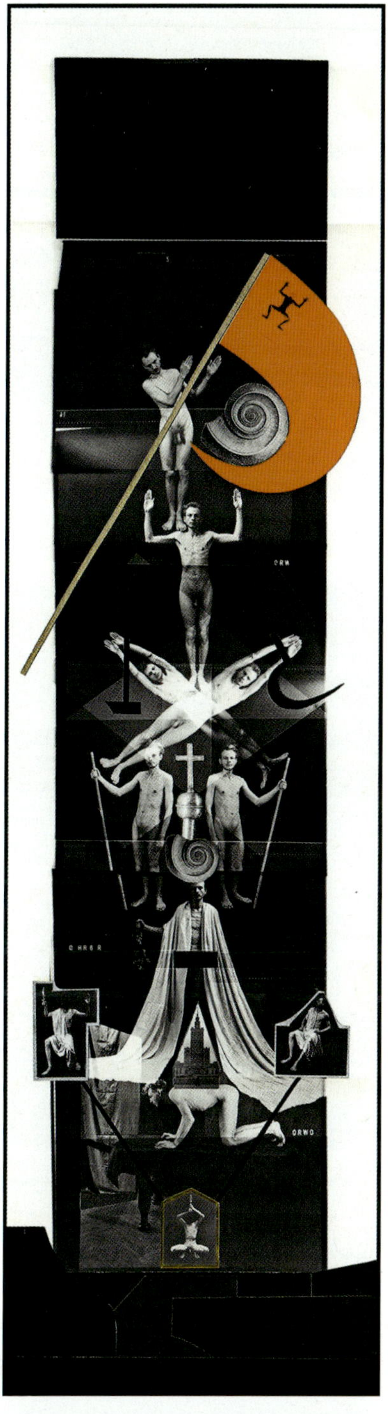

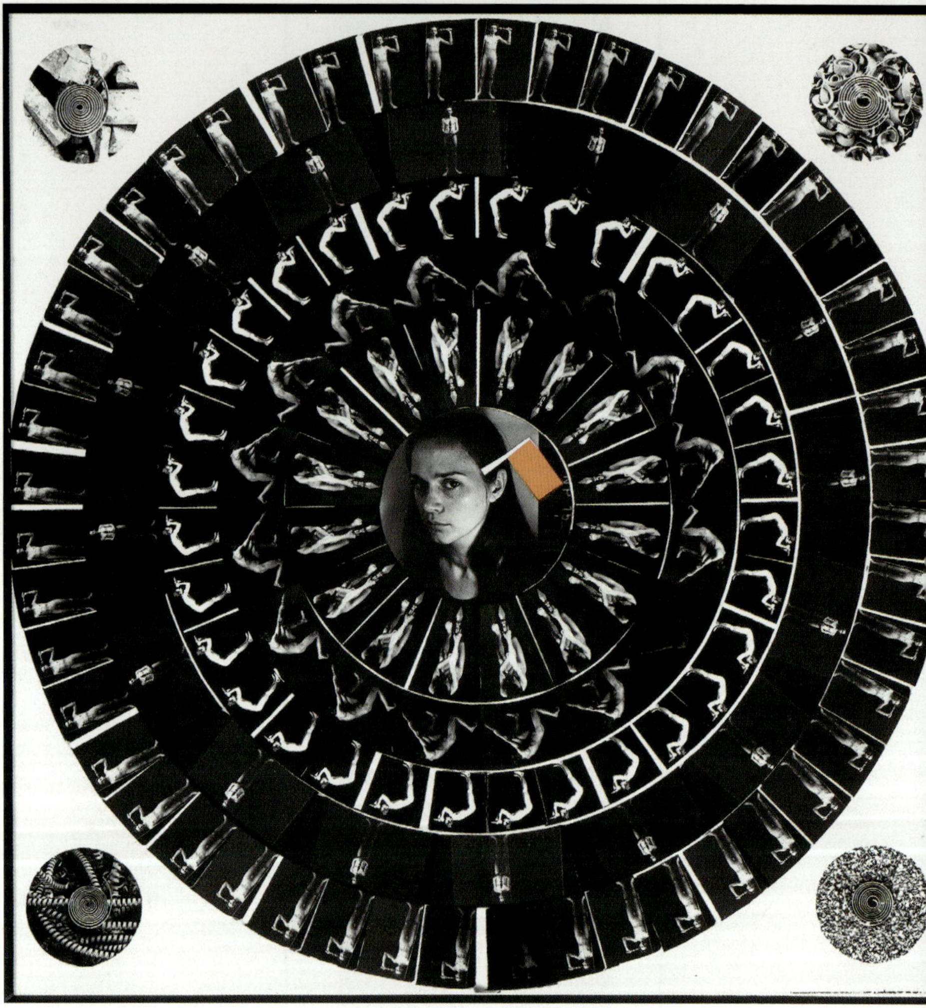

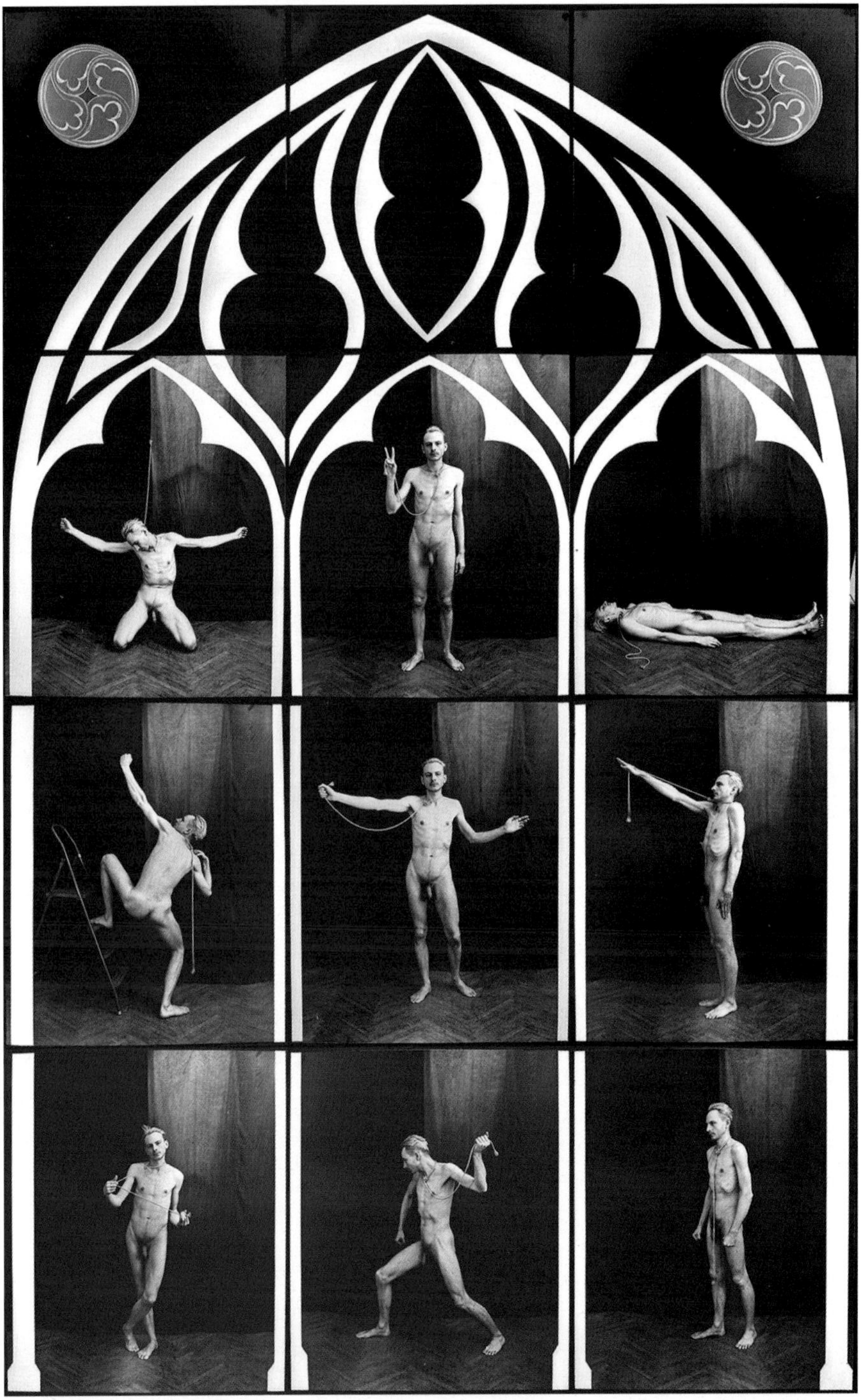

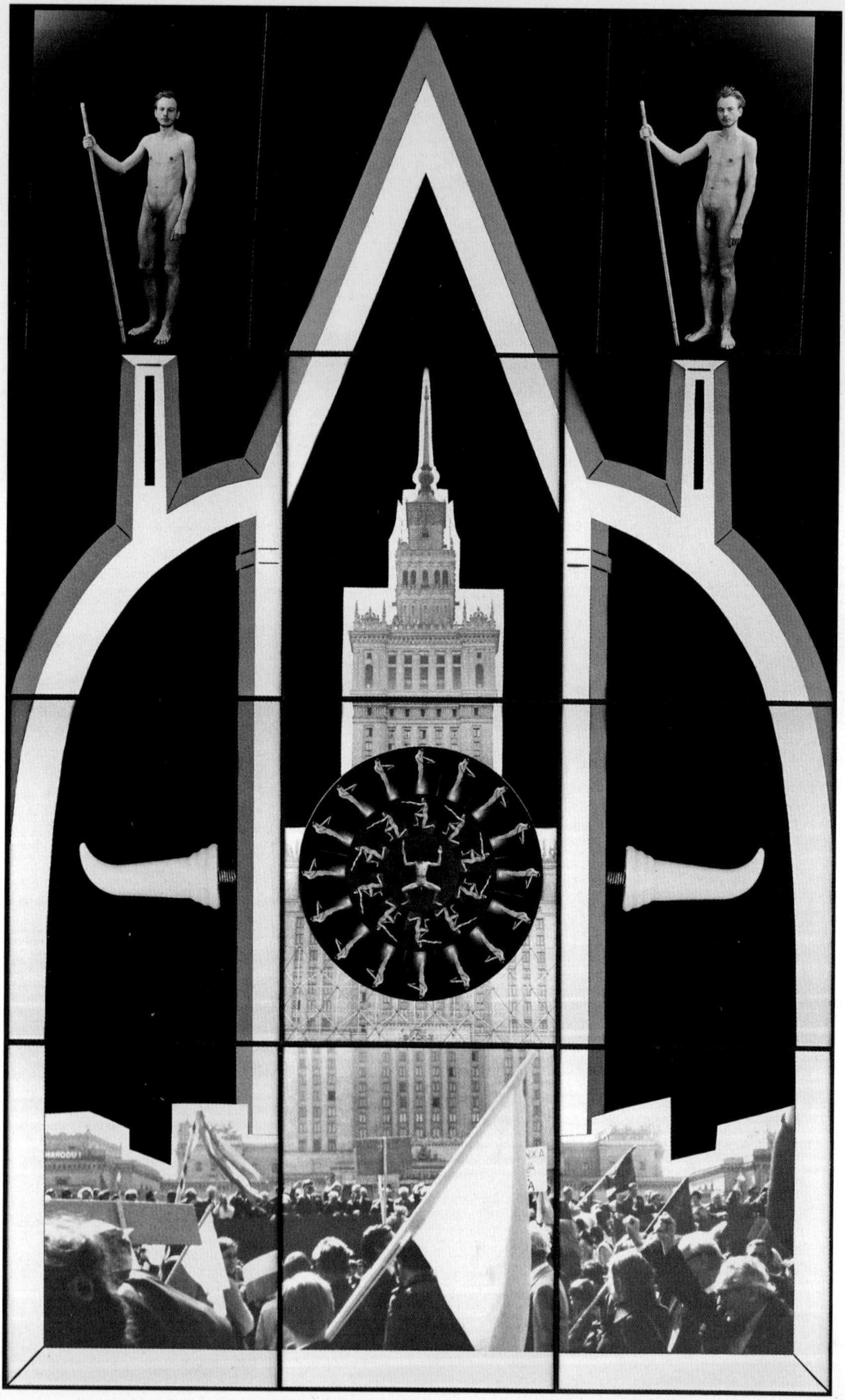
NARODU!

PART I

ZOFIA KULIK SELECTED WORKS

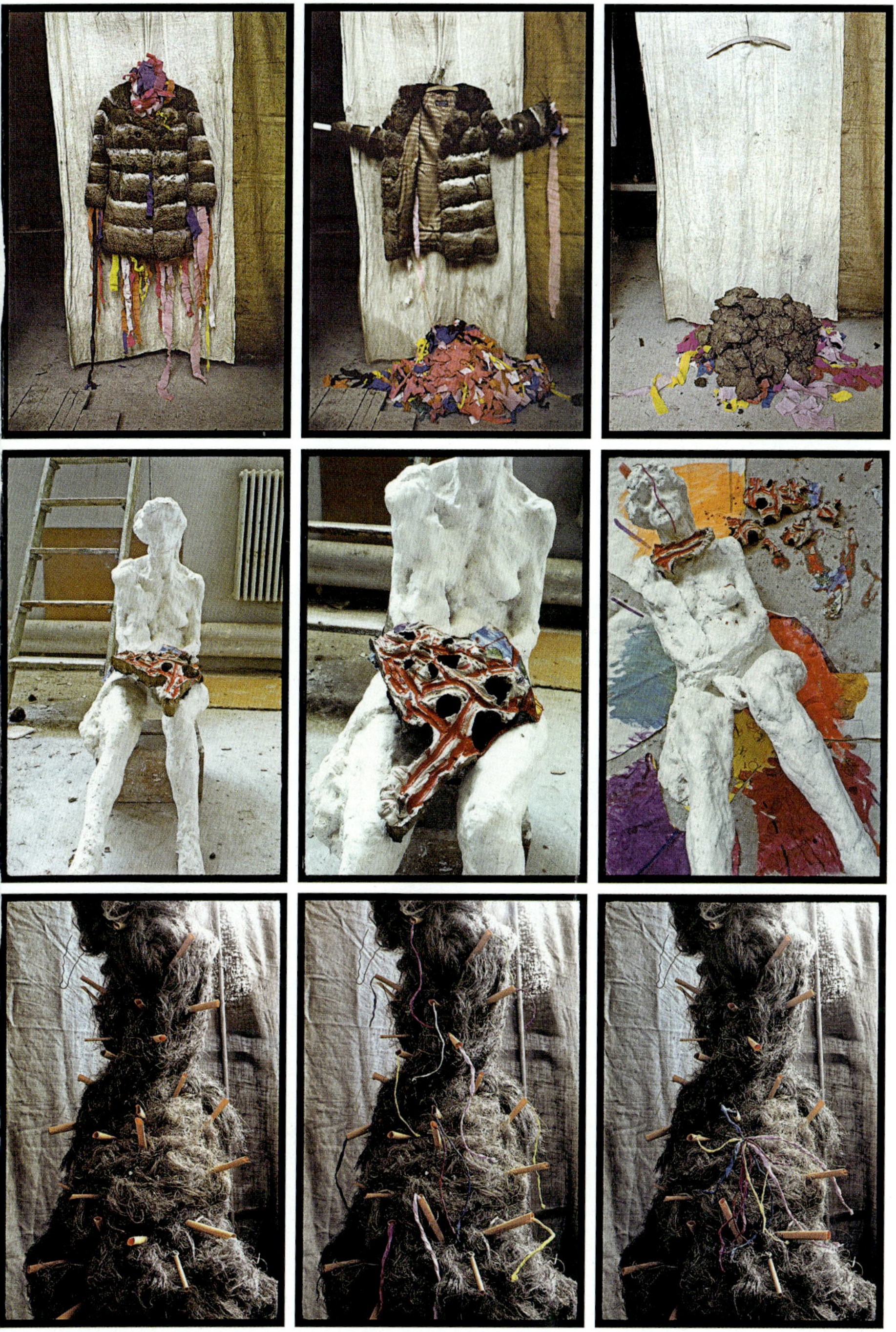

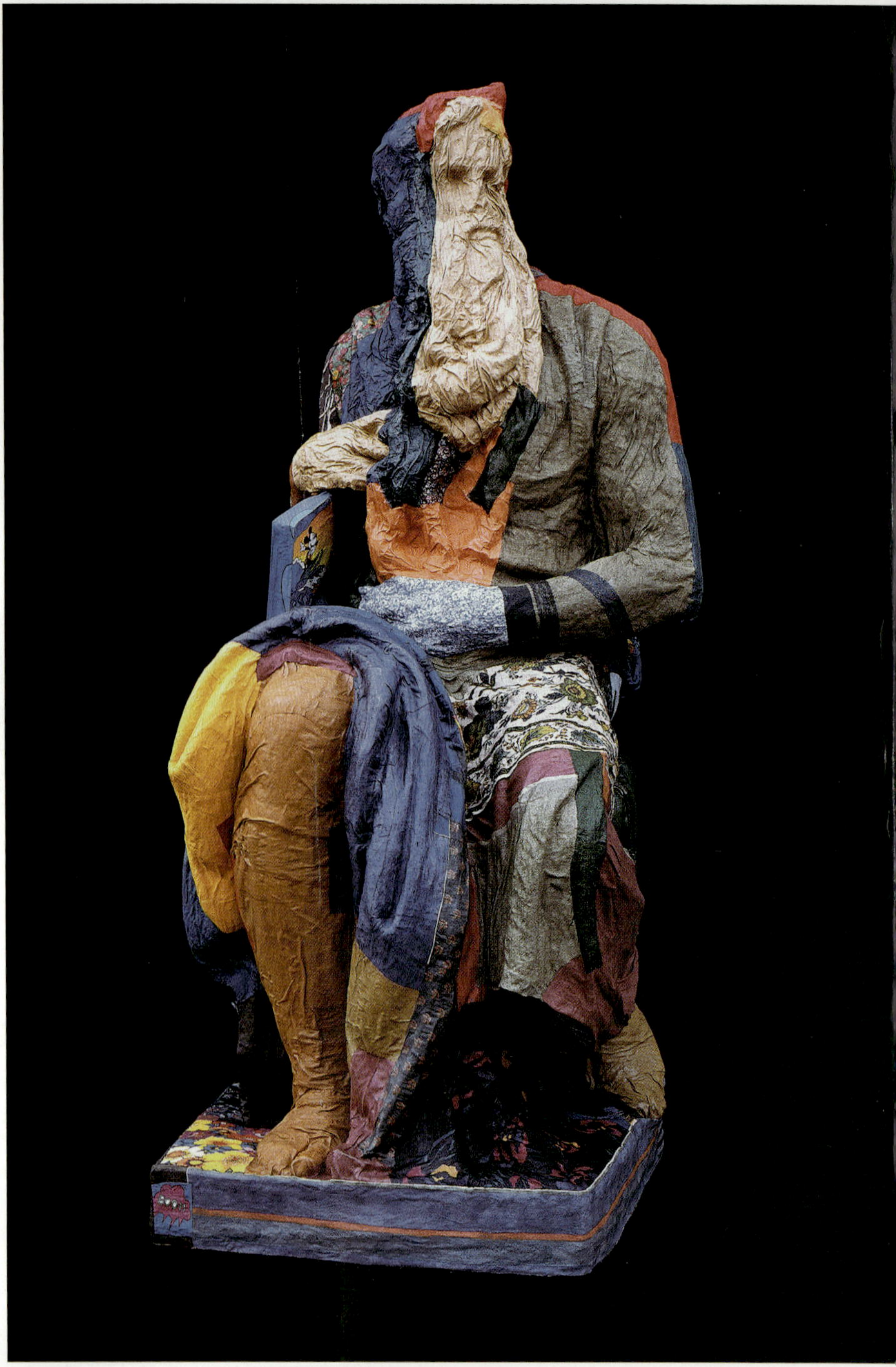

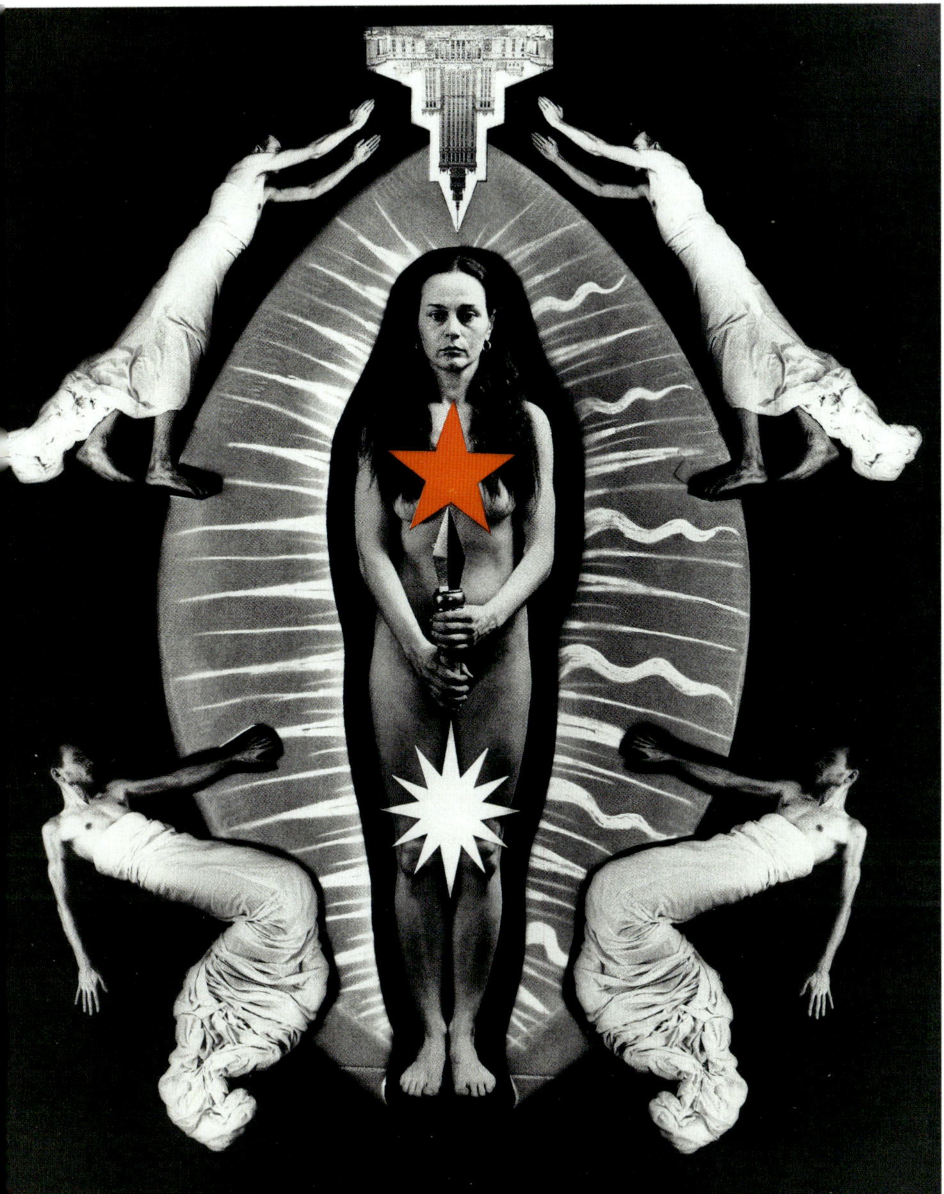

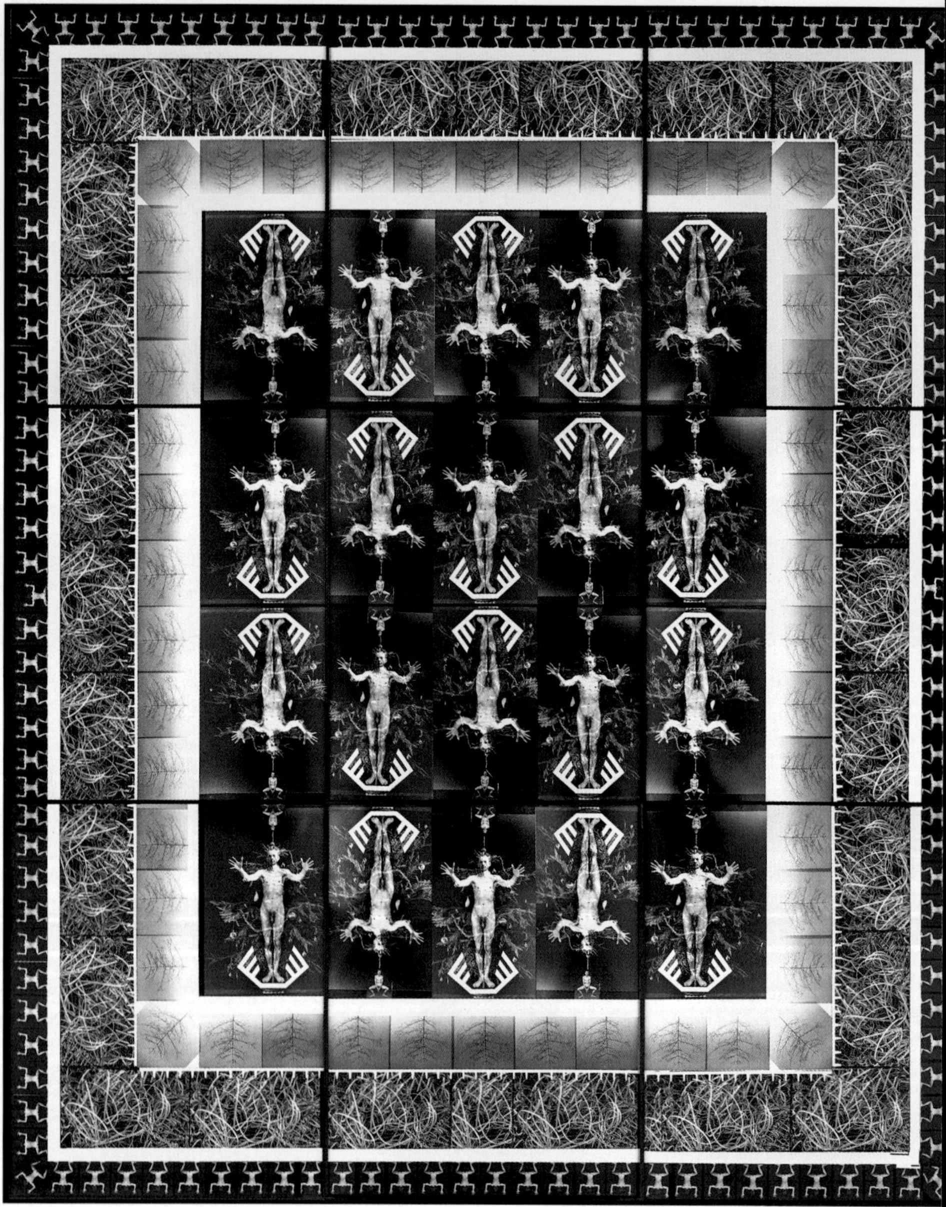

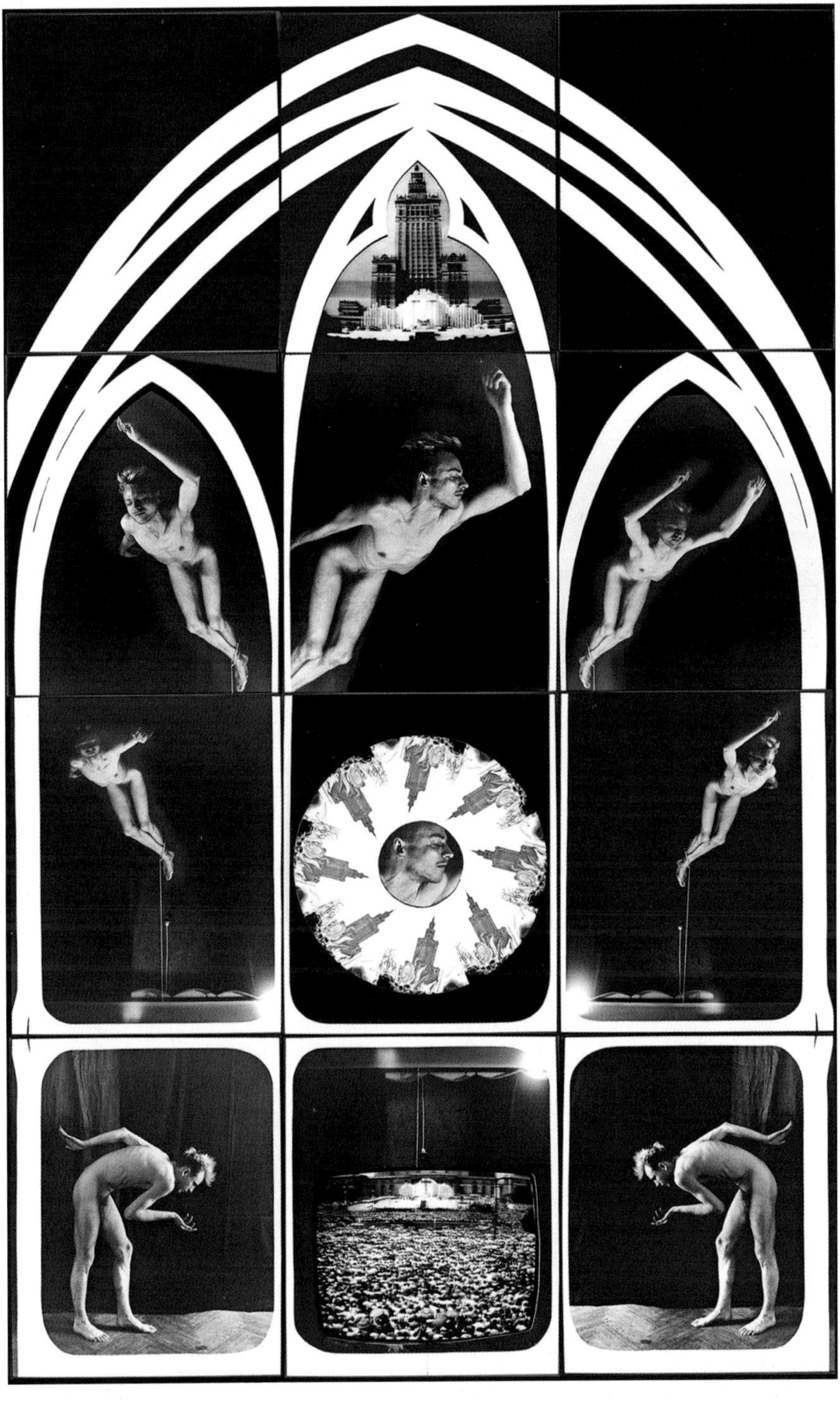

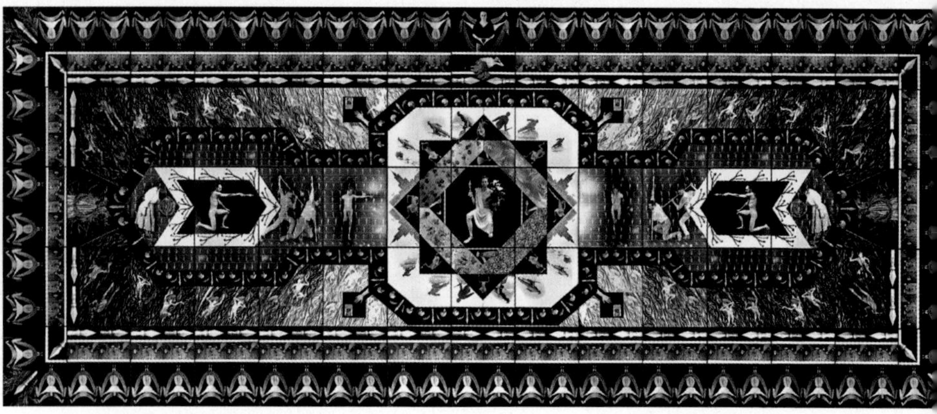

ALL THINGS CONVERGE IN TIME AND SPACE; TO DISPERSE, TO CONVERGE, TO DISPERSE, AND SO ON I, 1992

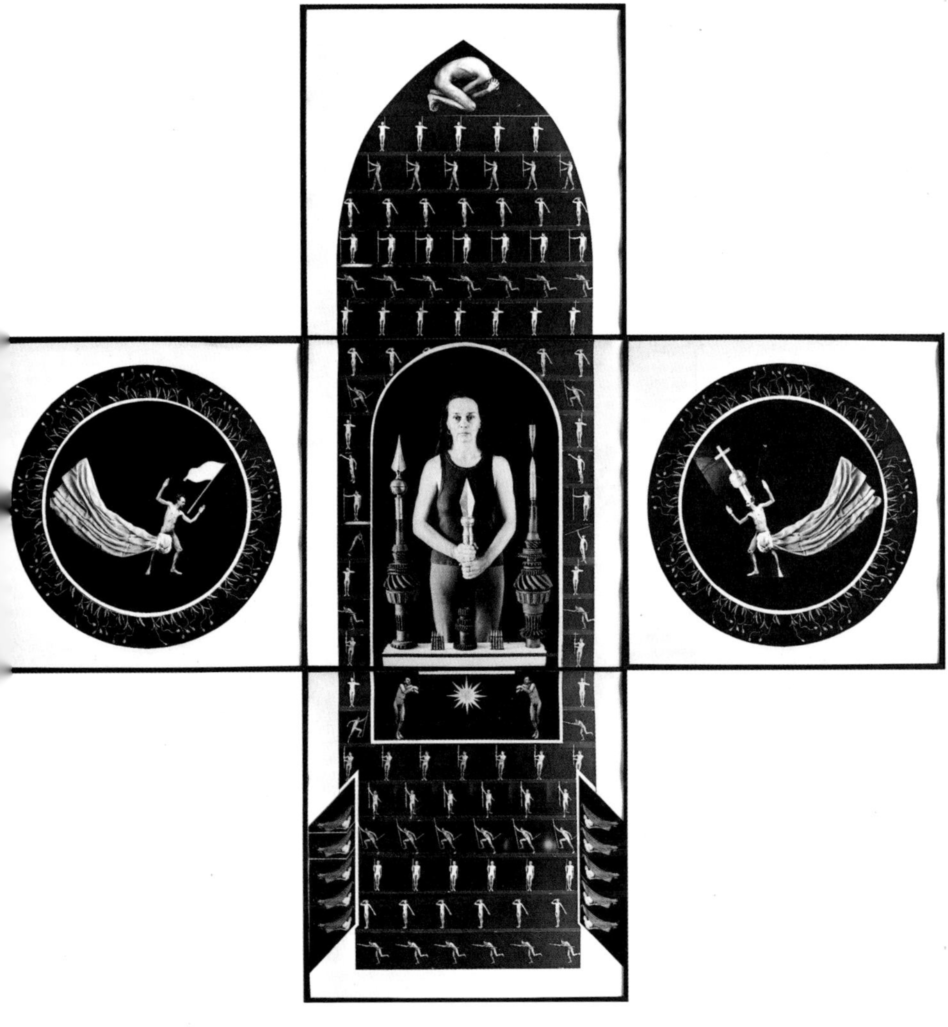

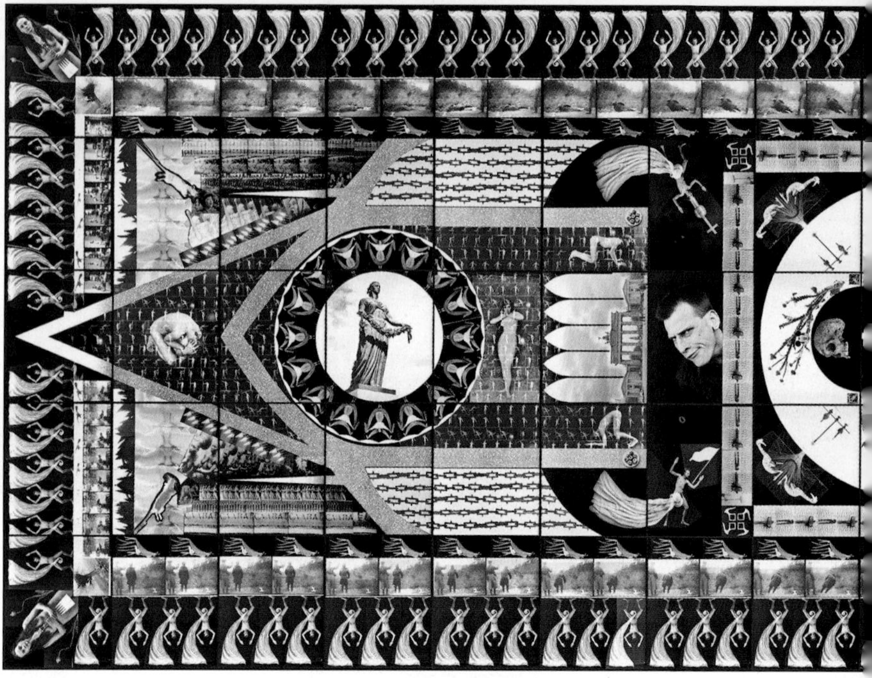

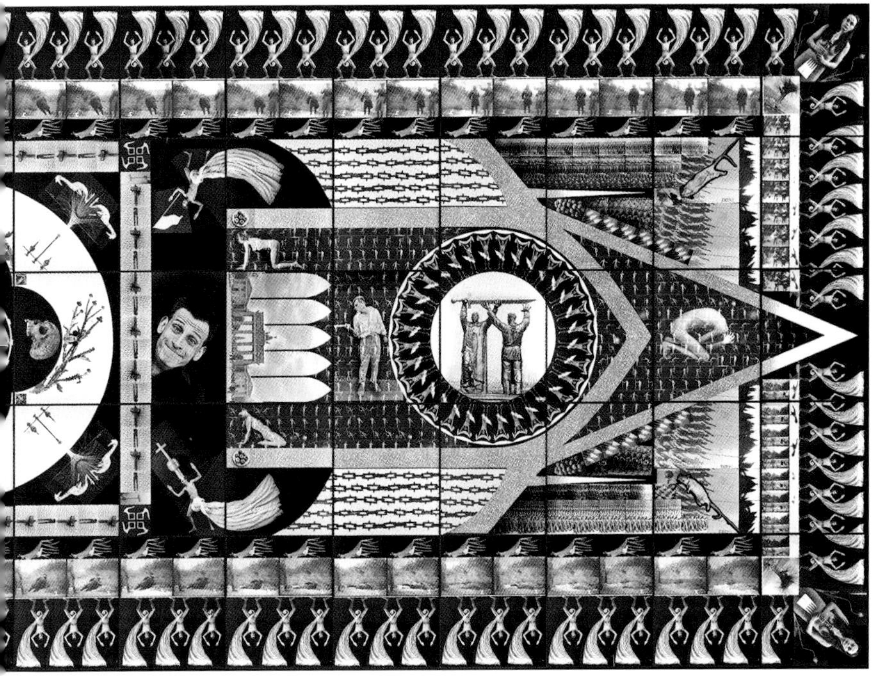

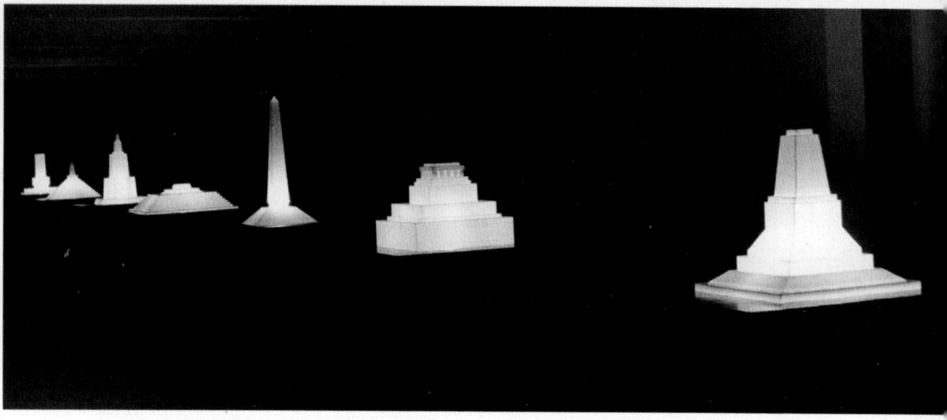

 MONSTRANCE I (LEFT), MOON-SKULL (RIGHT), FROM THE SERIES *COLUMNS*, 1995

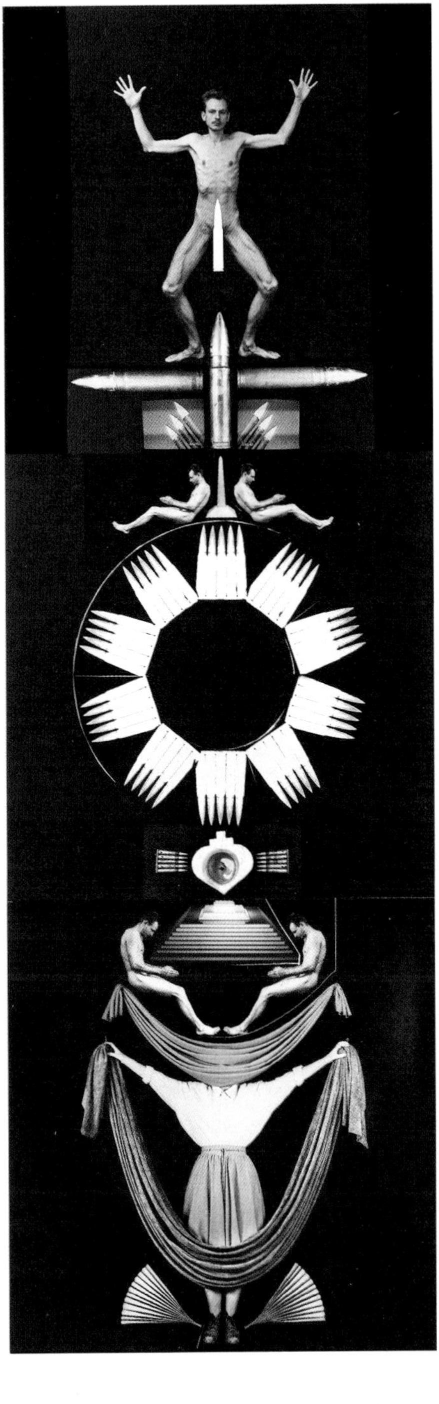

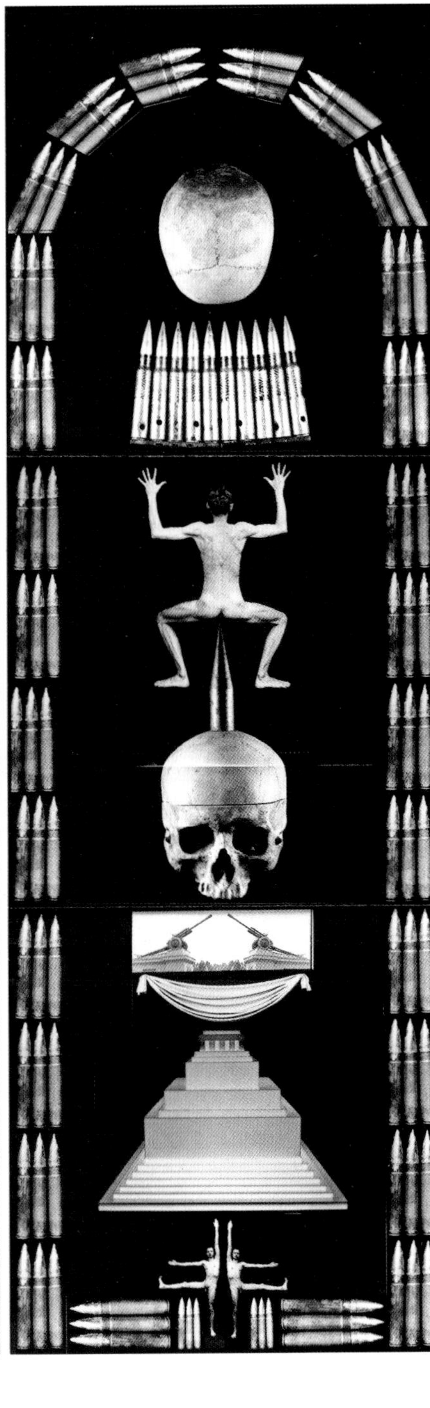

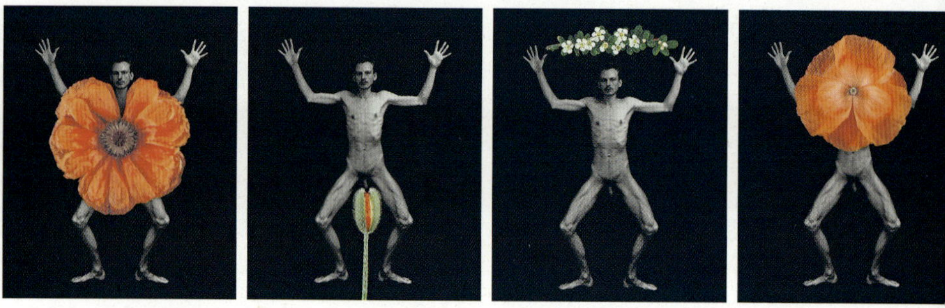

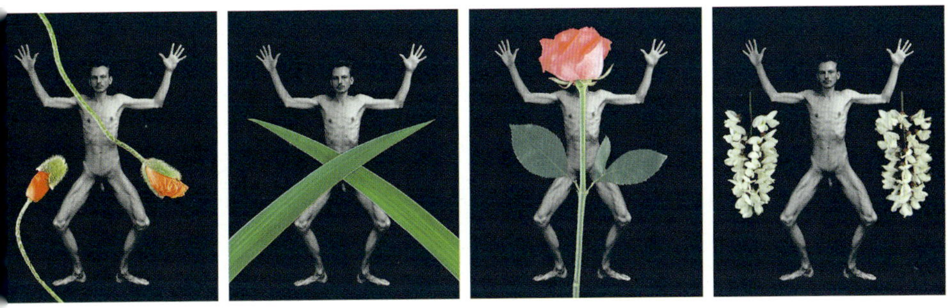

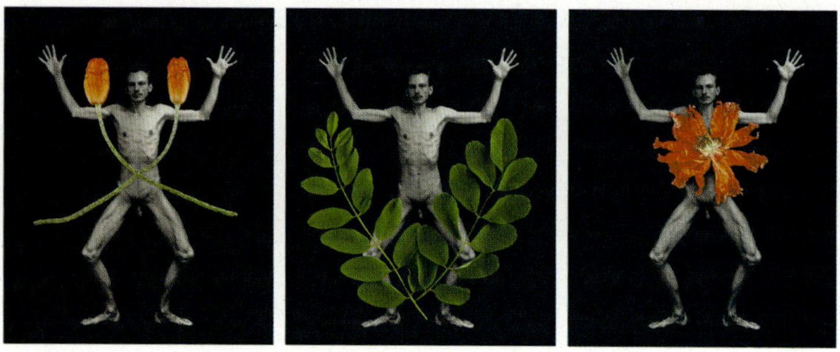

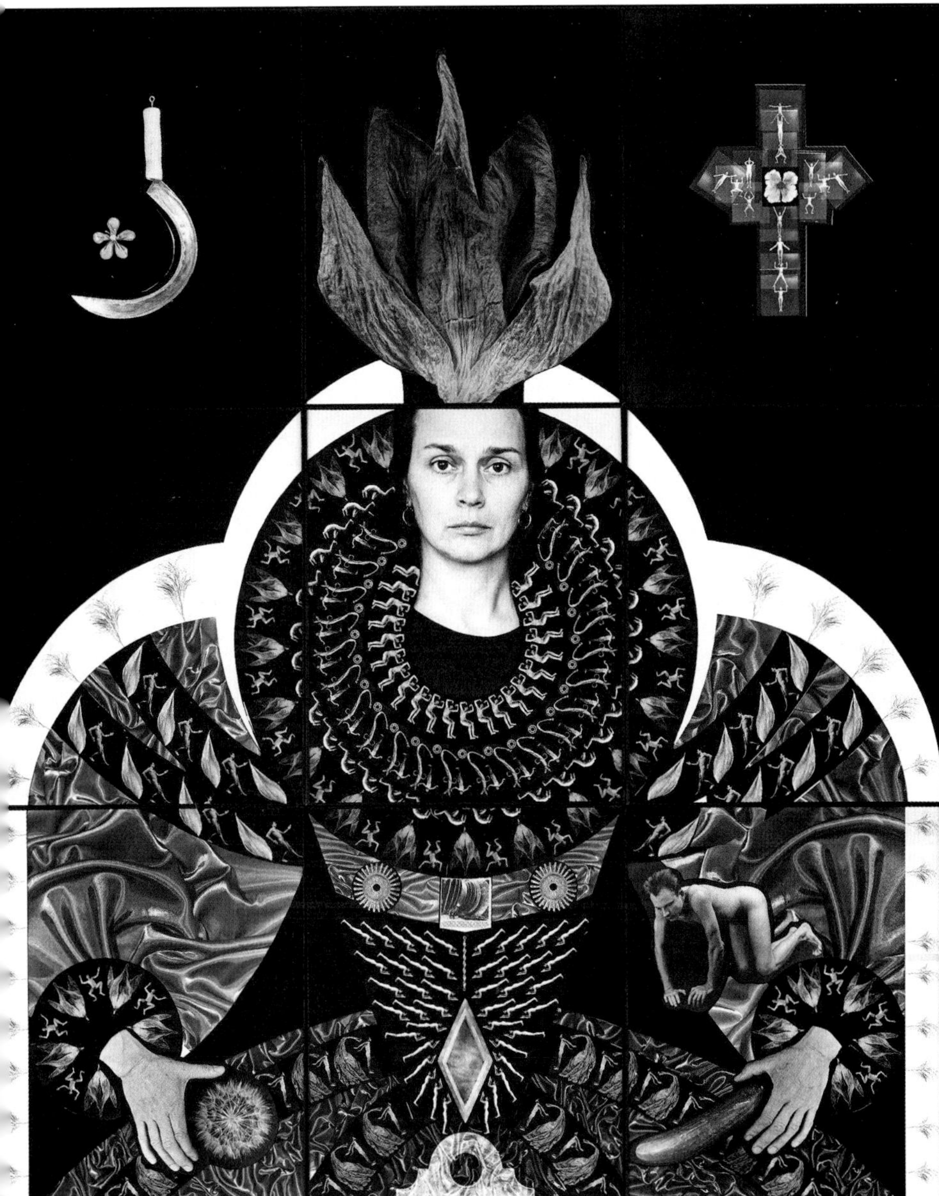

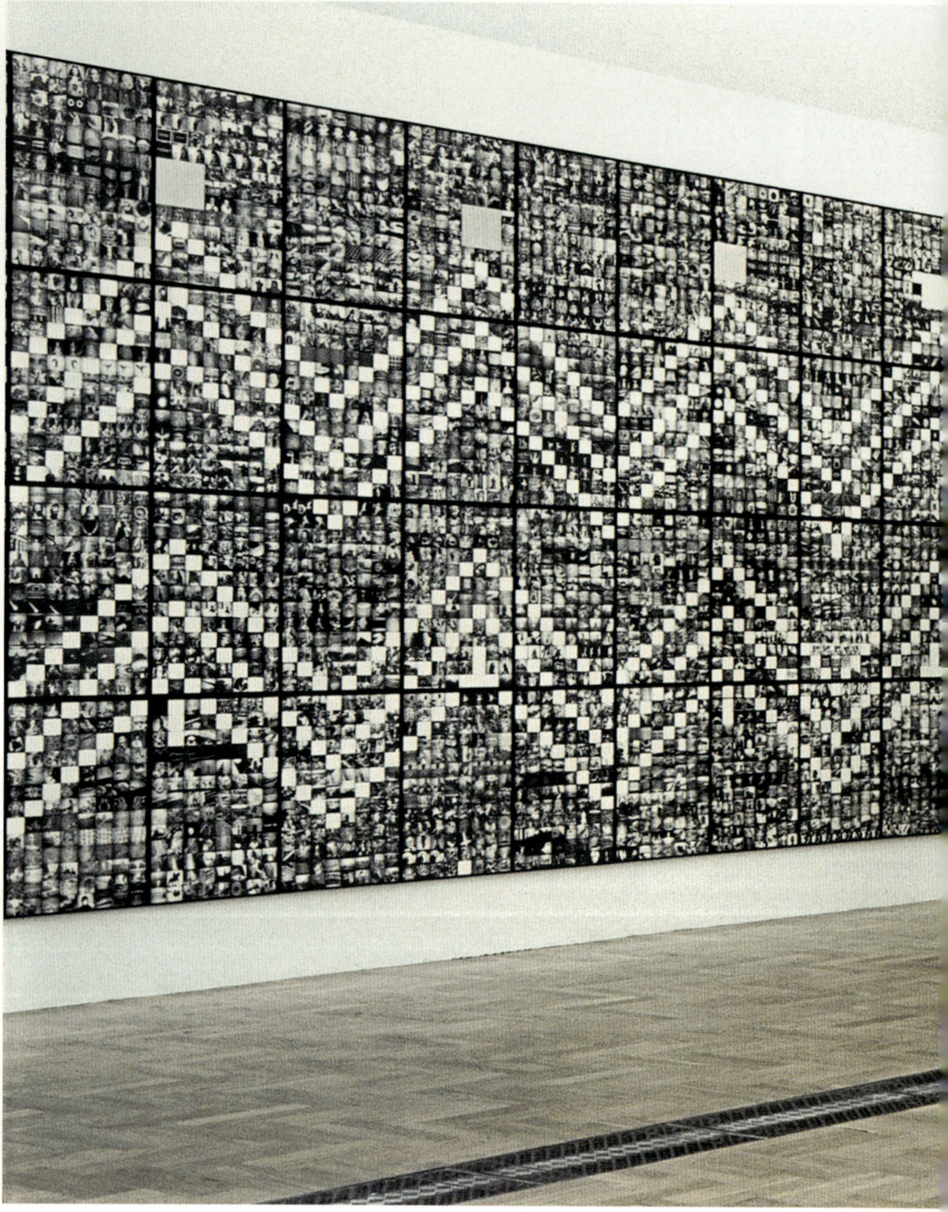

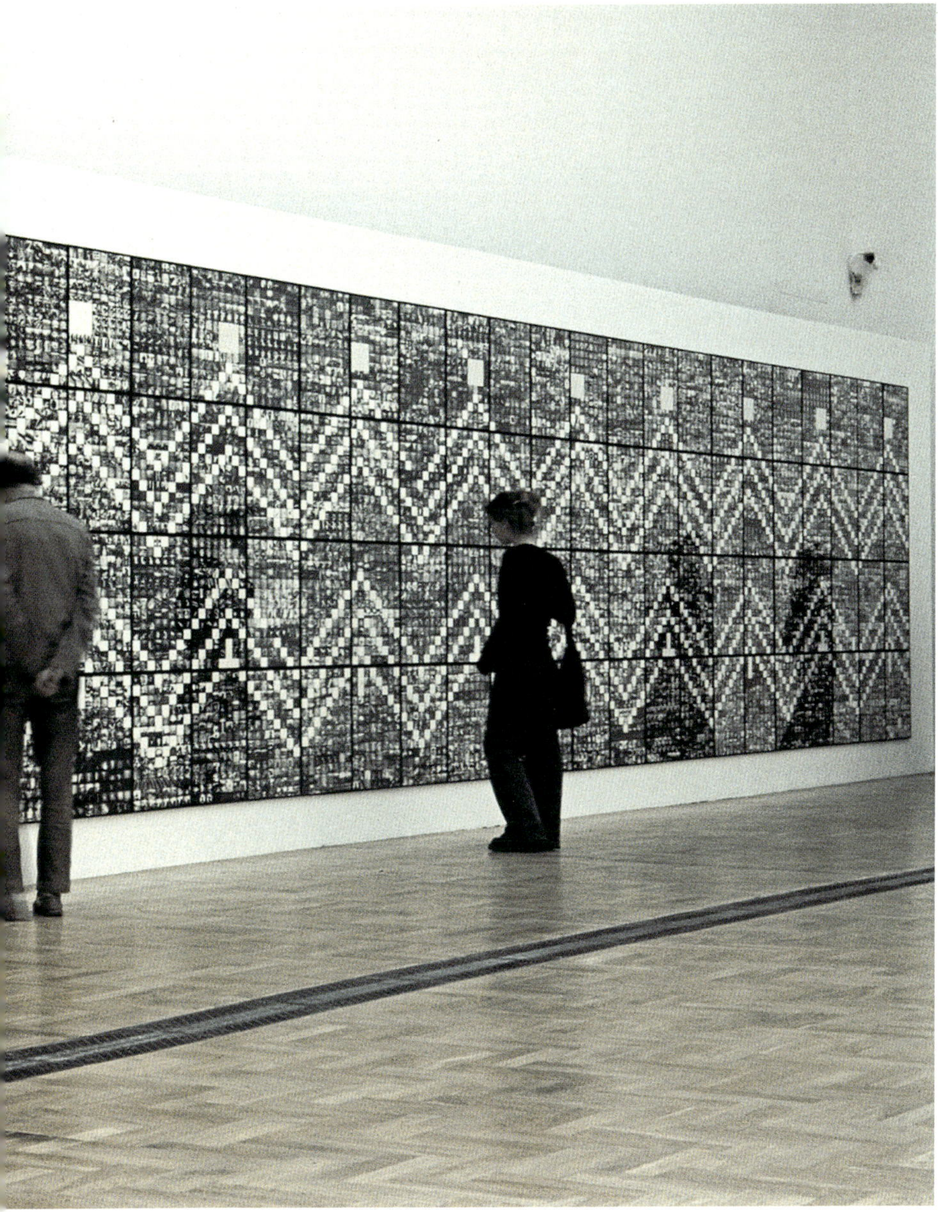

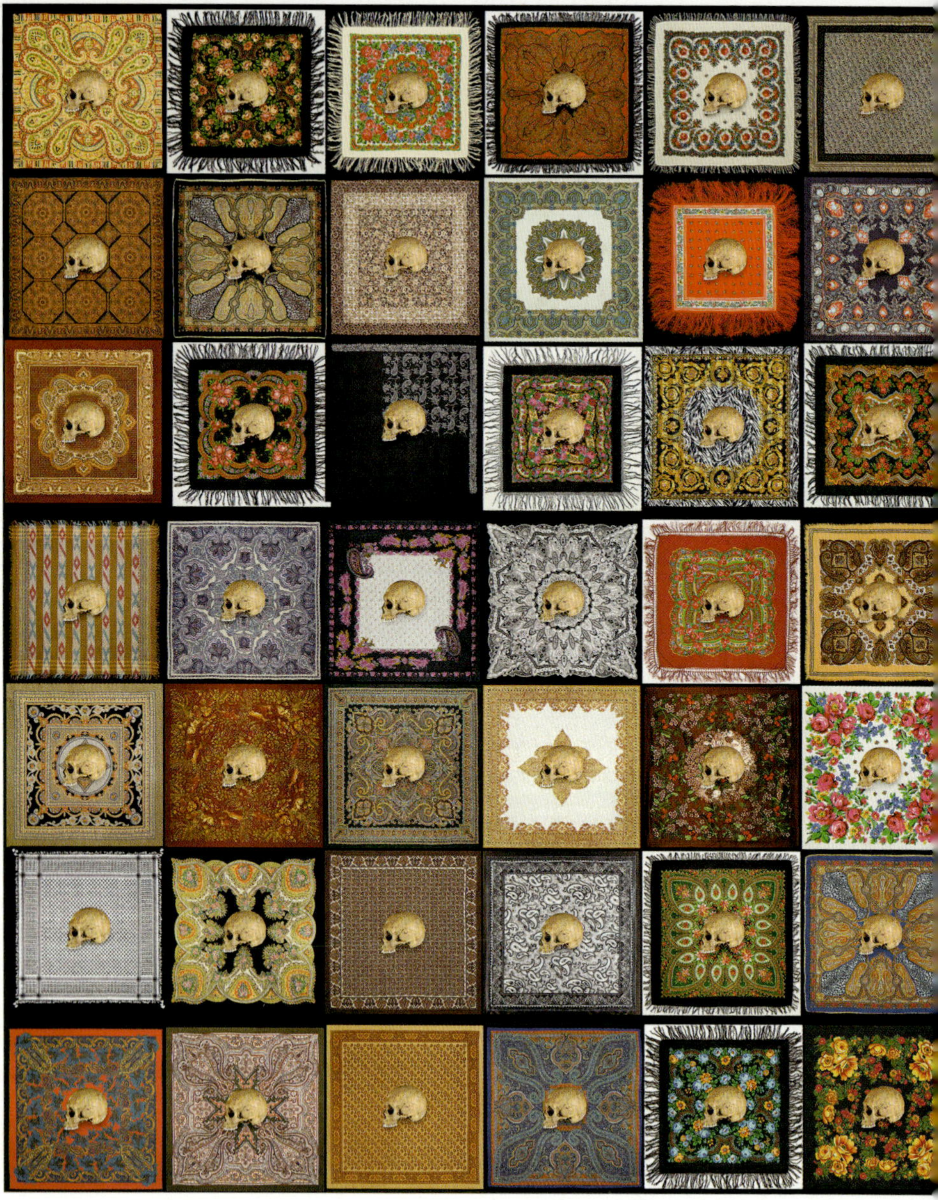

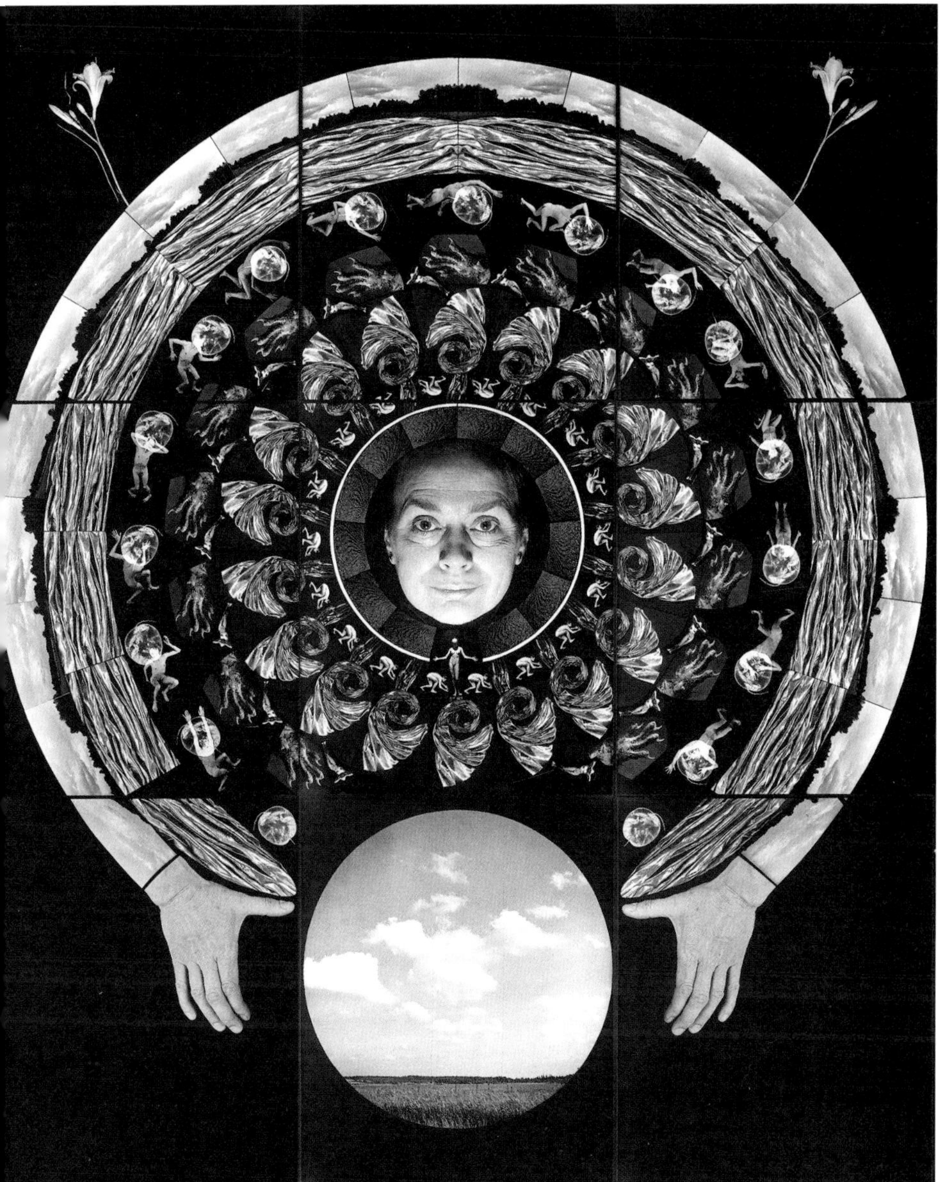

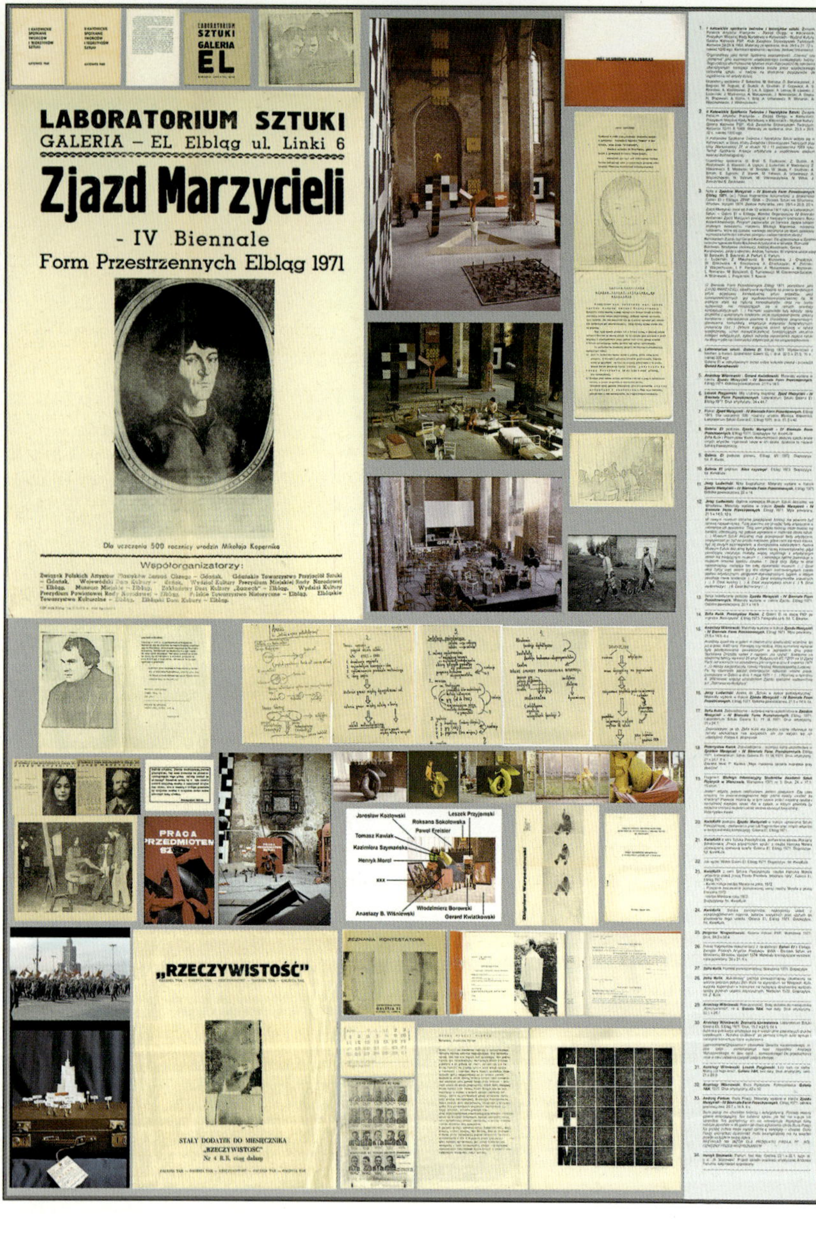
LABORATORIUM SZTUKI
GALERIA EL
LABORATORIUM SZTUKI
GALERIA – EL Elbląg ul. Linki 6
Zjazd Marzycieli
- IV Biennale
Form Przestrzennych Elbląg 1971
Dla uczczenia 500 rocznicy urodzin Mikołaja Kopernika
Współorganizatorzy:
PRACA PRZEDMIOTEM
Jarosław Kozłowski
Leszek Przyjemski
Roksana Sokołowska
Paweł Freisler
Tomasz Kawiak
Kazimiera Szymańska
Henryk Morel
XXX
Włodzimierz Borowski
Anastazy B. Wiśniewski
Gerard Kwiatkowski
ZEZNANIA KONTESTATORA
„RZECZYWISTOŚĆ"
STAŁY DODATEK DO MIESIĘCZNIKA
„RZECZYWISTOŚĆ"
Nr 4 B.K. ciąg dalszy

47 AMBASSADORS OF THE PAST (MADE IN GDR, USSR, CZECHOSLOVAKIA, AND POLAND), 2006

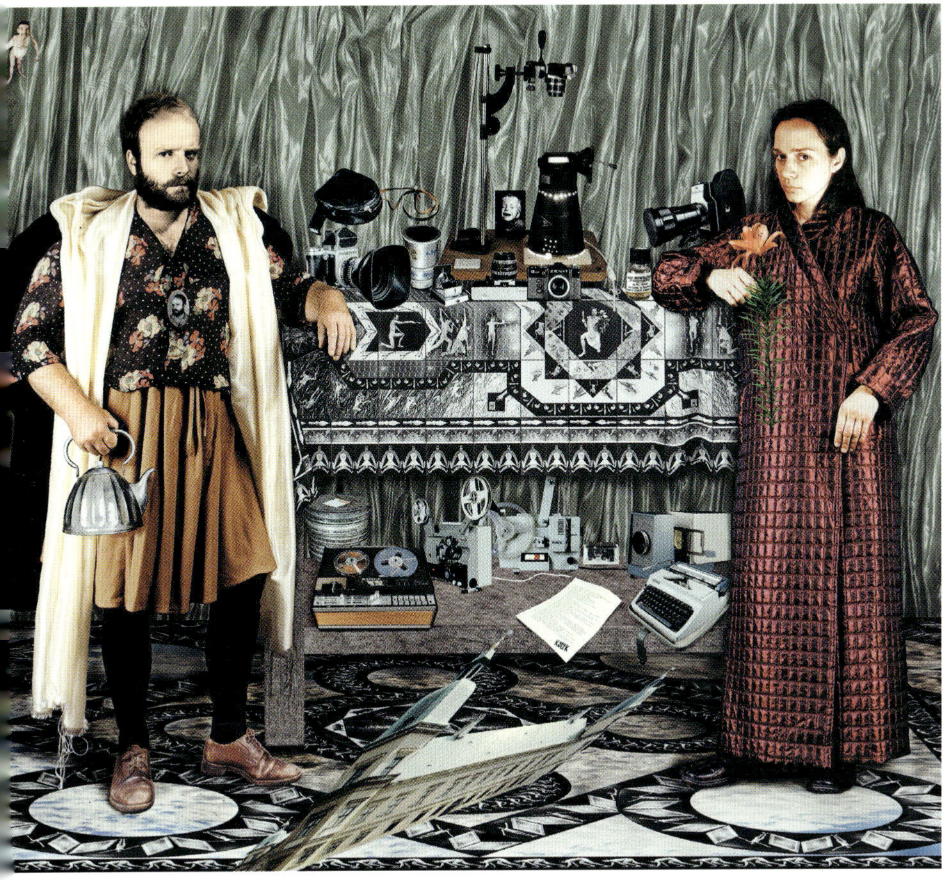

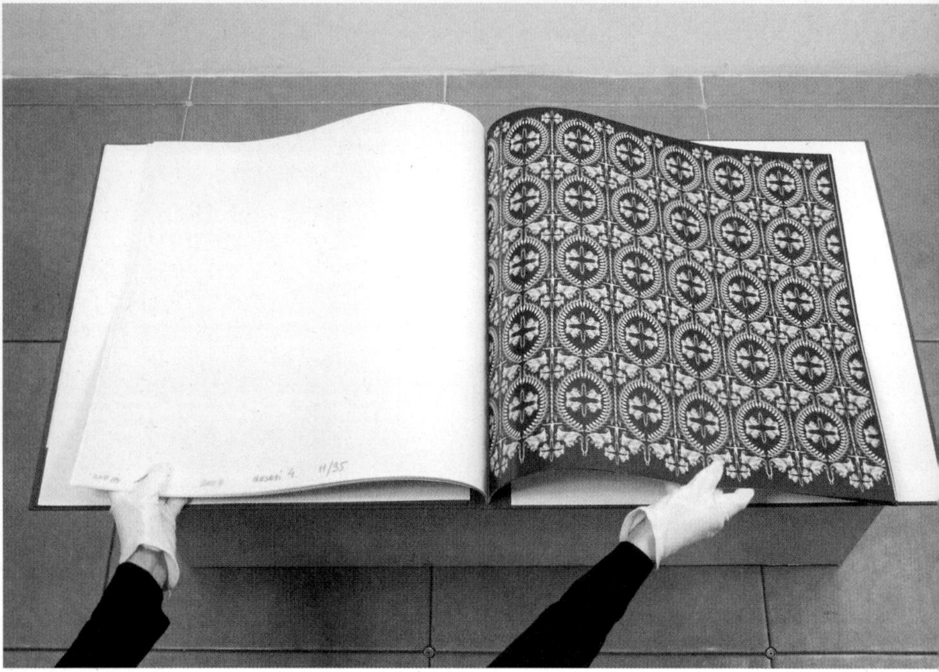

PART II

ESSAYS

Tomasz Załuski, PhD, is an art historian and philosopher. He is assistant professor at the Department of Media and Audiovisual Culture, University of Łódź, Poland, and the Department of Art History and Art Theory, Władysław Strzemiński Academy of Fine Arts, also in Łódź. His research interests include modern and contemporary art; social, political, and economic contexts of artistic culture; artistic activism and self-organization; documentation and artistic archives; configurations of aesthetics, ethics, and politics in the sociocultural project of modernity; and contemporary French philosophy. He is the author of the book *Modernizm artystyczny i powtórzenie: Próba reinterpretacji* (Artistic Modernism and Repetition: An Attempt at Reinterpretation) (2008), and editor of the volumes *Sztuki w przestrzeni transmedialnej* (Arts in Transmedial Space) (2010), *Skuteczność sztuki* (The Effectiveness of Art) (2014), *Socrealizmy i modernizacje* (Social Realisms and Modernizations) (with Aleksandra Sumorok, 2017), and *Wideo w sztukach wizualnych* (Video in the Visual Arts) (with Ryszard W. Kluszczyński, 2018), and *Galeria Wschodnia: Dokumenty 1984–2017 / Documents 1984–2017* (with Daniel Muzyczuk, 2019). He has researched and published widely on the KwieKulik duo, including "KwieKulik and the Political Economy of the Potboiler," in *Third Text* (2018). His recent published work also includes "Reworking Effectiveness: Art as a Politic of Redistribution—Some Remarks from a Polish Perspective," in *Zeitschrift für Kunstgeschichte* (2018).

HOW TO LIVE AND WORK WITH TWO ARTISTIC BIOGRAPHIES: ZOFIA KULIK'S ARCHIVAL DRIVE

Over the years, Zofia Kulik has repeatedly described herself as an artist with two distinct and divergent biographies.[1] Between 1970 and 1987, together with Przemysław Kwiek, she formed a neo-avant-garde duo named KwieKulik.[2] The artists discarded a deeply rooted tradition of object-based art and turned to ephemeral "Activities" that were supposed to reveal the creative process and its various conditioning factors. In 1987 the duo separated and Kulik slowly started to develop her individual career, which has continued until now. On the surface, this other artistic biography has been marked by a return to what KwieKulik vigorously contested—namely object-based art. These are indeed the terms by which the artist often

1 See, for example, "An E-Mail Conversation between Zofia Kulik and Marek Bartelik," *Kulik-KwieKulik Foundation*, accessed June 9, 2018, http://kulikzofia.pl/en/archiwum/rozmowa-internetowa-z-zofia-kulik-rozmawial-marek-bartelik.

2 On the KwieKulik duo and their "Art of Activities," see the sourcebook edited by Łukasz Ronduda and Georg Schöllhammer, *KwieKulik: Zofia Kulik & Przemysław Kwiek* (Warsaw: Museum of Modern Art in Warsaw and KwieKulik Archive; Wrocław: BWA Wrocław Galleries of Contemporary Art, Awangarda Gallery; Vienna: Kontakt: The Art Collection of Erste Group and ERSTE Foundation, 2012).

defined her major artistic shift in the early 1990s.[3] Nevertheless, the actual relationship between the two periods seems to be much more complex—and more important. In order to understand certain aspects of Kulik's individual creative practice after 1987 from a historical perspective, it is necessary to refer to her previous artistic biography. Reference to the KwieKulik period can shed interesting light on her individual art, show its genealogical contexts, and provide a deeper understanding of its development. Furthermore, this reference simply cannot be avoided when it comes to interpreting Kulik's work after 2000, when the artist began to work on the massive documentation generated by KwieKulik and brought her two biographies into a closer and more manifest dialogue with each other.

What is, therefore, the relationship, or rather, what are the multiple relationships between Kulik's two biographies? What "inherited elements" were passed on, transferred, and transformed, from one biography to the other? This is precisely the issue that I want to address here. I will try to establish possible continuities between the two biographies, tracing their points of contact and trajectories of passage. Yet, in order to do so, a more complex division of Kulik's overall artistic history must be introduced. I propose to distinguish five periods or phases in it: individual practices during the artist's studies, which culminated in the diploma piece of 1970–71; the period of cooperation with Przemysław Kwiek as the KwieKulik duo between 1970 and 1987; Kulik's individual career from 1987 onwards; an overlapping post-2000 return to the KwieKulik Archive in order to process and present it using certain modes of practice from Kulik's individual career; and the recent full integration or synthesis of Kulik's two biographies, beginning in 2017. This division is premised on some of Kulik's self-descriptions—to be discussed in what follows—and an analysis of

3 "Being Nothing But an Obedient Psycho-Physical Instrument: Ryszard Ziarkiewicz Talks to Zofia Kulik," trans. Marzena Beata Guzowska, *Kulik-KwieKulik Foundation*, accessed June 9, 2018, http://kulikzofia.pl/en/archiwum/badz-tylko-poslusznym-psychofizycznym-instrumentem/. First published as "Bądź tylko posłusznym psychofizycznym instrumentem: Wywiad z Zofią Kulik; Rozmawiał Ryszard Ziarkiewicz," *Magazyn Sztuki*, no. 1 (1993): 12–21.

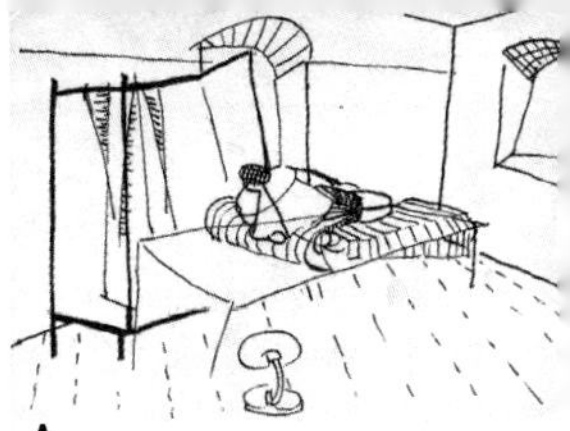

A

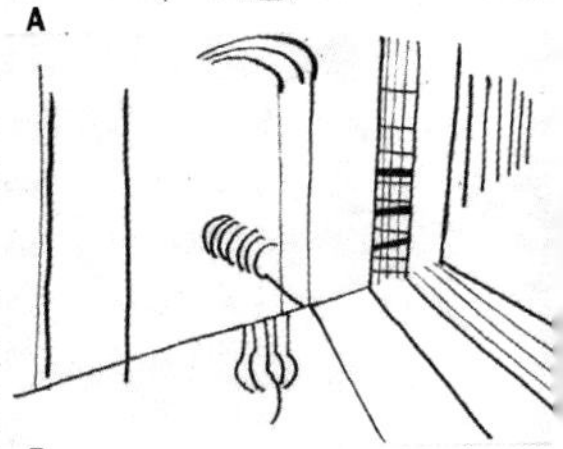

B

the decisive changes in her ideas and practices. Inevitably, an attempt at establishing links between Kulik's two biographies turns into drawing an overall "map" of her artistic pathways.

In the earliest phase of her artistic practice, during studies in the Department of Sculpture at the Academy of Fine Arts in Warsaw, Kulik showed immense fascination with photography. She treated the medium in its different aspects: as a tool for registering and documenting reality, both encountered and staged, ready-made and reconfigured; as an autonomous image that presents various configurations of visual data; and finally, as a material object that can be interfered with using other material objects and substances—scraped off, tinted, overlaid with clay, etc. She also engaged herself in experiments with generating a non-camera photographic image. This took the form of her student work **COMBINATORIAL DRAWINGS** A + B (1969–70), in which she made drawings on several sheets of semi-translucent paper and used them as quasi-photographic negatives; by putting them in layers in the photographic darkroom, and moving and rotating them in relation to one another under the enlarger, she made contact prints on photographic paper. Apart from the aspect of technical invention, this work proved her growing interest in variations and combinatorics, or more precisely, in creating new images from combinatorial or juxtapositional configurations of existing imagery. Another phenomenon connected with technical media that caught her attention was projection—both light projection onto a three-dimensional screen and the multi-projection of photographic slides. Last but not least, the artist was eager to photographically register her experience of the everyday—to create a kind of visual notebook, diary, or chronicle of visual memories from her student life, artistic activities, and journeys. This somewhat compulsive urge was already a symptom of what might be called an "archival drive," a drive for building up "image banks" that could later be restructured according to various categories and treated as a repertoire of items for creating proper artistic statements.

The synthesis of all these threads was fully manifested in Kulik's diploma piece of 1970–71. The work took the form of a multi-projection of about five hundred diapositives onto three spatially positioned screens. The slides had been carefully chosen and arranged according to a meticulously prepared score that programmed their juxtapositions, sequences, and the overall structure of the show. What related the images to one another were mainly their formal analogies or correspondences. Such formal (or formal-and-semantic) relationships contributed to generating surplus meanings, visual metaphors, and even fragmentary, multi-linear narrations.[4]

The diploma piece summarized Kulik's individual interests as a student and prefigured what she would soon contribute to the KwieKulik duo. All the same, it is quite difficult to completely separate Kulik's early work from that of Przemysław Kwiek,[5] especially from his own diploma piece of 1969–70. This consisted of a series of material and spatial transformations of a sculpture, which were recorded on over two hundred color diapositives and later presented as a single-stream slide projection, without any selection and in chronological order. Another part of the piece was a written journal used for recording details connected to the creative process, its accompanying life events, as well as a self-analysis of the author's mental states. A number of obvious similarities between the two diploma pieces, most notably a triad of activity, documentation, and projection, cannot help but put into relief the individual differences in the artists' respective approaches. To oversimplify things somewhat, it can be said that while Kwiek was more interested in the very process of creation in its various, ever-multiplying possibilities and self-generating ramifications, and the construction, use, or reuse of

4 A digital reconstruction of this work, made by the artist in 2015, is available online. "Zofia Kulik Instead of Sculpture," YouTube video, 31:55, posted by *Kulik-KwieKulik Foundation*, November 9, 2017, https://www.youtube.com/watch?v=MoWKob1ixMM&feature=youtu.be.

5 Przemysław Kwiek and Zofia Kulik first met in 1961, at the Youth House of Culture (Młodzieżowy Dom Kultury, MDK) in Warsaw, where they were both taking sculpture lessons. They met again in 1967 at the Academy of Fine Arts in Warsaw while they were both studying in Jerzy Jarnuszkiewicz's studio at the Department of Sculpture.

a photographic archive was of secondary interest to him, Kulik was more interested in building up photographic collections or archives and reorganizing their elements into narrative multi-projections. Furthermore, Kwiek's creative process could be described as more intuitive, marked by a certain "ad-hocism,"[6] in which the moments of reflection, decision, and action closely overlap. Kulik, in turn, tended to perform her creative process in two stages, the first of which was more intuitive as it was dominated by the abovementioned "archival drive," while the second was based on careful premeditation, reflection, planning, and programming, making scripts or scores to determine the choice of visual materials from the archive, and their arrangement within a well-articulated, multi-projected narrative.[7] In stark contrast to Kwiek, who was more suited to initializing actions and letting them develop in every possible direction—even those that might not prove artistically valuable, Kulik carefully analyzed the various artistic possibilities that her archived materials offered, and chose those she found convincing for the final projection piece. Finally, Kwiek was more interested in generating quasi-sculptural material and spatial situations that he called "pre-semantic" "aesthetic time-effects," whereas Kulik wanted to go a step further and turn images of these "pre-semantic" elements into inventive visual metaphors and narrations.

These interests, which soon proved to be compatible in some respects and in others divergent, were the contributions the artists made to the KwieKulik duo. Nevertheless, it seems that Kulik's individual interests never played an equal role in the duo's process-based practices, which became known as "the Art of Activities." These Activities were performed "for the camera": they were

6 Kulik's expression. See "Anatomia KwieKulik: Z Zofią Kulik i Przemysławem Kwiekiem rozmawia Tomasz Załuski," in *Zofia Kulik prezentuje KwieKulik: Dobromierz X*, ex. cat. (Łódź: Galeria Atlas Sztuki, 2008), http://www.atlassztuki.pl/pdf/katalog_36.pdf. An abridged English version of this interview has been published as "KwieKulik Anatomy: An Interview with Zofia Kulik and Przemysław Kwiek by Tomasz Załuski," in Ronduda and Schöllhammer, *KwieKulik: Zofia Kulik & Przemysław Kwiek*, 535–45. Unfortunately, the abovementioned expression has been omitted from this version.

7 For more information on Kwiek's and Kulik's diploma works see Ronduda and Schöllhammer, *KwieKulik: Zofia Kulik & Przemysław Kwiek*, 44–47, 72–77.

recorded (most often) on color slides or black-and-white photographic negatives and (infrequently) on film and video. Documentation was not treated as an external addition to the performative process, but became part of the idea and execution thereof. Aside from their own Activities, KwieKulik registered actions performed by other artists. Afterwards they not only presented such archived documentation to different audiences in order to disseminate and propagate information about ephemeral art, but also used the documents as a source of visual material for their own archive-based projection works, so-called "directed" screenings for the public.

KwieKulik's major concept-term—"Activities"—was indeed the most succinct way of describing the duo's artistic agenda. It helped them to integrate art with life and expand their notion of art, which they eventually defined as "continuous, efficient behaviors in specific existential, artistic, social, political, mental, material, or spatial situations."[8] Consequently, "Activities" aimed at the analysis of the multiple, diverse factors that determined artistic and everyday life practices in the Polish People's Republic of the 1970s and 1980s, expose the narrowed possibilities of action that they offered, and finally, transform a framework of conditions defining the field of art production in Poland and generate within it certain broader possibilities of action. The artists not only put a lot of effort into calling for change in the existing forms and conditions of creative practice, but also strove to design and develop new ones. They organized group activities, collective work, and short-lived coalitions, cooperated with other artists, and designed visual games aimed at turning art viewers into active participants and co-creators of artistic events. All of this was supposed to break with the individualism and egoism inherent in the traditional figure of the artist. KwieKulik also tried to establish alternative artists' associations and unions, waged a persistent and often harsh critique of state cultural institutions and policies, demanded improvement in the economic conditions of artistic practice, and struggled to redefine the status of the artist and bring it closer to that of an "innovator" or "researcher."

8 Przemysław Kwiek and Zofia Kulik, "Arnhem, Separate Whole," in Ronduda and Schöllhammer, *KwieKulik: Zofia Kulik & Przemysław Kwiek*, 453.

Last but not least, they designed a project for a new alternative institution: the Studio of Activities, Documentation and Propagation (Pracownia Działań, Dokumentacji i Upowszechniania, PDDiU), which was to be financed by the state and devoted to performing, documenting, and popularizing ephemeral art. Failing to win the state's support for this grassroots initiative, they had to confine themselves to running an alternative art gallery in their private flat in Warsaw.

In many cases KwieKulik's "efficient behaviors" proved to be unimplemented plans, unfinished actions, or ones that missed their goals, documents of defeat, or testimonies to confrontation with adverse living conditions and collisions with the external limitations that curbed the freedom of artistic practice. A symbolic victory came with the artists' ability to turn these limitations into a source of strength and creative stimuli. In effect, KwieKulik's testimonies of defeat were at the same time critical expositions of the institutional, economic, and sociopolitical realities of communist Poland, achieved by means of inventive visual and performative idioms.

Apart from external limitations, there were also internal reasons behind the fact that many of KwieKulik's ideas remained unimplemented and some of their enterprises were left unfinished. The artists incessantly chased new possibilities of action, which indeed seemed to emerge from one another. The "chase" frequently provided Kulik and Kwiek with cause for conflict. Kulik wanted to pursue her interests in working with the archival materials that the duo had managed to produce and gather to date. She tried to persuade her partner to devote more time and effort to organizing the archive and using it to create well-articulated statements that would enable them to effectively propagate previously generated forms of activities.[9] Yet Kwiek chose to press ahead, persisting with the necessity of engaging in ever-forthcoming initiatives and the exploration of new forms of action. He was satisfied with the sheer discovery, cognition, and chronicling of a new possibility of action, and cared less than Kulik about studying its archived documentation, processing it, and rearranging items selected from the archive into new configurations.

9 Kulik, conversation with the author, 2012.

This was why *Activities with Dobromierz*, one of their major projects from the 1970s, remained unaccomplished at the time. During the period 1972–74, at home and outside, the artists documented, arranged, and encountered situations involving their toddler son Maksymilian Dobromierz, along with objects of everyday use and elements of their surroundings [FIG. 1]. The archive thus created comprised nearly nine hundred color slides and black-and-white photographs. Initially, KwieKulik planned to use the slides to prepare a three-channel multi-projection that would be arranged according to a written score, as had been the case with Kulik's diploma piece. This didn't happen, though, as they became involved in new enterprises and couldn't find enough time or strength—or will—to work on the slides and prepare the show.[10]

Not being able to fully pursue her "archival interests," Kulik began to feel growing tiredness and disappointment, as well as resistance to the process-based, ephemeral activities, with their "ad-hocism," open-endedness, and non-conclusiveness.[11] This negative attitude was reinforced in the 1980s, when the duo made several artistic journeys to Western Europe, the US, and Canada. During their presentations there, KwieKulik usually reenacted activities and performances that they had already developed and shown in Poland. Even though the pieces were modified and mixed into new configurations called "multiperformances," Kulik felt the duo were simply repeating themselves instead of discovering something new.[12]

Aside from artistic differences, there were also existential, gender-related reasons for Kulik's growing unrest, which eventually prompted her to end her relationship and cooperation with Kwiek. As their life partnership involved—at least in some respects—gender inequality, Kulik felt subordinate and considered herself treated unfairly by her partner in terms of the unequal distribution of "invisible" domestic labor: mundane activities, everyday duties, and household chores, especially when they had to be

10 It was not until 2008 that *Activities with Dobromierz* was turned into a three-channel digital multi-projection by Zofia Kulik. I return to this work further in the text.

11 "Being Nothing But an Obedient Psycho-Physical Instrument."

12 "KwieKulik Anatomy," 545.

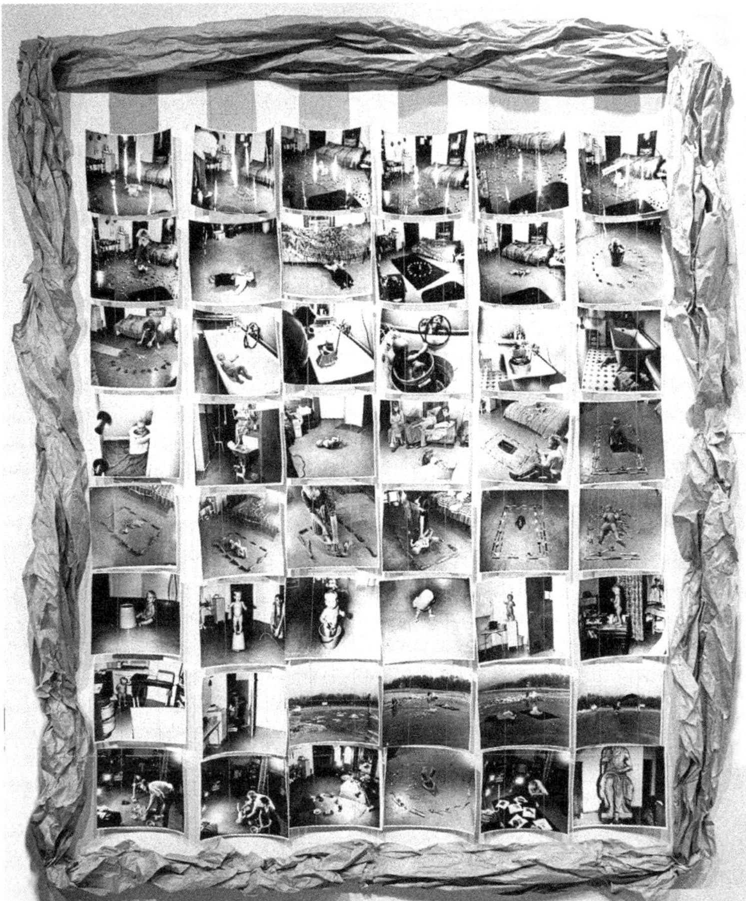

FIG. 1
KWIEKULIK, *ACTIVITIES WITH DOBROMIERZ*, 1972–74

performed within the conditions of the socialist shortage economy.[13] Both "threads," artistic and existential-feminist, came to be interlaced in the slow and lengthy process of Kulik's self-emancipation.

The process was marked by a few individual artistic statements. One cannot help but notice that Kulik drew on KwieKulik's method of "efficient behaviors in specific existential, artistic, social, political, mental, material, or spatial situations," and more specifically on their frequent strategy that could be described in terms of subversive overidentification, in order to critically testify to her subordinate position in the duo and begin building her own subjectivity. As early as 1974, during an artists' meeting in Osetnica, Kulik made the question of her female domestic labor part of her artistic identity. For a self-presentational leaflet, as one of the images that were to characterize her, she chose a photograph of herself on the pavement at a bus stop, with her toddler son, baskets filled with food and photo equipment. In 1977, invited by Antonio Ferro to contribute to his mail-art project *La Post/Avanguardia*, Kulik created *Alice's Adventures in Fucked Wonderland*, which included a photograph—seemingly covered with dust and dirt—of herself cleaning the floor with a big broom. Finally, in 1978, at the Dziekanka Gallery in Warsaw, after yet another performance by the duo, Kulik performed her individual piece *Zofia Kulik's Begging for Forgiveness*. Wearing a white gown, she approached the audience several times and knelt before them. She commented on the event many years later:

> The Duo did suffocate me too much: all of these repetitions; we were speaking always the same things, we were doing always the same things. Strange emotions accumulated within me. [...] I wanted to plea[d] [for] pardon from the public, making the same gesture as the actress and falling on my knees before it. What was the public supposed to forgive me? I didn't know exactly. Probably that I was not present in person, even if I seemed [to] be. I was nothing but a part of a

13 "Anatomia KwieKulik." I am referring again to the full Polish text of the interview, as the relevant fragments have been omitted from the abridged English version.

> dimorphic hybrid in which my role was not clear, nor how much space I occupied, what my shape was. [...] I must have been really pathetic, [...] I felt totally humiliated but... I asked for that. I needed such a situation and I had it.[14]

This proves that, at the end of the 1970s, she was already thinking about breaking free from the "dimorphic hybrid."

In 1982 Kulik made a decisive gesture towards existential self-emancipation, as she decided, without her partner's consent, to sell her mother's apartment, move away from Warsaw, and buy an old, damaged house in nearby Łomianki-Dąbrowa. Kwiek protested against the decision, but finally joined her, and together they started rebuilding and renovating the house by themselves (with a little help from temporary workers). This lasted for almost six years. Even though KwieKulik gave some of their best and most iconic performances during this period, such as *Polish Duo* (1984), *Hammer-Sickle* (1985), and *Banana and Pome-grenade* (1986), Kulik was already detaching herself from her partner and their common artistic agenda. In 1987 she ended her relationship with Kwiek, left the duo, and started, not without effort and hesitation, to follow her individual artistic path. She needed to redefine and reinvent herself. In the process, a major role was played by her confrontation with artists from a younger generation, namely Zbigniew Libera and Jerzy Truszkowski, as well as a somewhat complicated love affair with the latter.[15] Being exposed to their worldviews, ideas, values, and sensibilities, quite different from what she had identified with since the early 1970s, Kulik could negotiate and transform her previous artistic stance.[16]

14 "The Rebellion of a Neo-Avant-Garde Artist: An Interview with Zofia Kulik Conducted by Joanna Turowicz," *Kulik-KwieKulik Foundation*, accessed June 9, 2018, http://kulikzofia.pl/en/archiwum/bunt-neoawangardowej-artystki/. First published as "Bunt neoawangardowej artystki," in *Artmix*, no. 9 (March 2005).

15 Zofia Krawiec, "Portrety trzech," in *Miłosny performans* (Warsaw: Lampa i Iskra Boża, 2016), 101–21.

16 "Being Nothing But an Obedient Psycho-Physical Instrument" and "The Rebellion of a Neo-Avant-Garde Artist."

At first, this redefinition and reinvention of herself took the form of manifest negation of KwieKulik's main artistic ideas, goals, and values. In her statement published in the catalog of her first solo exhibition, *Idioms of the Soc-Ages* of 1989, Kulik drew on a conceptual opposition that was of utmost importance for KwieKulik, namely Open Form vs. Closed Form. At the beginning of the 1970s this opposition, taken from Oskar Hansen's theory, helped the duo to express their need to leave the Closed Form of traditional object-based art and promote the Open Form of process-based Activities. Entering her own path at the end of the 1980s, Kulik decided to turn this conceptual language against KwieKulik's ethos, and described her new artistic interests in terms of Closed Form. She wrote: "I am fascinated by Closed Forms. Centricity, symmetry, multiplication, order, figural ornament, imposing upon myself certain preexisting patterns of structures (monuments, medals, mandalas, carpets, and gates) that I try to fill with my own madness—these constitute my formal and constructive rules of composition."[17] In passing, and somewhat elliptically, she also seemed to suggest that imposing Closed Form was a kind of therapeutic self-treatment, a way of distancing herself from what she had learned to despise in KwieKulik's chaotic openness and the unfinishedness of every action: "In the beginning I look for a scheme, then while composing exactly according to this scheme I start to feel the sense of what I am doing. Ordering and submission constitute compulsion, so strong for me, to behave and work in so-called life and so-called art."[18]

This manifest negation of KwieKulik's heritage was still present at the beginning of the 1990s. In 1992, in an interview conducted by Ryszard Ziarkiewicz, Kulik stated that her individual career was a continuation of what she had been doing alone, without Kwiek, while preparing her diploma piece in 1970–71. She went as far as to say that "the beginning of the 1970s and my present practice are the supports of a bridge span that overhangs the [period of] work in the KwieKulik duo."[19] This statement, with its exclusionary rhetoric,

17 *Zofia Kulik: Idiomy socwiecza*, ex. cat. (Łomianki-Lublin, 1990), 1.
18 *Zofia Kulik: Idiomy socwiecza*, 1.
19 "Being Nothing But an Obedient Psycho-Physical Instrument."

although no doubt vital for Kulik's self-definition at the time, needs to be clarified when it comes to describing the actual complexity of links between the KwieKulik period and Kulik's solo career.

As previously stated, it is quite difficult to completely separate Kulik's early work from Kwiek's and, consequently, from KwieKulik's. To be more specific, there was already some of the duo's future agenda in her diploma piece, in which she also documented her own quasi-sculptural material and spatial activities. Furthermore, the main feature of Kulik's individual artistic strategy after 1987—a creative process consisting of generating, as if out of compulsion, a photographic archive, then configuring items selected from it into well-articulated visual structures—was undoubtedly already present in her early diploma piece. Yet it did not disappear completely during the KwieKulik period; it was surely pushed back, subordinated, and withdrawn in order to give priority to improvised ephemeral Activities, but it still managed to find its expression on several occasions, especially in preparing "directed" screenings for the public or in combining objects and materials to form visual idioms and metaphors for the duo's performances. From this perspective, Kulik's individual career after 1987 can be seen as resulting from a need to fully pursue this line of creation, to fully unleash her "archival drive," which was already present (but largely suppressed) during the KwieKulik period. Finally, if we take a closer look at the manifest negation of KwieKulik's agenda on which Kulik built her new artistic self-definition at the beginning of her solo career, we can see that it was KwieKulik, with their critical stance, which equipped her with the very strength and tools to self-emancipate and eventually cut herself away from the duo's agenda. This means that, paradoxically enough, the duo's heritage was operative even in Kulik's very gesture of discarding her previous artistic biography.

There were also some more positive points of contact. Kulik's works after 1987 are usually described in their technical and media aspects as "multiple-exposure photographs." They are also, in a sense, photograms, and as such they are always unique. In her double-staged creative process, Kulik first used human models[20] to build up an archive of photographic negatives showing the naked body in various carefully arranged postures and gestures, then utilized items from the archive to compose quasi-ornamental images that exposed the visual structures of power and submission. Still, her highly emblematic technique of "multiple-exposure photographs" took some time to develop. The artist initially experimented with photo-collage, cutting out pieces of photographic prints and pasting them onto larger pieces of photographic paper or other surfaces. Gradually, she started to feel the need to make this process more closely connected with the immanent potentialities of the photographic medium, and also more "automatic," or "machine-like."[21] As a result, she treated photographic negatives as reusable "puzzles" that could be, under the enlarger, transferred onto a piece of photographic paper, multiplied there if necessary, and combined with one another according to a preestablished design. This meant that even though she turned to object-based works, she was still looking for a way to make the manual aspect of their execution less artistically important.[22] This need to reduce the artistic importance of manual execution in favor of using the potentialities of technical media was a hallmark of KwieKulik's theory and practice.

But that isn't all. The technique of creating "multiple-exposure photographs" allowed Kulik to proceed in a way that partly resembled KwieKulik's procedure of using items from the archive for arranging "directed" projections. There was a crucial difference: while the duo's projections were quasi-ephemeral—they could be easily rearranged, and had to be assisted and performed by the artists each time—Kulik sought to configure items from her photographic archive into a fixed and enduring form that could "work" without her presence. At the same time she managed to retain a certain

20 Among Kulik's models were Zbigniew Libera, Robert Rumas, Joanna Stańko, Joanna Szymczyk, Urszula Kwiek, Robert Kucharski, Marek Kijewski—and herself.

21 Kulik, conversation with the author, 2018.

22 I could go as far as to speculate that, if she had been given access to advanced computer tools at the very beginning of her individual career, she would have decided to make digital photomontages, as she did much later in the new millennium.

changeability or variability of structures, so characteristic of the duo's Activities. Namely, when she made several "copies" of a particular multiple-exposure photograph—which is always, by virtue of the very technique, a unique image—she would usually reconfigure the "puzzles" and produce a series of slightly different variations of the original design.

Beneath all these points of contact that concern matters of artistic technique and procedures of execution, a much more profound continuity between Kulik's two biographies can be discerned. It lies in certain "habits of thought"—in theoretical and scientific inspirations that, having played a crucial role in the development of KwieKulik's notion and practice of process-based Activities, later proved to be equally important for Kulik's individual path. Along with Hansen's theory of Open Form, the duo drew inspiration from structuralist semiotics, generative grammar, information, communication and game theory, cybernetics, and praxeology. These helped the artists to develop an interest in the complex formal and real structures of things or actions, to acquire an ability to locate their common or similar elements, and finally, to perceive and analyze their interrelations and configurations as capable of generating and conveying meanings. The scientific inspirations offered an epistemic approach that strongly appealed to KwieKulik. It consisted of discerning—even in seemingly chaotic phenomena—basic elements, in order to classify and categorize them, create their generalized abstract models, and verify them practically. These "habits of thought" remained operative in Kulik's individual art, not only in how she created her basic, reusable archival items and composed them, according to prearranged cardboard models, into complex, modular, ornament-like, repetitive structures, but also in the way she approached the question of visual structures in their connection to history and memory. It might be said that Kulik, as she had become critical towards the ephemeral and obsessed with the durable, concentrated on a kind of *longue durée*: she began looking for and using visual forms, schemes, and patterns—repetitive figures, postures, and gestures that had lasted for centuries as enduring vehicles of power, ideology, and submission—as carriers of collective habits and affects, media of cultural memory that made all past images come back in a present one. In other words, the artist's approach consisted of finding the archetypal in the changeable, the most ancient in the most contemporary, and trying to construct general visual structures that would keep, in a kind of "internal archive," a memory of all their particular historical instances. This attitude is probably best expressed in the titles of two of her works: *All Things Converge in Time and Space; To Disperse, To Converge, To Disperse, and So on* (1992), and *All the Missiles Are One Missile* (1993). One cannot help but notice that, on different ground, such an "internal archive" was often a feature of KwieKulik's Activities, many of which referred to previous ones by incorporating their material and visual components, treated as multilayered vehicles of autobiographical memory.

Other common ground between KwieKulik's Activities and Kulik's individual works can be found in their thematic content. One of the most obstinate problems that KwieKulik repeatedly addressed in their art was the question of the institutional and political power relations that shaped art production and life in the Polish People's Republic of the 1970s. The artists tried to expose those existing power relations and change their negative impact. They not only sent letters of complaint and petitions to the authorities, but also, increasingly, made symbolic performances, by means of which they informed audiences about "bad situations" they had experienced and protested against the unfair treatment they had received. In the late 1970s and early 1980s these "protest performances" became increasingly metaphorical, as the duo no longer referred to specific situations and problems they had experienced, but commented on the more general economic and sociopolitical power structures that made individual lives subject to oppression. To that end, the artists used visual and gestural idioms—mostly invented and configured by Kulik[23]—that subversively evoked monumental propaganda sculptures. Playing the roles of such "living monuments," they at once embodied and exposed the submission of individuals to dominant forces and

23 *Zofia Kulik: Idiomy socwiecza*, 1, and "KwieKulik Anatomy," 545.

structures. After 1987 Kulik seemed to pursue this practice in her own way when she photographed naked models reenacting postures and gestures taken from political and military iconography, and later framed the images of their bodies into ornamental structures evoking power and subjugation.

Last but not least, what seems to link Kulik's early work from the beginning of the 1970s, the KwieKulik period, and Kulik's individual artistic path after 1987, is an interest in documenting and archiving the flow of the everyday—of what passed through the artist's eyes. As previously stated, large numbers of slides from the artist's diploma piece were produced by documenting her visual experience of everyday places, situations, journeys, and actions. The need for the integration of art and life made the everyday equally important for KwieKulik. Some of their works, the most notable examples being *Activities with Dobromierz* of 1972–74 and *KwieKulik's Circle* of 1976 [FIG. 2], showed their Activities performed in connection with their everyday life conditions, places, and objects, and became visual diaries of their singular experience of the world. This autobiographical dimension of documenting the everyday was also important for Kulik after 1987. In the 1990s she registered, photographically and on video, not only the events and situations that were part of her individual life, but also a stream of images from TV broadcasts that gave her access to facts, events, places, people, and habits from different regions of the world during a time of decisive transformation. The archive thus produced was later used to create the monumental photographic panneau *From Siberia to Cyberia* of 1998–2004. As Kulik declared, its mosaic-like structure, composed of thousands of TV screenshots, was to testify to what her eyes had seen.[24] It was also a way of taking a firm grip on the chaotic flow of the everyday, introducing order into it by means of the selection of images, their chronology, formal affinities, and the overall ornamental structure of the composition.

24 Bożena Czubak and Zofia Kulik, eds., *Zofia Kulik: Od Syberii do Cyberii* (Warsaw: Zachęta National Gallery of Art, 2004). See the artist's statement located after Panel 168.

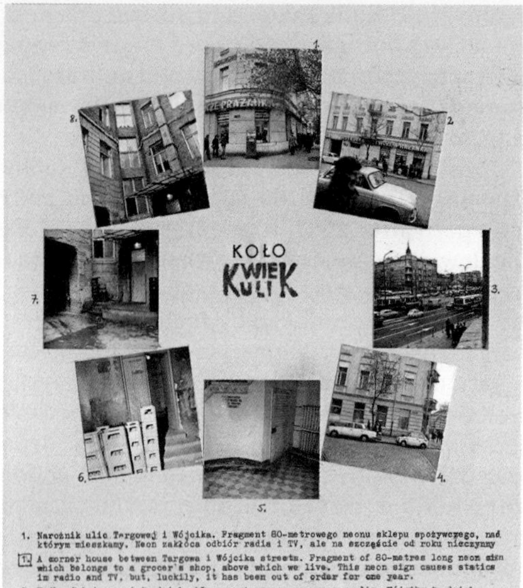

1. Narożnik ulic Targowej i Wójcika. Fragment 80-metrowego neonu sklepu spożywczego, nad którym mieszkamy. Neon zakłóca odbiór radia i TV, ale na szczęście od roku nieczynny

[1.] A corner house between Targowa i Wójcika streets. Fragment of 80-metres long neon sign which belongs to a grocer's shop, above which we live. This neon sign causes statics in radio and TV, but, luckily, it has been out of order for one year.

2. Najbardziej wysunięty dział sklepu spożywczego na prawo w ulicę Wójcika to dział "Wódki". Kolejka po wódkę ciągnie się od 3 do 20 metrów. Wódka ściąga pijaków i degeneratów. W bramie na lewo są drzwi na naszą klatkę schodową.

[2.] The "wodka" department is the farthest on the right into Wójcika street jutting department of the grocer's shop, Wodka line measures from 3 to 20 metres. Wodka appeals to drunkards and degenerates. There is a door to our staircase in the gate which is visible on the left.

3. Ulica Targowa z naszego okna. Cały dzień niebieskie spaliny, hałas i tłok. /Zdjęcie zrobione w niedzielę/. Niemożliwe jest otworzenie okna między 5 rano a 1 w nocy.

[3.] Targowa street from our window. Blue fumes, a noise and crowd during a whole day. /This photo was done on Sunday/. It is impossible to open the windows from 5 oclock in the morning to 1 oclock in the night.

4. Okna parterowe należą do restauracji "Wisła". Muzycy + solista pracują tam do 1-ej w nocy. Okna, zwłaszcza latem, otwarte. Przez nasze zamknięte okna słyszymy trąbkę, gitarę, bębny, "Czikitę", "Kalkutę", szczęk sztućcy, gości opuszczających lokal.

[4.] The ground floor windows belong to "Wisła" restaurant. Musicians + soloist work till 1 o clock in the night there. Open windows, particularly in a summer. Through our close windows we hear a trumpet, a guitar, drums, "Chiquita", "Calcutta", knives, forks and spoons clash, quests leaving the place.

5. Prawa strona naszej klatki schodowej - W.C. dla klijentów sklepu z wódką. Ciemne plamy na podłodze to mocz. Mocny smród.

[5.] Right side of our staircase - W.C. for customers of the wodka shop. Dark spots on the floor mean urine. A strong stenhh.

6. Wejście do naszej klatki schodowej z bramy. Brama pełna skrzynek po butelkach.

[6.] Entrance to our staircase from the gate. The gate is full of boxes empty from bottles

7. Czarna wnęka po lewej stronie to drugi koniec bramy widzianej na zdj. 2. Okrągła lampa świeci nad drzwiami, przez które przerzuca się z hukiem cały towar do sklepu w metalowych pojemnikach przez cały dzień. Widoczne okno wychodzi na klatkę schodową.

[7.] Black niche on the left. It is the second end of the gate, noticeable on the photo 2. Round lamp is shining above the door, through which one throws with rumble all articles in metal boxes to the shop during a whole day. Visible window leads into staircase.

8. Nad drzwiami /patrz zdjęcie 7/ po prawej stronie jest przewód głównej wentylacji sklepu Trzy potężne silniki do wentylacji umieszone w piwnicy powodują cichy, ale uporczywy gwizd w naszym mieszkaniu.

[8.] There is a ventilatione-line on the rigt side above the door /photo 7/. Three huge engines placed in the basement cause low, but persistent whistle in our house.

Znaczenia wyrazu "koło" - meanings of word "koło" : 1. blisko-near. 2. koło-circle.
Translated by authors.

Kulik ·X·1976 ©

FIG. 2
KWIEKULIK, *KWIEKULIK CIRCLE*, 1976

Having built her individual artistic biography in the 1990s after distancing herself from KwieKulik's agenda, around 2000 Kulik engaged once again in working on the duo's archive and preparing its items for presentation. She began scanning slides, photographs, and paper documents from the archive and using them to make narrative sets: photographic installations and digital emulations of slide projections. She came back to those archival materials as she wanted to intervene in an ongoing process of the institutionalization and historization of 1970s and 1980s Polish neo-avant-garde art—to counter certain official and canonical narratives with the story of the phenomenon as seen and rewritten from KwieKulik's perspective.[25] At first, she wanted to do this with Kwiek, but it quickly proved to be impossible as they "entered the same old routine of arguments and quarrels that threatened to thwart the project altogether."[26] After that, Kulik decided to act on her own, and in 2000 she prepared her first narrative set dedicated to the duo and its Activities—the monumental panneau *Autobiographical Aggregate* of 2000. In order to reveal the complex structure of authorship behind the piece, she used the phrase "Zofia Kulik presents KwieKulik." This label was supposed to indicate that, first, the initiative belonged to a different sphere of Kulik's creative engagement than her individual artistic career and, second, that the structure of the presentation and the ensuing narrative were to be understood as her individual account, her own interpretation of KwieKulik's history. Some of the presentations, such as *Variations of Red/The Path of Edward Gierek* of 1971 (digitized 2005), were simple digital reconstructions of slide projections from the 1970s and 1980s. Others, like *Game on Morel's Hill*, were filmed as digital slide projections accompanied by a commentary read by Kulik and Kwiek, whom she sometimes managed to involve in her project; these pieces could also be classified as reenactments of the artists' verbally narrated slide screenings, which they used to propagate the practices of ephemeral art. Finally, digital multi-projections like

25 "Notes in the Margin of the Theory and Practice of the Archive. Transcription of a discussion from Galeria Le Guern prepared by Justyna Kowalska," *Obieg* 75/76, nos. 1/2 (2007): 16–17.

26 Zofia Kulik's remark, see "Notes in the Margin," 26.

Activities with Dobromierz (1972–74/2008) were newly composed, contemporary pieces made with archival slides, which were selected and arranged in a way that not only echoed one of KwieKulik's concepts created along with the original Activities in the early 1970s, but were also strongly reminiscent of Kulik's diploma piece.

In an e-mail conversation with Marek Bartelik, Kulik observed that, while working on the KwieKulik Archive, she was actually combining aspects of her two artistic biographies.[27] That already seems to be the case in *Autobiographical Aggregate* [FIG. 3], where she took advantage of the expertise in creating monumental panneaux she had gained from her own work, especially during the early stages of working on *From Siberia to Cyberia*. Generally speaking, she treated the preexisting KwieKulik Archive in a similar way to the archives she had built up for the purposes of her individual art; namely, she used it to produce Closed Forms—fixed and durable structures that could be perceived as well-articulated narrative accounts.

It is worth recalling two works that epitomize this procedure and its effect. *From the KwieKulik Archive* of 2005 consisted of nine panels with montages made of printed digital reproductions of selected archival documents and their printed descriptions. The items were composed chronologically so as to create an insider overview of a large part of the 1970s and 1980s production in the field of alternative arts in Poland. On the one hand, the piece was rooted in how KwieKulik used to exhibit their archive. In 1979, during the famous *Works and Words* show in Amsterdam, they attached black-and-white photos and other documents to several vertical strips of fabric hung on a wall, each strip presenting one year of their artistic practice, while in 1985, in Banff, they distributed a large number of Polish artists' books, posters, prints, and catalogs on several desks for the audience to browse through. On the other hand, *From the KwieKulik Archive* represented Kulik's contemporary need for giving her historical narrative a fixed form that could be read and understood independently of her presence.

27 "An E-Mail Conversation between Zofia Kulik and Marek Bartelik."

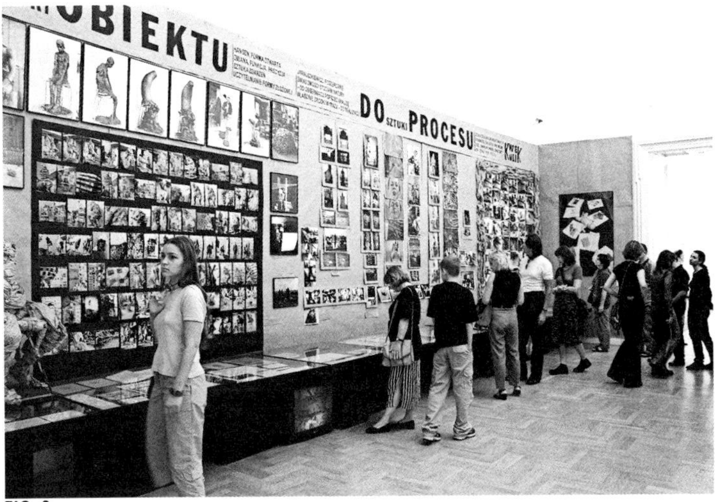

FIG. 3
ZOFIA KULIK, *AUTOBIOGRAPHICAL AGGREGATE*, 2000, EXHIBITION VIEW, ZACHĘTA NATIONAL GALLERY OF ART

Kulik's two artistic biographies were brought even closer to each other and remixed in *Ambassadors of the Past (Made in GDR, USSR, Czechoslovakia, and Poland)*. This digital photomontage, a transposition of Hans Holbein's *The Ambassadors*, depicted Kulik and Kwiek standing next to a table with photo and movie cameras, slide and film projectors, a typewriter, a tape player, an enlarger, etc.—pieces of equipment that the duo had been using to perform, document, and propagate artistic ideas and activities. The images of the artists' heads were archival passport photographs from the 1970s, but the equipment was "staged" and photo-documented for the occasion. Furthermore, the "cloth" that covered the tabletop in the montage was actually the image from Kulik's multiple-exposure photography *Favorite Balance* of 1991. Its title seemed to take on an additional—autobiographical and somewhat ironic—resonance if taken as a reference to the tense relationship between Kulik and Kwiek as former art and life partners.

At this stage, even though Kulik's two biographies became intertwined, they never reached full integration or synthesis, since the artist still wanted to keep a clear dividing line between them. In private discussions she often complained that instead of concentrating on her individual career, she devoted most of her time to working on the KwieKulik Archive, turning its items into narrative sets, organizing their exhibition, and preparing a monumental source book on the history of the duo.[28]

This attitude has changed only very recently. In 2017, in Warsaw, during a seminar entitled "Cultivating the Archive,"[29] Kulik showed five[30] new works—film "clips" that had been edited and prepared for screening that year, but were based on footage she had been shooting for two decades. In the mid-1990s she began recording on video various actions and activities connected with her

28 Ronduda and Schöllhammer, *KwieKulik: Zofia Kulik & Przemysław Kwiek*.

29 "Kultywowanie archiwum—projekcja filmów artystycznych Zofii Kulik," a seminar at the Institute of Art at the Polish Academy of Sciences, Warsaw, October 10, 2017. Participants: Agata Jakubowska, Marta Leśniakowska, Dorota Sajewska, Agnieszka Szewczyk, Tomasz Załuski.

30 In a sense, there were not five, but eight pieces, as one of the works had two parts and another was a three-part "miniseries."

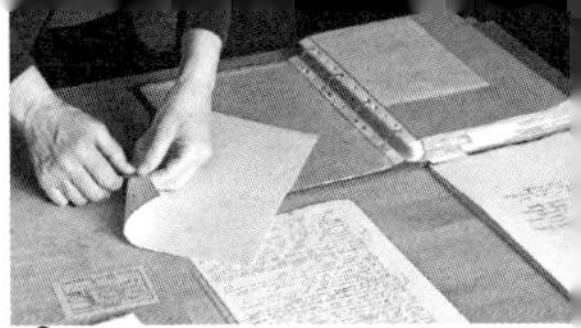

C

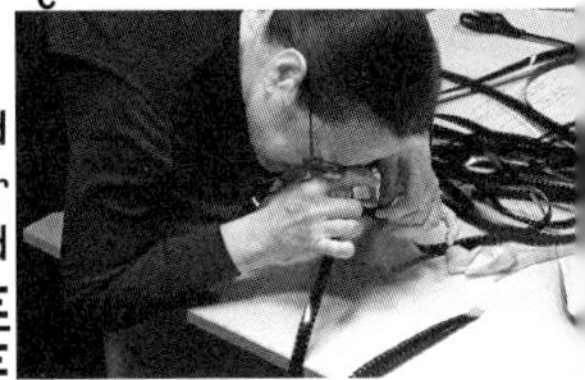

D

everyday life, domestic chores, family relations, and artistic work with both archives: the one she built for the purpose of her individual art, and the one produced or gathered by KwieKulik. The films (**CULTIVATING THE ARCHIVE, OR, IN OTHER WORDS, A PERFORMATIVE WORK**) C + D (2016) presented during the seminar showed both areas of Kulik's archival practice as an integrated, continuous sphere of creative engagement. Additionally, the artist finally dropped the label "Zofia Kulik presents KwieKulik," admitting—in an interview conducted by Wiktoria Szczupacka—that she treated her work on the duo's archive as an immanent part of her individual artistic enterprise.[31] This may have been the beginning of a new stage in Kulik's art, one in which her previously separate biographies will become fully integrated due to her seemingly all-embracing archival drive. The latter indeed seems to have reached new territories, because in one of the films the artist made an improvised performance that brought recollections of the past, while in another she embarked on reenacting the process of making an early student clay sculpture.[32] Kulik's unexpected turn (or return) to process-based activities, if only momentary, indicates that this major Polish representative of "the archival turn" in the visual arts has begun to expand her notion and practice of the archive so as to include her own body, with its gestures, postures, motoric skills, and creative habits—its material, involuntary, performative, and affective memory.

31 Wiktoria Szczupacka, "Poprzez sztukę dokumentuję swoje życie: Rozmowa z Zofią Kulik," in *Miejsce: Studia nad sztuką i architekturą polską XX i XXI wieku*, no. 4 (2018): 82.

32 All films are available online at the *Kulik-KwieKulik Foundation* website, accessed August 8, 2018, http://kulikzofia.pl/en/archiwum/cultivating-the-archive-films-by-zofia-kulik/.

Edit András, PhD, is an art historian, and a senior member of the HAS Research Center for the Humanities, Institute of Art History, Budapest. She focuses on Eastern and Central European contemporary art and theory, gender issues, socially engaged art, public art, the post-socialist condition, and nationalism in the region. She was a member of the Advisory Board and the researcher of Hungary for the exhibition *Gender Check: Femininity and Masculinity in the Art of Eastern Europe* (mumok, Vienna, 2008–09). She was a core member of the international seminar series *Art History in East-Central Europe*, organized by the Research and Academic Program at the Clark Art Institute (Williamstown, MA, 2010–11). She curated the exhibition *Imagined Communities, Personal Imaginations* (Budapest Gallery; Kiscell Museum, Budapest, 2015); co-curated the *Universal Hospitality* exhibition in Vienna and Prague (2016–17); and organized the international conference "Visualizing the Nation: Post-Socialist ImagiNations" (Budapest, 2015). She edited the anthology *Transitland: Video Art from Central and Eastern Europe 1989–2009* (2009). Recent essays have been published in *Former West: Art and the Contemporary after 1989* (2017), *Art and Theory of Post-1989 Central and Eastern Europe: A Critical Anthology* (2018), and *Art in Hungary 1956–1980: Doublespeak and Beyond* (2018).

"YES" FOR GENERAL AND SOCIAL ISSUES, "NO" FOR ANYTHING PRIVATE: MATRIX P (THE PUBLIC, THE PRIVATE, THE PERSONAL, AND THE POLITICAL) IN ZOFIA KULIK'S ART

Contemporary art criticism consciously tries to avoid the traps of intentionalism, the method by which the artwork is interpreted alongside the original idea and intention of the artist. Given that artists might formulate their narrative in order to position themselves in the current art-historical discourse—even applying it retrospectively—the cautiousness of art critics and historians is justified. However, in rejecting intentionalism, the baby is frequently thrown out with the bathwater, as the saying goes: through fear of the interpreter becoming the mouthpiece of the artist, the artist's explanation can be totally ignored or contradicted.

As for the geopolitical attitude of art criticism, the center-periphery binary is disqualified at present for not being contemporaneously relevant.[1] Still, when a slogan or precept emerges from the local conditions of the center, yet is applied blindly to a dissimilar marginal scene, the very dichotomy denied by the theory is affirmed or taken for granted in art-historical practice.

1 Terry Smith, *What Is Contemporary Art?* (Chicago: University of Chicago Press, 2009).

The title of this essay comes from an interview with Zofia Kulik conducted by Joanna Turowicz in 2004, in which the interviewer states: "As we can see, the feminist slogan of the 1970s 'what is private is political' has remained up-to-date."[2] In her reply, Kulik gives a self-reflective (but not at all attuned) description of the socialist art scene of that decade. She provides the key terms of the paradigm within which she and her fellow artists operated:

> In the 1970s the obligatory model of an artist was that of a universal person, which probably also implied a sexless one. While we were sunk in the avant-garde trance, there were no personal sentiments. Even if we, that is I and Kwiek, took "conditions" into account in our art. We would reveal many details from our lives and external "necessities"; however, that was an attempt at the construction of a certain objective model, as science did, or create a universal warning for the so-called "society." Such things, however, were not meant to pertain to an individual experience. "Yes" for general and social issues, "no" for anything private. No way. This would mean derision. Therefore, I subdued these things for so long.[3]

In another interview she puts it differently, but claims the same attitude: "I give myself no permission to expose private things."[4] In yet another statement, she pinpoints that "I'm not a person who will instantly reveal all of her private matters,"[5] and that "One can confess very intimate things to the world. Whatever it is, I never do it directly."[6] Despite her persistence, which resonates with other art-

2 "The Rebellion of a Neo-Avant-Garde Artist: An Interview with Zofia Kulik conducted by Joanna Turowicz," *Kulik-KwieKulik Foundation*, accessed June 15, 2018, http://kulikzofia.pl/en/archiwum/bunt-neoawangardowej-artystki/.

3 "The Rebellion of a Neo-Avant-Garde Artist."

4 Comment made by Zofia Kulik to Sarah Wilson in 1998. Sarah G. Wilson, "Discovering the Psyche: Zofia Kulik," *n.paradoxa* 4 (July 1999): 62, https://www.ktpress.co.uk/nparadoxa-volume-details.asp?volumeid=4.

5 "The Rebellion of a Neo-Avant-Garde Artist."

6 "Self-Portrait: I Am, However, Myself, Not Somebody Else; Bożena Czubak Interviews Zofia Kulik," in *Zofia Kulik—Self-Portraits and the Garden*, ed. Bożena Czubak (Warsaw: Galeria Le Guern, 2004), 50.

ists' positions of the time in the region,[7] the popular feminist slogan "the personal is political" is applied to her œuvre as a general guideline, and perceived as evident without being confronted with the local context or tested against her actual artworks.[8] The same thing applies to another basic tenet of feminism, which is that the connotation of public space is masculine, while private space is feminine—again taken for granted and used by default, and also neglecting its confrontation with local context.[9]

According to Piotr Piotrowski's ideas, the method of the smooth integration of art from the margins into the Western canon, along frameworks and key terms elaborated in the center, not only results in accepting the submissive position, but also in giving up local specificities and nuances.[10] I share his conviction that, instead of tailoring the art of East-Central Europe into a preformulated, default canon, the task of the regional art historian is to elaborate the nuanced differences, based on the different historical-political context. Therefore, I do not wish to buy into these taken-for-granted assumptions; instead, I aim to take a closer look at the socialist context of the 1970s: How does the different sociopolitical context modify those ready-made concepts, and how are they sublimated into the artworks of the time?

In a broad sense, modern Western culture demarcates the private realm of personal life (the realm of domesticity and intimacy) from the public realm (social and/or civil society). In the Western sense, the private not only connotes a particular interest—as opposed to the common, communal, nonpartial interest—but also

7 Dóra Maurer, Ilona Keserü (Hungary), Geta Brătescu (Romania).

8 "...the personal is evidently the political for Kulik..." Sarah G. Wilson, "Zofia Kulik: From Warsaw to Cyberia," *Centropa* 1, no. 3 (September 2001): 240. Reprinted in this volume.

9 Izabela Kowalczyk, "The Geometry of Power in Zofia Kulik's Work," *n.paradoxa*, online issue no. 11 (October 1999): 19–25, https://www.ktpress.co.uk/pdf/nparadoxaissue11.pdf.

10 Edit András, "Provincializing the West: Interview with Piotr Piotrowski," *ARTMargins online*, October 2012, http://www.artmargins.com/index.php/5-interviews/691-provincializing-the-west.

designates privacy, a rights-shielded realm of personal life.[11] The feminist understanding of the public/private dichotomy is that "the separation of the private domestic life of women from the public world of men has been constitutive of patriarchal-liberalism from its origins since the mid-19th century."[12] The hierarchical nature and the gender connotations of the division between (masculinized) public and (feminized) private space, both in concept and practice, are emphasized. The public/private distinction also corresponds to the distinction between political/nonpolitical. The meaning of the powerful slogan "the personal is political," aimed at bridging the two distinct realms, is that if personal factors are structured by public factors (the law, the welfare system, the sexualized division of labor and wage, etc.), then personal problems can be solved only through political means and political actions.[13] However, the analytical account of the theory and politics of the public/private distinction warns us that many feminist writers treated it as an essential key to understanding women's oppression, but "tended to forget that there are important versions of the public/private distinction that could not be mapped directly onto a female/male opposition."[14] I propose that important versions are also produced by geopolitical localities; therefore, one cannot agree more with Weintraub's claim that "the public/private distinction is not straightforwardly universal in its applicability [...] but is sociohistorically variable."[15]

It could safely be claimed that the public/private dichotomy in socialist countries differed significantly from contemporaneous Western variants. Comparing the Western and Eastern meanings of these concepts and practices, Marc Garcelon states that "Under communism, one simply cannot speak of either in terms of the normatively recognized pursuit of legitimate civil interests [...]

11 Marc Garcelon, "The Shadow of the Leviathan: Public and Private in Communist and Post-Communist Society," in *Public and Private in Thought and Practice: Perspectives on a Grand Dichotomy*, eds. Jeff Weintraub and Krishan Kumar (Chicago: University of Chicago Press, 1997), 323–24.

12 Carole Pateman, *The Disorder of Women: Democracy, Feminism, and Political Theory* (Stanford: Stanford University Press, 1989), 132.

13 Pateman, *The Disorder of Women*, 131.

14 Jeff Weintraub, "The Theory and Politics of the Public/Private Distinction," in *Public and Private in Thought and Practice*, 29.

15 Weintraub, "The Theory and Politics of the Public/Private Distinction," 37.

or in terms of an institutionally secured realm of personal life [...] social dependency under communism effectively prevented the institutionalization of secure spaces for an autonomous personal life."[16] Although his research is based on Soviet Russia, the basic tenets hold true in the satellite countries as well.

The Soviet satellite countries also had different formulae for public and private polarization than those of modern Western societies. Party-state domination meant the monopolization of the public sphere; thus, no publicly available space remained for political life outside of the official discourse. All manner of autonomous, socially visible forms of critical political discourse were subjected to strict control. Regarding Poland, this is clearly reflected in Kulik's reply to the question of why she wanted to apply to the (Polish United Workers') Party (although she was never accepted): she stated that "the Party seemed to be the only legal way of being outside the private grounds."[17]

The spatial conception of power is equated with the public sphere, which is traditionally regarded as a masculine space. However, public space in socialist countries, where all aspects of life were oversaturated by high politics and observed and controlled by the regime, was not available to those who were not involved in the common delusion of communism, least of all those who operated (or were accused of operating) outside the state-controlled dream machine. Thus, the separation between private and public realms occurred more along the lines of (political) power than by traditional gender division; hence, alienation and exclusion from politics and the public sphere applied equally to men and women.[18] As for the other side of the dichotomy, no such thing as a rights-shielded realm of personal life existed in socialist countries. Since neither the public nor

16 Garcelon, "The Shadow of the Leviathan," 323–24.

17 "The Rebellion of a Neo-Avant-Garde Artist."

18 Edit András, "Do I Dream Freely or on Command? Imagined Masculinity in Socialist Hungary," in *Gender Check: Femininity and Masculinity in the Art of Eastern Europe*, ed. Bojana Pejić (Vienna: Museum Moderner Kunst Stiftung Ludwig Wien, 2009), 100–4.

private space in socialist countries could be described using Western categories, the local situation jumbled gender roles as well, so neatly described in the Western feminist and art-historical canon.

The phenomenon of converting a private space into a semi-public space by converting private apartments into galleries for artists' activities (and their mostly limited audiences) existed in almost all the countries of the Eastern Bloc, even if in different measures in various countries.[19] However, in this essay I am not interested in the alternative spaces created for art activities, but rather in art-making practices and the imaginary alternative spaces created by the artworks.[20]

As for testing the applicability of feminist terms and key notions to Eastern conditions, Zofia Kulik once again provides clues. When she is asked about Polish artists such as Ewa Partum and Natalia LL, "who had contacts with the world feminism"—a statement implying that she did not—she replied: "They used Western terms; yet, this was incomprehensible in the Polish Communist reality. They were radical in their commonplace texts but they did not reveal any single bit of the secrets of their own experience and thoughts."[21] In complete agreement with her, I argue that if the Western feminist claim that the personal is political is weighed against the claim of artists operating behind the Iron Curtain, we find that the exact opposite is relevant, i.e. the political is personal![22] This means that instead of the issues of segregated, degraded, and invisible private life being pushed into the public arena and thereby upgrading questions of

19 Łukasz Ronduda, "Art, Love, Politics, Science," in *KwieKulik: Zofia Kulik & Przemysław Kwiek*, eds. Łukasz Ronduda and Georg Schöllhammer (Warsaw: Museum of Modern Art in Warsaw and KwieKulik Archive; Wrocław: BWA Wrocław Galleries of Contemporary Art, Awangarda Gallery; Vienna: Kontakt: The Art Collection of Erste Group and ERSTE Fundation, 2012); József Havasréti, *Alternatív regiszterek: A kulturális ellenállás formái a magyar neoavantgárdban* (Budapest: Typotex, 2006).

20 Edit András, "Out of Private Public Opinion into Shared Personal Opinion: The Public, the Private, and the Political," in *Art in Hungary 1956–1980: Doublespeak and Beyond*, eds. Edit Sasvári, Sándor Hornyik, and Hedvig Turai (London: Thames and Hudson, 2018), 229–50.

21 "The Rebellion of a Neo-Avant-Garde Artist."

22 The concept was first elaborated by the author at the symposium "Reading Gender: Art, Power, and Politics of Representation in Eastern Europe" (Vienna: mumok, November 14, 2009); then expanded in: András, "Out of Private Public Opinion."

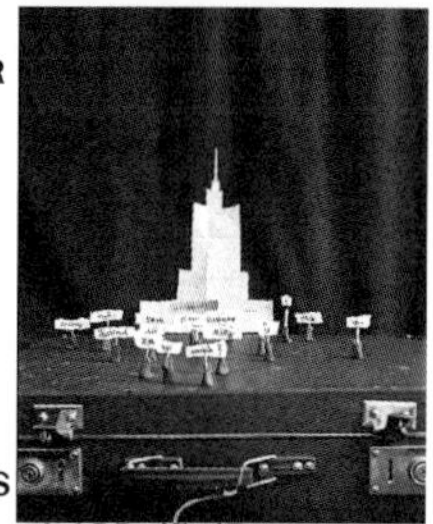
A / PP. 15–17

micro-power, (macro-)political issues are treated as highly personal concerns. The creation of various imaginary alternative spaces by artists in different parts of the region counteracted the exclusion from public space and public politics, and served as a substitute both for personal involvement in public life and for the politics lost in personal life. In a Freudian slip, Ewa Lajer-Burcharth notes, in her piece analyzing Kulik's and her own attitudes towards socialism, that "we wanted to personalize" the socialist utopia, which supports my thesis.[23] However, she and several other writers focus on the artist's retrospective critical rethinking in Kulik's post-socialist works that address the issues of socialism.

I am interested in the artist's critical and subversive attitude during socialist times, which offers more than safe post-socialist critical reflection and irony, and restores the agency of the artist, implemented through an act of—as I call it—the imaginary transgression of public space. The works analyzed here appropriate and internalize politics, turning it into intimate private property, and smuggle the political into art in an era when the public was infantilized and excluded from politics.

Compared to the huge works made in the 1990s, **LETTER FROM MILAN** [A (1972)] —long-overlooked, small-scale (but very complex)—sits at the center of my case study. This work had remained omitted from the studied œuvre; it has only lately, after forty years, moved into the spotlight.[24] However, it offers ample opportunity for uncovering the issue of agency beyond the official discourse during the time of socialism.

The work is an accumulation of color slides, black-and-white negatives, and sketches. It was also exhibited as a sequence of twenty-one small color prints mounted on a wall in sequential order like a storyboard.[25] The location of the story is defined by the first photo, a cutout from a handwritten letter of Kulik's partner, Kwiek,

23 Ewa Lajer-Burcharth, "Old Histories: Zofia Kulik's Ironic Recollections," in *New Histories*, ex. cat. (Boston: Institute of Contemporary Art, 1996), 119–36. Reprinted in this volume.

24 It was exhibited for the first time at the KwieKulik retrospective exhibition *Form Is a Fact of Society*, BWA Galeria Awangarda, Wrocław, 2010.

25 *Love Performance*, Galeria Labirynt, Lublin, 2016.

forming the silhouette of the Palace of Culture and Science in Warsaw. It provides the background, as in real life, to a May Day parade, enacted by small clay figurines carrying placards. The stage for the miniaturized theater is the artist's luggage—placed on a couch (to be psychoanalyzed) and covered by a blue curtain. There are paper skies appliqued on the blue textile background, a cutout paper heart is pinned on the paper building, and paper flowers cover the ground, in imitation of the communist ritual. As the event unfolds, with its phases being documented in carefully arranged photographs, the cheerful, idyllic scene turns into a dystopia of total devastation.

The work permits different readings; Luiza Nader most recently analyzed it within the discourse of conceptual art, wondering whether the work changes the established historical-artistic image of conceptual art in its materialized and emotional form.[26] She relies on Roland Barthes' *A Lover's Discourse: Fragments* as a theoretical guideline, considering *Letter from Milan* a non-verbal "love letter" to her partner, Kwiek, in which "love is registered in all its shades."[27] Her sensual and insightful interpretation concludes that "the artist not only speaks up, but, above all, operates on her own terms, setting the rules of the game. She acts and speaks as a strong subject emerging from the murmur of love. In doing so, she establishes a new paradigm of love, drawing from the space of actioning—constant, persistent work and mediation focused on the process of communication, leading to the subject's transformation and sometimes, potentially, to social and political change."[28] I would like to begin my interpretation where Nader's finishes, namely with the social and political potential involved in the work.

From this perspective, we should start with the May Day parade around which the plot revolves. Ceremonies had a ritualistic nature in socialist states. Publicly staged political rituals were the basic form of reinforcing or even sacralizing power in commu-

26 Luiza Nader, "Materializing Conceptual Affects: The Love Discourse of Zofia Kulik's *Letter from Milan* (1972)," in *Conceptualism and Materiality: Matters of Art and Politics*, ed. Christian Berger (Leiden: Brill, 2019). I am grateful for having been able to read the manuscript prior to publication.

27 Nader, "Materializing Conceptual Affects."

28 Nader, "Materializing Conceptual Affects."

nist states. "Public manifestations, adorned with political and ideological symbols, provide a means of self-representation of the state-power."[29] For the individual to be controlled, they had to be on public show at all times.[30] The totalitarian model is built on the discipline of an all-powerful sovereign center.[31] In the carefully orchestrated displays, its own power is demonstrated, and therefore the "unspoiled image of the public parade" held utmost importance.[32] This applied even in Yugoslavia, which, when compared to Soviet Russia in this regard, could be found at the other end of the spectrum. That is why all deviant objects (books, whiskey, cigarettes) and subjects (a woman feigning masturbation—a taboo under socialism) had to be removed from Sanja Iveković's balcony during Josip Tito's 1979 parade in Zagreb, immediately after having been spotted by the secret police from a roof opposite. Her performance took place in an in-between space, her balcony, which linked the privacy of the apartment with the outside world.[33] As Ruth Noack observes in her close reading of that work, there is an "agonistic coupling between the male statesman in a populist projection of his self into public" and a female artist "inwardly focused, engaged in intellectual pursuit"; that is to say, a man in public office and an artist with a limited public role—a woman in her privacy.[34] Iveković's method here is termed "argumentative juxtaposition"[35] by the writer. In my reading, the *Triangle* (the performance and its photo documentation) is also a nuanced demonstration of the reverse validity of the Western feminist slogan "the personal is political." It strongly suggests that the political (in local meaning: high politics) saturates all aspects of personal life on the most intimate, bodily level, and that the personal and private could not exist outside of politics—not even in Yugosla-

29 Katarzyna Ruchel-Stockmans, *Images Performing History: Photography and Representations of the Past in European Art after 1989* (Leuven: Leuven University Press, 2015), 138. See also excerpts from Ruchel-Stockmans' text in this volume, 247–66.

30 Ruchel-Stockmans, *Images Performing History*, 10.

31 Garcelon, "The Shadow of the Leviathan," 311–12.

32 Garcelon, "The Shadow of the Leviathan," 139.

33 Ruth Noack, *Sanja Iveković: Triangle* (London: Afterall, 2013), 2.

34 Noack, *Sanja Iveković: Triangle*, 5, 6.

35 Noack, *Sanja Iveković: Triangle*, 7.

via, the freest country within the Bloc. The work mounts a powerful artistic resistance towards suppressive state power by its transgressive action.

If independent political and public life was in short supply in the Soviet satellite countries, carefully orchestrated mass celebrations attempted to maintain the illusion of the collective cohesion of a community, politically and ideologically loyal to the leaders. Even though, in these mass celebrations, the public was involved in politics simply by being on display, politics were neither discussed nor negotiated with the people. These rituals were supposed to provide a carnivalesque image of freedom, and generate euphoria through collective marching and singing surrounded by flags and ribbons. Attendance was obligatory and organized meticulously through workplaces. Artists interested in the issues (or the loss) of politics were especially attracted to the most spectacular of all celebrations: the May Day parades. Hungarian artist Dóra Maurer's *Private May Day Demonstration in an Artificial Field* (1971) [FIG. 1] is a kind of privatization of the public celebration, the direct opposite of the official one. This parade took place in an isolated, claustrophobic private space, and resembled the monotonous physical exercise one might undertake for survival in a solitary cell, rather than the cult of physical fitness of the new kind of human advocated by communist ideology. This was not a triumphal march towards a bright future, but effectively a standstill—a circular movement turning back on itself again and again as a symbolic comment on the country's ideology. Coming from socialist Yugoslavia, Bálint Szombathy, a minority Hungarian artist in Vojvodina, staged his performance reflecting on the May Day parade in public space. He joined the end of a parade in Budapest when the crowd and its enthusiasm were dissipating, and documented the performance in the photo series *Lenin in Budapest* (1972) [FIG. 2]. Communist heroes are in abundance in socialist mass celebrations; the obligatory distance is emphasized by the enormous size of their portraits, raised high above the heads of ordinary people. Szombathy breaks the unwritten rules when he carries a pole with a placard showing Lenin's head, much like those carried by the marchers, but instead of leading the

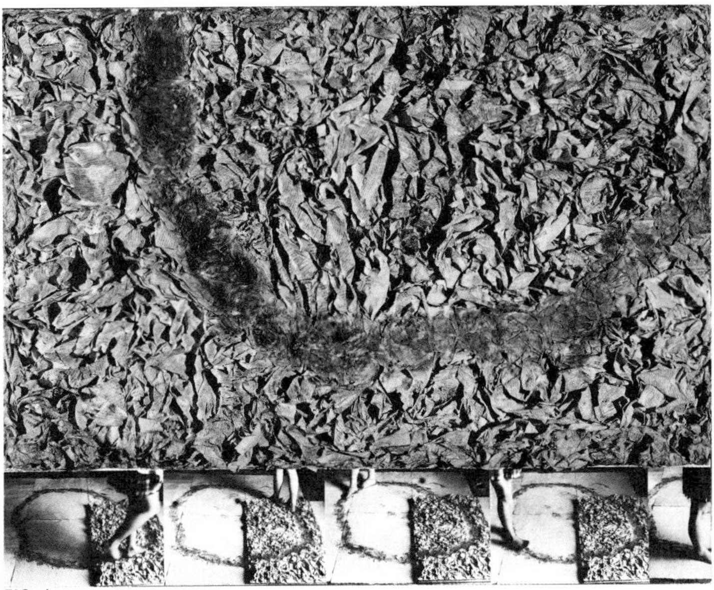

FIG. 1
DÓRA MAURER, *PRIVATE MAY DAY DEMONSTRATION IN AN ARTIFICIAL FIELD*, 1971

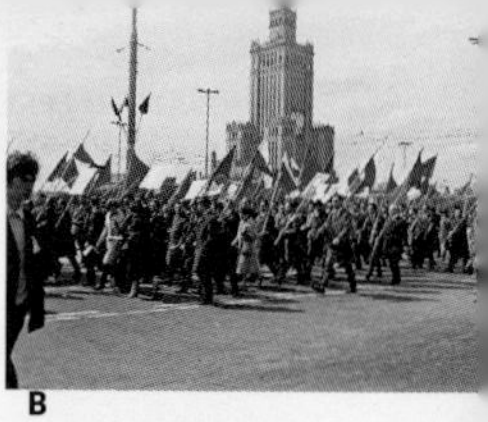

B

masses, Lenin is marching in the opposite direction, turning his back on the people. The untouchable hero, the symbol of the regime, is demystified and commercialized.

Concerning socialist Poland, "a particularly symbolic role in the ceremonial calendar was played by the May Day celebrations—'the festival of festivals'—symbolizing fundamental principles of the new system. [...] The May Day parade remained intact over many decades, as a metaphor conveying the rules of social and political order embedded in Marxist-Leninist ideological projects."[36] Zofia Kulik, a socially and politically conscious artist, was deeply attracted to the celebratory decorations of rituals held in Moscow (which she visited as part of a student group, organized by the Academy of Fine Arts in 1971) and in Warsaw. These rituals combined the visual heritage of her childhood, her experience of life in a military barracks, the military exercises organized by her father, and the colorful textiles of the domestic environment created by her seamstress mother. Out of curiosity and attraction she invaded public space like Szombathy, yet she remained invisible. In Moscow she was fascinated by the enormous scale of the political propaganda[37] and took photos from a bird's-eye view. During **MAY DAY PARADES** **B (1972)** held in Warsaw she was an observer of the political orgy, and as a flâneuse[38] she mingled with the crowd and took hundreds of snapshots of the celebratory mass. She felt it was her duty to document these events. The slides were stacked up and later served as the repertoire of her activities. The memory of these rituals was still vivid during her stay in Milan.[39]

36 Piotr Osęka, "Ritual of the May Day Parade in Poland between 1945 and 1989," *Centropa* 12, no. 1 (January 2012): 65.

37 "The Rebellion of a Neo-Avant-Garde Artist."

38 She states in an interview that "the only role which I consciously act is the role of the observer." "Self-Portrait: I am, However, Myself, Not Somebody Else," 43.

39 "In 1972, Zofia Kulik received the prestigious Stella Sas Korczyńska Bottoni scholarship, a biannual award given to the 'most gifted female graduate of the Faculty of Sculpture' in Poland. She stayed in Italy from May 17 to August 28." Ronduda and Schöllhammer, *KwieKulik: Zofia Kulik & Przemysław Kwiek*, 118–22.

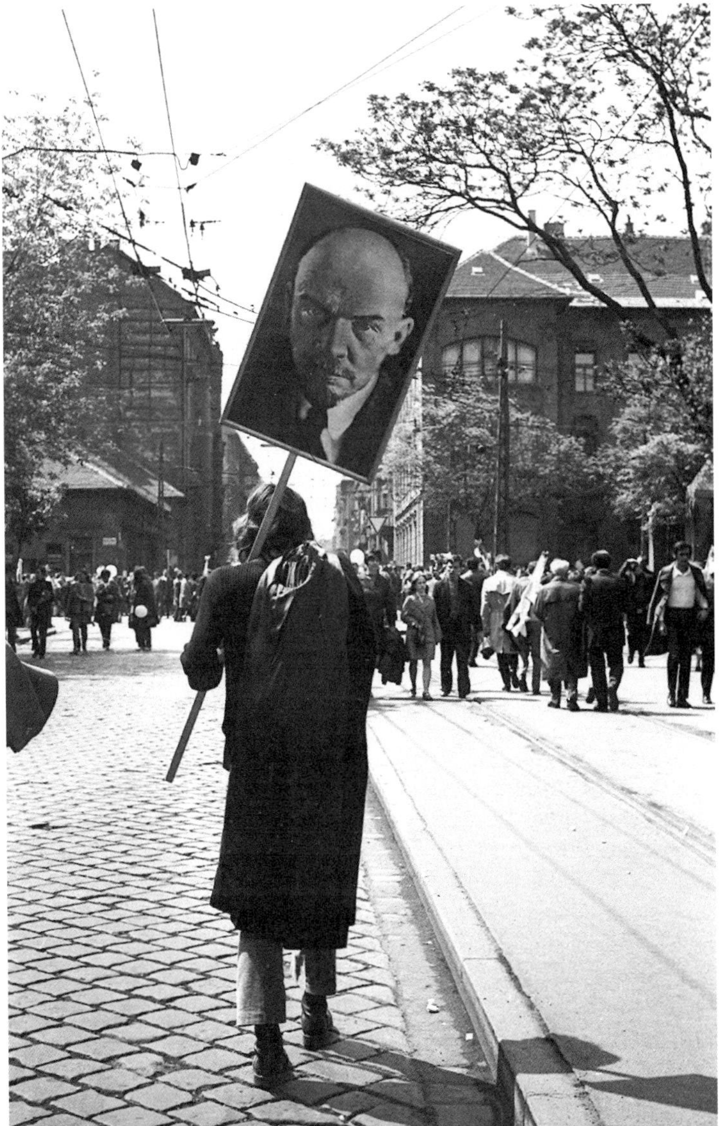

FIG. 2
BÁLINT SZOMBATHY, *LENIN IN BUDAPEST*, 1972

In Poland, the May Day parades "were transformed into propaganda spectacles over which the administrators—beginning in 1945—had increasingly effective control."[40] Kulik took control and agency into her own hands when she created her private, miniaturized version of the parade, combining elements of the festive city witnessed in Moscow and the parade she experienced many times in Warsaw, intertwined with her personal life. Her conceptual performance piece, the phases of which were documented by photographs, was made in an "extraterritorial territory," by Kulik's definition, which is, in my terms and the context of this essay, a semi-private space:[41] a not-quite-private but also not-quite-public space. Although it was a private space, it was not her own, as she was not at home, but rather in a foreign city—Milan. The piece could be perceived as a miniaturized theater performance, or rather its script, documented in photographs, or even as a sketched comic book. Although the May Day parade imitated in front of the Warsaw Palace of Culture and Science is made from colorful cut-outs on top of a suitcase, the content is not simply a public ceremony rearranged and reenacted in a private space. A public event transformed into a personal one could be the visualization of the passages of a human emotion—love—so eloquently elaborated in Luiza Nader's writing, or, on the contrary, in my reading, could be a kind of appropriation of a public event for personal and political ends—in Kulik's words, a "universal warning for the so-called 'society'."[42]

Zofia Kulik's entire life is full of politics, or, to put it another way, her "dowry"[43] consists of political symbols and political visions. "I was born for ideals not for myself,"[44] as she declares. So much so that even the letter written by her lover, the father of her

40 Osęka, "Ritual of the May Day Parade," 66.

41 "My stay was possible thanks to the scholarship. I received money, but I had to organize my stay in Italy by myself. In Milan I lived in a private flat—somebody in the Academy introduced me to a woman and she agreed to rent a room to me. In one of the attached slides the window and the street can be seen..." Kulik, e-mail to the author, July 4, 2018.

42 "The Rebellion of a Neo-Avant-Garde Artist."

43 "An E-Mail Conversation between Zofia Kulik and Marek Bartelik," *Kulik-KwieKulik Foundation*, accessed June 9, 2018, http://kulikzofia.pl/en/archiwum/rozmowa-internetowa-z-zofia-kulik-rozmawial-marek-bartelik.

44 "The Rebellion of a Neo-Avant-Garde Artist."

unborn child (with whom she was already pregnant in Milan), is transformed into the Palace of Culture and Science. There is little to distinguish private from public: private life is transparent and literally projected into public space. It is not some hidden personal issue that qualifies for political reasoning, but the other way round: the personal is fully saturated with politics. Politics is personalized, drawn deep into private life.

All the elements in this monodrama oscillate between the two spheres. The window is the border between inside and outside; with a blackout curtain, one is shut out of the perspective of the other. When the curtain is metamorphosed into the curtain of a theater, it is supposed to insulate reality from fantasy and imagination; however, this curtain is taken from the window hook, line, and sinker—that is to say, along with its rod, but used as the background for a private theater, not for segregation and for defining the boundaries. The domestic environment is enhanced, eliminating the borderline; the artist floats freely between private and public, and between personal and political.

The suitcase, the stage for the plot or pedestal for statues made of clay and paper (the material she took from the sculpture studio of the Academy of Fine Arts in Milan), is a transportable object, able to bridge the gap between private and public space. It is associated with privacy, and serves as a vessel for carrying mostly personal items while moving from one public/private place to another. In its static function it is used for hiding and preserving the most precious personal treasures and memories. It could also be a container for the goods of a vendor, or the attribute—"the cross of so many 20th-century passions"[45]—of the homeless, refugee, migrant, or victim. For artists, it is perfect for miniature or unfinished works.[46] According to Marcel Duchamp, everything important he had ever done could be put into a little suitcase, referring to *Box in a Suitcase*, his suitcase artwork, and "to the inherent ability of these objects to compress our

45 A very telling phrase, used by Hungarian scholar Zsuzsa Hetényi, a historian of Russian literature.

46 Amy Lin, "These Artists Create Microcosms with Suitcase as Art," *Widewalls*, December 11, 2016, https://www.widewalls.ch/suitcase-art/.

entire lives in small rectangular space."[47] In societies lacking free speech, the suitcase serves as a "closet" for forbidden ideas, thoughts, or identities.[48] What are those ideas in the case of Zofia Kulik, whose suitcase is personified by her luggage tag left on it? We may have some insights as the story advances.

The monumental dimensions of socialist celebrations[49] were obligatory. Kulik's, however, is a downscale, miniaturized version built on top of a suitcase. Enlargement, miniaturization, and the changing of scale are traditionally tools of social critique.[50] So, if we are inclined to associate the scene with a theatrical production, then it is more likely a flea circus, not to be taken seriously, or should be read as an ironic commentary. Taking into consideration the traditional gender connotation of private space—that it is supposed to be a feminine realm—the construction is a doll's house; however, no dolls are present. She is playing with politics—a better fit for boys, in conventional thinking. Not only are the gender roles turned upside down, but so is the "concept of a hierarchized and militarized social order,"[51] when she creates a randomly arranged, disorganized mess. The playfulness, mocking humor, and infantilized, childish execution involved in this small-scale, private version of the May Day parade are elements that are not tolerated by high politics.

The Palace of Culture is a cutout of Kwiek's letter to Kulik—from a plain, factual, professional letter, not a personal, intimate one (a love letter). In my reading, the content does matter, and is not "out of touch with the scenography of Kulik"[52] (i.e. when viewed from a personal perspective). The letter is about ideas for artists addressing social and political issues, along with topics that present then-current political-ideological matters, such as *The Path of Edward Gierek*, *The Achievements of the Avant-garde and Political Art*, *Using the*

47 Lin, "These Artists Create Microcosms with Suitcase as Art."

48 Károly Halász, a Hungarian neo-avant-garde artist, whose art evolved around his hidden homosexual identity, often uses bundles and luggage in his art.

49 Osęka, "Ritual of the May Day Parade," 71.

50 See Jonathan Swift, *Culliver's Travels*.

51 Osęka, "Ritual of the May Day Parade," 66.

52 Nader, "Materializing Conceptual Affects."

Internationale *in Actions*, *Think Communism*, *Lenin Superstar*, etc.[53] The topics listed and the aims to be achieved (to be didactic and optimistic) strongly resemble the attitude of the revolutionary avant-garde of the 1920s, who aimed to take part in building the social utopia of a more just future in which artists would have their share.[54] So, the artistic activity projected onto the facade of the Palace (which embodied all aspects of official culture) is an imaginary transgression, an imaginary appropriation of a symbolic space that was not assigned to the artists from her circle, and not assigned to her either. The personal letter with public content is mutilated, and the truncation results in a fragmented text similar to a free poem. However, dissection does not mean castration—quite the opposite in fact: the phallic character of power is made obvious by the transformation of the letter, written by the dominant member (at the time) of the artistic duo. It becomes architecture with phallic dimensions alongside its authoritarian character, representing the "Stalin-era articulations of theories about 'architectural power.'"[55]

Although the Polish words on the banners carried by the clay figurines (which translate as "My lovely... My dear... Do you think about me?... I want to be with you... I miss you so much... I often think about the child...") are certainly those of a person in love, the love object is rather ambiguous, taking into account the visual environment where the parade unfolds. It could be Kwiek, but it could also be deep-seated love for social utopia or a strong commitment to "change reality," as Kulik defined her stance in an interview. I share the perception of the interviewer, Joanna Turowicz, for whom the artist's attitude resembles the Russian avant-garde of the 1920s, but Kulik, although accepting the analogy, puts emphasis on the difference, stating that "we did not want to destroy; we wanted to reform

53 Przemysław Kwiek, "Proagit 2," in *KwieKulik: Zofia Kulik & Przemysław Kwiek*, 431–36.

54 Richard Stites, *Revolutionary Dreams: Utopian Vision and Experimental Life in the Russian Revolution* (New York: Oxford University Press, 1989).

55 Michał Murawski, "Big Affects: Size, Sex, and Stalinist 'Architectural Power' in Post-Socialist Warsaw," in *Elements of Architecture: Assembling, Archeology, Atmosphere and the Performance of Building Spaces*, eds. Mikkel Bille and Tim Flohr Sorensen (New York: Routledge, 2016), 65.

and reorganize."[56] This sentiment or desire, however, remained platonic, never able to blossom in real life, and remained a personal longing, an object of fantasy, as she was not allowed to take part in its public realization. And so the private letter (with public content) is transformed into a kind of sociopolitical manifesto of a socially committed artist who is dissatisfied with the cultural climate she lives in.

After the collapse of socialism, revenge was wreaked so obsessively and in so many works on the official totalitarian culture that had been imposed on all fields of art and culture during its existence, but Zofia Kulik might also have been seeking revenge for the aborted utopia of transforming society with the help of artists. There is an ambiguity or hesitation in this terminated love—a mixed feeling of admiration and betrayal, an emotional state where the ideas of communism had not yet been completely rejected,[57] but their metamorphoses into monstrousness are already present in the visual form of the (phallic) Palace. It was "a Stalinist model for transformative acculturation through architecture,"[58] a powerful example of the Stalinist sublime, with its intention to terrify but also with a magnetic (even sexual) attraction due to its enormous size and astonishing dominance. Artists were regarded as scientists;[59] however, in the scientific process of breeding a new kind of humanity, those lacking absolute and unconditional love, hesitating, or having their own ideas were not invited. "In his parental role, Stalin as father is motherly more than punitive, nurturing rather than disciplinary. The Soviet family drama is pre-Oedipal. It is for not loving the mother/leader that the child is punished"[60]—which applies to the satellite countries as well.

56 "The Rebellion of a Neo-Avant-Garde Artist."
57 Wilson, "Zofia Kulik: From Warsaw to Cyberia," 238.
58 Murawski, "Big Affects," 70.
59 In the socially committed Eastern European avant-garde, and partly in the neo-avant-garde, artists considered themselves scientists—"engineers of the future"—as seen in various artists' manifestos. Kulik also refers to this: "we were prepared to be scientists." Comment made by Kulik to Wilson in 1998. Wilson, "Discovering the Psyche," 63.
60 Susan Buck-Morss, *Dreamworld and Catastrophe: The Passing of Mass Utopia in East and West* (Cambridge, MA: MIT Press, 2002), 197.

The idyll and adoration of the first few photos of the narrative, evolving in consecutive acts documented in the carefully arranged photos, evaporates for the finale, when the remains of the cutout Palace are transformed into wings, and the Palace (which had become "the most powerful material legacy of state-socialism"[61]) disappears, flying out of the scene of political fantasy. The clay figures grow enormously, taller than the paper Palace, and the decoration becomes trampled during the ominous, frightening events. And, after the ideology vanishes, a completely ruined, devastated scene remains, leaving a mass of clay on top of the luggage. For the final scenes a black-and-white photograph is added, showing a human figure trying to imitate the Palace, but his/her wings, made of white fabric, can't lift the body into the air, leaving it unable to fly away. It remains on top of the heap with similar, smaller photos. This is a dystopian fantasy that was totally forbidden, and as such had to be hidden during socialism. If we are witnessing an act of the imaginary killing of a loved one, as Nader claims,[62] the victim in my reading is the dominant, masculinized political force; it is more akin to a secret political voodoo ritual directed against the symbols of the system that would fall two decades later. Kulik, asked why she continued to rely on the topic of socialism, its imagery and symbols, well after the collapse of the regime, when all other artists had left it behind as its currency was lost, replied that "it must be my strong will to refer to the political past and to my own lifetime as well." [63] In a text written in 1991, she declared that "I take an artistic revenge by grabbing all sorts of weapons (symbolic and formal) directed against me."[64] Although she is referring to her post-1989 activity, the seeds of the idea of revenge were already with her in 1972 in Milan, and fueled her private performative action. This early form of revenge might correspond with the anthropological understanding of revenge as a destructive and abrupt violent response to anger or humiliation. After the collapse of the socialist system she plotted a full-fledged

61 Murawski, "Big Affects," 77.
62 Nader, "Materializing Conceptual Affects."
63 Kulik, e-mail to the author, July 4, 2018.
64 "The Rebellion of a Neo-Avant-Garde Artist."

and very sophisticated revenge—not just on patriarchy and the dominant, submissive masculinity present in "her own lifetime," but equally on the "political past" that was also dominant and submissive. In the articulated post-socialist revenge, the scale once again shifts, but now in the other direction: masculinity is miniaturized, decreasing into decorative pattern,[65] while the Palace is degraded into a toy, losing its power by being transformed from its erect stance into a small, loosely hanging version.[66] The "Palace Complex"[67] is analyzed and treated on the couch of the artist. Both revenges—though in embryonic form—are inscribed into this early solo work. The two are not rendered in hierarchical order, each having its place in Kulik's life and art.

I claim that the two major lines defining Kulik's own art beyond the KwieKulik duo, blossoming in post-socialist times, are advanced in this small-scale, condensed work. It is placed in Matrix P, as I name it: the public, the private, the personal, and the political, blurring and reversing the canonical distinctions between them. Its immense complexity makes it accessible from a private, personal perspective, and available to interpret from within "her own lifetime"—as in Nader's interpretation—as well from a public perspective, from the "political past"—in my interpretation. The imaginary transgression of an artist-agent manifested in the work also proves that the Western assertion of the total division and sharply opposed character of the Soviet-style spheres ("passive victimized societies and victorious, omnipotent and relentlessly oppressive party-states") does not hold true.[68] Artists, Zofia Kulik among them, were able to go beyond these binaries via their imaginary transgressions.

Ewa Lajer-Burcharth's insight—that the masculinity of official power was reflected in unofficial discourse—is highly relevant with regard to the East-Central European region as a whole,

65 Wilson, "Discovering the Psyche," 61.
66 Kulik, *Self-Portrait with the Palace*, 1990.
67 Murawski, "Big Affects," 76.
68 György Péteri, "Introduction," in "Patronage, Personal Networks and the Party-State: Everyday Life in the Cultural Sphere in Communist Russia and East Central Europe," special issue, *Contemporary European History* 11, no.1 (February 2002): 1.

not just to Poland. The "sad corpus," as she names the phenomenon, of Eastern European myth that equates the dissident artist with a man,[69] is only just starting to be dissolved. Behind the myth, strong women artists emerged, even during socialism[70]—in our case, Zofia Kulik outside the KwieKulik duo. Kulik's own voice may have become more robust after the collapse of socialism, but her speech-act was articulated well before the political and personal life change, deep in the times of socialism. The *Letter from Milan* of 1972 is powerful proof of this.

69 Lajer-Burcharth, "Old Histories," 131.

70 Sanja Iveković and Katalin Ladik in the former Yugoslavia; Jana Želibská in Slovakia; Dóra Maurer and Ilona Keserü in Hungary; Geta Brătescu and Ana Lupas in Romania, to name just a few.

Wiktoria Szczupacka is an art historian, currently a PhD candidate at the Institute of Art at the Polish Academy of Sciences. Her research focuses on the neo-avant-garde art of the 1970s, and the feminist perspective. She has published in exhibition catalogs and art magazines such as *Magazyn Sztuki*, *Obieg*, and *Szum*. Her recent published work includes "Foksal Gallery, Women and Labor of Love in the 1960s and 1970s" in the post-conference volume *Revisiting Heritage* (2018) and "Poprzez sztukę dokumentuję swoje życie: Rozmowa z Zofią Kulk" (Through Art I Document My Life: Conversation with Zofia Kulk), published in *Miejsce* journal (2018). She is director of the Kulik-KwieKulik Foundation.

RESPONSIBILITY IS AN ACTION, NEVER SIMPLY A FEELING: ZOFIA KULIK'S *ALICE'S ADVENTURES IN FUCKED WONDERLAND*, OR, CLEANING INSTEAD OF TALKING IN THE CONTEXT OF THE POLISH NEO-AVANT-GARDE OF THE 1970s

During the 1970s, when Zofia Kulik was a member of KwieKulik, an artistic duo (1970–87) comprised of Zofia Kulik and Przemysław Kwiek, she produced only a handful of solo works. One of those was the mail-art composition titled *Alice's Adventures in Fucked Wonderland*. This was one of two works prepared by Kulik and Kwiek for Antonio Ferro's mail-art project *La Post/Avanguardia*. It is precisely this work, in the context of Zofia Kulik's position in the Polish neo-avant-garde of the 1970s, which I wish to make the central focus of this essay.

The critic Marceli Bacciarelli called the landscape of the artistic initiatives of the era in Poland a "printed artistic life." Galleries were begun by sending out letters, and art labs and centers were initiated with manifestos.[1] "As if artists sought to move

1 Marceli Bacciarelli, "Drukowane życie artystyczne," *Współczesność*, no. 12 (1971).

backwards and forwards on the borderline of doing nothing,"[2] to cite Jerzy Ludwiński, who in his famous lecture "Art in the Postartistic Age" characterized artistic practices in the late 1960s and early 1970s as striving towards "zero" level. During the period's numerous symposiums and panels, both Ludwiński himself and many other artists and theoreticians formulated manifestos that established institution-ideas. From semiofficial propositions such as Ludwiński's Center for Artistic Research (1969) and the Art Documentation Center (1970–71), through private art-exchange networks such as Jarosław Kozłowski and Andrzej Kostołowski's NET, Andrzej Partum's Poetry Office (later morphed into the Pro/La Gallery), or Ewa Partum's Adres Gallery,[3] to ironic gallery-manifestos such as Anastazy B. Wiśniewski's "Non-Existent Self-Affirming Gallery Yes," Jerzy Treliński's 100×40 Gallery, and Andrzej Pierzgalski's A4 Gallery.

While the mail-art dispatch of *Alice's Adventures in Fucked Wonderland* can also be described as an example of "printed artistic life," I perceive the work as Kulik's critical commentary on the functioning of the Polish neo-avant-garde art movement and her own position within it.

The composition's central element is a photograph showing a woman sweeping the floor. Similar imagery can be found throughout much of the feminist art of the 1970s, such as in Mierle Laderman Ukeles' famous performance *Hartford Wash: Washing, Tracks, Maintenance* (1973), where she mopped a gallery's stairs, pointing to

2 Jerzy Ludwiński, "Art in the Postartistic Age," in *Notes from the Future of Art: Selected Writings by Jerzy Ludwiński*, ed. Magdalena Ziółkowska (Eindhoven: Van Abbemuseum; Rotterdam: Veenman Publishers, 2007), 17.

3 At the time of writing, the first Adres Gallery retrospective, *My Gallery Is an Idea*, is showing at the Studio Gallery in Warsaw. The curator, Karolina Majewska-Güde, has stressed the "pre-feminist" nature of Ewa Partum's institutional initiative, while asking whether "there can be anything more feminist than starting your own institution and controlling its message"; Tomasz Załuski characterizes Partum's gallery in similar terms in his essay, "Kobieta walcząca o pozycję w polu produkcji artystycznej: Samoidentyfikacja, samoorganizacja i samoemancypacja według Ewy Partum," in *Zagadnienia Rodzajów Literackich* 61, no. 2 (126) (2018): 75–89. This additionally points to the context of the male-dominated field of artistic production within which Partum functioned. Besides short-lived initiatives such as Barbara Kozłowska's Babel Gallery or galleries run by larger artist collectives, such as the Actual Art's Gallery, Partum's Adres seems indeed to be the only woman-run gallery among the Polish neo-avant-garde gallery-ideas.

cleaning as invisible, low-paid work performed for the art world; and in other floor-cleaning performances that sought to acknowledge the significance of women's domestic work, e.g. *Scrubbing* (1972) by Chris Rush or the Les Nyakes performance at the First Catalan Women's Conference (1976). Drawings showing floor-washing as a chore typically performed by women, such as Birgit Jürgenssen's *Bodenschrubben* (1975), should also be mentioned here.

In Polish art of the 1970s, such images and motifs are hardly found. In Poland at the time, women's emancipation was a cliché—an official communist slogan, rather than a postulate actively pursued by any kind of grassroots social movement.

In her essay "The Gender Issue in the Works of KwieKulik: *Cherchez la femme*,"[4] Ewa Majewska described the *La Post/Avanguardia* dispatches as one of the rare moments in the duo's history where KwieKulik were being emotional—where they gave up calculated scenarios on behalf of spontaneity and affect. For a researcher, Zofia Kulik's composition appears in the first place to express frustration and anger. This, however, is not anger at domestic chores, but at the reality of communist Poland—the oppressive prose of life, which stifled art-making. Agata Jakubowska approached the work from a different perspective. In her essay "The Existential and Economic Dimensions of the 'Actioning' of Zofia Kulik and Her Mother"[5] she analyzed the recent *Cultivating the Archive* series of films, citing Kulik's mail-art piece as one of the artist's representations of her own work. Jakubowska compared Kulik's artistic work with her mother's work in her garden, highlighting the existential dimension of the essentially similar works of the artist and the retired seamstress, as well

4 Ewa Majewska, "The Gender Issue in the Works of KwieKulik: *Cherchez la femme*," in *KwieKulik: Zofia Kulik & Przemysław Kwiek*, eds. Łukasz Ronduda and Georg Schöllhammer (Warsaw: Museum of Modern Art in Warsaw and KwieKulik Archive; Wrocław: BWA Wrocław Galleries of Contemporary Art, Awangarda Gallery; Vienna: Kontakt: The Art Collection of Erste Group and ERSTE Foundation, 2012), 518–20.

5 Agata Jakubowska, "Egzystencjalne i ekonomiczne wymiary 'czynnościowania'
Zofii Kulik i jej matki Heleny," *Miejsce: Studia nad sztuką i architekturą polską XX i XXI wieku*, no. 4 (2018): 12–24.

as stressing the relationship of economic dependence. The artistic work of KwieKulik was made possible by the work and financial support of Zofia's mother, Helena Kulik.

Although both perspectives are feminist, and Jakubowska addresses the work of women, thus setting a line of interpretation that is of interest to me, the analyses conducted so far have not referenced a later performance in which the artists, this time as a duo, reused their *La Post/Avanguardia* mailings with added artistic content. Noticing a relatedness between *Alice's Adventures in Fucked Wonderland* and the context of functioning in the 1970s neo-avant-garde art community, I will focus in this essay on the question of the responsibility involved in launching and running artistic initiatives.

Even though *Alice's Adventures in Fucked Wonderland* is a solo work by Zofia Kulik, it is one that shows the "backstage" of living as an artist, thus resonating with the practices of KwieKulik, which existed at the fringes of, but still within, the neo-avant-garde art community. What made KwieKulik different was that they problematized the sociopolitical context of their work, showed everyday life, and commented critically on artists' living conditions. They had the courage to present and critically analyze propaganda ceremonies, their professional situation—the hackwork—and also their family life: their son, Kwiek's disabled sister, housing (*KwieKulik's Circle*, 1976),[6] and existential conditions (*Art Out of Nerves*, 1975).[7] They also ran the home-based Studio of Activities, Documentation and Propagation (Pracownia Działań, Dokumentacji i Upowszechniania, PDDiU). The duo was unlike any other in Poland, because KwieKulik were the only ones to seriously reflect on Marxist concepts and on their relationship with state institutions such as the Visual Arts Studios (Pracownie Sztuk Plastycznych, PSP) or the Ministry of Culture and Art. They wanted to change the system from within, and at the same time, almost in line with the feminist slogan that the "personal is political," they exposed the underside of being an artist in the Polish People's Republic, bringing to light the realities of artists' everyday socioeconomic struggles.

6 Ronduda and Schöllhammer, *KwieKulik: Zofia Kulik & Przemysław Kwiek*, 235.
7 Ronduda and Schöllhammer, *KwieKulik: Zofia Kulik & Przemysław Kwiek*, 214.

The PDDiU published theoretical texts—manifestos—but being located in a private home and running a program of shows and visits initiated by KwieKulik, its existence was significantly more "real" than that of the institution-ideas mentioned at the beginning of this essay. KwieKulik long sought to ensure the preservation of their collection and, aware of the amount of work involved in pursuing the PDDiU mission, repeatedly applied for funding—grants that would allow them to document art. The many letters, entreaties, and cost estimates to that effect in the KwieKulik Archive show how much their thinking about the institution and its operation was anchored in material reality. This was a material reality not only of petitions and budgets, but also of ordinary dirt, fatigue, and toil.

In a 1975 PDDiU exhibition,[8] comprised of a text enlarged to the size of an entire wall, KwieKulik provided a gritty account based on their daily experience:

> Weary, we walked downstairs to buy oil at the grocery store. We took an empty bottle and eighteen zlotys. The saleswoman: "What? This dirty bottle? No way can we take it! Wash it and bring it back; if you use washing powder, the wax and sticker will come off easily!" Our chests grew hot. We said, "We know!" and there was nothing else we could say. We shuffled back upstairs. We scraped off the wax, washed the fat away, and there was nothing else we could do.[9]

This is just one of many examples showing how directly the art of KwieKulik drew on the events of everyday life.

Such daily hurdles were also the stuff of the duo's mail-art dispatches to *La Post/Avanguardia*. In 1977 KwieKulik were invited by artist Antonio Ferro to join his international mail-art project, alongside some three hundred other artists such as Ben Vautier, Daniel Spoerri, Jiří Kolář, László Beke, Pierre Restany, and Ernesto

8 *Fruits of the Earth* by Edward Dwurnik and *Art Out of Nerves* by KwieKulik, PDDiU, December 18–28, 1975.

9 Ronduda and Schöllhammer, *KwieKulik: Zofia Kulik & Przemysław Kwiek*, 215.

de Sousa. The invitation was in the form of a large sheet of stiff paper (ca. 40×50 cm), with the caption "La Post/Avanguardia" at the top, and a frame marked "reserved for your creation" below.

Kulik and Kwiek each came up with their own responses. Kwiek's work is called *My Two Projects Rejected by All*, and shows precisely that, plus the artist's commentary. In the burned-out central section of the sheet there are two color drawings showing details of a design—scenographic elements of a traveling exhibition called *The October Revolution and Poland*—pieces of artistic hackwork commissioned by the Lenin Museum in Warsaw. One shows entwined flags, the other a red star. Kwiek filled the remaining intact paper space with the following text: "I kept my eyes fixed on the place 'for my creation,' many ideas were running through my head—then this place began to burn and my two recent designs, rejected by all, appeared in [the] burnt [out] hole." The fantastic situation suggested by the artist—the self-ignition of the central part of the sheet—was juxtaposed with the reality of his artistic existence, where, in order to earn his living he had to do hackwork. Such artistically unrewarding jobs were commissioned mostly by the Visual Arts Studios, and later by private and state payers (Warexpo, in this particular case). One first had to win the commission, and then in successive stages of production the design and the work-in-the-making itself were evaluated. The evaluating committee could reject the work or pay only a part of the agreed remuneration if it found the final effect to be wanting. The designs proposed by Kwiek—the entwined flags and the star—weren't accepted, and so he received no money for his work on them. He became frustrated, having spent his creative energy doing hackwork—for nothing, as it turned out.[10] The piece is analogous to many KwieKulik works where the artists presented their hackwork projects.

A more personal allusion to work can be found in the dispatch prepared by Zofia Kulik. A collage fills the "reserved for your creation" space. It shows a woman leaning over a large broom in a dimly lit domestic interior, with spots of light illuminating her hair, hands, feet, and the broom, so it is hard to say what we are actually looking

10 Ronduda and Schöllhammer, *KwieKulik: Zofia Kulik & Przemysław Kwiek*, 274.

at. It can be guessed that this is the artist photographed while sweeping the floor. The central section of the composition has been clearly delineated with a white circle. By placing specks of dirt and fluff on the negative, and printing them using the photogram technique, Kulik created abstract, irregular forms on the edge of the circle; she then painted them in rainbow colors. Despite the mundane theme of cleaning, the composition brings to mind astronomical maps, images of the sky, and outer space. This was intended by the artist, who says that she was inspired by a "feeling of transcendence, without the need for naming it."[11] Kulik describes her inspirations as relating to meditation in movement, such as, for example, monotonous physical work. She defines this state as a connection between the mind and the material body.

Below, outside the circle, Kulik wrote a caption in decorative script: *Alice's Adventures in Fucked Wonderland* (in Polish and English). Asked about it today, she replies that she calligraphed names on documents for a living, but refuses to elaborate on the choice of that particular title.[12] The composition of *Alice's Adventures*, with a portrait of the broom-wielding artist in the center, surrounded by rainbow "dust," suggests that she can be identified with Alice in Wonderland here. A literary figure of iconic status, Alice's characteristics —kindness, rationality, courage, assertiveness—seem to be shared by Kulik too. At first lost in the fantasy world, Alice soon realizes that the only fixed and immutable thing is that her expectations and preconceptions about the world around her meet with rejection, in particular the rejection of the logical rules governing reality as she knows it. In Wonderland, cause and effect aren't what they are elsewhere, and this is why Alice feels frustrated.[13]

Zofia Kulik too seemed to be venting her frustration, especially through the formulation of the title. *Alice's Adventures in Fucked Wonderland* is an artwork that, like the practice of KwieKulik, has been fundamentally informed by daily experience. Kulik has

11 Kulik, e-mail to the author, March 6, 2017.
12 Kulik, e-mail to the author, March 6, 2017.
13 Andrzej Z. Makowiecki, *Słownik postaci literackich* (Warsaw: Państwowy Instytut Wydawniczy, 2000), 23.

stressed in numerous interviews that cleaning and the logistics of everyday life were her main chores. Some of the hackwork-documenting photographs [FIG. 1] show her in the background, in work clothes, as well as offering a glimpse of her kitchen—a space that had many purposes, serving as a guest room, dining room, and atelier, and therefore requiring thorough cleaning before and after every job.[14] Functioning in such conditions, in a single space that required cleaning "around the clock," became the basis for making *Alice's Adventures*.

In my view, this isn't a voice in the debate on women's domestic work, but the frustration of a rational artist functioning in the neo-avant-garde art world, which, according to her, was governed by absurd laws. Starting a gallery didn't entail maintaining it; an institution-idea on a piece of paper didn't have to be cleaned.

I earlier described Kulik's attitude towards cleaning as affirmative—she perceived domestic chores as "meditation in movement"—but at the same time she was frustrated by how underappreciated this kind of work was in "printed artistic life." The ambivalent attitude towards women's domestic work in Western culture (on the one hand, disparaging it—on the other, demanding financial payment for it) was brought into focus by a black feminist. bell hooks, in her framing of work "from margin to center" undid the monolith of feminist critique, allowing for a different approach to work—one much closer to the attitude embodied by Zofia Kulik. hooks, distancing herself from the second-wave "wages for housework" feminist movement, nonetheless demanded more respect for this kind of work. She compared cleaning to love; she argued that too little had been written about the value of service work, in particular domestic work. Notwithstanding studies such as Ann Oakley's *The Sociology of Housework* (1974) or Rae André's *Homemakers: The Forgotten Workers* (1981), there were very few feminist analyses, according to hooks, that recognized how well-performed housework contributed to the overall well-being of individuals. Criticizing Western feminists, hooks wrote:

14 See "KwieKulik Anatomy: An Interview with Zofia Kulik and Przemysław Kwiek by Tomasz Załuski," in Ronduda and Schöllhammer, *KwieKulik: Zofia Kulik & Przemysław Kwiek*, 535–45.

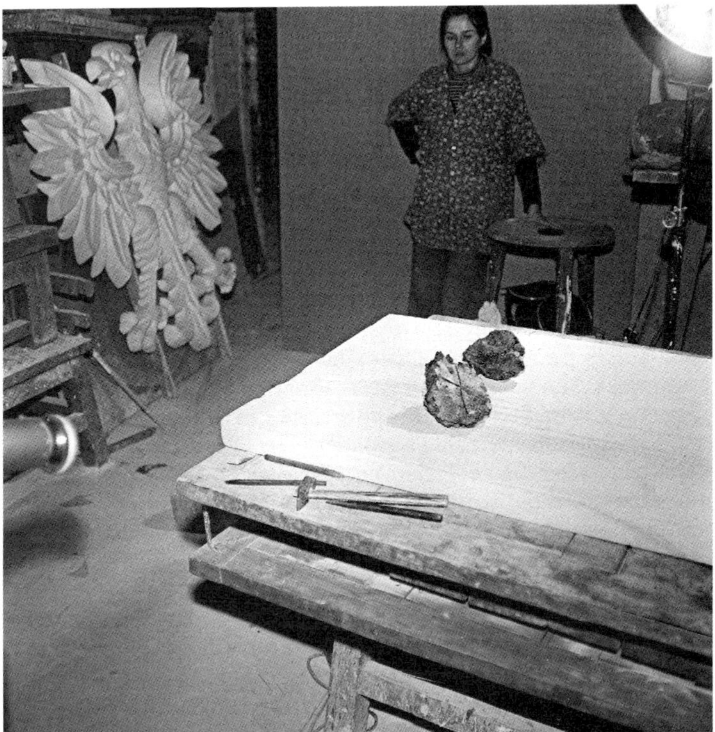

FIG. 1
KWIEKULIK, *AK KINGA PLAQUE—EARNING AND CREATING*, 1974

> By learning housework, children and adults accept responsibility for ordering their material reality. They learn to appreciate and care for their surroundings [...]. Girl children, though usually compelled to do housework, are usually taught to see it as demeaning and degrading. These attitudes lead them to hate doing housework and deprive them of the personal satisfaction that they could feel as they accomplish these necessary tasks [...]. Today, many young Westerners, female and male, follow the teachings of varied Eastern religious and philosophical thought in the hopes of experiencing self-realization. During this process, they learn to rethink their attitudes towards work, especially service work. They learn that discipline begins with careful performance of all tasks, especially those deemed "menial" in this culture.[15]

Zofia Kulik's public comments suggest a similar attitude towards housework. She appreciated its "meditative" monotony, and at the same time called for it to be appreciated in the creative process. "Menial" work also became a subject of her theoretical reflection. Kulik originated the neologism *czynnościowanie* (actioning), denoting monotonous, repetitive tasks.[16] As she has said, "Getting involved in work stifles your fears."[17] At this point, one could ask what kind of fears did Kulik seek respite from in housework? Speaking in interviews about her position in the 1970s neo-avant-garde art community, Kulik has stressed that she "didn't speak," that she didn't like the situation where the most charismatic (or loudest) person always led the field. In a conversation with Joanna Turowicz, Kulik remembers her rebellion against that, which materialized in the 1980s. "I did not want to go to all these events and symposia 'starring' Kwiek, Józef

15 bell hooks, *Feminist Theory: From Margin to Center* (Boston: South End Press, 1984), 104.
16 A definition of "actioning" in an interview with Kulik, in the author's archive.
17 Kulik, e-mail to the author, March 6, 2017.

Robakowski, Andrzej Partum, and others."[18] Interesting evidence of this is found in a document from the Dreamers' Congress[19] [FIG. 2]. Anastazy B. Wiśniewski produced a kind of catalog of the event—taking pictures of the participants, collecting their comments and proclamations—which he then published in the form of sheets with artists' pictures and texts—a collection of individuals and their manifestos. But when Wiśniewski asked Kulik if she wanted to say something for the record, she just shook her head. That gesture obviously wasn't captured by the voice recorder, so Wiśniewski asked whether Kulik was too embarrassed to speak up, to which she shook her head again. As a result, the sheet devoted to Zofia Kulik features her photographic portrait and a small, absurd-sounding note: "Let it be known that citizen Zofia Kulik has some very important information about things that matter to us all, but isn't too embarrassed to share them. Signed: A. Wiśniewski."

Talking to Joanna Turowicz, Kulik remembered the cause of her silence: "I was never pushy about speaking. I couldn't gather my thoughts whenever someone expected me to say something; although, [very] often everything would simmer inside me." She also said she preferred a different kind of modus operandi: "I think that if we lived in the time of a revolution, my role would be next to some leader fighting for beautiful ideas. I would organize things, carry pamphlets, bombs or whatever."[20] Kulik didn't comment on KwieKulik's practices; talking to the public, polemicizing, and commenting was Kwiek's domain; Kulik was in charge of the logistics of their trips and meetings.

An unwillingness to take the floor during debates conducted in the neo-avant-garde art community—as a phenomenon characteristic for the experience of women artists—has been described by a researcher of the Wrocław scene, Zofia Reznik. Citing

18 "The Rebellion of a Neo-Avant-Garde Artist: An Interview with Zofia Kulik Conducted by Joanna Turowicz," *Kulik-KwieKulik Foundation*, accessed February 27, 2019, http://kulikzofia.pl/en/archiwum/bunt-neoawangardowej-artystki/. First published as "Bunt neoawangardowej artystki," in *Artmix*, no. 9 (March 2005)

19 A five-day artistic congress, from September 8 to 12, 1971, in Elbląg.

20 Ronduda and Schöllhammer, *KwieKulik: Zofia Kulik & Przemysław Kwiek*, 284–85.

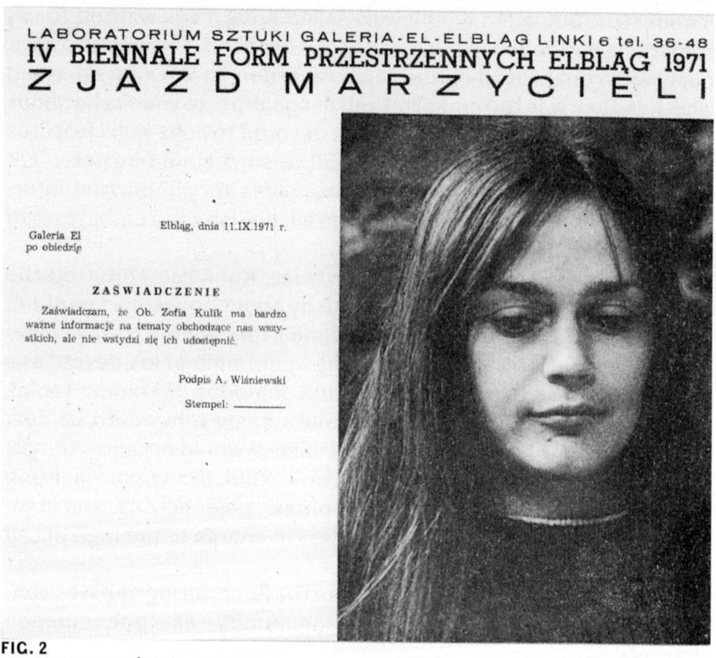

LABORATORIUM SZTUKI GALERIA-EL-ELBLĄG LINKI 6 tel. 36-48
IV BIENNALE FORM PRZESTRZENNYCH ELBLĄG 1971
Z J A Z D M A R Z Y C I E L I

Galeria El
po obiedzię

Elbląg, dnia 11.IX.1971 r.

ZAŚWIADCZENIE

Zaświadczam, że Ob. Zofia Kulik ma bardzo ważne informacje na tematy obchodzące nas wszystkich, ale nie wstydzi się ich udostępnić.

Podpis A. Wiśniewski

Stempel: ________

FIG. 2
ANASTAZY B. WIŚNIEWSKI, CATALOG ENTRY FOR ZOFIA KULIK, THE DREAMERS' CONGRESS, 1971

her interviews with artists Katarzyna Chierowska and Anna Kutera, Reznik pointed out how they would opt out of the men's discussions and busy themselves with service work: "When asked directly about their activeness in the group, both women answered jokingly and rather evasively: 'I helped at the gallery; I swept the floor [...] When [the men] came to discuss, I made them some tea and minded my own business.'"[21] The example of Zofia Kulik suggests that this wasn't a specifically Wrocławian issue, but rather a larger phenomenon bound up with the position of women in the art world at the time.

Working in a collective—namely a duo—was also problematized by Kulik. This experience is the theme of another of her solo works, the emancipatory performance *Zofia Kulik's Begging for Forgiveness*, presented at the Dziekanka Gallery in 1978 following the KwieKulik performance *Heavy Complaints Kill Life*,[22] which offered a pessimistic take on the reality of life in the Polish People's Republic and dealt with individual responsibility. Inspired by the 1938 Hollywood melodrama *Jezebel*, Kulik rented a wedding gown and knelt before the audience, begging for forgiveness. For her, this was a moment of self-humiliation, but also of emancipation—a liberating act of expressing her mute presence in KwieKulik. This was the first such radical outlining of the artist's "contours," as well as one of Kulik's few solo presentations during KwieKulik's career. Asked why she and Kwiek made separate works for *La Post/Avanguardia*, the artist says that it was the result of chance. "We received two identical sheets, so we did two works," she shrugs. An unwillingness to waste one of the sheets—as well as the opportunity to make a statement in international company—translated into Kulik's solo piece for the mail-art project.

21 Zofia Reznik, "The Fifth Beatle and the Mother of Success: Female Artists of the RAG Collective in the Light of Oral History," in *Galeria Sztuki Najnowszej / The Recent Art Gallery*, ed. Anna Markowska (Wrocław: Contemporary Museum, 2014), 332.

22 *Heavy Complaints Kill Life*, Dziekanka Gallery, Warsaw, June 20, 1978. From among two hundred invited guests, twenty-three were selected to participate in the performance. They were asked to stand up and talk briefly about a "painful hardship, discrepancy, botchery, irregularity, or inconvenience" they had experienced or noticed in real life. Those "complaints" were recorded on heavy objects, which were added to a bag suspended from a string. When the string finally broke, the bag fell onto a drinking bowl, killing a laboratory rat, at which point the words "You are all responsible for that" were projected on a screen.

All the responses Ferro received from the invited artists were exhibited in 1977 at the Numerosette Gallery in Naples, and then at the Museo del Sannio in Benevento.[23] KwieKulik, rather than content themselves with that, and driven perhaps by a desire to get their message across to the Polish neo-avant-garde art community, recreated their dispatches and showed them at the Mospan Gallery in 1978 [FIG. 3], addressing the remade *La Post/Avanguardia* compositions to the Warsaw audience.[24] The reproduced text-and-image paper compositions were displayed on the wall and in frames, linking them to the traditional art of painting. The show was complemented by the presence of the artists themselves, both with certain accessories. Kwiek wore an eye patch with a drawing of a photo camera stuck on it, referencing the duo's documentary practice as part of the PDDiU and making a jocular allusion to "winking an eye." Kulik appeared wearing a special construction on her head—a wire frame hidden by her hair that held in place a bullet pointing at her temple. The construction stressed Kulik's frustration, already present in the title of the mail-art composition. Kwiek treated the guests to vodka and *bigos*[25] and initiated discussions, whereas Kulik recorded the proceedings using a tape recorder. But the presentation of the remade *La Post/Avanguardia* dispatches was accompanied by one more element, which appears particularly significant in the context of Kulik's non-speaking.

Like any other KwieKulik show, this one included an open discussion. This time, however, anyone willing to speak had to put a pebble in their mouth. Making it difficult for others to speak, Kulik, as the event's co-creator, projected her own experience of having difficulty articulating her thoughts onto those present at public debates. An archival photograph shows Andrzej Partum—one of the most charismatic figures of the neo-avant-garde movement, an active participant in numerous symposia and debates—who, about to join the discussion, is pictured putting a pebble in his mouth [FIG.

23 A printed catalog was also published, but it didn't feature the dispatches by Kulik and Kwiek. Antonio Ferro, *La Post/Avanguardia*, Museo del Sannio, Benevento, Italy.

24 Ronduda and Schöllhammer, *KwieKulik: Zofia Kulik & Przemysław Kwiek*, 300.

25 Traditional hunter's stew of slowly cooked cabbage and meats.

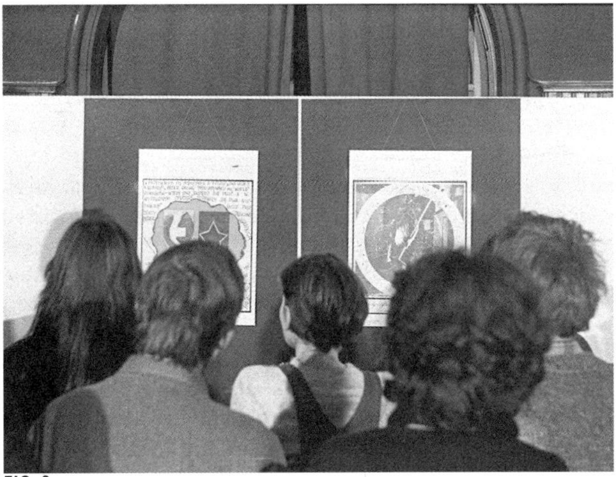

FIG. 3
KWIEKULIK, *PERFORMANCE, A MINIMUM—LA POST/AVANGUARDIA*, EXHIBITION VIEW, MOSPAN GALLERY, WARSAW, 1978

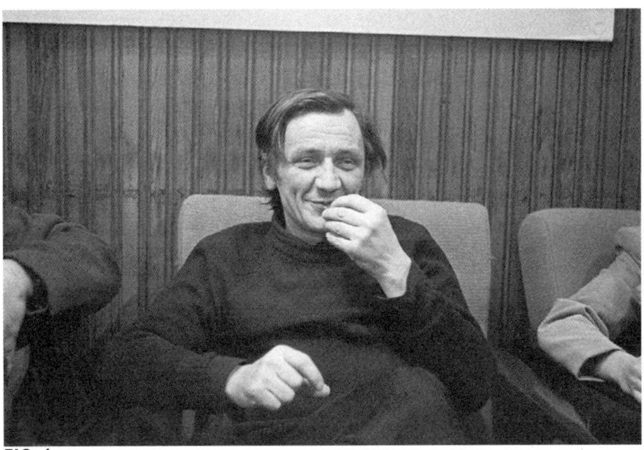

FIG. 4
ANDRZEJ PARTUM PUTTING A PEBBLE IN HIS MOUTH, MOSPAN GALLERY, WARSAW, 1978

4]. No recording or other documentation of the discussion has been preserved, but the KwieKulik monographic publication states that the "presentation seemed to be a self-reflective critical commentary on [the duo's] own work, [on] documentation, [on] discussions on art in artistic circles, and the techniques applied during their earlier presentations, etc."[26]

My view of *Alice's Adventures in Fucked Wonderland* is that the work is a critical commentary on the forms of the art world's functioning at the time, and on its inability to acknowledge the "menial" work necessary for its own survival. An Alice in a neo-avant-garde Wonderland, Kulik was frustrated by her work in a reality where the rules she knew did not apply. Cause wasn't related to effect; calling a gallery into existence didn't require maintaining it. According to KwieKulik and according to Kulik, an institution's realness manifests itself only in its struggles with reality.

In the action at the Mospan Gallery, the pebble in the mouth was meant to prevent the usual speakers from all-too-easily verbalizing their concepts and designs, and to make them feel the weight of material reality. Long debates on the medium of art, its ideas, its recipients, and other such abstract themes were part and parcel of artistic conclaves and powwows. Everyday reality and actual work, however, which had to be performed in order for artistic ideas to be turned into reality—from tea-making, through the constant cleaning of the studio, to organizational efforts and negotiations—were missing from those gatherings altogether.

The title of this essay paraphrases bell hooks' famous dictum, "Love is an action, never simply a feeling."[27] Zofia Kulik's attitude towards cleaning seems akin to that presented by hooks. Both call for recognizing it as an important form of contributing to collective well-being—as commitment expressed in a different

26 Ronduda and Schöllhammer, *KwieKulik: Zofia Kulik & Przemysław Kwiek*, 300.

27 "Ever since I started writing about love, I have defined it in a way that blends M. Scott Peck's notion of love as the will to nurture one's own and another's spiritual and emotional growth, with Eric Fromm's insight that love is action and not solely feeling. Working with men who wanted to know love, I have advised them to think of it as a combination of care, commitment, knowledge, responsibility, respect, and trust." bell hooks, *The Will to Change: Men, Masculinity, and Love* (New York: Atria, 2004).

language, in different forms, other than by excelling in public debates. They understand cleaning, quite simply, as a rightful form of responsibility.

Translated by Marcin Wawrzyńczak

This text was originally published in Polish in Aspiracje*, no. 51/52 (2018); it is published here in a revised version.*

Angela Dimitrakaki, PhD, is a writer and senior lecturer in contemporary art history and theory at the University of Edinburgh, where she directs the MSc in modern and contemporary art. She works on social reproduction, globalization, gender, and labor in relation to art and its institutions, having published over sixty articles and book chapters. Her academic books include *Gender, artWork and the Global Imperative: A Materialist Feminist Critique* (2013), *Art and Globalization: From the Postmodern Sign to the Biopolitical Arena* (in Greek, 2013), *ECONOMY: Art, Production and the Subject in the 21st Century* (co-edited with Kirsten Lloyd, 2015), and *Politics in a Glass Case: Feminism, Exhibition Cultures and Curatorial Transgressions* (co-edited with Lara Perry, 2013), and she is currently completing a book titled *Feminism, Art, Capitalism*. She is a Corresponding Editor of *Historical Materialism*, for which she co-convenes the London Annual Conference's Marxist-Feminist Stream and co-edited the special issue on Social Reproduction (2016), and an editor of *Third Text*, for which she co-edited the Social Reproduction and Art special issue (2017) and the Anti-Fascism/Art/Theory special issue (2019). An award-winning novelist in her native Greek, she was a recipient in 2017 of an Athens Academy Award for her fiction on themes connected with her scholarly work.

THE STRUGGLE FOR NON-ALIENATION: ZOFIA KULIK'S WORK IN TERMS OF LABOR

Zofia Kulik's art-making is often seen as "labor-intensive." We can begin by observing the work's imaginal complexity (the intricacy arising through the capacity of image-making).[1] This complexity tends to be articulated through the tropes of detail and juxtaposition—social detail and formal juxtaposition in artworks that often entail a noted monumentality: Kulik's celebrated *All the Missiles Are One Missile* (1993) and *From Siberia to Cyberia* (1998–2004) are relevant examples. Secondly, Kulik's is a practice that insists on the dialectic between the messy wealth of visual culture and the artwork's adequacy for ordered, synthetic exposition. Much has been said about Kulik's artworks incorporating the televised image, as well as her turning of voluminous three-dimensional public monuments into two-dimensional miniature references in tapestry-like artworks based on a meticulously planned, symmetrical arrangement of

1 Philosopher Chiara Bottici has argued for the need to develop "a theory of imaginal politics"—that is, a theory connecting the civilizational capacity of making images to politics. See Bottici, "Imaginal Politics," *Thesis Eleven* 106, no. 1 (2011): 56–72.

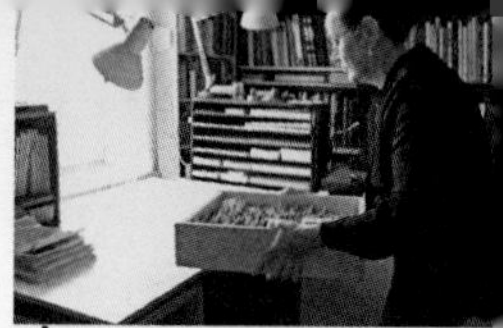

A

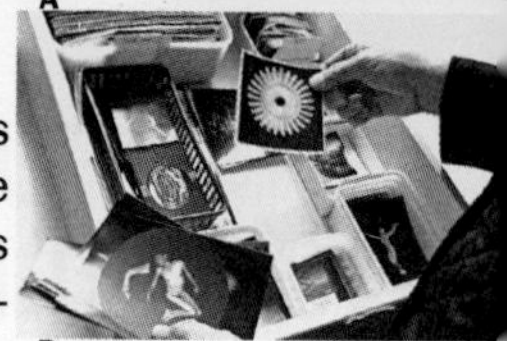

B

motifs.[2] And finally, the evolution of this work compels clarifications pertaining to a time frame. Kulik's time frame is marked by major historical events as well as events in her life as an artist—in this case, a "woman artist"—an unstable yet provocative political category in feminist imaginaries since at least the turbulent 1960s.

These feminist imaginaries have been grappling with a contradiction that also necessarily informs the present analysis: on the one hand, there is the political need to foster a *plural* subject of creative capacities and in-common militancy through the abstraction "woman artist"; on the other, there is the pragmatism that dictates the equally political need to grasp the work-life circuit of a *singular* "woman artist," given that the actual art field is populated by stories of individual achievement. Feminist art history has not resolved the methodological issues that arise from this contradiction. In the majority of cases, it continues to address the outputs of artistic labor known as "artworks" when these are made by "women artists"; it has also elaborated biographies of individual female artists (irrespective of these women's relationship to feminism). Yet feminist art history has not so far developed what we might call a biopolitical method, whereby the productive life of a gendered singularity acquires its direction—its continuities, discontinuities, and leaps, its negations and compromises—through social processes affecting a gendered multitude. In short, feminist art history has not pursued, through its salient militant category (woman artist), a *life-work dialectic* with analytical persistence.

In the "former West," from where I approach Kulik's work, feminist imaginaries have persistently negated the derogatory connotations of the "woman artist" category in histories of

2 Kulik's film **KYOTO: HOW KULIK, WITHOUT LEAVING HOME, EXPLAINS HER WORK TO AN AUDIENCE THOUSANDS OF MILES AWAY AND SEEKS OUT A RELATIONSHIP WITH A JAPANESE ARTIST** [A+B (2016)], 16:00, available at http://kulikzofia.pl/en/archiwum/cultivating-the-archive-films-by-zofia-kulik/, is very helpful as a document of this process, in particular as regards the motifs embedded in *All the Missiles Are One Missile*.

modernism.[3] Yet, for the most part, such feminist imaginaries have focused more on persistent divides (such as between art and craft) or strategic reorientations of feminist art-making (towards video or photography, for instance), and less on why and how a creative subject socialized as a woman in a given context would pursue or effect changes in her labor, as opposed to choices made by a "woman artist"—a term of often-privileged class connotations. There are many reasons for this oversight, including that feminist art history emerged during the hegemony of postmodernism as a cultural narrative in the 1970s and 1980s—a narrative that flagged its aversion to anything regarding histories of labor and the "economy," and that, in contrast, heavily promoted what Fredric Jameson dubbed a "cultural logic."[4] At the same time, in the "former East," categories such as "labor," including artistic labor, were (typically, yet not always) hijacked by the oppressive discourse of what Ewa Lajer-Burcharth has referred to as "the nomenclature";[5] while later on, during the so-called "transition" of the 1990s, there was a feminist reservation towards the explicit politicization of labor in art, as if such a pursuit would lead straight to the economic reductionism connected with

3 I borrow the term "former West" from the homonymous eight-year research project run by BAK in Utrecht. This transnational project investigated the impact of 1989 on shaping what we call contemporary art and society. See "About," *Former West*, accessed July 15, 2018, http://www.formerwest.org/About. See also the selection of texts in Maria Hlavajova and Simon Sheikh, eds., *Former West: Art and the Contemporary after 1989* (Cambridge, MA: MIT Press; Utrecht: BAK, 2017).

4 Fredric Jameson, *Postmodernism, or, the Cultural Logic of Late Capitalism* (Durham: Duke University Press, 1991).

5 See Ewa Lajer-Burcharth, "Old Histories: Zofia Kulik's Ironic Recollections," in *New Histories*, ex. cat. (Boston: Institute of Contemporary Art, 1996), 119–36. Reprinted in this volume.

the "rejected" political past.[6] Overall, feminist critique in art history, and likewise in film studies, focused mostly on sexual difference and the consumption of the over-sexualized sign of the feminine.[7] Kulik has talked publicly about her own questioning stance towards the female body's sexualization, with regard to how feminism was practiced by (a limited number of) women artists in Poland during state socialism.[8] Reading her 2005 interview "The Rebellion of a Neo-Avant-Garde Artist," where those comments were made, is instructive: Kulik's uneasiness in relation to feminism concerns how feminism appeared as *artwork content*, whereas she saw feminism as belonging more to a social field where women's problems required solutions. But what then lies between artwork content and the social field? What indeed connects the two? In the same interview, Kulik offers an oblique answer to this: What connects them are women artists' "experience and thoughts," which tended, and tend, to remain "secret"—or, as feminist theory would say, suppressed and possibly self-censored in the public domain. The reflections that follow on

6 Bojana Pejić, chief curator of the major transnational, research-based art exhibition *Gender Check: Femininity and Masculinity in the Art of Eastern Europe* (mumok, Vienna, November 13, 2009–February 14, 2010; Zachęta National Gallery of Art, Warsaw, March 19–June 13, 2010), notes in a 2009 interview her desire to revisit gender relations in Eastern Europe in terms of "power" as elaborated by Michel Foucault—that is, power as *diffused*—and in a way that departed from the majority of the critiques of state socialism, which focused on nationalism and/or totalitarianism. See Hedvig Turai, "Bojana Pejić on Gender and Feminism in Eastern European Art (interview)," *ARTMargins*, December 18, 2009, http://www.artmargins.com/index.php/interviews/540-bojana-pejic-gender-feminism-eastern-european-art-interview. Foucault's complex notion of power became very useful to feminist critique under postmodernism, but recent debates have brought forth his relationship to liberalism and indeed neoliberal economics. Indicatively, see "Can We Criticize Foucault? An Interview with Daniel Zamora," *Jacobin*, October 12, 2014, https://www.jacobinmag.com/2014/12/foucault-interview/, and Daniel Zamora and Michael Behrent, eds., *Foucault and Neoliberalism* (Cambridge: Polity Press, 2015).

7 On this, see the special issue on social reproduction and art, co-edited by Kirsten Lloyd and myself, of *Third Text* 31, no. 1 (January 2017) in print, and online at https://www.tandfonline.com/toc/ctte20/31/1.

8 Kulik wonders: "After all, if we speak of feminism why did Partum put mascara on her eyelashes and applied make-up foundation to her body when she undressed, preparing for a performance? She would put on her stiletto [heels] and only then was she a 'feminist'?" See "The Rebellion of a Neo-Avant-Garde Artist: An Interview with Zofia Kulik Conducted by Joanna Turowicz," *Kulik-KwieKulik Foundation*, accessed June 9, 2018, http://kulikzofia.pl/en/archiwum/bunt-neoawangardowej-artystki/.

Kulik's "labor-intensive" practice take shape within feminist art history's methodological gap—with this suppression and, I would argue, repression in mind.

Yes, but No: On the Effort to Be a Traditional (Woman) Artist

In the aforementioned interview (which I will draw on heavily), Kulik stated that, at a certain point, she wished to be merely a "traditional artist"—a role that, for her, implied not a fantasized-as-free engagement with form, but rather self-organized, "cognitive" (her word) labor: she immersed herself in the study of art's "epochs," "gathering knowledge" so as to find her way in the "forest" she had decided to enter. Yet the role of a traditional artist came with two caveats: first, Kulik connected the role with how she wished to be in her relation to the art institution;[9] second, she was hesitant about the role of the traditional artist and did not "feel at home" in it.[10] And all of this was happening in the late 1980s, when Kulik's world had accelerated: her personal reorientation, following the dissolution of KwieKulik,

9 By "art institution" I mean the complex of practices and organizations that have been the object of analysis (and in many ways the target) of institutional critique—as an artistic practice and theory-led investigation—at least since the 1960s. In the present analysis, the art institution is *art as an institution* that entails both an ideological and a material register. Despite understandable differences in the historical formation and trajectory of the art institution (thus defined) of the East and West, the term denotes in both contexts the mechanisms of reproducing the art field in its known form and function. The form and function were, and are, largely permeated with patriarchal values and exclusionary mechanisms explicitly opposed by feminists working in the art field—so far, I would argue, with limited and variable results. On institutional critique see, indicatively, Alexander Alberro and Blake Stimson, eds., *Institutional Critique: An Anthology of Artists' Writings* (Cambridge, MA: MIT Press, 2009).

10 Kulik explains her work at the end of the 1980s: "I started to behave in a 'conservative' way and demanded from various institutions to treat me as a regular traditional artists. I envied my younger colleagues, who worked with the new media, that they entered into official relations just after graduation—galleries, museums, press, etc. They never questioned these institutions and relations, probably there was no need for that any longer. Even when they were criticized by some right-wing centers, they had already enjoyed the status of a professional artist. One could not even dream about such a situation in the 1970s. So that was the reason why I craved the role of the 'traditional' artist for myself even stronger. Which, however, did not mean I felt at home in this role. All the time something hesitated in me whether I should, perhaps, go back again into this alternative independence of the previous period." Kulik, "The Rebellion of a Neo-Avant-Garde Artist."

was matched by that of Poland and the upturn of the premises on which her art-life nexus had so far been built. There was certainly a sense of adventure—Kulik uses this word—but the pursuit of adventures is typically realized outside the home, whereas Kulik's reinvention of herself was connected with buying (in 1982) a new, attention-seeking house (that is, one in need of refurbishment) [FIG. 1]. Moreover, adventures are also typically seen to belong to men, or at least to the women working alongside (or even under) "exceptional" men. (Kulik herself appeared aware of this convention, in speculating on the life she might have lived in "revolutionary times.") Yet working alongside a man was the very context from which this woman artist had escaped by ending the art-and-life KwieKulik partnership.

In hindsight, knowing what post-transition, neoconservative Poland held in store for women (in tandem with a major authoritative, pro-patriarchal turn in the Global North at large, especially evident after the global financial crisis of 2008), it would be justified to assume that Kulik's earlier, positive sense of adventure was not free from contradictions. Indeed, the articulation of her newly found artistic freedom as a woman and an artist in terms of a desired return to the "traditional artist" role can be seen as symptomatic of this. Yet this contradiction did not arise in Kulik's *subjective* relationship to the art world; it was rather the *objective* condition on which the relationship had to be enacted. To be a "traditional artist" was to be a *professional* artist: embracing the role expressed the claim to the right of undertaking a particular kind of labor, institutionally ratified as "art," and entering, as a woman, the web of professional relations that came with the claim. In the aforementioned interview, Kulik notes her organizational skills, which had already sustained KwieKulik, and yet, when the moment to realize KwieKulik's Open Form, spontaneous, performative actions had arrived in the past, Kulik (the woman artist) was assigned the role of the non-speaking Significant Other. The renunciation of "Open Form" by Kulik was declarative: it was one way of realizing, in material terms, her opposition to the hierarchy and oppression that often shapes male-female creative collaborations that are also life partnerships in a patriarchal context. In such situations, the inextricability of "life" and "art"

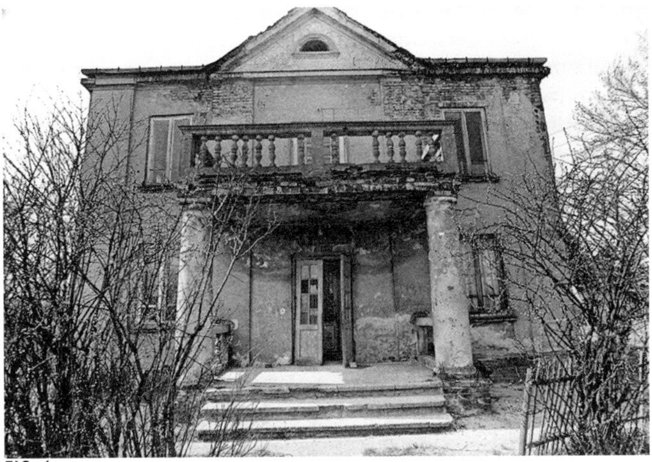

FIG. 1
EXTERIOR VIEW OF ZOFIA KULIK'S HOUSE, ŁOMIANKI, POLAND, 1982

occurs in terms quite different to those sought after (but never achieved) by the historical avant-gardes. But where was Kulik to go after this declarative renunciation? What was on offer in the forest she was entering?

The self-identification with the "traditional artist" makes us confront a limit that mainstream art history—including mainstream feminist art history—often refuses to speak of: that artistic labor in capitalist patriarchy, delivered as modernity (historical or extensive),[11] acquires fairly specific forms; that, rather than art in modernity being an open field of endless possibilities and potentialities, when it comes to the kinds of labor made available at a given juncture, it is rather a field of prescriptive and often forced choices drawn from a delimited spectrum.[12] Kulik's appeal to the traditional artist identity was, on some level, a covert acknowledgement that being an artist was not just a matter of producing a labor output called "artwork" (material or immaterial). In that respect, Kulik proved unable to remain traditional, and observed with irritated disbelief the return to conservative painting that became the *sine qua non* of the 1980s art scene (as we know, not just in Poland)—a return that, on top of everything else, was advanced through male-dominated group shows.[13] Rather, her somehow puzzling self-identifi-

11 On the concept of extensive modernity see Dimitrakaki, "Extensive Modernity: On the Refunctioning of Artists as Producers," in *A Companion to Modern Art*, ed. Pam Meecham (Oxford: Blackwell-Wiley, 2018). The chapter discusses the continuity of the modern art paradigm, despite the postmodern parenthesis of the 1970s and 1980s, in relation to how capital impacts the shaping and social perception of artistic labor.

12 This is why, despite the investment in "personal visions," the art of modernity is always populated by artistic movements and marked by technological developments often defining the "new"—for example, "video art" or, recently, "post-internet" art. It is in this sense that art has, indeed, a history.

13 Feminist art historians extensively criticized the Royal Academy of London group show *A New Spirit in Painting*, 1981, featuring thirty-six men and no women. The show was deemed particularly important for introducing "the return to painting" in a contemporaneous art paradigm (led by conceptualism and performance in the preceding decade), and was largely seen as symptomatic of a conservative turn in art and society at large. See Janet Wolff, *Feminine Sentences: Essays on Women and Culture* (Cambridge: Polity Press, 1990), 56. The "return to painting" effected in the 1980s had repercussions on how a contemporary art paradigm, still with us to date, was to be shaped, as painting was never again met with such opposition, instead retaining its status in the art market.

cation with the "traditional artist" formula betrayed the understanding that being a professional artist required an *infrastructure*. Overall, women themselves had provided part of this infrastructure to the creative males in their lives. Lara Perry's recent article on the artist's home in 19th-century London indicates that much research remains to be done on elucidating how and why women agreed to be the auxiliaries in providing a supporting "labor of love" that carried on into the 20th century.[14] Yet since the end of the 20th century, when neoliberalism went full steam ahead with its global expropriation project through the debt economy, art was en route to being openly described as merely a different "labor of love"—a passion to be followed with much sacrifice, with subsidizing oneself through other sources and "day jobs," and with enduring what women had been told to endure: the provision of free labor for the assumed rewards of a noble cause—raising children, cleaning the room after the revolutionary meeting, and, yes, also making art.[15] Kulik's desire, then, to operate as a "traditional artist" was far from counterintuitive. In hindsight, it can be seen as reflective of three interconnected things: her accumulated work experience in the actual art field, where she grasped the significance of infrastructural labor;[16] a sensing of the developing conditions in the global art field, where being an artist required, for instance, mastering English (she spoke it; her

14 Lara Perry, "The Artist's Household: On Gender and the Division of Domestic and Artistic Labor in Nineteenth-Century London," *Third Text* 31, no. 1 (2017): 15–29.

15 Opening with the phrase "They say it is love. We say it is unwaged work," the emblematic text in the context of second-wave struggles led by anti-capitalist feminists is Silvia Federici's pamphlet *Wages against Housework* (Power of Women Collective and Falling Wall Press, 1975), last modified September 15, 2010, https://caringlabor.wordpress.com/2010/09/15/silvia-federici-wages-against-housework/. On how these debates are impacting the art field see, indicatively, Danielle Child, Helena Reckitt, and Jenny Richards, "Labors of Love: A Conversation on Art, Gender, and Social Reproduction," *Third Text* 31, no. 1 (2017): 147–68.

16 On this see Marina Vishmidt, "The Two Reproductions in (Feminist) Art and Theory since the 1970s," *Third Text* 31, no. 1 (2017): 49–66. Vishmidt draws her examples from a Western context.

ex-partner did not);[17] and a disdain for performing in terms of a "labor of love"—a euphemism for women's and feminized subjects' low- or no-cost service and servitude—in any context.

It is, of course, far easier to see and say all of this today—when most artists, no matter where they are based, complain about precarity, entrapment, institutional dependency, and reforms that continue to give us the familiar male-female ratio of art success—than it was in 1989, when the "sense of adventure" previously noted carried individuals and masses towards political optimism, and when capitalism could still be argued for by serious scholars in terms of the happy "end of history" and the unmitigated advance of democracy.[18] Yet from today's vantage point we must also consider Kulik's stated discomfort in her effort to embrace the "traditional artist" identity—her confession that she did not feel "at home" in this effort. From this point on, we can follow different threads.

First, as feminist art history has demonstrated, women were paradigmatically prevented (as a group) from having access to this central identity, being forced instead into satellite identities (such as "amateur artists"). Writing in particular about women art-

17 I am obviously alluding here to Mladen Stilinović's landmark piece *An Artist Who Cannot Speak English Is No Artist* (1992). The work captured the terms in which the "transitioning" Eastern Bloc's art scenes would have to be incorporated into the global art world, where mobility and communication were to play an unprecedented role. On the impact of globalization on art, see in particular Hans Belting and Andrea Buddensieg, eds., *The Global Art World: Audiences, Markets, and Museums* (Karlsruhe: ZKM; Ostfildern: Hatje Cantz, 2009), and Jonathan Harris, ed., *Globalization and Contemporary Art* (Oxford: Wiley-Blackwell, 2011).

18 See Francis Fukuyama, *The End of History and the Last Man* (London: Hamish Hamilton, 1992). There are numerous investigations into the conditions of labor in the art field. Indicatively, see Hans Abbing, *Why Are Artists Poor?* (Amsterdam: Amsterdam University Press, 2002); Gregory Shollete, *Dark Matter: Art and Politics in the Age of Enterprise Culture* (London: Pluto Press, 2010); Julieta Aranda, Brian Kuan Wood, and Anton Vidokle, eds., *Are You Working Too Much? Post-Fordism, Precarity, and the Labor of Art* (Berlin: Sternberg Press, 2011). Nonetheless, at the time of writing (2018), I am not aware of a book-length study of the gender division of labor in relation to art under the conditions imposed by global capital. My own book *Gender, artWork and the Global Imperative* (2013) includes relevant chapters rather than providing an overall focus on the subject, and Angela McRobbie's important research focuses more broadly on the creative industries. See in particular her *Be Creative: Making a Living in the New Culture Industries* (Cambridge: Polity Press, 2015) and *The Aftermath of Feminism: Gender, Culture and Social Change* (London: Sage, 2009).

ists' desire to paint, Griselda Pollock has examined the psychic mechanisms that boost rather than dissolve women's attachment to tradition, "when everyone else has moved to another room."[19] But Kulik's case differs, precisely because she was, as part of KwieKulik, a major builder of the once-new and fairly radical room named "process art." She made it, inhabited it, and at one point, blasted an exit through it. But then again, what *is* an exit?

In asking this, we may first pursue similar threads. There are cases in art where women experienced such an irresolvable conflict between the radical creativity they wished to explore and the framework provided by the art world that they ended up leaving the latter altogether. In Poland, Jolanta Marcolla, an artist associated with conceptualism, withdrew from the art world in the 1980s to become an illustrator of children's books, but her case remains little researched and little known within the broader narrative of women's refusal to abide by normative channels of creativity.[20] The two best-known cases come from the Western capitalist context: in Italy, Carla Lonzi gave up being an art critic and also ended her long relationship with a male sculptor in order to channel her creativity into feminism as a real-world politics and "life"; in the US, Lee Lozano, a woman artist who met with partial success in the New York art scene, while not identifying as feminist, dropped out of art altogether, turning this act into a "process" piece; in parallel, she also stopped talking to women for the rest of her life (at least on paper, through her *Boycott Women* piece). Research on these women's life-and-art exchange has only recently been provided on a substantial

19 See Griselda Pollock, "Painting, Feminism, History," in *Destabilizing Theory: Contemporary Feminist Debates*, eds. Michèle Barrett and Anne Phillips (Cambridge: Polity Press, 1992), 151.

20 See "Jolanta Marcolla," artist entry, *Arton Foundation*, accessed July 31, 2018, http://repozytorium.fundacjaarton.pl/index.php?action=view/category&catid=5&lang=eng.

level,[21] but it is hard in both cases not to discern a degree of self-punishment that arose precisely from the fact that these women were ultimately forced to act alone, as *individual* women: there was no feminist army of art critics withdrawing their labor from an art world that thrived on cut-throat competition, nor were there scores of conceptualist women artists who knew success only to give it up out of intellectual dissatisfaction. Unsurprisingly, the art world carried on without them, and their radicalness is now under the threat of institutional recuperation—a recuperation that perhaps they would themselves welcome, as leaving-in-protest can hardly be equated with the desire to join the long litany of invisible women within the broader domain of culture production. (Refusal also contributes to making culture, to crafting a milieu, lest we forget.)

An exit can take then the form of dropping out, but the organization of the art world has strong mechanisms of incorporation. An experienced woman artist in search of agency (such as Kulik in the late 1980s) may take this route at great risk, or may turn to soul-searching, through which she would question precisely *how* she has thus far performed artistic labor, what emotional labor was co-constitutive of any "success," and to what extent she might be able to develop not a "language," as post-structuralist art criticism would have it, but a *material* process of work that would satisfy, at least to an extent, the quest for agency. In this respect, a much longer essay would be needed to explore what, in the US of the early 1970s, pushed Mierle Laderman Ukeles to drag maintenance labor into the art institution and what, in mid-1980s Poland, pushed Zofia Kulik to experiment with becoming a singularity by performing the labor of the

21 See Giovanna Zapperi's *Carla Lonzi: Un'arte della vita* (Rome: DeriveApprodi, 2017), not translated into English at the time of writing; Francesco Ventrella, "Carla Lonzi's Artwriting and the Resonance of Separatism," *European Journal of Women's Studies* 21, no. 3 (2014): 282–87; Claire Fontaine, "We Are All Clitoridian Women: Notes on Carla Lonzi's Legacy," *e-flux journal* 47 (September 2013), https://www.e-flux.com/journal/47/60057/we-are-all-clitoridian-women-notes-on-carla-lonzi-s-legacy/. Also, Sarah Lehrer-Graiwer, *Lee Lozano: Dropout Piece* (London: Afterall, 2014) and Jo Applin, *Lee Lozano: Not Working* (New Haven: Yale University Press, 2018). Indicatively, Lee Lozano exhibitions took place in Moderna Museet, Stockholm, in 2010, Museo Nacional Centro de Arte Reina Sofía, in 2017, and the Fruitmarket Gallery, Edinburgh, in 2018.

meticulous, tireless archivist of her historical moment (one also scripted by her). Neither, however, opted to operate outside the institution, though in both cases a new relationship was demanded from it. Kulik's ambivalent appeal, then, to the "traditional artist" (a "yes" nurturing a "no"), as part of her emergent self-consciousness, was not exempted from the gender determinations defining the circuit of "art" and "life" in historically specific terms.

"Begging for Forgiveness": On Gendered Alienation

That Kulik did not feel "at home" while making the claim to the figure of the "traditional artist" must therefore be posited against this background—except that this is not a background that can in any way be detached from the actual scene of performed action: Kulik herself as a living, laboring subject, always and necessarily shaped through the contradictions that comprise the so-called background. Kulik's spectrum of (limited) choices instructs feminist art history to engage with the complex alienation a woman artist can face, and with what might constitute a *struggle against such alienation*. Alienation figures prominently in Marx's work and Marxism overall, but traditionally (sic), artistic labor has been connected with non-alienation.[22] This deeply problematic—from a contemporary vantage point—schema is, as expected, premised on the distinction between the industrial worker not owning the means and outputs of his labor, and the male artist, often a bohemian figure inherited from the 19th century, feeling free to conduct his anti-bourgeois critique by frequenting brothels (Picasso), or making the most of his sexuality by drifting to the colonies (Gauguin), or roaming urban space (the Impressionists; the Surrealists; the Situationists, to name but a few).[23] The art field never gave up its promise of non-alienated

22 See the classic 1970s studies: Bertell Ollman, *Alienation: Marx's Conception of Man in Capitalist Society* (Cambridge: Cambridge University Press, 1976) and Ann Foreman, *Femininity as Alienation: Women and the Family in Marxism and Psychoanalysis* (London: Pluto Press, 1977).

23 For an analysis of the gender relations (especially in relation to the infrastructure provided to male members) of the Situationists, see the chapter "The Situation of Women" in Frances Stracey, *Constructed Situations: A New History of the Situationist International* (London: Pluto Press, 2014).

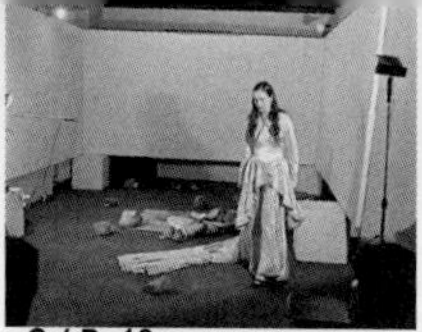
C / P. 19

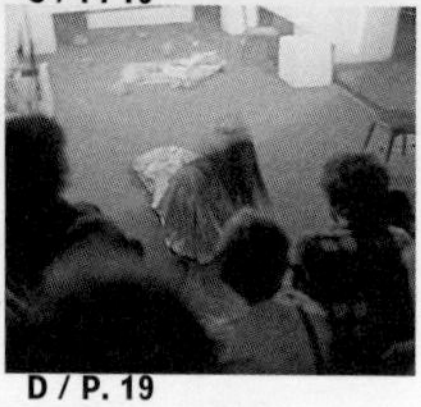
D / P. 19

labor, as doing so would have made it a far less central and persuasive mythology of freedom under capital—a mythology that was, and remains, operative beyond the gender divide. Women craved access to art for the same reasons as men, but we must look with greater care at the conflict produced for women artists between art's promise of non-alienation and their gendered experience of work. It is hard to come across male artists who would describe their labor as follows:

> In 1978 I made an independent mini-gesture entitled **ZOFIA KULIK'S BEGGING FOR FORGIVENESS** C+D (1978). For the first time [...] I [tried] to do something without Kwiek. The Duo did suffocate me too much: all of these repetitions; we were speaking always the same things, we were doing always the same things. Strange emotions accumulated within me. [...] What was the public supposed to forgive me? I didn't know exactly. Probably that I was not present in person, even if I seemed [to] be. I was nothing but a part of a dimorphic hybrid in which my role was not clear, nor how much space I occupied, what my shape was. I was tired with that muteness of myself. "Zofia Kulik's Begging for Forgiveness." Look [at] the title [...]: a concrete person with a given name and surname asks her public for pardon. [...] I approached the public several times to fall onto my knees. I must have been really pathetic [...]. When I made a few bows I felt totally humiliated but... I asked for that. I needed such a situation and I had it.[24]

And, regarding the new labor Kulik opted for after the mid-1980s:

> For years, I was with Kwiek who always cooked. Later, Kwiek moved to the utility building at the back of our garden so, there was nobody to cook for me. I was left alone with our son. I began to learn cooking. The TV set

24 "The Rebellion of a Neo-Avant-Garde Artist." [The citation has been modified to reflect the change in the work's title. It has been referred to as "Plea for Pardon." —Ed.]

> was in the kitchen. I would install a camera on a tripod opposite the set. And, here was I peeling potatoes, and here—I push the camera button. Later, I bought a video recorder and started systematic recording. I developed a kind of addiction: lunch or supper time and I look up what's on TV in the newspaper to know what time precisely is worth going to the kitchen to have an interesting recording at the same time. It was like that for several years. Were it not for my kitchen duties, this work would not appear.[25]

The quotes above pose a conundrum for feminist art theory. On the one hand, the pattern described in the second departs from, as much as it fulfills, expectations about women's roles in the domestic sphere. Kwiek, a male artist, provided part of the infrastructure required for KwieKulik's artistic labor, and yet single motherhood eventually returned Kulik to the kitchen—the space where care labor and artistic labor had to intersect for the female artist. But nothing in this quote signals alienation; rather, Kulik's emphasis is on accepting the material conditions within which she would have to work (not so relevant, obviously, to the "traditional" male artist).

The first quote, on the other hand, is rife with intimations of alienation, stemming from Kulik's marginalization within the KwieKulik art-life partnership. It refers to a performative piece in which she tried to address her instances of perceived public humiliation—not in the abstract, but in the Open Form of "spontaneous" collaborative artworks. She did not mince her words when admitting: "Przemek [Kwiek] would indeed humiliate me in public. I have never discussed it in my interviews but this may have been the main reason of our split. [...] At home, you could pass over it somehow but in public it was terrible."[26] We would be remiss to disregard here the

25 "The Rebellion of a Neo-Avant-Garde Artist."

26 See "Contradiction 3: Work and Nonwork," in Angela Dimitrakaki, "Feminism, Art, Contradictions," *e-flux journal* 92 (June 2018), https://www.e-flux.com/journal/92/205536/feminism-art-contradictions/, and Marion von Osten, "Irene ist Viele! Or What We Call 'Productive' Forces," *e-flux journal* 8 (September 2009), https://www.e-flux.com/journal/08/61381/irene-ist-viele-or-what-we-call-productive-forces/.

well-known divide between public and private on which second-wave Western feminism erected its critique; and Kulik remembers, all these years later, that the temptation of dropping out also took hold of her.[27] If she managed to overcome it, this again had to do with art, upon her realization that Kwiek was not interested in investing much in his solo career. It is therefore at least debatable to what extent Kulik's refusal to drop out (a personal, if political, protest-gesture emanating from her position specifically as a woman artist in a male-dominated art scene) was not subverted by her (conscious or perhaps initially unconscious) desire to also maintain the legacy of the KwieKulik collective and the milieu in which it existed. This long-term commitment was already evident in the Studio of Activities, Documentation and Propagation (Pracownia Działań, Dokumentacji i Upowszechniania, PDDiU), an independent project run by KwieKulik in their Praga-district apartment in Warsaw, and it was illuminating that, in 2018, my personal communication with the artist, in an effort to understand the trajectory of her post-collective labor, occurred just as she was preparing a major KwieKulik exhibition.[28]

The appeal made here to this commitment to "maintenance" is not politically innocent: the term is strongly associated with women's work, but, as social reproduction theory insists, maintenance work is not just limited to the domestic sphere. Rather, women maintain communities; they maintain activist politics and networks; they maintain art reputations and histories. Women are reportedly given to maintaining life—even keeping episodes of art alive. In a 2018 article I specifically discussed the conflicts that arise for emancipated women (like Kulik) whose self-consciousness is shaped through the demands of patriarchal modernity *and* the rebellious demand for agency.[29] As Marion von Osten convincingly argued

27 "It was more or less 1982 when I did not want to deal with art at all. I did not want to go to all these events and symposia 'starring' Kwiek, Józef Robakowski, Andrzej Partum and others. Therefore, I had the idea to move from Warsaw to Dąbrowa," Kulik says in "The Rebellion of a Neo-Avant-Garde Artist."

28 This was *KwieKulik: She and He*, Badischer Kunstverein, Karlsruhe, May 4–July 1, 2018. For a description of the intentions and the included works, see the press announcement, *e-flux*, April 30, 2018, https://www.e-flux.com/announcements/182760/kwiekulikshe-and-he/.

29 Dimitrakaki, "Feminism, Art, Contradictions."

a decade ago, the problems of this composite (or, alternatively, divisive) self-consciousness were not unknown to young women artists and filmmakers in the 1970s—when Kulik performed her piece on gendered humiliation. These problems, however, precisely because of the trajectories of second-wave feminism (which at some point lost its social-movement momentum), ultimately had to be addressed personally, if at all. Yet becoming conscious of a problem does not amount to solving it. Women artists and intellectuals have not so far managed to overcome the atomization techniques endemic in capitalist patriarchy; and to the extent that future communist subjectivity was defeated by Stalinism, neither did state socialism manage to undo this fundamental ideological determination of the artistic subject. This specific ideological determination has shaped modernity and whatever one understands by "modern art" at all points of the compass; this, however, is a different discussion, though far from unrelated to Kulik's choice to engage in archiving labor, and experimenting with whether and how her formidable organizational skills could prove useful in the long-term maintenance project her archive was willed to become. It is hard not to see the latter as an exercise in gaining at least a degree of control over the forces shaping her life—switching places from private to public and back again.

And it is startling to observe in a recent 2016 film the discrepancy between Kulik's prioritization of ordering and recollection, and Kwiek feeling enlivened by the prospect of realizing "spontaneous" ideas: in the film, he encourages Kulik (who has the mad idea) to stand on a narrow, high pedestal of stacked concrete slabs in a private garden and place a bucket (a smelly one, which Kulik first had to empty) over her head, depriving her of sight and eventually making her dizzy.[30] Once again, Kulik needs to follow Kwiek's instructions, and must rely on his eyesight if she does not wish to put herself at physical risk. But it is okay now for Kulik to be filmed (by Kwiek) with a dirty bucket covering her head, for not only does she speak incessantly (unlike their early performances, where she stayed silent), but the film, publicly

30 Kulik, *Cultivating the Archive, or, in Other Words, a Performative Work*, YouTube video, 15:38, posted by the *Kulik-KwieKulik Foundation*, November 10, 2017, https://www.youtube.com/watch?time_continue=396&v=PBuHGix4oDw.

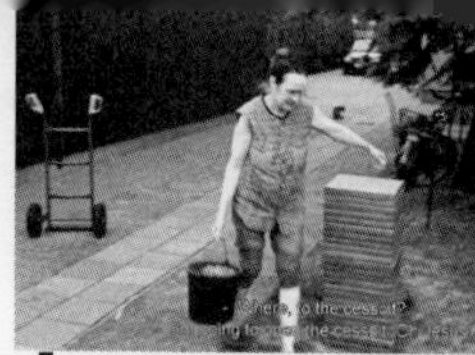
E

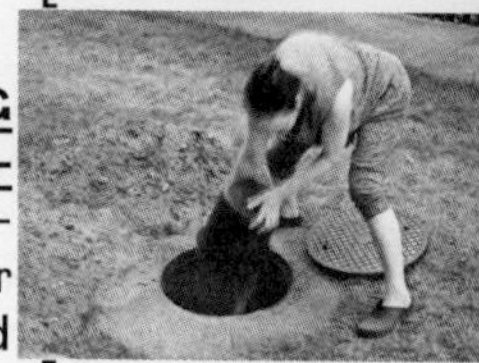
F

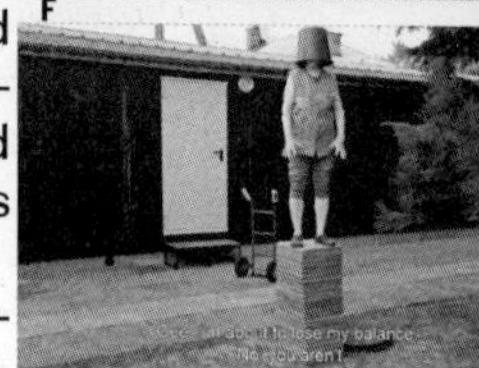
G

available on the artist's website, is called **CULTIVATING THE ARCHIVE, OR, IN OTHER WORDS, A PERFORMATIVE WORK** E–G (2016). The specific, collaborative, "performative" action (a term both artists mock in the film for its presently ubiquitous deployment in the Polish and international art world) is documented in the second section of the film, subtitled *How Everyday Activities Unexpectedly Stimulate the Archivist's Memory*. Kulik has discussed the use of props, and specifically buckets, in KwieKulik's actions of the 1970s and 1980s as follows:

> So, in 1978 I had the idea of this performance with a washbasin. We were thinking then what we could do during the "Performance and Body" even[t] at the Labirynt Gallery in Lublin. Later, we developed the idea, adding buckets on our heads and the heads on chair seats. Finally, our appearance was in three parts. In the second part I was sitting on the floor, my head projecting through the hole cut-out in the washbasin. Kwiek poured water into it and, next, he washed his face and legs in this water. Then he wielded a knife at the back of my head and yelled: You bitch! Say something! Say! From the moment of that appearance I started to feel better. Yet, I think that Przemek [Kwiek] still slighted such prearranged appearances. He preferred the things which looked spontaneous.[31]

In short, Kulik has come a long way in the 2016 film: not only is she able to return to the once-disparaged "Open Form," but she does so with confidence, subsuming performative, ephemeral work under the archivist's durational work that has been her choice since the late 1980s. We can detect in Kulik's current confidence the realization that a woman artist does not experience humiliation simply because the male artist she works with washes his face and feet in a washbasin, from the bottom of which her head is protruding; nor

31 See "The Rebellion of a Neo-Avant-Garde Artist."

from the male artist placing a knife at the back of her head and screaming "You bitch! Say something!" [FIG. 2]. The humiliation arises through a *durational process* as such, but one that exceeds the space-time of any given artwork; it arises from the repeated instances of marginalization and silencing that cross from the social world to the art world as a matter of course and as a manifestation of the status quo. And should one wish to move against the latter, this would not require small, ephemeral acts of self-assertion articulated in consecutive artworks, but an active overthrow, a clean break, a publicly announced rupture such as that declared symbolically by Kulik's move from "process" to "object." I would suggest that in effecting this move, Kulik did not so much break with Kwiek, but rather with the normative history of art, scripted in the male-dominated avant-gardes and identifying a progressive disentanglement from the object as a de facto marker of social progress and emancipatory politics. We know that the very accommodation of the erstwhile avant-gardes within the "art collection" disputes this narrative,[32] but we need a far more radical art-historical paradigm to investigate how art's history *as a history of labor* would be written from the standpoint of a renewed feminist radicalism.

On Contesting Closure: Gender, Class, Labor Experiments

In a Skype conversation I had with Kulik, I was curious about one thing, knowing that her mother was a seamstress—that is, a working-class female subject in the context of state-socialist Poland, bearing in mind that a "working class" identity is not limited to a conventionally

32 Criticisms of the avant-garde's taming within the art institution have been widespread at least since the publication, in German, of Peter Bürger's *Theorie der Avantgarde* (*Theory of the Avant-Garde*) in 1974 (English translation 1984). Bürger revisited his argument in a special issue of *New Literary History* on the avant-garde in 2015. See Peter Bürger, "Avant-Garde and Neo-Avant-Garde: An Attempt to Answer Certain Critics of 'Theory of the Avant-Garde,'" *New Literary History* 41, no. 1 (Autumn 2015): 695–715.

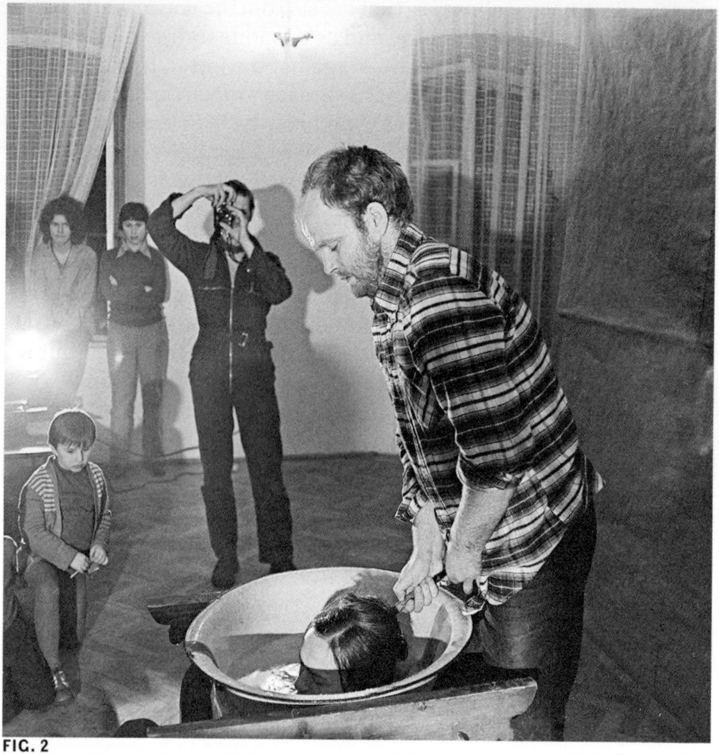

FIG. 2
KWIEKULIK, *ACTIVITY FOR THE HEAD: THREE ACTS*, 1978

defined proletariat composed of factory workers[33]—I wanted to know if her mother, Helena Kulik, "understood" what her daughter made for a living in being an artist. "No, she doesn't," replied Kulik. "Neither does my mother understand what I do as a writer," I replied, and we laughed, possibly thinking of our mothers, whose remunerated labor relied on delivering concrete outputs.[34] What, however, both our mothers always understood was, and is, "hard work," and as my mother does for me in the capitalist 2010s of normalized overwork schedules, Kulik's mother also supported her daughter's hard work by preparing food for KwieKulik in 1970s Warsaw. Living in the Praga district (in a 19th-century house rather than the neighborhood's legendary state-socialist apartment blocks, which were sometimes topped with artists' residence-ateliers), Kulik had to carry heavy baskets of food, prepared by her mother, who respected hard work: "Everything was in the baskets: soup, chops, cakes—mostly processed food because I was ashamed to take raw food like fresh potatoes. My mother believed that this was the way to save our time and work, not that we did not have anything to eat."[35]

As Zofia Kulik is exactly my mother's age, but from a different national-historical context, this transmission of maternal labor as part of an infrastructure that permits educated daughters to invest their time in intellectual "hard work" channeled into the

33 The efforts to rethink and expand the definition of the "working class" are particularly prominent today within the framework of social reproduction theory, led by Marxist feminists. Tithi Bhattacharya has attended specifically to the need to rethink the recomposition of the global working class from a feminist perspective for the 21st century, though such an endeavor necessarily revisits and questions the certainties of dominant strands of Marxism over the history of labor and working-class identity. See Tithi Bhattacharya, ed., *Social Reproduction Theory: Remapping Class, Recentering Oppression* (London: Pluto Press, 2017).

34 My mother, from a rural background in Greece, was a civil servant from the 1970s until 2006. At the time, entry into this profession required passing state exams, but not necessarily having a university degree. In 1960s Greece, university education among young women from rural areas (unless from a middle- or upper-class background) was not common. Given the absence of state support, a family from a rural context could often sponsor the higher education of only one child, and this was normally the first-born son.

35 Kulik describes the Praga period during the KwieKulik collaboration in "The Rebellion of a Neo-Avant-Garde Artist." Notably, the Praga apartment blocks accommodated residents from diverse social strata, including academics.

public sphere offers food for feminist thought; and, indeed, it helps us approach from a different angle what Kathi Weeks has called a globally hegemonic "work society," as well as the generational transmission of this ethos of labor-intensive "making" in which mothers, invested in social reproduction work in addition to their remunerated labor, are apparently also implicated.[36] For different reasons perhaps, both my mother and Kulik's placed great value on women's work in the public sphere, where such work is not, however, defined strictly as "work outside the home" (an artist, a seamstress, and any digital laborer may well work from home), but rather as women's potential to make stuff that is *publicly* recognized as labor. Even if the precise complexity of this labor may appear obscure to anyone not doing it, "hard work" carries enough ideological clout to generate the hope that this work matters outside the domestic sphere, where many women have disappeared as into the proverbial black hole. The class dimension underpinning such a position must not be lost: in both the former East and West, self-worth was claimed by a working-class individual through this commitment to contribute to a "work society." A feminist insurgence against women's unquestioning subjugation to endless work did exist in the 1960s, but it has gained new traction in recent years, in light of the fact that contemporary capital's accumulation processes no longer need armies of workers (rather, capital and society at large are faced with millions of redundant people, if participation in production is the criterion). Yet the feminists who advocate women's liberation from work tend themselves to work around the clock—which is another way of saying that there is some distance between theory and/or art imagining the remaking of the world and the material conditions determining women's participation in, and reproduction of, the "work society." Kulik, it must be said, has not engaged in a critique of "work society"; rather, her labor-intensive practice, mentioned in the opening sentence of this essay, has sought possibly to explore whether object-based art-making could be dislodged from its usual connotations of serving an *authority*, and be combined with a woman art-worker's right of access

36 See "Introduction," in Kathi Weeks, *The Problem with Work: Feminism, Marxism, Antiwork Politics, and Postwork Imaginaries* (Durham: Duke University Press, 2011).

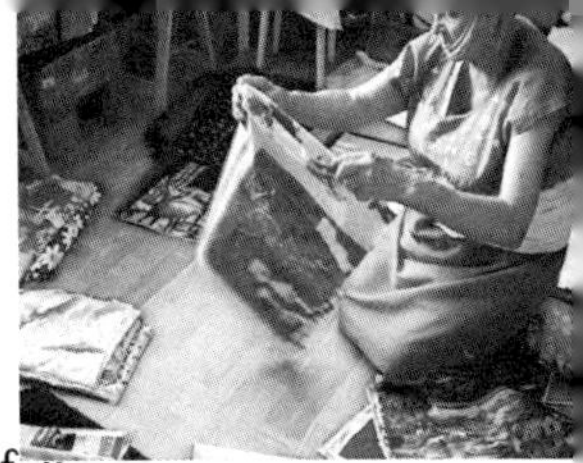

H

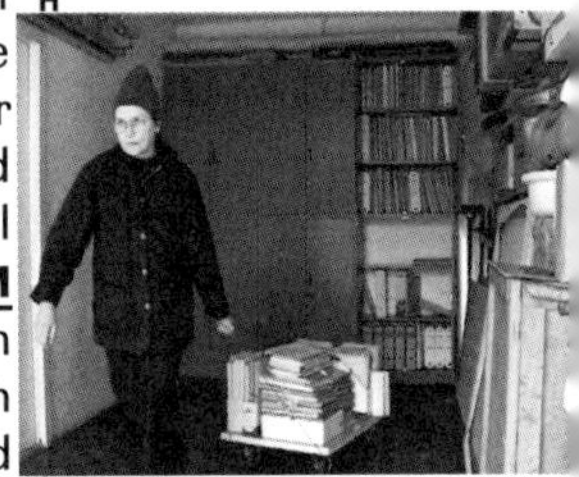

I

to cognitive labor. And this can also be seen as part of Kulik's struggle against alienation—this time, the one engendered through the transition from manual labor (Kulik's mother) to the intellectual activity associated with artistic labor, often denoting the successful achievement of upward social mobility. The film **A SUM OF RAGS AND AN ARCHIVE NEXT DOOR** H + I (2017), in which Kulik appears with her mother, going through piles of fabric, discussing images and motifs, would suggest that this engagement with materiality was perhaps necessary in extending the mother-daughter bond, which had been subverted by the two women's different (and hierarchically constructed) relationship to work.[37]

State socialism tried to erode this distinction, at least in some contexts, but the ease with which it reemerged in post-transition Poland suggests that this remained an unfinished project at best: in 2015, the Free/Slow University of Warsaw published a research-based report titled *The Art Factory*, where we are cautioned against equating artists' precarious income with poverty, as "precarity" in the art field can (and tends to) be mediated by class. Among its summary findings, the report also states that "the matters of gender and gender-based injustice remain concealed and unexamined."[38] Yet one does not really need intersectionality theory to grasp that "gender-based injustice" is always entangled with class stratification: the reproduction of classed-gendered subjects is a "live," ongoing social process in modernity, constitutive of what we know as the social fabric. Such subjects are, of course, dynamic,

37 See Kulik, *A Sum of Rags and an Archive Next Door*, YouTube video, 15:38, posted by the *Kulik-KwieKulik Foundation*, November 10, 2017, https://www.youtube.com/watch?v=Nslpx25mebQ. On Kulik's films that feature her mother, see Agata Jakubowska, "Egzystencjalne i ekonomiczne wymiary 'czynnościowania' Zofii Kulik i jej matki Heleny," *Miejsce: Studia nad sztuką i architekturą polską XX i XXI wieku*, no. 4 (2018): 12–24. English translation of the text ("The Existential and Economic Dimensions of the 'Actioning' of Zofia Kulik and Her Mother"), unpublished, made available by the author.

38 The publication was the outcome of the project "Division of Labor and Related Distribution of Social and Economic Capital in the Field of Visual Arts in Contemporary Poland," led by Michał Kozłowski, Kuba Szreder, and Jan Sowa, https://issuu.com/beczmiana/docs/fabryka_sztuki.

and to speak of class and gender does not imply the recognition of closure on the level of consciousness. Rather, what I am suggesting is that a reading of Kulik's efforts to develop a critical artistic practice (critical of the spectacle; critical of technology; critical of a modernity delivered through a rift between "feminine" and "masculine"; critical of the war principle), through bringing together manual and (so-called) immaterial-cognitive labor, must also address the socially scripted class-gender relations that have filtered into her personal-political history.

In a 2018 essay on maintenance and the gendering of art labor, Marina Vishmidt wrote:

> It is long past time to start dismantling the opposition of novelty and maintenance in order to develop a feminist politics of creativity which does not dissociate care from the capacity to engage in worldmaking. [...] As the architectural theorist Maria Giudici has written, we can reimagine maintenance as a radicalisation [...] This starts to give us some of the tools to reimagine maintenance not just as reproduction—that is, as maintaining what already exists in a state as self-similar as possible, cut off from any idea of novelty or disruption—but rather as resistance.[39]

Although further in her essay, Vishmidt mentions maintenance in connection with negativity, linking it to the terrain of struggle, I would argue that negativity is not always a requirement for recasting maintenance in this light. In Kulik's case, the enactment and maintenance of archives, of art histories that are always threatened with peripheralization, of class links woven into family histories, of life narratives dragging "women's experience and thought" out of the drudgery of self-repression in the public sphere, and much more, are all mediations of the specter of alienation in its gendered manifestation in art. Kulik opted—in the way that options can be said to exist when one sets out to cross a forest—to combat this specter by investing her energies in reinventing herself as a laboring subject, rather

39 Marina Vishmidt, "Pure Maintenance," *South as a State of Mind* 10 (June 2018): 81–89, 82.

than doing patriarchy the favor of evacuating herself from the (art) scene. In doing this, she has offered feminist imaginaries in art history the opportunity to explore the life-art contradiction—the principal contradiction faced by generations of avant-gardes—as it bears specifically on women's claims on worldmaking activities, including art. Should this be seen in terms of a refusal of the refusal? Or, rather, as the never-settled, lifelong process of self-definition that feminism once promised and capitalist patriarchy continues to pervert? It is hard to tell, but if the popular slogan on the struggle that continues is to be taken seriously, it would dictate an affirmative answer to the latter question.

Ewa Lajer-Burcharth is the William Dorr Boardman Professor of Fine Arts in the Department of History of Art and Architecture at Harvard University. Specialist in 18th- and 19-century French art, she has also written extensively on contemporary art and film, such as the work of Mona Hatoum, Mary Kelly, Pipilotti Rist, Cornelia Parker, Krzysztof Wodiczko, Amy Sillman, and Chantal Akerman, among others. Her books include *Necklines: The Art of Jacques-Louis David after the Terror* (1999), *Chardin Material* (2011), *Interiors and Interiority* (with Beate Söntgen, 2015), *Painting Beyond Itself: A Medium in the Post-Medium Condition* (with Isabelle Graw, 2016), *Drawing: The Invention of the Modern Medium* (a catalog of the exhibition she curated with Elizabeth Rudy at Harvard Art Museum, 2017), and, most recently, *The Painter's Touch: Boucher, Chardin, Fragonard* (2018).

OLD HISTORIES: ZOFIA KULIK'S IRONIC RECOLLECTIONS

Memory may take the form of a cultural montage shaped by the scissors of personal experience.

First cut: Copenhagen, May 1, 1982. I am standing at a window looking down, through the fog of the Scandinavian spring, at a colorful and cheery, if rather small, batch of people crossing a bridge. Realizing that what I am seeing is my very first "Western" May Day parade, I become wrapped up in my own somewhat foggy mixture of feelings and involuntary recollections. I am at once surprised, impressed by, and a bit envious of the people on the bridge; of the authenticity of their enthusiasm, its color, and its confident gestures. Here they are, the people who have both their beliefs and a language in which to articulate them—their *own* culture. But, as I also register a certain sadness of this small crowd of May paraders barely noticed by the passersby, their actions a mere colorful comma in the sentence of yet another gray and foggy day in Copenhagen, I feel my first surprising pang of an exile's nostalgia. (I didn't even realize that I had already become an exile.) Suddenly vivid in my mind stood what *would* have been going on at the very same time in Warsaw, had it not been for martial law: the colossal spectacles of officialdom that froze all forms of daily life in the city, stopping or rerouting the traffic to make way for the obligatory march of The People across town. I recalled the preceding days' frantic searches for a friendly doctor who could provide a certificate attesting to one's serious indisposition and thus a release from the injunction to march. And yet, what I also recalled was that if one did not manage to get a doctor's certificate and had to march anyway, it was mostly *kind of* fun. Once, for example, I happened to march with a group of (male) poets and writers who had just produced the journal of a new literary generation called *Nowy Wyraz* (New Articulation). We were handed a generic red banner with a white inscription that said something like "Onward We March Towards Socialism!" (socialism being a step towards the higher, utopian order of communism, not to be confused with the Western European notion of social democracy), and we decided that we wanted to, well, personalize it. Who knows, maybe the benevolent eye of power would notice us from the viewing tribune—since we were stuck with marching, we might as well be recognized for fulfilling our civic duty. Because no one had any tools or paint, I offered my eyeshadow, an import from the "rotten West," with which we proceeded to scribble the shaky letters of *Nowy Wyraz* onto the banner. And we could not help but enjoy the double irony of this truly New Articulation: the pearl-green pigment from Max Factor on the red banner of communism, and a woman's makeup as the official face of the new (male) literature. So, refocusing on the Copenhagen parade, it occurred to me that, back in Poland, "we" (an elusive category established chiefly through opposition to the imaginary "they" of the *nomenclatura* system) also had "our own" culture—not exactly the signs and gestures of officialdom, but rather our ironic experience (or negotiation) of them.[1]

Second cut: Bologna, early March, 1990. By one of those strange accidents of fate, I found myself at the last Italian Communist Party Congress, a guest in the press gallery above the plateau of delegates. After the debacle of the Eastern Bloc, and following the

1 For an excellent discussion of the imaginary communities designated by the "we" as opposed to the "they" of officialdom as typical creations of Eastern Europe, see Svetlana Boym, *Common Places: Mythologies of Everyday Life in Russia* (Cambridge, MA: Harvard University Press, 1994).

political changes within Italy, Partito Comunista Italiano was about to change its name to Partito Democratico della Sinistra (Democratic Party of the Left) and to become a different party, swapping its red emblem of the hammer and sickle for a new, ecologically correct and politically accommodating symbol: a green oak tree. As had happened years previously, at the very outset of my voluntary odyssey of exile in Copenhagen, I was witnessing, if on a larger and emotionally louder scale, an impressive spectacle of other people's beliefs. There came a moment in which everyone in the convention hall rose to their feet and, in unison, burst into song, the majestic "Internationale." And I, to my great surprise and embarrassment, burst into tears. And, what's worse, I could not stop, both crying and laughing at myself, as the more-than-familiar song that I used to sing by rote, a tune inseparable from the protracted boredom of endless high-school *academiae* (as the celebrations of various official anniversaries were called, and for which we were plucked en masse from classes and herded into the gymnasium, looking not unlike the party delegates now crowding below me), wreaked havoc in my emotional universe. Some friends standing by, witty journalists from an oppositional leftist paper *Il Manifesto* (anti-Partito Comunista), teased me: "crying is the game of the guilty ones; come now, closet communist!" It was not the inaccuracy of their diagnosis, but the difficulty in offering my own, alternative explanation of my reaction, that bothered me most. ("Anti-communists from a paper called, of all things, *Il Manifesto*—look who's talking," I am now musing disgruntledly when, alas, it is too late for a repartee.) Was I a communist? No. But *who* was I, swept by a wave of sympathetic identification with the crowd singing the "Internationale"?[2]

What my Bolognese episode made me realize amounts to this: communist culture was not some context in which I happened to have lived my own separate life—ironic though it may be—for some

2 It is the difficulty of negotiating one's position as an emergent postcommunist and/or exile subject that I am trying to foreground here, for I did not feel the label "anti-communist" would define me either. To begin with, the very term "communism" is misleading. One could argue that Eastern European countries were never really communist, but rather *nomenclatura* regimes: countries ruled by the excessive (and inevitably corrupt) state bureaucracy, based on Communist Party membership rather than communist ideals. This is what may be said at least of pre-1989 Poland.

twenty years; it was more of a text (or should I say song?) of my life. Whether I wanted it or not, I was part of this culture, and what's more, this culture was—*is*—somehow (the question is how) part of me. I am a subject inscribed by the communist signifier: my sense of self, my unconscious, harbors a shadow—an ambiguous one, to be sure—of the system in which I grew up. And so it was with the deep pleasure of instant recognition that I greeted the sulking woman, a red flag stubbornly stuck in her head, at the center of one of Zofia Kulik's photomontages from her *Idioms of the Soc-Ages* series (1989). There it was—an allegory of the postcommunist subject's ambiguous predicament. What this image of the artist spinning a Muybridgean wheel of her ironic fantasy of communism as a male pose visualized for me was both the deeply psychic level of my cultural inscription and its deeply ironic dimension. But if it reminded me of the irony in my past, it also suggested the productively unsettling potential of recollection.

As a figure of the artist, the woman with the red flag stuck in her head situates Zofia Kulik's work in this imaginary cultural territory, so-called Eastern Europe, the provisional yet long-lasting creation of the Cold War (and thus haunted by the ghosts of the Second World War), which, to most people's relief, is now gone. But with it, gone too is part of "ourselves," the men and women born under the twinkling Red Star, leaving "us" with a strange kind of loss. For few would want the lost object to return, and yet its absence (and the psychic hole it has created) makes itself felt. Kulik's art emerges from within this absent territory, missed only at its disappearance, to speak with a kind of nostalgic passion, as obsessional as it is ironic, of its past existence and complex afterlife. Her photomontages are, in a sense, the imaginary museums erected on the ruins of communist or, to be more precise, *nomenclatura* culture, documenting its paradoxes, its inconsistencies, its contradictions, and its all-pervading *former*-ness. Critical re-collections, they do not simply seek to preserve the past, but rather submit it to ironic revision, exposing its psychocultural mechanisms. And, as such, they are a woman's deconstructive re-collections: visualizing lovingly only to ruthlessly undo the masculinist assumptions behind the cultural mask of the *nomenclatura*, thus teasing out the logic of desire that had shaped it.

After the fall of the communist regime in Poland in 1989, Kulik embarked on the production of a series of photomontages that have now become quite familiar to international art audiences.[3] In all of these works, images of the male nude are arranged into complex patterns and structures that resemble mosaics, carpets, mandalas, Gothic windows, and altars, as well as other forms that foreground the idea of visual order. Part academic model, part object of some dark erotic fantasy, her mock-heroic male nudes are shown obediently rehearsing an array of poses that evoke, more or less directly, the rhetoric of Polish fêtes, celebrations, and monuments of the communist era. Many of their accessories—including flags, banners, poles, pikes, commemorative wreaths, and war medals—refer explicitly to May Day and the military parades of the communist past. Other attributes, such as loincloths, crosses, and censers, evoke Catholic ritual. The male model is frequently superimposed on or intercut with images of Second World War memorials and the mythic buildings of the communist political empire, such as the Palace of Culture, Stalin's detested gift to the city of Warsaw, or Berlin's Brandenburg Gate, the sublimated architectural emblem of the Iron Curtain. At times, in works such as *Favorite Balance* (1991), instruments of death and torture, from ropes to bullets, as well as skulls and other vanitative motifs, appear.

Kulik's male protagonists, the guardians of the spire, standard-bearers, wreath-holders, and other kinds of compliant performers, represent the idea of the communist subject as the function of a *system*—neither an anonymous state apparatus nor a mere ideological abstraction, but rather a system of cultural signification defined as a repertory of specific signs and poses.[4] It is the

3 While Kulik lives and works in Poland, her work has also been shown at international exhibitions, such as *Wanderlieder*, organized by the Stedelijk Museum in Amsterdam (1991–92), and *Beyond Belief* at the Museum of Contemporary Art in Chicago (1995). She had a retrospective show at the Zone Gallery in Newcastle upon Tyne, England, in 1995. Her photomontages have also entered museum collections in Poland and abroad.

4 For an important discussion of the theories of a nation as cultural system, and of the subject as a product of such a system, see Homi K. Bhabha's introduction to his anthology *Nation and Narration* (New York: Routledge, 1990), 1–8.

masculinist rhetoric of this system, as much as the maleness of the subject it assumes, that Kulik's work makes apparent. Not only are its motifs conspicuously phallic (not by chance is Warsaw's spired Palace of Culture the artist's favorite architectural motif), but its formal structure also insistently aligns the idea of composition with the symbolic order defined as the invisible but omnipresent Law governed by the phallic signifier. This alignment organizes the subject's appearance, but at the cost of his partial disarticulation (castration), which at times is quite comical. Note, for example, the negative images of the headless bodies that surround the prostrating male nude at the center of *Gate*. The fork in the key of the arch, in place of the escutcheon, as well as the torture implements underneath it, are the parodic emblems of this exacting Law that turns the man into pliable flesh, a mere morsel of meat about to disappear in the mouth of the cannibal "system." Similarly, the motif of sharp bullet cartridges in *Moon-Skull* and *Monstrance* from the *Columns* series inscribes the male model with a literally phallic signifier, at once highlighting the virile prowess of his pose and rendering it ludicrous. But what the *Gate* image also parodically suggests, through the little cupids placed on both sides of the fork, is the "amorous" (seductive) appeal of this Law, its power to interpellate—to call and coax—the subject into assuming the pose. Thus, Kulik envisions the "system" in psychosexual terms, wittingly foregrounding its capacity—its *desire*—to define the subject as a pose, a kind of phallic fiction based on the aggressive-heroic ethos of masculinity.[5]

If Kulik's arrangements expose the male subject's entrapment by the system, they also foreground the equivocal nature of his predicament: the naked man is as much "caught" by the controlling network of poses as he is willingly "acting out" an

5 In other words, it is not a matter of visualizing ideology, but of representing the psychic impact of the ideology on the subject, or the way in which the subject is interpellated by ideology through specific devices such as the repertory of signs that constituted the dominant fiction of the post-Second World War communist self. Kaja Silverman's theoretical elaboration of the complex relation between phallicity and the dominant fictions of masculinity was important to the development of my argument here; see her *Male Subjectivity at the Margins* (New York: Routledge, 1992).

internalized mode of behavior. His body conveys pain, but also a degree of pleasure in submission. This is clear, for example, in the martyrological delight with which men present themselves to the viewer in *Inter-National Gothic*, and in the quasi-ecstatic reverence of the two male figures flanking, like orants, the somber, fully clothed "madonna" in the very center of *All Things Converge in Time and Space; To Disperse, to Converge, To Disperse, and so On* (a photographic self-portrait of the artist with spears and bullet cartridges). The erotic tension between the submissive male and the "cold and cruel" dominatrix spells out the nature of their relation in terms of masochistic desire. Yet the image also reveals that masochism here is less a matter of an interpersonal dynamic than the male subject's *relation to the signifier*. The alignment of the dominatrix with the Palace of Culture that the male nude below her carries on his back makes it clear that the subject is bending under the weight of the communist sign, not an actual woman. (Just as in *Gate*, he prostrates under a fork as a mocking emblem of the subsuming or, to be exact, consuming power of the system.) What the somber madonna represents is the Law that governs the communist fiction of masculinity. And it is in the same role that she appears as the "key" image in the compositional architecture of *Favorite Balance*.

This is to say that Kulik's montages, notwithstanding their seemingly exclusive focus on the male figure, are also diagrams of a certain scheme of gender relations—of the "favorite balance," as it were—which, however, has nothing to do with the empowerment of women. It addresses, rather, male psychosexual dependence on a certain cultural ideal of masculinity, the authority of which is what Woman is asked to embody in order to secure Man's subjective coherence, to support his *maleness*. Assuming the mantle of a dominatrix, Kulik ironically identifies herself here as the guardian of a certain order of things: a masquerade of gender secured by the specific logic of desire at the core of the communist subjective ideal. Conveying a sense of mutual dependence between victim and oppressor, she presents herself as the key term in the metaphonic relation between the communist subject and the state, which she thereby reveals to be essentially masochistic. (As Gilles

Deleuze reminds us, in the masochistic fantasy the symbolic Law, traditionally identified with the Father, is transferred onto a maternal figure.[6]) In addition to staging herself as a dominatrix, Kulik introduces other devices that suggest the masochistic dimension of the communist imaginary by figuring the idea of the symbolic frame or compositional order as feminine. Thus, in *Favorite Balance*, the man in a toga kneeling at the center with a spear in one hand and a funerary bouquet in the other—yet another figure of male abjection under the auspices of the system—is framed by an orthogonal made of a flowery "feminine" fabric. From each of the frame's four corners a (female) hand extends, pointing towards a book cover of Maxim Gorky's *Matka* [*Mother*] [FIG. 1], the obligatory reading of every adolescent in pre-1989 Poland, and a thinly veiled literary metaphor for the communist state. The supportive-metaphoric function of femininity as the frame of symbolic reference is also hammered home by the repeated, rhythmic sequence of feminine figures that runs like a frieze of triglyphs and metopes around the entire composition; each of the women, dressed in a spoof of the Communist Youth uniform (white blouse, flared skirt, and heavy boots), holds a drapery swag in an alternating position (i.e. either raised above her head or obliterating it from view).

The masochistic, though, is not simply Kulik's iconography, but also the psychosexual logic behind the formal quality of her arrangements. Deleuze, who suggested that masochism is less an erotic or moral economy (of pleasure/pain or guilt/punishment) than a particular kind of *formalism*, emphasized qualities of the masochistic fantasy such as arrested movement, lack of narrative, and extreme stylization.[7] It is easy to see that these are precisely the aesthetic features of Kulik's photomontages. Her static, repetitive (i.e.

6 "The masochist experiences the symbolic order as an intermaternal order in which mother represents the law under certain prescribed conditions; she generates the symbolism through which the masochist expresses himself." Gilles Deleuze, *Coldness and Cruelty*, trans. Jean McNeal (New York: Zone Books, 1991), 63.

7 "Masochism is above all formal and dramatic; this means that its peculiar pleasure-pain complex is determined by a particular kind of formalism, [and its experience of guilt by a specific story]," Deleuze explains in *Coldness and Cruelty*, 105.

no narrative progress), highly formalized, and oddly harmonious montages (nothing like, say, Hannah Höch's deliberately incongruent visual amalgamations), function as an aesthetic support—a carpet of psychic comfort—for a masochistic male subject. What then does such an aesthetic of masochism amount to? Where exactly is the critical dimension of Kulik's vision?

The answer lies in its irony. Deleuze argued that masochism as such constitutes an ironic subversion insofar as it reveals the absurdity of Law. What is supposed to punish and prevent pleasure does precisely the opposite—it produces it. Insofar as, precisely through a *formal* process, the masochist identifies Law with the figure of the Mother, he threatens the Law of the Father and thus, again, may be seen as a challenger of the symbolic order.[8] From the Deleuzian perspective, it is the masochist himself who is ironic, his obedience concealing a criticism and provocation of sexual (and thus also societal) norms.[9]

Zofia Kulik's aesthetic play upon the idea of masochism asks, however, for a somewhat different reading. For the irony in her work is not the property of the male subject, but rather of the feminine teller of the masochistic tale, the woman in charge of the formal process: the Mother and/*as* the artist. It is, in other words, her aesthetic irony that reveals masculinity to be a man's comical effort, at once the aspiration and failure to assume the pose. And it is her ironic distance from herself that allows her to assume the preposterous role of the dominatrix from the masochistic fantasy. This feminine (and feminist) perspective on communist culture reveals masochism as the central psychocultural mechanism in the formation of Eastern European subjectivity: the logic that shaped the dominant ideal of the subject as a *man avowed to a system*. And insofar as Kulik's work may be seen as a critical insight into a specifically Polish inflection of this exemplary ideal, it suggests that its masochistic logic may have

8 Identified as the latter is with the figure of the Father. See *Coldness and Cruelty*, chs. VII and VIII, especially 88–91.

9 Deleuze, *Coldness and Cruelty*, 88. Thus it may be argued that Deleuze's provocative analysis serves only to return the lost glory of the fallen Father to that of his gloriously transgressive masochistic son—a subversive gesture that remains inscribed within a masculinist ideal of subversion.

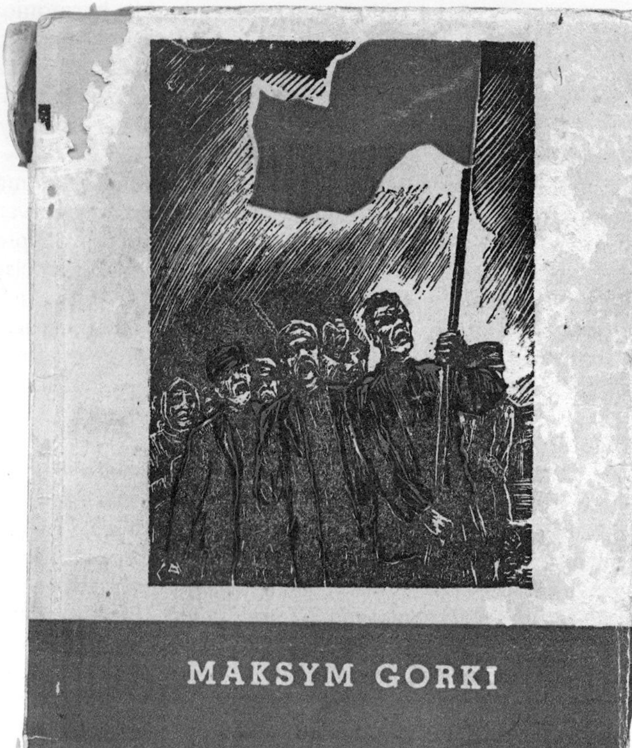

FIG. 1
POLISH EDITION OF MAXIM GORKY'S *MOTHER*,
IN THE LIBRARY OF ZOFIA KULIK

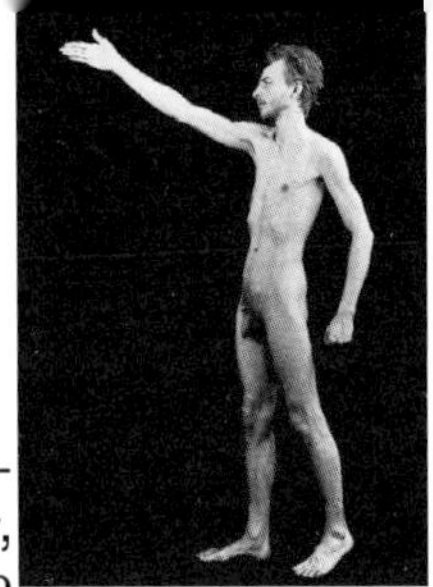

A

something to do with the Catholic underpinnings of Polish culture.[10] (What I have in mind here is, specifically, the martyrological image-repertory of Catholicism to which Kulik herself explicitly refers, for example in the *Inter-National Gothic*.)

What Kulik's aesthetic irony reveals is not the male masochist's "criticism and provocation of law," as Deleuze put it, but rather his frail body's inadequate attempts at mimicry, at conformity with the Law. Throughout her work, Kulik exposes this ridiculous incommensurability of the male body with the ideal it tries to enact. Can you believe in the aggressive posture of the skinny naked man charging forward with a spear while his ribcage is showing and his sadly pendent penis is exposed in its full vulnerability? Kulik's men are repeatedly staged as ironic signifiers of phallic mastery, marked as they are by the internal distance between their meager physical bodies and the exemplary masculine poses they take on.

The effect of this ironic disjunction may be better grasped by a comparison between the nude model from a detail of Kulik's **FACADE OF 500 EXPOSURES** A (1995), and its iconographic source, G. D. Alekseev's 1924 statue of Lenin as the *Calling Leader* [FIG. 2], one of the early masterworks of Russian socialist realism. While the pose and gesture of Kulik's model testify to the power of the socialist-realist body as an identificatory model, his nakedness underscores the incompleteness of his identification. Note specifically the eloquence of the male genital organ in Kulik's figure, and the distance its detumescence articulates from the symbolic Phallus embodied by Alekseev's safely clothed (and thus unimpaired) confidently gesturing leader. Expropriating the male anatomical part

10 The cultural amalgamation for which the Italians, commenting on the paradoxes of their own political culture, have an apt term: *Cato-comunismo* (used affectionately by Italian communists themselves).

to challenge its symbolic equation with the Phallus, Kulik makes masculine frailty resurface here, as she does elsewhere, from under the cultural pretense of the socialist-realist pose.[11]

In doing so, Kulik's photographic enterprise casts an ironic shadow on socialist realism as the specific (often disavowed), aesthetic legacy of communism.[12] The Lenin-bound mimicry of her male protagonist addresses the broader issue of the cultural assimilation of the aesthetic paradigms generated by the former Soviet Union in the Eastern Bloc. In defining this mode of assimilation as exposure (literally, by her work's title: *Facade of 500 Exposures*), the artist points to the critical, deconstructive dimension of her choice of photography as a technique for rewriting the old Eastern European

11 The distancing, ironic-masochistic logic of the pose is comically illustrated by the male nude in one section of *Inter-National Gothic*, standing with an arm extended in a military salute while holding a hanging rope, with its noose around his neck. (The title of this work is an ironic reinscription of the internationalist rhetoric of the Soviet-generated socialist discourse as a kind of Gothic tale.) Similarly, in the middle of another work from the *Columns* series (1995), a man is shown rehearsing heroic postures, but the fiction of his pose comes apart. He is shown trying on a wreath or striking a celebratory posture with a banner, his face thrown into profile for posterity, but his distinctly unheroic nudity, with his penis as prominent as it is unimpressively pendent, defines masculinity as vulnerable and frail rather than triumphant and controlling. Finally, on the border of *Favorite Balance*, under the frieze of female figures with drapery pendants, there runs a series of images of two "real" Polish men, as opposed to academic models, sitting in a restaurant, their bodies slumped in what seems either to be deep meditation or, more likely, drunken stupor, quite eloquently articulating their incompatibility with (or refusal of) the heroic ideal of masculinity paraded elsewhere in the work.

12 It is well known that socialist realism, developed in the Soviet Union, functioned as the aesthetic idiom of the Eastern European communist countries in the 1940s and 1950s. Yet its character, development, and cultural importance were not exactly the same as in Russia. In Poland, for example, it was only a brief episode, although, it may be argued, of crucial importance for constructing a (hole-ridden) shared cultural memory. For a provocative assessment of Polish socialist realism, see Ryszard Ziarkiewicz, *Raj Utracony*, ex. cat. (Warsaw: National Museum, 1990). For an extensive discussion of socialist-realist aesthetics in a cultural context, see Wojciech Włodarczyk, *Socrealizm: Sztuka polska w latach 1950–1954* (Kraków: Wydawnictwo Literackie, 1982).
An insightful analysis of its complex after-effects on the Polish artistic culture of the late 1950s is offered in Waldemar Baraniewski, "Okolice odwilży," in "Wokół rzeźby współczesnej," special issue, *Zeszyt Naukowy Akademii Sztuk Pięknych w Warszawie* 19, no. 1 (1987): 52–65.

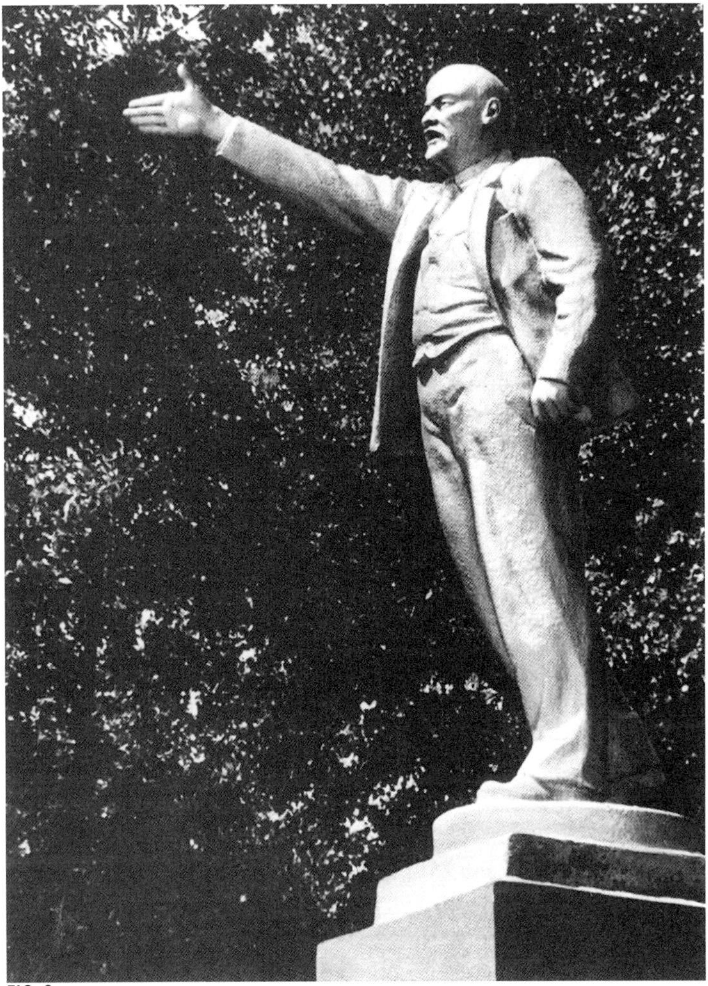

FIG. 2
G.D. ALEKSEEV, *CALLING LEADER*, 1924

story through, precisely, a *formal process*.[13] At the same time, taking on socialist realism, Kulik's work also retells an older story, calling forth as it does the long artistic tradition of narrative painting, of which the official aesthetic idiom of the communist era was but one installment. As a matter of fact, the gestures of both Alekseev's Lenin and her own male model send us down memory lane to the very moment when this narrative tradition was first put to the service of revolution: with Jacques-Louis David's *The Tennis Court Oath*.[14]

David's sketch for the work allows us to peek behind the curtains of this tradition, specifically into the structure of its masculinist assumption in the making. Envisioning the founding moment of the French Revolution through an image of an exclusively male community, the sketch documents the construction of the male body as the privileged signifier of a subjective ideal, exemplary in both its moral and physical excellence—the Revolutionary subject as maleness par excellence. Not only are the Third Estate deputies transformed here into athletes of the Revolution, their gestures borrowed from the antique oratory tradition, but they are also shown "seized," as it were, by the system of one-point perspective adopted by the artist to convey this "pregnant moment" of the Revolution. The unerased orthogonals seem to pull these contingent bodies into complete identification with an invisible ideal of unity (i.e. the *fraternité* as the backbone of the Jacobin ideology that shaped David's commission), and it is precisely insofar as their bodies conform to this unifocal spatial structure, with their gestures echoing the direction of the lines, that these figures represent the Revolutionary subject. What we witness here, then, is a visual construction of the *orthopsychic* subject of the Revolution: a corporeal representation of the

13 As a technique it is quite interesting: it is not exactly a photomontage, but rather a photographic tapestry created by manually assembled, individually exposed photographs. When asked why she does not use a computer to generate her imagery, Kulik answered that it offered too much control to the artist.

14 A standard work of the art-historical canon, but also especially familiar to Poles through a copy drawn by Jean-Pierre Norblin de la Gourdaine, an artist who was active in Poland from 1774–1804. One version of the drawing is now in the collection of the National Museum in Warsaw; others are at the Fogg Art Museum, Cambridge, MA.

ideologically desirable, "correct" psyche.[15] At one with their pose, these men are sustained by, and therefore able to project forth, a certain normative fiction of masculinity.

If Kulik's compositional structures evoke order, they are also images of disarray and dispersal—of uncontrolled, kaleidoscopic multiplication without beginning or end. In contrast to the unifocal composition of the David, Kulik's works—whether her *Favorite Balance* or another entitled *All the Missiles Are One Missile* (1993)—often confront us with a rhythmic series of flat patterns that, despite the accentuated center, invite the eye to laterally scan the whole image without prescribed order, in a kind of scattered perusal.[16] In other words, while in some sense orderly, her unrelentingly repetitive spatial organization of bodies at once evokes and erodes the narrative paradigm of history painting that focused on a sole, noteworthy "pregnant moment." Instead, Kulik situates the old stories of communism in an ironic frame of disordering order.[17] (This is also true of her elaborate architectural compositions such as *Facade of 500 Exposures*, where the overall structure remains essentially anti-narrative.) By locating her ever-posing men in this multifocal, rhythmic structure, she both illustrates and ridicules the idea of identification—envisioning a kind of continuous (because repeatedly unsuccessful) mimicry, a process without beginning or end. Caught in the grip of the heroic posture that fails to embrace them, yet never lets them go, the dominant subjects of Kulik's stories are a poignant testimony to the masculine pathos of the communist era.

It is this pathetic male protagonist that links Kulik's art to the more broadly understood new artistic production that has emerged from the former precincts of the Eastern Bloc. It seems that, after the fall of communism, it was specifically women artists

15 For an important discussion of the Lacanian notion of the orthopsychic subject (a term Lacan borrowed from Bachelard), see Joan Copjec, "The Orthopsychic Subject: Film Theory and the Reception of Lacan," ch. II, in *Read My Desire* (Cambridge, MA: MIT Press, 1994). I have discussed David's canvas in these terms in my *Necklines: The Art of Jacques-Louis David after the Terror* (New Haven: Yale University Press, 1999).

16 An ironic paraphrase of T. S. Eliot's "all the women are one woman."

17 In accordance with the Greek etymology of the word (*eironicos*, meaning both dissimulating and disassembling).

and writers who took on the creative responsibility of exposing the gender assumptions behind the dominant cultural fictions of the *nomenclatura*. Their concerted efforts gave shape to a phantom of the unbearable frailty of masculinity that hovers above the new horizons of European art and literature—a harbinger of the difficult process of shedding the past. We find it, for example, in the novels of Croatian writer Dubravka Ugrešić, who excels in laying bare and poking fun at the unsuspected fragility of Eastern European manhood. While under Ugrešić's warmly ironic gaze, the pretensions and poses of both genders melt away, yet it is her gallery of dubious male characters—the impotent sexual prowlers, the neurotic bureaucrats of the communist apparatus, and the calculating careerists of the 1980s *nomenclatura*, who turn into wimps at the slightest withdrawal of feminine support—that constitutes a distinctive mark of her writing.[18] In one of her most recent novels we witness a feminine parody of rape performed by three women writers on a misogynist literary critic. In this hilarious scene, which takes place in a hotel room during an international literary conference in Zagreb, Ivan Ljustina, the pet critic of communist officialdom, known for his sarcastic remarks on feminine creativity, succumbs to an outburst of parodic Bacchanalia staged by a team of enraged but inventively playful Eastern and Western European women of letters. We are introduced to him as he lies naked and spread-eagled on a bed, with his arms and legs bound to the bedpost and his mouth gagged. Having covered his entire body with sticky glue, the three women release feathers from a pillow all over him, turning him into a deplorable snowman. Then, attaching his penis by a string to a small balloon, the women enjoy the spectacle of the male organ's slow emergence from under the feathers, first peeking through with detumescent uncertainty and then bursting into an involuntary erection.[19]

18 See, for example, a literal gallery of such imperfect men encountered by the female protagonists in Dubravka Ugrešić, *In the Jaws of Life*, trans. Celia Hawkesworth and Michael Henry Heim (London: Virago Press, 1992).

19 Dubravka Ugrešić, *Fording the Stream of Consciousness*, trans. Michael Henry Heim (London: Virago Press, 1991), 132–35.

What peeks out from underneath the plucked feathers of official masculinity is also the sad corpus of the Eastern European myth of the dissident artist as a man. While the deconstructive efforts of artists such as Zofia Kulik and Dubravka Ugrešić, who expose the invisible gender assumptions in the cultural past, are of crucial importance, the crumbling of the mythic oppositional artist has to be seen as part of a broader process of the waning of cherished Eastern European ideologies of cultural subversion, a waning due to factors such as the pressure of the market, which has emerged as a relatively new aspect of artistic life, and a broader transformation of artistic discourse and institutions after the fall of communism.[20]

What, then, is the place of a subversive *woman* artist in the new artistic landscape of the nascent democratic, consumerist societies of the former Eastern Europe?[21] Kulik's practice may be seen as a response to this query, formulated from the perspective of a "veteran" member of the Polish oppositional avant-garde—the generation of artists who came of age in the 1970s and whose critical practice defined the paradigm of cultural subversion. Her current deconstructive activity may thus be seen not only as a critical reexamination of the cultural history of the Polish *nomenclatura*, but also, in a sense, as an auto-ironic revision directed at her own artistic history. Between 1970 and 1987 the artist was engaged in post-conceptual performance work in collaboration with Przemysław Kwiek, with whom she created a public persona functioning under

20 For the discussion of the transformation of the art world in post-*nomenclatura* Poland, see my "Warsaw Diary," *Art in America* 82, no. 2 (February 1994).

21 This complex problem cannot be solved by ready-made discursive or aesthetic imports from the West, for the post-Second World War gender arrangements in Eastern Europe were radically different (that is, *differently* asymmetrical) than those of the West, i.e. most women in postwar Eastern Europe worked, and the efforts of both men and women were measured against the ethos of an exemplary, more or less genderless, constructor of the new order. Yet the communist discourse of gender equality was driven by hidden tensions and inconsistencies in the ways men and women were being situated in relation to this dominant subjective ideal, and especially in the ways in which the bourgeois notion of the exemplary nuclear couple lingered on uneasily beside the fiction of a more or less genderless *community*.

the symbiotic name KwieKulik.[22] As the artist put it in a recent interview, theirs was a kind of "strange personal-artistic collage," important and in many ways rewarding, but also, in the long run, stifling her own proper artistic voice.[23] In this context, Kulik's current photomontages may be seen as an ironic reconfiguration of her earlier work with Kwiek. The binary, gendered structure of her photographic arrangements featuring a submissive male and a dominant female registers the ambivalent process of separation from her artistic past, both restaging and exorcizing her former symbiotic relation with her artistic partner. The submissive male actor, however, should not be viewed literally, as an image of a person (i.e. Kwiek), but rather as a figure of the unspoken assumption that underlay the kind of subversive practice in which they were *both* involved: i.e. the conception of the dissident artist as a victim of the system, and the unacknowledged masochistic desire that shaped it. Including images of herself in her work, Kulik is thus not exempting herself from the legacy of the past, but ironically reconfiguring its masochistic premise, seeking distance from the self-immolating male desire with which she used to identify as an artist.

The implication of Kulik's practice—namely that the alternative cultural ideal of the oppositional avant-garde may not have been as far removed from the exemplary subject of the

22 Their work, and the larger critical-artistic practice to which it belonged, was supported by an alternative gallery system that flourished in Poland from the 1970s until martial law (imposed on December 13, 1981), under semi-tutelage or semi-tolerance by the Office of Art Exhibitions (Biuro Wystaw Artystycznych). Their performances targeted the obstacles and constraints imposed on critical cultural activities in Poland and on their authors. *The Monument without a Passport* [FIG. 3], presented in 1978 at one of the alternative spaces in Sopot, offered a satirical commentary on KwieKulik's position as artists impeded by state bureaucracy; as punishment for their critical activity they were denied passports between 1975–79.

23 See *Magazyn Sztuki*, no. 1 (1993): 15.

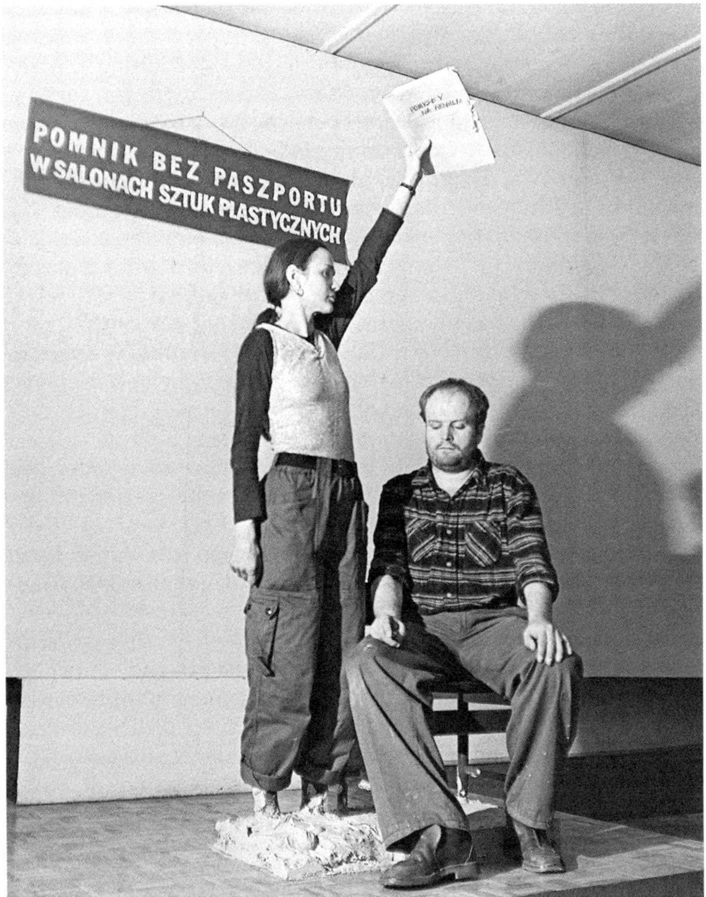

FIG. 3
KWIEKULIK, *THE MONUMENT WITHOUT A PASSPORT*, 1978

nomenclatura as one would have suspected—is provocative.[24] Reaching beyond signs and accessories to the logic that shapes one's relation to them, Kulik's deconstructive work exposes the psychosexual mechanism that operated across different levels of cultural practice in pre-1989 Poland and, at least to some extent, in the former Eastern Europe as a whole. It is exactly because it is a psychically based cultural mechanism that its shedding is a complex and difficult process. If the critical dimension of Kulik's photomontages extends beyond the parameters of the communist era to the present, it is precisely insofar as they acknowledge and examine the afterlife of the Soc-age idioms in the postcommunist psyche. Rather than simply offering new signs and trappings, this work suggests another kind of relation to signs based on a critical rethinking, rather than a forgetting, of the past. Its irony is thus a mode of formulating a cultural memory of the expired system that may help provide new imaginary bases for the self, including that of the artist, emerging from its ruins.

Kulik's most recent work, however, casts a shadow of doubt on the possibilities of any fast-and-easy renewal, whether aesthetic or subjective. Titled *Still Life* (1995), her new series of Cibachrome photographic collages combines, with a kind of brutal elegance, images of human skulls, blood sausage (the Polish *kiszka*, designating both a common culinary treat and human entrails), animal bones and teeth, chunks of raw meat, root vegetables, an occasional lemon, and, in one case, heavy chains in a form suggesting the human brain. While departing from her earlier black-and-white poetics, these colorful and bold combinations offer us a glimpse of what resurfaces from behind the symbolic facade of subordination when it crumbles: a disembodied postcommunist subject, at a loss of self-image and identity. At once beautiful and difficult to look at, Kulik's

24 For a critical rereading of the Polish alternative avant-garde of the 1970s, which accuses the oppositional artists of perpetuating the very ideological models they opposed, see Piotr Piotrowski, *Dekada* (Poznań: Wydawnictwo Obserwator, 1992). I have briefly discussed its merits and limitations in my previously mentioned "Warsaw Diary." The difference between Piotrowski's (in a sense disciplinary-Foucauldian) diagnosis and Kulik's ironic perspective on the oppositional artistic past is precisely the latter's psychosexual rather than institutional or discursive dimension, and a much greater emphasis on the ambiguity of the artists (and thus her own predicament).

mise-en-scènes of death hark back to Théodore Géricault's notorious images of severed heads and amputated limbs, the tableaux of post-Napoleonic melancholia. But hers is melancholia with a bite, an aggressive and humorous rearticulation of loss. Both gruesome and comic, her arrangements of disparate motifs eat away at the vanitative decorum of the still life tradition. For one, her motifs bite at *one another*—skulls nibbling at *kiszka* or, cannibalistically, at each other. Staging the idea of death in a mode that is at once disturbingly literal and exceedingly stylized, these are macabre spoofs on the time-honored visual metaphors of vanitas. Furthermore, if we see the still life tradition, as art historian Norman Bryson has urged us to, as an appropriative vision of feminine space, Kulik's work is a striking reappropriation: flaunting the foodstuff signs of domesticity, her *Still Life* is a feminine vision with a vengeance—death and life after communism served with black culinary humor.[25] Under the symbolic auspices of the Polish *kiszka*, these pictograms of consumption gnaw, moreover, at the consumerist promises of fulfillment spun by the new visual culture of advertisement that has flourished in the former Eastern European countries. Horns of plenty *à rebours*, they rub against the grain of the newly dominant fantasies of 1990s Poland, where Mercedes Benz showrooms have mushroomed next to shops offering the paraphernalia of the Soc-age on sale. And as ironic advertisements, they are a kind of symbolic weapon of a woman artist winking from behind the Iron Curtain, after its fall.[26]

This text was originally published in New Histories, *ex. cat., Boston: Institute of Contemporary Art, 1996; it is published here in a revised version.*

25 See Norman Bryson, "Still Life and 'Feminine' Space," *Looking at the Overlooked: Four Essays on Still Life Painting* (Cambridge, MA: Harvard University Press, 1990), 136–78.

26 The term "symbolic weapon" has often been used by the artist herself in relation to her earlier, Soc-age-related work.

Sarah G. Wilson is Professor of the History of Modern and Contemporary Art at the Courtauld Institute of Art, University of London. Her recent publications include *Figurations ± 68—Le monde visuel de la French Theory* (2018), *The Visual World of French Theory: Figurations* (2010), and *Picasso / Marx and Socialist Realism in France* (2013), based on decades of research and interviews. She continues to publish on women artists: Zofia Kulik, Germaine Richier, or those less well-known, such as Myriam Bat-Yosef, while performance is another interest. At the Courtauld, her MA course, Global Conceptualism, was created in 2011 with Professor Boris Groys. She is an active member of CCRAC (Cambridge Courtauld Russian Art Centre). She was the principal curator of *Paris: Capital of the Arts 1900–1968* (Royal Academy of Arts, London; Guggenheim Bilbao, 2002–03), *Pierre Klossowski and the Vicious Circle* (Whitechapel Art Gallery, 2006) (exhibited as *Klossowski* in Cologne and Paris), and co-curator of the First Asia Biennale / Fifth Guangzhou Triennale (Guangzhou, China). She was appointed Chevalier des Arts et des Lettres by the French government in 1997, and received the AICA Award for Distinguished Contribution to Art Criticism in 2015.

ZOFIA KULIK: FROM WARSAW TO CYBERIA

Warsaw-based Zofia Kulik, with her partner Przemysław Kwiek, as the duo KwieKulik, were among Poland's most prominent performance artists in the 1970s and 1980s, playing constantly with national symbols such as the national flag.[1] Yet by the time the show *Idioms of the Soc-Ages* opened in New York City in 1990 at the Postmasters Gallery, she had abandoned performance, abandoned Kwiek, and was making large photopieces based on the designs of both oriental carpets, known as polonaises in Poland, and the arched structures of stained-glass windows, referenced in works such as *The Guardians of the Spire*, which she called, ironically, "Inter-National Gothic." These post-Stalinist works, often dominated by kaleidoscopic images of the Soviet Palace of Culture in Warsaw, were "Soc-art" productions; the New York gallery show was typical of the popularity of post-Soviet, Eastern European postmodernism in the West at the time.

1 See the comprehensive study by Jerzy Truszkowski, *Sztuka krytyczna w Polsce = Critical Art in Poland / Kwiek, Kulik, KwieKulik 1967–1998* (Poznań: Galeria Miejska "Arsenał," 1999).

In the international exhibition *Wanderlieder* held in Amsterdam in 1991, Kulik felt herself to be "a 'quotation' from the East," involving all the problems of "double identity" as she took her place among a constellation of Western artists.[2] At the 57th Venice Biennale in 1997, Kulik represented her country in the Polish Pavilion. There the postmodernism/postnationalism equation was epitomized by the epic frieze *All the Missiles Are One Missile* of 1993. Like all of Kulik's work, this was highly political. Much of its imagery relates, in a deliberately arbitrary way, to television images culled from Western European sources. Subsequently, Soc-art as socialist-realist memory, rather than piquant, post-Soviet kitsch, combined with the broad sweep of Cold War history within the context of globalized media "infotainment," was presented in the vast photomural, *From Siberia to Cyberia*, shown in Kulik's Poznań retrospective, and in Stockholm and Berlin, in *After the Wall: Art and Culture in Post-Communist Europe*, 1999–2000.[3]

If postmodernism and postnationalism may be equated, to what extent does it follow that one can equate modernism and nationalism? As a Europeanist fascinated by the cosmopolitanism of the so-called School of Paris before and after 1945, I would contend that the concepts are indeed linked, but are passionately antithetical. The crystallizing moment of modernism, hermetic cubism, witnessed the coming together of Picasso from Spain and Braque from France, working together and renouncing their signatures; more pertinently, the avant-garde consensus around grid-based cubist painting and sculpture was shattered almost immediately, not only by war but by the eruption of the Central European and the performative, with Tristan Tzara's Parisian Dada movement (significantly, the Romanian pseudonym "Tzara" referred in his exile

2 See *Doppelte Identität: Polnische Kunst zu Beginn der neunziger Jahre* (Wiesbaden: Landesmuseum, 1991), and *Wanderlieder* (Amsterdam: Stedelijk Museum, 1991–92).

3 Zofia Kulik and Piotr Piotrowski, eds., *Zofia Kulik: Od Syberii do Cyberii / From Siberia to Cyberia* (Poznań: National Museum, 1999); Bojana Pejić and David Elliott, eds., *After the Wall: Art and Culture in Post-Communist Europe* (Stockholm: Moderna Museet, 1999). Kulik's work was also featured in the exhibition *L'autre moitié de l'Europe (mémoire, histoire, biographie projet, utopie, construction réalité sociale, existence, politique énigme, secret, ésotérisme)*, Galerie nationale du Jeu de Paume, Paris, 2000.

to Tzara's patria or homeland). And as a way of returning, circuitously, to Kulik, let us consider a major source that she ironizes: the dynamic imagery of pioneer photomontage artists within modernist, revolutionary Russia. Modernist photomontage, in itself the origin of the modern political poster, celebrated the construction of nationhood, national myth, and glorified impersonality: see the photomontages of Rodchenko, El Lissitzky, and particularly Gustav Klutsis, with his duplicated, miniscule Lenins, the characteristic repetition of heads in a crowd, and of gymnasts, strikers, soldiers and bayonets. The oblique camera angles captured a peopled fragment that stood for the masses at large, the entire Soviet collective. Number under socialism was therefore celebratory, a sign of the will to power. Yet the nationalist message implicit in the formula Sovietization = modernization was disrupted by the performative: the repeated gestures of the leader as mannequin were too obviously linked to propaganda. Too soon, patriotic photomontage would come to signal the rhetoric of the lie: not hope, but despair; not life, but the liquidation of the "enemy" within. Modernist tropes as a form of control thus preceded both the slippage towards socialist realism and the Gesamtkunstwerk Stalin in the USSR, and generated the "reactionary modernisms" confronting nationalist realisms and the internationalist modernism of the 1930s.[4]

Before using and perverting Soviet photomontage motifs in her critical photopieces, Kulik made sculpture, photographs, mail art, and then, as KwieKulik, turned to performance, using art as the critique of a regime in which nationalism as a concept was totally bewildered—made wild, made savage—not only by the status of Poland as a Soviet satellite, but as a country whose borders had been unstable since 1795. Occupied first by the Nazis and subsequently by the Soviets, with over six million war dead, Poland's boundaries shifted radically once more as it became a one-

4 Consider the confrontations suggested by *Abstraction-Creation*, Musée d'Art Moderne de la Ville de Paris, 1978 (Paris-based international abstraction c. 1930–38); Jeffrey Herf, *Reactionary Modernism: Technology, Culture, and Politics in Weimar and the Third Reich* (New York: Cambridge University Press, 1984); and Boris Groys, *The Total Art of Stalinism* (Princeton: Princeton University Press, 1992).

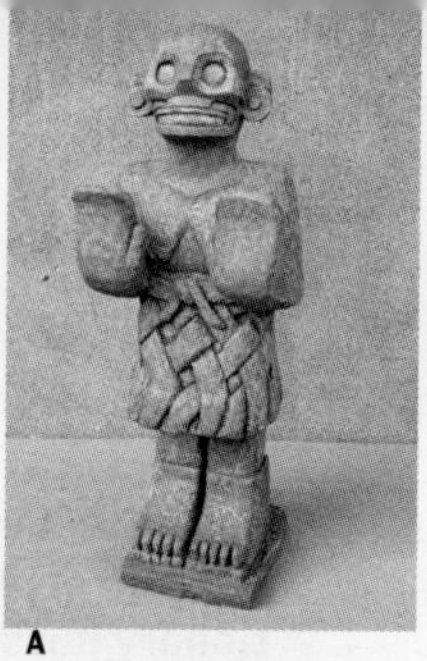
A

party, Stalinist state in 1946. Yet the "Polish October" of 1956 and the subsequent liberalization allowed for the accommodation of postwar existentialism with some Eastern regimes, giving rise to an "absurd" so recognizable in the work of a Jan Kott or a Tadeusz Kantor. In the context of the 1970s' "dematerialization of the art object," performance provided the perfect arena for the critique of totalitarianism, since both discourses focused on the body as metaphor. As the exhibition *Body and the East* (held in 1998 in Ljubljana) demonstrated, performance art was a widespread (if covert) phenomenon all over Eastern Europe.[5] "I am an artist of the 1970s. [...] For us 1981 started in 1974."[6] Kulik's childhood and artistic youth under communism preceded the performance years, in this freer but still politically repressive Poland: what she called, to use the title of a rayogram made with dust and her hair, *Alice's Adventures in Fucked Wonderland*. From the outset, Kulik's art was resolutely antipatriarchal.[7] Her first sculpture was a copy of a stone Aztec snake goddess, **COATLICUE** A (1961), her skirt a braided plaiting of live serpents. She worked in clay as her mother had worked with needle and thread; conversely, her ironic pastiche of Michelangelo's **MOSES** B (1971) at art school duplicated the noble marble with a version in exuberant patchwork cloth.[8] Her diploma piece comprised five hundred slides, very many of a naked woman in academic poses—sometimes wearing or playing with a red sash. Taken over a year, these constituted the first of her subsequent photoarchives. The red sash, the "sign of official celebrations," which appears in photographs draped upon her drawings and on or with her model, seems to exemplify *à la lettre* what Renata Salecl calls "the red thread" running through her own, "post-socialist" analy-

5 Zdenka Badovinac, ed., *Body and the East* (Cambridge, MA: MIT Press, 1998).

6 Unsourced quotations by Zofia Kulik are comments made to the author in Łomianki, November 21–23, 1998.

7 See Jerzy Truszkowski, "The Structure of Kulik," *Magazyn Sztuki*, no. 10 (1996).

8 The Michelangelo piece has been reconstructed several times: by KwieKulik (three copies) for the exhibition *Sorcerers and Mystics*, Center for Contemporary Art, Ujazdowski Castle, Warsaw, 1991; and by Kulik (two copies) for the exhibition *Architectures of Gender. Contemporary Women's Art in Poland*, Sculpture Center, NYC, 2003. [The latter copy is reproduced on p. 14 of this volume. —Ed.]

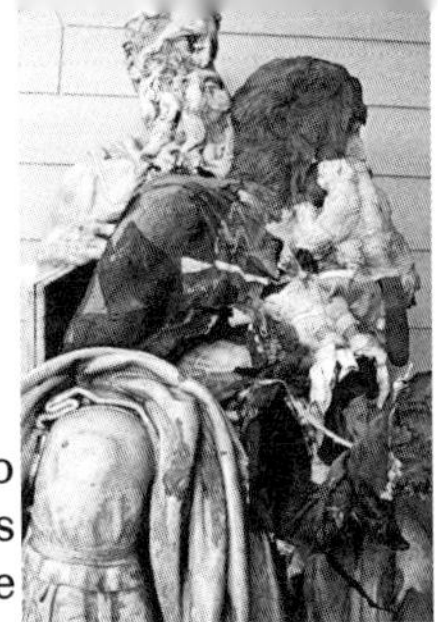

B / P. 14

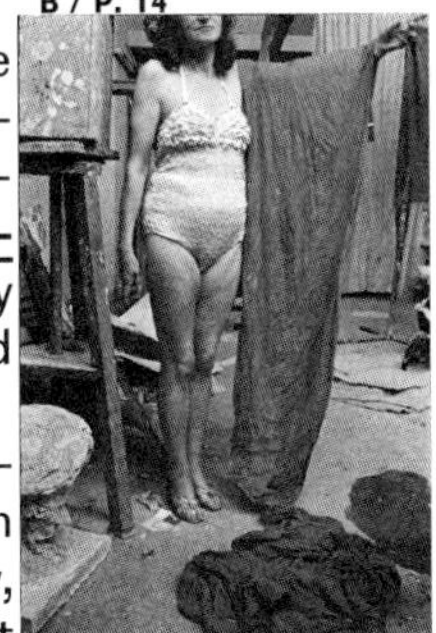

C / P. 13

ses: "the notion of fantasy, not as a supplement to 'actual' power relations, but as an agency that always already structures these relations [...] the structure of power is inherently fantasmatic."[9]

Kulik's photographs of a model whose white swimsuit is covered with the red sash demonstrate an eroticized, female body fantasmatically displacing the totalitarian state (**INSTEAD OF SCULPTURE** C [1968–71]): see Kulik's own photographs of May Day in Warsaw, showing state buildings similarly decorated with vast red banners.

By 1971, Kulik was working with her partner Kwiek as the artistic couple KwieKulik. With the film *Open Form*, which involved five people in group activity, Kulik experienced a release from traditional art objects. She described the experience as a new "opposition to officiality, building a private base for independence." But the freedom of expression signified by Open Form was both compounded and belied by disturbing images of silencing: the film stills the couple labeled *Game on an Actress's Face* involve blobs of clay stuck onto the skin; another shows a bay leaf—one thinks of the poet's laurels—glued to the actress's mouth by a gloved hand. Even the extraordinary experimental pieces with their baby son Maksio (Maksymilian Dobromierz), created within their apartment from 1972–74 and constituting, remarkably, over two hundred images [FIGS. 1–2], obtained highly emotional effects via images of containment.[10] Far from psychologically based—they make an extraordinary comparison with the psychoanalytically informed work of Mary Kelly at the same time in the West—these works were, according to Kulik,

9 Renata Salecl, *The Spoils of Freedom: Psychoanalysis and Feminism after the Fall of Socialism* (London: Routledge, 1994), 7.

10 Unframed slides presented in strips were mounted in a window frame as *Logical Window*, 1973; forty-eight black-and-white photographs were "framed" with crumpled brown paper and shown several times. The large Cibachrome images of the series are a new development, shown in *The Missing Link*, Galeria Miejska "Arsenał," Poznań, 1999.

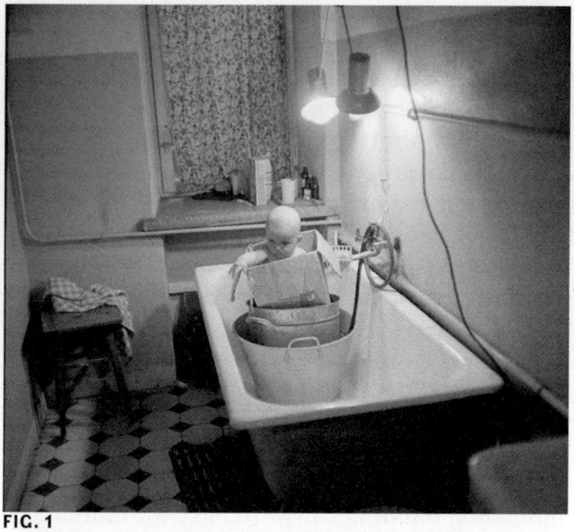

FIG. 1
KWIEKULIK, *ACTIVITIES WITH DOBROMIERZ*, 1972–74/2008

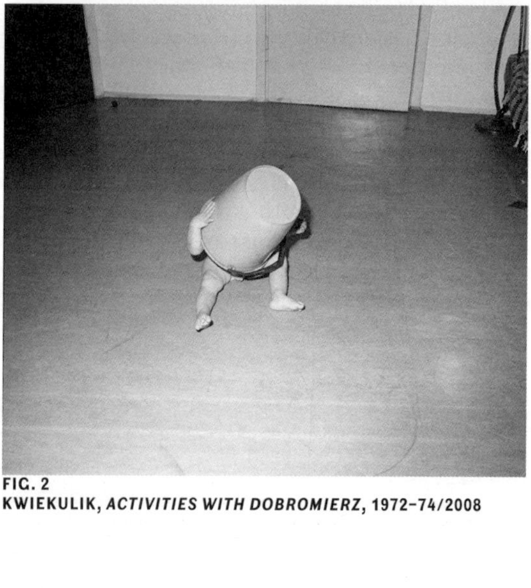

FIG. 2
KWIEKULIK, *ACTIVITIES WITH DOBROMIERZ*, 1972–74/2008

mathematical and abstract in conception.[11] Despite their inadvertent comedy and pathos—Dobromierz, a name that means "a good measure," is surrounded by onions, knives and forks, and blocks of ice from the nearby Vistula river—they anticipated KwieKulik's later performance pieces, with devices such as the bucket on the baby boy's head, and the use of sharp instruments. Overtones of potential sadism held at bay, or at least a disturbing spectacle made of the bewilderment of innocence, mirror KwieKulik's adult political critiques. Constructed situations symbolizing imprisonment and suffocation continued as the work of KwieKulik became more public and then international: international by default when, refused passports to participate in a behavior workshop in Arnhem, the Netherlands, they performed *The Monument without a Passport* at the Biennale of Young Artists in Sopot in 1978. Kulik first put her head through a table top, supporting a surface upon which slides of postcards sent from Arnhem were projected; Kwiek plastered her legs to the floor, symbolizing her now "double imprisonment." Lastly, a declamatory banner was revealed, as Kulik, in a quasi-triumphant gesture, brandished her portfolio Projects for Arnhem.[12] The photographs commemorating the piece demonstrate why KwieKulik preferred the term *działania*, "activities," to performance. The relationship to documentation—still photographs—what KwieKulik called "aesthetic-time-results," was all-important.[13] The *działania* have been appropriately called "tableau-pieces."[14]

11 From 1972–74 both artists attended "logic-humanistic" seminars and chess theory seminars at the University of Warsaw and, in 1975, seminars at the Studio of Design Methodology at the Polish Academy of Sciences. Mary Kelly's *Post-Partum Document*, 1973–79, was shown as a book project with slides and a discussion at the ninth Kraków festival of performance in 1981. See *Spotkania Krakowskie IX, 1981* (Kraków: BWA Contemporary Art Gallery, 1995), 30–31.

12 Linda Novak, "The 'Działania' of Zofia Kulik and Przemysław Kwiek," *High Performance* 38 (1987): 54–58. The juxtaposition of Kulik and a Polish national eagle in plaster, captioned "Commentary Art: A Bird of Plaster for Bronze in the Slums of the Fine Arts," together with a phallus sculpture labeled "Commentary Art: 'Man Dick'" in the Malmö Konsthall catalog *Seven Young Poles* in 1975, led to a four-year travel prohibition.

13 "The full name for our Actions is: documented Actions of material-time-space-life." From *Actions with a Tube*, 1976, in "KwieKulik," *EXIT New Art in Poland* 5 (1991), 152.

14 Cynthia Carr, "Poles Apart," *The Village Voice*, March 31, 1987, 93.

At *Performance and Body*, Lublin, 1978, where the public entered the hall with little red flags stuck behind their ears—a parody of May Day behavior—both image and action became unexpectedly violent. The specter of state interrogation and torture was parodied and echoed by the brutality of relations between the sexes: Kwiek thrust Kulik's head into a bowl, threatening her with a knife and shouting, "You bitch! Say something! Say!" The action ended with the powerful image of their heads being suffocated in buckets of garbage. Brown paper curtains were used to conceal and reveal the tableaux. At this point, the images of doubling and the work of KwieKulik as partners coincided with an international interest in "artist-couples."[15] Yet significantly, it was during *Performance and Body*, with many significant *działania* ahead, that Kulik first experienced feelings of rebellion against the "process-like quality" of the actions, and was tempted to make an art object.[16]

By 1981, with the coming of Solidarity, KwieKulik achieved the status of cultural pioneers.[17] The ninth Kraków festival, held that year, heralded a completely international East-West dialogue: KwieKulik performances joined those of Mary Kelly, Stuart Brisley, and a host of by now well-known Polish contemporaries such as Jerzy Bereś, and powerful female artists such as Ewa Partum and Christine Chiffrun.[18] Again, the most striking image of KwieKulik was that of an abject and uncanny twinning. With clay stuck over their

15 See the exhibition *Artistic Couples*, Kunstverein, Karlsruhe, 1978. Michael Schwarz's catalog appeared as a special issue (no. 28) of *Kunstforum International*. See also Ewa Kuryluk, "The Journey to the Limits of Art," *Projekt* 4 (1979): 35–38, and for a brilliant comparison with the more body-conscious and less political work of Marina Abramović and Ulay, Katarzyna Michalak, "Performing Life, Living Art: Abramović/Ulay and KwieKulik," *Afterimage* (Nov–Dec 1999), 15–17.

16 See "Being Nothing but an Obedient Psycho-Physical Instrument: Ryszard Ziarkiewicz Talks to Zofia Kulik," trans. Marzena Beata Guzowska, *Magazyn Sztuki*, no. 1 (1993), 6.

17 A special issue of *Sztuka* (the Polish *Artforum*) juxtaposed their work with Joseph Beuys and Sue Coe—but only one hundred copies were saved by Kwiek from subsequent censorship and destruction.

18 For the performance context involving major Polish figures, see also Jerzy Bereś, *Zwidy, wyrocznie, ołtarze, wyzwania* (Poznań: National Museum, 1995), and Zbigniew Warpechowski, *Zasobnik* (Gdańsk, Słowo/Obraz terytoria, 1998). For women artists, see also *Artystki polskie* (Warsaw: National Museum, 1991), and *Voices of Freedom: Polish Women Artists and the Avant-Garde* (Washington: National Museum of Women in the Arts, 1991).

duplicated, smothered heads, they shuffled around on chairs, and blindly attempted to sculpt their own and each other's faces—ending up on the floor with their heads stuck together in the monstrous *Activities for the Head*, alluding to a Polish term for indoctrination. Concurrently with this greater internationalism, their work with the Polish national flag intensified. Kulik's own words most eloquently describe *Polish Duo* [FIG. 3], performed at the Dziekanka Gallery, Warsaw, in 1984:

> White and red flags attached to the heads of two performers are fluttering in the wind produced by a fan. / The fan blows only for one of the performers, the other must run to have her flag fluttering. / Both performers must run to have their flags fluttering. / She and He connected with the white and the red. They bend over backwards and two white and grey [flags] appear...[19]

An element of the conjuring trick intensifies an absurdity that is always pragmatic, despite its existentialist residue. While *Hammer, Hand, Ice; Sickle, Hook, Shadow*, performed at the same venue in 1985, played with Soviet insignia and metaphors of glaciation and shadow play, *Semantic Monster*, performed abroad in Banff, reverted to the Polish flag, as did *Banana and Pome-grenade*, back in Warsaw in 1986. This involved a tableau-piece in which the seated performers held a Polish flag and a white-and-gray flag respectively, while the halves of a dead pig's head were placed on the buckets that covered both of their heads. In a different tableau they also held mirrors, scales, stones, and books, with, on their heads, cubes, more buckets, and even a Golgotha arrangement of crosses on the bucket-head pedestal. Just as Czesław Miłosz analyzed language's function within the gray universe of Eastern doublethink in *The Captive Mind* (1953), so Kulik has reflected upon the "graying" of Poland, the destruction of the Polish language under Stalinism, and the brutal excisions and simplifications, creating "a surrounding fog which also you have in you." "I was so silent, I could not speak. I needed someone [Kwiek] to

19 Kulik's description in a handmade brochure, an inestimably precious labor of love, sent to the author.

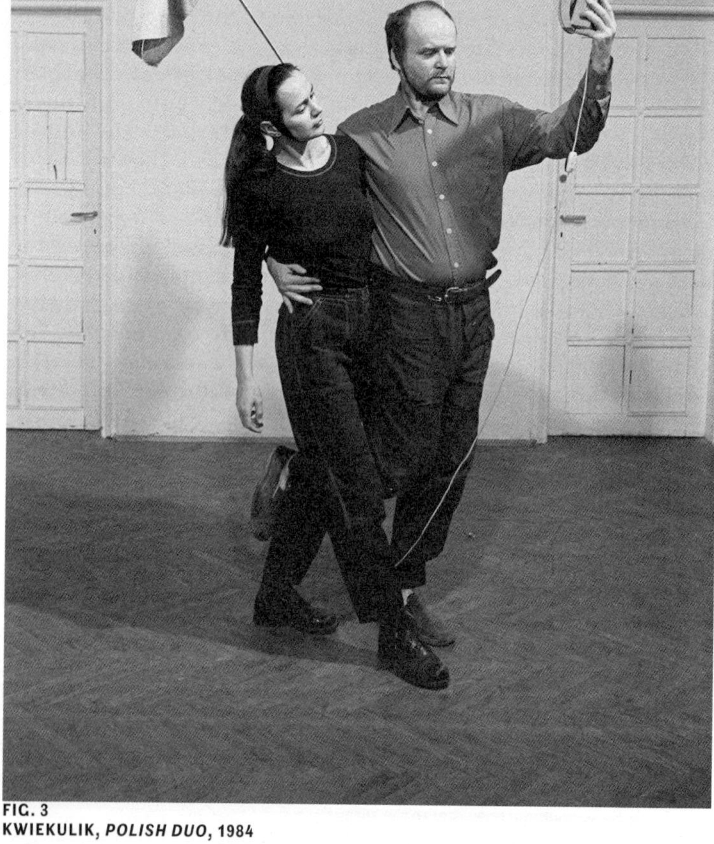

FIG. 3
KWIEKULIK, *POLISH DUO*, 1984

be between me and the world," Kulik said retrospectively.[20] Yet strangely, she explains that these images of personal repression, stifling, and suffocation were part and parcel of a passionate critique engaged with the state, a critique that aimed at reparation in the face of "events, especially bad events." Kulik has spoken to me of her desire to "test" Communist Party dicta at a time when both artists were still positioned against notions of personal subjectivity and had not completely rejected communism as a system of ideals and aspirations.[21] The Soviet eradication of the introspective, post-Romantic, post-Freudian individual—a shared European heritage before 1939—was one of the Eastern Bloc's greatest tragedies: "The psyche under Communism didn't exist. [...] We were trained to be scientists," Kulik says. Personal motivation, or the driving force of a private relationship, were inadmissible in terms of a communist epistemology that transmuted desire into abstract nouns: *Sława*, *Miłość*, *Nadzieja* (Fame, Love, Hope). The abject antitheses of these ideals were worked through in the performance pieces, in situations exemplifying abjection and humiliation, hatred, or despair, created concurrently, at one period, with the couple's daily labor as conservators at the Lenin Museum in Warsaw! In the later photopieces—not photomontages, but black-and-white multiple-exposure photographs[22]—Fame, Love, and Hope are transmuted, ironically (nostalgically?) into emblems of swords, medals, and aureoles: "a traditional art object, always accepted by official power, became a better weapon against those who were regularly armoured with metal and mass media."[23] Hence my essay "Discovering the Psyche," for Kulik's 1999 Poznań

20 Kulik, fax message to the author, March 9, 1999. See Piotr Piotrowski, "The Grey Zone of Europe," in *After the Wall*, 35–38.

21 "They want to include such actions in the conceptual and administrative system of the official Polish art, fighting for it organizationally..." Biographical note, *EXIT new art in Poland*, 150.

22 "I expose image after image according to cardboard stencils which I do earlier in daylight, but in a darkroom I am totally determined by stencils." Kulik, unpublished letter, October 5, 1999.

23 "...The avant-garde stance became a paper mock-up in the context of martial law" precedes this statement, "Being Nothing but an Obedient Psycho-Physical Instrument," 7.

retrospective, was premised upon poetry (in particular the impact of T. S. Eliot in Poland) and the image. It aimed specifically to respect the pre-psychoanalytical nature of Kulik's experience.[24]

I believe that there is a certain ironic pathos—as well as incisive justice—in the fact that now, younger theoreticians such as Renata Salecl, coming from Central Europe (in her case Slovenia) have reinscribed the experience of pre- and post-communist women, post facto, within a psychoanalytical framework.[25] And Ewa Lajer-Burcharth, like Kulik a Polish woman from Warsaw, offered a penetrating psychoanalytic and indeed feminist reading of Kulik's photopieces for the 1998 *New Histories* show at the Boston Institute of Contemporary Art—a brilliant "performance" on Lajer-Burcharth's part within the recognized paradigms of American art history. Zofia Kulik, who is interested in schizophrenia and melancholy (as in the works of Antoni Kępiński) claims not to have read psychoanalytic texts per se—despite experiencing an inchoate feeling of "lack" in this area, she says—and deliberately omitted to mention Lajer-Burcharth's text to me when I first visited her in Łomianki. The central point of this text applies as much to KwieKulik's actions as to Kulik's photopieces: this feminine (and feminist) perspective on communist culture reveals masochism as the central psychocultural mechanism in the formation of an Eastern European subjectivity: the logic that shaped the dominant ideal of the subject as a man avowed to a system.[26]

The ephemera of the performances became the archive of performance events, named the Studio of Activities, Documentation and Propagation (PDDiU). Kulik needed a rebirth as an artist. Moving out of Warsaw under martial law, and abolishing partnership and reciprocity, "man" became subject to her artistic will as she constructed the elements of her huge photopieces. Yet similar motifs, similar gestures, continue through from the *działania* into this new work, such as the Polish flag (both as ensign and shape), or

24 Sarah C. Wilson, "Discovering the Psyche," in *Zofia Kulik: Od Syberii do Cyberii*, 53–73.

25 Salecl, *The Spoils of Freedom*.

26 Ewa Lajer-Burcharth, "Old Histories: Zofia Kulik's Ironic Recollections," in *New Histories*, ex. cat. (Boston: Institute of Contemporary Art, 1996), 119–36. Reprinted in this volume.

motifs such as Kulik's raised arm from *The Monument without a Passport*. And now Kulik, working with the model Zbigniew Libera, plied his body to her system, as she, the artist, became the demiurge, controlling representation.[27] Libera, Kulik's model, was photographed, for example, with an arm outstretched, rather pathetically parodying, in his limp nakedness, the rhetorical gesture of the Roman sculpture *Aulus Metellus*, as adapted by countless sculptures of Lenin: typical is G. D. Alekseev's sculpture *Calling Leader*, 1924. This socialist body became demonstrably interchangeable with the fascist body when Libera parodied Arno Breker's sculpture for Hitler's Reich Chancellery. The caprices of arrangement were exercised after the pleasures, strains, and frictions of the posing sessions: Libera naked under strong lights in a bare room; Libera as a tumbling figure from Memling; as a kneeling figure from William Blake; Libera as swastika, as Catherine wheel, as fallen angel; Libera dragging an inordinate amount of drapery knotted in a huge bulge over the genitals, then ruched to resemble a crustacean's tail; Libera holding swags of cloth aloft while the negative imprint of spearheads conjure a giant erection, or, with his body multiplied into a circle around the great patriotic, socialist-realist sculpture from Magnitogorsk, making a series of cogs in a wheel—pleats of ribbon around an old, discarded medal. Significantly, the Slovenian Renata Salecl does not consider the case of Poland in *The Spoils of Freedom* (see footnote 10), while the Polish Lajer-Burcharth develops the psychoanalytic case for the body under communism at the expense of any investigation of the structures of Catholicism. Kulik, however, plays each repressive structure against the other. And curiously, her own most "masochistic" statement relates not to the state—derided yet essential for the fostering of a certain avant-garde—but to the church: "But in front of whom is one to be humiliated nowadays? There is no god, no leader, no mystery. So whom is one to serve? That's it. I am afraid of myself—I am scared that I can feel subordination so perfectly and can visualize it."[28]

27 Zbigniew Libera is now notorious for his *Lego Concentration Camp*, 1996, shown in *After the Wall* (1999).

28 Zofia Kulik, "1989," in *Zofia Kulik: Idiomy socwiecza*, ex. cat. (Łomianki--Lublin, 1990).

This statement is surely challenged by Kulik's saucy, self-exultant self-portrait with a red flag, or the extraordinary placement of Kulik herself, rather than the Virgin, within the luminous flares of a mandorla—which becomes obscene vaginal lips. Here, in *Self-Portrait with the Palace (Mandorla)* (1990), where Kulik grasps an inverted Soviet Palace of Culture, she is just as "blasphemous" towards the latter as towards the repressive, misogynistic Catholic Church; she is tempting Providence, surely. Kulik claims to see her model as "a scientist, doing gesture after gesture." Yet there is evidently a certain delight in this sporting with the male body; at will doubled, trebled, multiplied, depersonalized, inverted, and distorted into strange symmetries, monstrous chimera, destroyed even: "a man is a splinter I can crumble at my own will."[29] Kulik's position as "preposterous dominatrix" (Lajer-Burcharth) is the obverse of her putatively "masochistic" position.[30] But Libera's body first and foremost evokes the body of Christ; Kulik's work, with its darkly Gothic evocations and arching, pointed structures, is framed by the eschatological: fluctuating, visually flickering between the blasphemous and an acknowledgement of power and tradition that evokes the cry of the unbeliever, or of Christ Himself: "Why hast Thou forsaken me?"

While the personal is evidently the political for Kulik, it is of course more problematic to apply psychoanalytic categories such as the return of the repressed to larger sociocultural phenomena—in particular as psychoanalysis, like Soviet communism, like Catholic Christianity, is a totalizing discourse that "masters" its objects. In speaking of a past always "unmasterable," Dominick LaCapra, reflecting upon the links between history and trauma, has left the psychoanalytic link with the larger framework of things as "a mooted question."[31] Does Kulik's practice aim to exemplify a paradoxical answer?

29 Kulik, "1989."
30 Lajer-Burcharth, "Old Histories," 126.
31 Dominick LaCapra, "The Return of the Historically Repressed," in *Representing the Holocaust: History, Theory, Trauma* (Ithaca: Cornell University Press, 1994), 169, ff.

Kulik questions, through parody and replication, all systems of ordering, of hierarchy, of discipline and punishment, of control over minds, over bodies (of women, especially), together with the demand for self-sacrifice and self-repression. As *May Day Mass* of 1990 demonstrates, the religious was inseparable not only from the political but the technological: in the rose-window structure, Kulik's own photographs of May Day 1971 are combined, at the base of the work, with images of Pope John Paul II celebrating a contemporary, televised Mass in front of the Palace of Culture. It is this communist, May Day Poland whose memory brought the "pang of an exile's nostalgia" to Ewa Lajer-Burcharth, at her first "Western" May Day parade, in Copenhagen in 1982. It is with this recollection, and (despite herself?) with the tears of the author, that she began her 1998 text on Kulik. But Lajer-Burcharth also mourns her former self: "Mine eyes dazzle: she di'd young." In Elizabethan English, for the eyes to dazzle meant to fill with tears.[32] Lajer-Burcharth's authoritative, psychoanalytic commitment to Kulik's postcommunist body precludes an investigation of the fact that her own work, like Kulik's, is, above all, a work of mourning. Structurally, the kilim-like photo-fragments in Kulik's work dazzle and disturb; the images have the crystalline fragility of a moment held in a kaleidoscope image. In English the current meanings of "dazzle"—"to confound with brilliancy, beauty, cleverness"—also have the military dimensions of deception and camouflage: the "dazzle painting" on the sides of ships; dazzle that conceals identity and number.[33] The body as sign and ensign exists in dazzling tension on the splintering photographic surface. Dazzle represents the Manichaean power of the dialectic between light and dark, good and evil, redemption and damnation, creation and destruction, exposure and hidden identity—and masculine and feminine—continually haunting Kulik's work, whose very basis, from a technical point of view, depends upon light itself, upon illumination and its withdrawal, on the

32 "Cover her face. Mine eyes dazzle: she di'd young," *The Duchess of Malfi*, Act IV, Scene 2, in John Webster, *Three Plays* (Harmondsworth: Penguin Books, 1972), 260.

33 *Chambers Twentieth Century Dictionary* (Edinburgh: Constable, 1973), 330.

"positive" and the "negative." The psychoanalytic dimension of this unresolved dialectic accounts for the feelings of both violence and impotence that Kulik has expressed: "In the form of my mother I put the content of my father." Kulik has described those different male and female universes, perceived at home as a child; her dressmaker-mother's domestic space, a "soft" world of carpets, kilims, textiles, embroideries, and printed cottons in the apartment within a military barracks, looking out on the parade ground where her father organized and participated in countless military exercises. She asks in a 1994 photomontage: *Who Conquered the World?*

Yet Kulik's kaleidoscope principle turns number into madness; her obsessive use of bilateral and rotational symmetries dissipates all linear rationality. The all-seeing eye of Christian humanist perspective has abandoned the scene; mad implosions and explosions negate any remaining remnants of a "logic of history" or the "truth of images." Indeed, the reference to madness becomes explicit in figures such as the draped female (Urszula Kwiek, Przemysław's mentally unstable sister, from *All the Missiles Are One Missile*).[34] Gilles Deleuze and Félix Guattari's *Anti-Oedipus: Capitalism and Schizophrenia* of 1972 is inverted; we confront "Totalitarianism and Schizophrenia" in which dissolved, pixelated, repetitious motifs, seemingly arbitrarily miniaturized or blown up: "women's crotches, camera in water, shot from underneath," become a counterpoint texture to foci of military episodes and Soviet wartime assassinations—equally arbitrary of course—within the logistics of the rationalization of slaughter.

How, finally, does one move from carpets to genocide, and from Siberia to the Cyberia of cybercafes, the title of Kulik's most ambitious postmodern/postnationalist photopiece? The history of ornament is a history of conquest and the rise and fall of empires. At the height of the British Empire, Owen Jones' 1856 *The Grammar of Ornament* demonstrated the structures and motifs of a history extending from "The Ornament of Savage Tribes" to "Italian Ornament" within an implicitly Hegelian and Darwinist framework of

34 Significantly, the title itself is a parody of T. S. Eliot's phrase "all the women are one woman" in his notes to "The Fire Sermon" from *The Waste Land,* 1922.

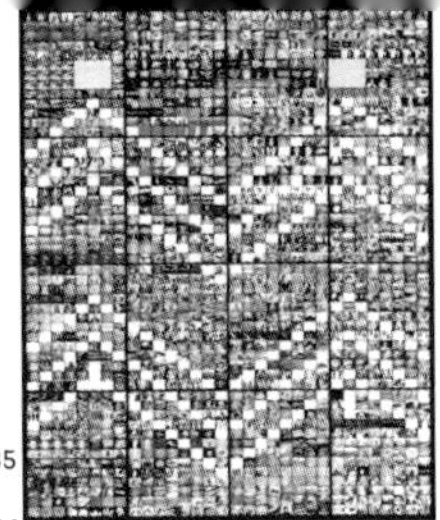

D / PP. 42–43

evolution: no place here for the concept of genocide.[35] The conjunction "ornament and crime" was made by the modernist Adolf Loos in 1909, with specific reference to the Ringstrasse in Vienna. Yet he could not possibly have envisaged the atrocities of the 20th century—or Austria's role therein. After Auschwitz, André Malraux, in "Le Musée imaginaire" of 1947, traced the stylistic passage of a smile from a Cambodian Buddha to the cathedral of Rheims—a passage, he proclaimed, that "transcended" millions of deaths. Just so, Kulik demonstrates the saga of the transmission of ornament, from the Turkish carnation in the carpet to the Polish national costume (a wholesale Turkish import).[36] And, in **FROM SIBERIA TO CYBERIA** D (1998–2004), from the prehistoric zigzag—the first sign for a man—to the repetitive dazzle of our TV screens, where historical atrocity lives atemporally and promiscuously with the pornographic.

From Siberia to Cyberia was Kulik's final 20th-century epic. Relatives of her family were sent by the Soviets to Siberia; she explained to me how Polish "enemies" were co-opted for a Polish army in the USSR after 1942. Siberia evokes camps, slave labor, incarceration, the long histories of a barbarous Other, and the over one million Polish civilians deported to Arctic Russia, Siberia, and Kazakhstan during the Second World War and occupation.

Kulik has shown me Jacek Malczewski's depictions of groups on their way to Siberia, and the history of Poland's uprising in lithographs by Artur Grottger from an old book belonging to her father; she spoke of the play *November Night* by Stanisław Wyspiański, about the insurrection of 1831, and the poetry of Adam Mickiewicz. Siberia itself is an old theme in Polish art. "Cyberia," the pun, already spawns a thousand websites. Poland's new cyber-elite shun the Soc-ages, accessing sites in a cyberspace light years away from Kulik's darkroom, where at home she wove together her Siberian fresco like a modern Penelope. Yet Kulik's pixelated surface of gray TV images

35 Owen Jones, *The Grammar of Ornament*, rev. ed. (1856; repr., London: Studio Editions, 1986).

36 See Anna Sieradzka and Krystyna Turska, eds., *Ubiory w Polsce* (Warsaw: Association of Art Historians, 1994).

serves as both warp and weft, as grid rather than content, the support of a meaning becoming ever more ghostly, the simulacrum of a simulacrum. Here, the heroic tradition joins the stich: the zigzag signs of prehistoric man—abstracted points of "heads" and "phalli"—lace together her surfaces, visually linking with the crochet pattern books, the *robótki ręczne* of a thousand Polish hearths.[37] The positive or negative electronic impulse equals the stich; "to keep or lose eyes" (to "drop stichs" in Polish) so often equates with losing lives, losing souls. Each trace stands, metonymically, for the acts, moments, and utterances that left no trace—what the modernist Adolf Loos called "ins Leere gesprochen," spoken into the void. The East/West story is one of delayed reception; so is the transmission of both ornament and technology. Working in Britain or America, Kulik would be working on a screen; *From Siberia to Cyberia* would be displayed on a video screen, or at least with light boxes or real television.

"The disasters which mark this end of millennium, are also the archives of evil [les archives du mal]" Jacques Derrida writes in *Mal d'Archive*, translated as *Archive Fever*.[38] Derrida reminds us that the word archive derives from *arkheion* (a house, in Greek), that archives take place within a context of "domiciliation," and that "the pain of the archive" is the necessary double of this "archive fever."[39] Kulik's house in Łomianki, outside Warsaw, restored after 1982, is a house of memory, reflection, and the site of her archives of the century. From the Soviet ideal of revolutionary, nation-building modernism, acknowledged in her photomontages, to postmodernism and postnationalism: concepts that cannot exist, perhaps, without their dark side of mourning. Out of what Derrida called "the burning evidence" of the 20th-century archive, Kulik has dazzled us with tears as well as postmodern irony: "I am organizer of the plenitude which

37 See Carl Schuster and Edmund Carpenter, *Patterns that Connect: Social Symbolism in Ancient & Tribal Art* (New York: Harry N. Abrams Inc., 1996) (in Kulik's library).

38 Jacques Derrida, "Priére d'inserer," in *Mal d'Archive: Une impression freudienne* (Paris: Gallimard, 1995), 1. The English title, *Archive Fever: A Freudian Impression* (Chicago, University of Chicago Press, 1996) conveys both enthusiasm and illness.

39 Derrida, "Priére d'inserer," 12.

attacks me." Forever caught between the sickle and the cross, her ironic self-referentiality nonetheless links up with mandalas of healing and of our archetypal memory.

This text was originally published in Centropa *1, no. 3, September 2001.*

Michał Murawski is an anthropologist of architecture and art, based at the School of Slavonic and East European Studies, University College London, where he is lecturer in Critical Area Studies. His book *The Palace Complex: A Stalinist Skyscraper, Capitalist Warsaw, and a City Transfixed* was published by Indiana University Press in 2019, and, in Polish, by the Museum of Warsaw in 2015. He is currently conducting research for a new book project on architectural aesthetics and politics in Putin-era Moscow. Along with Jane Rendell, he coedited *The Social Condenser: A Century of Revolution through Architecture, 1917–2017*, a special issue of *The Journal of Architecture* (2017), and he has published in scholarly and media outlets, including *Third Text*, *Comparative Studies in Society and History*, *Anthropology Today*, *Social Text*, *Laboratorium*, *Focaal*, *The Calvert Journal*, *Strelka Magazine*, *Forbes*, and *The Architectural Review*. In 2018, at the Shchusev State Museum of Architecture in Moscow, he co-curated the exhibition *Portal Zaryadye*, featuring eighteen new works by Russian artists exploring the relationship between architecture, politics, and ecology in contemporary Russia.

ZOFIA KULIK'S PALACE COMPLEX: REVEALING THE COMPLEXITY OF CLOSED FORM (FILLING IT WITH HER OWN MADNESS)

> I am fascinated by Closed Forms.
>
> Centricity, symmetry, multiplication, order, figural ornament, imposing upon myself certain preexisting patterns of structures (monuments, medals, mandalas, carpets and gates) that I try to fill with my own madness—these constitute my formal and constructive rules of composition.[1]

The Palace of Culture and Science—the Stalinist skyscraper gifted to Warsaw by the Soviet Union in 1955—features prominently in at least eighteen of Zofia Kulik's works: eight executed together with her partner Przemysław Kwiek while part of the KwieKulik duo between 1970 and 1987, and ten of Kulik's own. These Palace-focused works—the majority of them executed at the time of the fall of the Polish People's Republic in 1989 or in the decade that followed—will be the focus of my attention in this essay.

1 Kulik, quoted in *Zofia Kulik: Idiomy socwiecza*, ex. cat. (Łomianki-Lublin, 1990).

Warsaw's "Palace Complex"—the dominance of the Stalinist Palace over the post-socialist city, and the corresponding "fixation" of the city's social life on this building—functions to a large extent by means of the building's symmetrical layout, its monumental appearance, and its uncontested location at the city's absolute center. These attributes—centrality, monumentality, and symmetry—are also key ingredients of what Kulik—after her teacher and mentor Oskar Hansen—calls "Closed Form." I argue in this text that, following the collapse of state socialism in Poland in 1989, Kulik developed a sophisticated and radical understanding of and interaction with Closed Form, which went beyond Hansen's own binary distinction between Closed and Open Forms (a binary to which Kulik herself subscribed, to an extent, in her earlier works).[2] Instead, in her 1990s works, Kulik "queered" the Palace, by questioning the commonsensical understandings of the relationship between aesthetics, form, geometry, politics, gender, and sexuality, which were typical not only of her time (the late-socialist and post-socialist periods) but also of her intellectual and artistic milieu. In doing so, Kulik's 1990s works attested to the latent subversive and critical potential within the Closed Form of Warsaw's Stalinist Palace, as well as anticipating (and perhaps actualizing) the current role of the Palace as an object of hatred for Poland's reigning nationalist government and their far-right allies—and a possible tool and symbol of resistance against the pervading ideological climate.

Crucially, I emphasize that the category of the Palace Complex is neither a "pathological" nor a "normal" phenomenon. The Palace Complex is not an ailment, which afflicts only some Varsovians—it is a political-aesthetic, ideological, and economic

2 It is instructive to note, given my concern in this text with Kulik's kinship with Russian conceptual art of the late-socialist and post-socialist period, that Hansen's binary is redolent of architectural historian Vladimir Paperny's high-structuralist division of Soviet architectural culture into a horizontal, dynamic, open Culture One (epitomized by the avant-garde of the 1920s), and the vertical, static, closed-off Culture Two (epitomized by the Stalinist period). Paperny's analysis of Culture Two (published in English in 2006) was first written as a PhD thesis in Moscow in 1972, but not published in full in Russian until 1996. Paperny, *Architecture in the Age of Stalin: Culture Two* (New York: Cambridge University Press, 2006).

conjuncture, whose contours were influenced by the historical context from which the Palace arose, its aesthetic and spatial characteristics, and today by the political-aesthetic realities of Poland's post-socialist condition. Kulik's Palace Complex, however, is not focused on erasure, mutilation, containment, and subordination, or on the "undermining" or "overcoming" of the Palace's "domination" over the city; instead, it explores and attempts to make sense of—to "reveal"—the Palace's social and aesthetic complexity. In their 1970s actions, Kulik and Przemysław Kwiek already sought to adapt a studio exercise of Oskar Hansen's, "Revealing Complex Form," into an artistic and activistic method, which they called "The Art of Revealing Complex Form." Kwiek and Kulik "tried to strip the exercise of its purely formal dimension and relate it to the complex socioeconomic situation."[3] Kulik's work with the Palace—both before and after 1989—continued in this vein, in an effort to disclose the "complexities of reality and the relationships constituting it, to knock the recipients out of their normal routine 'rhythms' or 'patterns' of behaviour, and to reveal the multidimensionality of seemingly defined relationships."[4] And today, the output of Kulik's Palace Complex—the archive of her revealings of Complex Form—can still work to defamiliarize our political-aesthetic commonplaces, among other things, by highlighting some of the ways in which aspects of Poland's socialist legacy—including its Closed Forms—can function as vectors of commonality, publicness, and collectivity in the privationary and stratified climate of the late-capitalist city.

The Palace, as I show in detail elsewhere, was built as an inherently and powerfully *public* building—the largest "House of Culture" ever constructed in the socialist world, existing as it did not only on the level of a city district, or work unit, but also on the scale of a large city and national capital. Moreover, unlike much of the rest of Warsaw, which has been—and continues to be—mercilessly restituted

3 Łukasz Ronduda and Georg Schöllhammer, eds., *KwieKulik: Zofia Kulik & Przemysław Kwiek* (Warsaw: Museum of Modern Art in Warsaw and KwieKulik Archive; Wrocław: BWA Wrocław Galleries of Contemporary Art, Awangarda Gallery; Vienna: Kontakt: The Art Collection of Erste Group and ERSTE Foundation, 2012), 466.

4 Ronduda and Schöllhammer, *KwieKulik: Zofia Kulik & Przemysław Kwiek*, 466.

and reprivatized since 1989, the Palace has, *somehow*, been able to maintain the myriad public functions condensed within it: concert and congress halls, four theaters, a gigantic Palace of Youth featuring elaborate sports and arts facilities (including a monumental, marble-decked swimming pool[5]), municipal offices, the headquarters of the Polish Academy of Sciences, and a viewing terrace, among many others.[6] The Palace is able to remain socialist in part because of the spectacular and far-reaching manner in which numerous elements of a socialist-realist "economic aesthetic" were built into it: gigantic size, bombastic style, symmetrical layout, and nodal positioning at the heart of the city's transport network and layout of communicational axes. Together, these aesthetic features—mapping precisely onto Hansen's understanding of Closed Form—ensure that there is enough room within the building for the Palace's myriad public functions to be gathered together under one roof. They secure for the building a prominent place in the city's symbolic universe, and also inspire a mixture of awe and fascination among the city's inhabitants.

However, none of this multifunctionality or collective use-value would have come into being had the land on which the Palace sits not been expropriated from its private owners by the Warsaw Decree on land use of 1945, and had the construction of the Palace itself not been motivated by its designers' and patrons' mission to "revolutionarily transform the city."[7] The complex of the Palace's spatial and aesthetic characteristics—the Closed Form that came to fascinate Kulik—works to consolidate the social and affective effects of this transformation, even long after the collapse of the political system that brought these morphologies into being.

5 Kulik points out that she would regularly attend diving training at the Palace of Youth's swimming pool between the ages of fourteen and sixteen. Kulik, personal communication with the author, 2018.

6 These functions are elaborated on in detail in Murawski, *The Palace Complex: A Stalinist Skyscraper, Capitalist Warsaw, and a City Transfixed* (Bloomington: Indiana University Press, 2019); the idea that the Palace functions as a fusion of the Soviet House of Culture and a "Social Condenser" is theorized in Murawski, "A Stalinist 'Social Condenser' in a Capitalist City," *The Journal of Architecture* 22, no. 3 (2017): 458–77.

7 Edmund Goldzamt, *Architektura zespołów śródmiejskich i problemy dziedzictwa* (Warsaw: Panstwowe Wydawnictwo Naukowe, 1956), 21.

The Palace Complex

The idea that Warsaw suffers from a "Palace Complex" —a pathological fixation on or obsession with a single building that represents the traumatic memory of Poland's communist past and Russian/Soviet domination—is regularly invoked in conversations about the Palace. Though this term has a complex usage, it is especially frequently encountered in conversations about the Palace's perceived architectural "domination" over Warsaw. Since the fall of the communist regime in 1989, countless attempts have been made to try and "overcome" the Palace's dominating presence in Warsaw; most of these conversations and proposed solutions focus their attention on the problem of the Palace's apparently overbearing symmetry and centrality.

One frequently encountered suggestion is to overcome the Palace Complex by demolishing the Palace or physically modifying it. For example, by chopping off its side wings, which reach like talons into the surrounding city; by removing some of its extravagant exterior decorations, thereby turning it into something more like a "normal" skyscraper; or by removing the spire, as in the suggestion of Warsaw architect Jerzy Skrzypczak, thereby making the Palace the same height as the later glass-and-steel towers built during the 1980s–2010s, the tallest of which are between 140 and 180 meters high.[8]

Another set of ideas aspires to keep the Palace's physical body as it is, but to "contain" its pathological presence by changing the nature of its surroundings. Professional and amateur architects (in most cases middle-aged men) have frequently suggested covering the Palace with glass pyramids or Buckminster Fulleresque geodesic domes. Official proposals for the Palace—those formally promoted by the municipality, whether as a result of international architecture competitions (1992) or the adoption of binding zoning ordinances (2010)—first entailed surrounding the Palace with a circle (or "crown," or *corso*) of even taller skyscrapers; this was the official plan for the empty space around the Palace during

8 See Murawski, *The Palace Complex*, for a detailed description and analysis of these and other "ideas" for the Palace.

1992–2006 and 2008–2010. Subsequently, the debate was won by those who suggested that crowning the Palace with a ring of towers would only under*line* its symmetry and dominance rather than under*mine* it, and thus the proper response was to diffuse the Palace's overbearing symmetry within an irregular jumble of high-, low-, and mid-rise structures.

As transcripts of the Warsaw mayor's advisory councils have shown, these discussions usually feature long back-and-forths between architects, accusing each other's ideas of under*mining* as opposed to under*lining* the Palace (and vice-versa). A few choice quotations from the period between 1992 and 2010 provide a vivid insight into the see-saw that characterizes Warsaw discussions about architectural responses to the Palace:

> If you stick a compass in the Palace and make a circle, then this magnifies the Palace, it doesn't diminish it. (actor and satirist Stanisław Tym, 1992)

> ... the *corso* is ... utopian ... an architectural megasculpture ... which raises the value of the Palace instead of depreciating it. (architect Czesław Bielecki, 2007)

> We must depart from the symbolism of crowning the Palace. (architect Andrzej Chylak, 2008)

> ... the attempt to form a symmetrical "wall" or "curtain" of tall buildings on the Palace's western side ... would strengthen its domination, and not weaken it. ... Symmetry is the aesthetic of fools. (planner Grzegorz Buczek, 2008)

> The elimination of the symmetry in the Palace's surroundings would be desirable. Ultimately, however [in all the variants presented so far for the council's evaluation], the Palace is underlined, and it has not been possible to avoid this. (architect Tomasz Sławiński, 2008)

> Our conscious strategy ... was the avoidance of the simple symmetry that is imposed by the Palace itself. (Deputy Mayor Jacek Wojciechowski, 2010)

> ... we really try to honor the axiality of the Palace and its ensemble. ... we have tried to reflect the Palace's symmetry in the panorama of the city. (municipal planner Małgorzata Sprawka, 2010)

Abhorring/Adoring/Erasing: Closed Form before 1989

Zofia Kulik's teacher and mentor, Oskar Hansen—the creator of the theory and practice of "Open" vs. "Closed" form that informed much of Kulik's work in its formative phase, during her time as a student at the Warsaw Academy of Fine Arts in the late 1960s and early 1970s—had his own ideas about how to deal with the Palace, which was, for him, the paradigmatic example of Closed Form.

Hansen formulated his clearest thoughts on the Palace itself while working on his final exhibition project—devoted to the Palace's relationship to Warsaw's cityscape—in 2005. "The Palace—uncontested in its enormity and aggressive in its form, subordinates to itself all the remaining elements of Warsaw's landscape by means of the contrast of form and scale."[9] He also saw the problem with the Palace as being related to its oneness: "The cityscape of Warsaw educates us. Now we live in a world dominated by a single element."[10] But the skyscrapers that have sprouted up in central Warsaw since the 1980s are of little help: "instead of weakening the effect of the Palace, they strengthen it. It looks a bit like the King surrounded by his servants."[11] Hansen's remedy was not to "destroy, conceal, or screen" the Palace, but to "polemicize" with it, to enter into a "conversation with it." His solution, the model of a proposed

9 Oskar Hansen, "'Koń trojański' XX wieku—PKiN im. Józefa Stalina w Warszawie," in *Zobaczyć świat* (Warsaw: Zachęta National Gallery of Art, 2005), 102.

10 Hansen, quoted in Artur Żmijewski, *Sen Warszawy / A Dream of Warsaw* (2005), accessed September 15, 2018, https://artmuseum.pl/en/filmoteka/praca/zmijewski-artur-sen-warszawy.

11 Hansen in Żmijewski, *Sen Warszawy*, 2005.

building—a high concrete shaft topped by a wide elliptical crown—took the form of a tall sculpture affixed to the branches of a tree providentially positioned just outside the Palace-facing windows of the Foksal Gallery Foundation [FIG. 1]. For Hansen, this constituted a "civilized," dialogic negation of the Palace: "The Palace of Culture grows wider at the base, and this grows wider all the way up. It's a sort of reversed pyramid."[12]

The ideas of Oskar Hansen—a generation older than Zofia Kulik—came out of a mid-century fascination with cybernetics and binary structural oppositions. Kulik shares many aspects of this fascination, but her relationship to it—both as part of KwieKulik and as a solo artist—is more ambivalent. Whereas Hansen, in his binary purism, seeks—however dialogically—to reject or "overcome" the Palace Complex, Kulik seeks to bury herself within the Palace Complex, to make sense—in a quasi-ethnographic manner—of the structures (in particular, the symmetries) constituting it. Furthermore, Kulik's approach seeks to harness the Palace Complex, to appropriate it, to "fill it with her own madness," and ultimately to deploy this mutated Palace Complex—this "activated" Closed Form—as an aesthetic and political weapon.

The manner of the Palace's appearance in Kulik's work is, on the one hand, quite steady, running through some of the ruptures or phases that art historians tend to demarcate her œuvre into. Katarzyna Ruchel-Stockmans writes of Kulik's photo-collages (those from 1989 onwards) that "many of these compositions are symmetrical, centralized, and geometrically organized, imitating the previously abhorred 'closed form' theorized by Oskar Hansen."[13] Yet they are foreseen in (and make explicit reference to) earlier works. Thus, perhaps Kulik's most explicitly Palace-centric work, *The Guardians of*

12 Hansen in Żmijewski, *Sen Warszawy*, 2005.

13 Katarzyna Ruchel-Stockmans, *Images Performing History: Photography and Representations of the Past in European Art after 1989* (Leuven: Leuven University Press, 2015), 127. Excerpts reprinted in this volume.

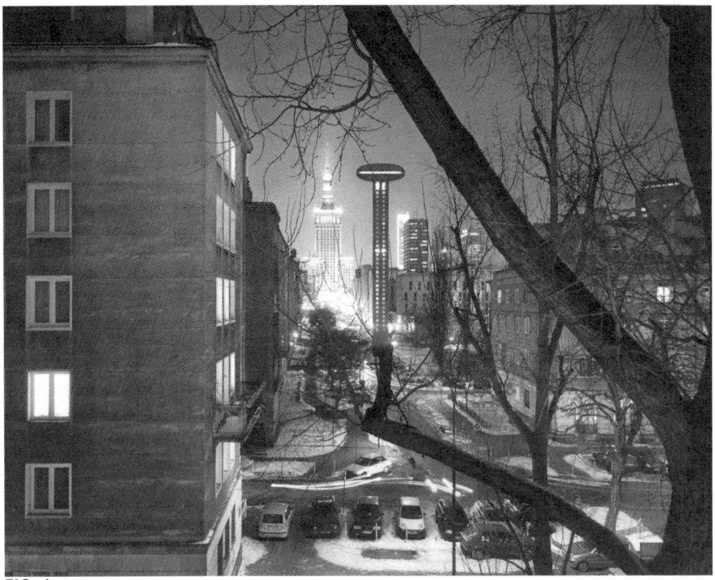

FIG. 1
OSKAR HANSEN, *A DREAM OF WARSAW*, 2005

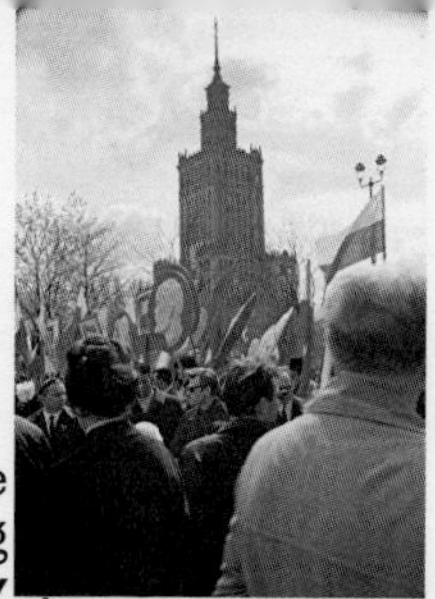
A

the Spire foregrounds a photograph of a crowd outside the Palace of Culture, one of a number taken during KwieKulik's documentation of the 1972 **MAY DAY PARADE** A (1972).

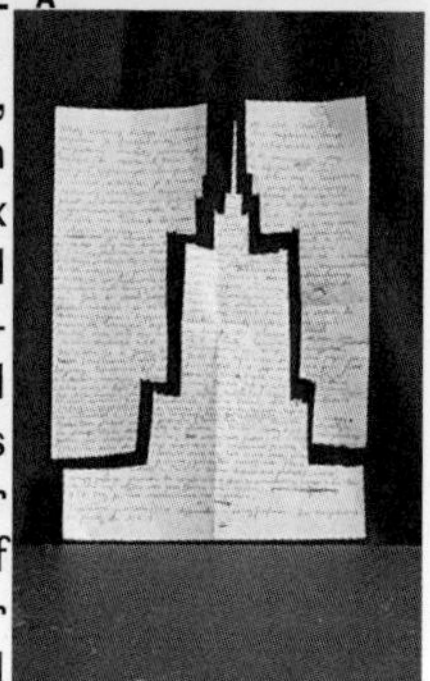
B/PP.15–17

Kulik's work **LETTER FROM MILAN** B (1972), an elaboration on her correspondence from Italy with Przemysław Kwiek, comprises a remarkably complex early series of activities on the figure of the Palace and its symmetries. The centerpiece of the work is a handwritten letter from Kwiek, onto which Kulik has sketched the silhouette of the Palace. The work consists of a series of photographs documenting successive stages or scenes, all taking place against the background of a navy-blue curtain (onto which several light-blue paper clouds have been attached), with the stage itself laid out on the surface of a brown imitation-leather suitcase. In the first act, the Palace—now cut from Kwiek's letter—has had a red heart attached to it, and appears to grow out of a little grass lawn that has been cut out of paper and stuck to its bottom reaches. The brown suitcase, standing in for Parade Square at the foot of the Palace, is the scene for a sort of May Day parade composed of amorphous clay figures carrying one-word love slogans, as if cut out of Kwiek's letter ("Dear," "Dream," "To You," "Was," "Think," "I Miss," "Yes," "For"). The slogan-bearing figurines are interspersed with extravagant decorations "made from colored paper used by children for cut-outs" and resembling—according to the catalog of KwieKulik's works[14]—"infantile decorations from state ceremonies in Communist Poland."

In the next scene, the Palace appears to grow wings, made from the two fragments of Kwiek's letter, which Kulik had excised in order to obtain the figure of the Palace itself. The Palace flies off into the sky, lifted by the flapping of its side wings. As the Palace flies farther and farther away, the cute little clay figurines grow and mutate into enormous, grotesque, golem-like vertical

14 Ronduda and Schöllhammer, *KwieKulik: Zofia Kulik & Przemysław Kwiek*, 119.

formations, while the May Day decorations and love/agitational slogans are scattered over the surface of the suitcase (or Parade Square). As the Palace retreats towards the horizon, the golems are flattened, and the suitcase-Square is turned into a wasteland of parched clay. Finally, a silhouetted photograph of a woman—stretching out her arms in mimicry of the symmetry of the flying Palace—is placed on the clay, accompanied in the concluding scene by a series of several smaller photographs of human silhouettes, as the Palace (and the sun under which it had been flying) disappears. (The motif of the disappearing Palace also appears in Kulik's diploma project, *Instead of Sculpture* [1968–71].)

In Luiza Nader's analysis, the first act "introduces the two subjects and their amorous, affective relationship."[15] The first subject is constituted by the inchoate multitude gathered at the foot of the Palace (clay figurines, paper slogans, and cutouts). In Nader's words, "this is a subject that expresses itself in fragments. She is dispersed, incoherent, surrendered, naive, childish, enthusiastic, disciplined, but first of all—in love." The second subject is the "phantasmatic, phallic structure of the Palace of Culture and Science." This subject is "powerful, institutional, political, it receives tributes, it deploys the expert language of art, and first of all—it is the object of love." We can identify this second Palace-subject, Nader writes, "as a human subject and an ideological nonhuman one: as a partner as well as a post-totalitarian political system."[16] As Nader points out, it is never clear whether the object of love (or obsession, or fixation—"affect" is Nader's chosen word for the sum of these feelings and drives) is a person or a political system—"the ambivalence is maintained" throughout the piece.[17]

15 Luiza Nader, "Materializing Conceptual Affects: The Love Discourse of Zofia Kulik's *Letter from Milan* (1972)" in *Conceptualism and Materiality: Matters of Art and Politics*, ed. Christian Berger (Leiden: Brill, 2019). First published as "Konceptualne afekty: Dyskurs miłosny *Listu z Mediolanu* (1972) Zofii Kulik," *Miejsce: Studia nad sztuką i architekturą polską XX i XXI Wieku*, no. 3 (2017): 176–204.

16 Nader, "Materializing Conceptual Affects."

17 Nader, "Materializing Conceptual Affects."

Kulik's apparently conscious conflation of her lover/ the father of her child/the Palace/the totalitarian system is remarkably redolent of the phenomenon of this "untypical" correspondence sent to the Palace, kept for decades in a special folder by the building's chronicler Hanna Szczubełek. The first letters in Szczubełek's folder date from 1972—remarkably enough, the same year as Kulik's Milan letter. The letters from the 1970s and 1980s connect the Palace to sacred, eschatological, and legal realms, as well as to love, dispute resolution, demonic and healing power, public and intimate abuses, and grievances. Many of the letters also contain references to the architectural or spatial (such as suggestions for alterations to the body of the Palace) and ideological realms (attacks against or defenses of the Palace on historical-political grounds). Notably, both the pre- and post-1989 letters frequently contain a strikingly gendered dimension.[18]

Kulik's "disappearance" of the Palace in the *Letter from Milan* is also redolent of the manner in which the Palace's eradication (or at least its deformation) was treated, during the late-socialist 1970s and 1980s, as a prerequisite for any sort of substantive reconfiguration of Warsaw's (and Poland's) social, political, and ideological landscape. During this time, artists, writers, musicians, filmmakers, and satirists produced visions depicting the Palace as codependent on the system that erected it. One of the opening lines of Tadeusz Konwicki's novel *A Minor Apocalypse*, for example, describes the Palace, once a "monument to arrogance, a statue to slavery, a stone layer cake of abomination," transformed into merely "a large, upended barracks, corroded by fungus and mildew, an old toilet forgotten at some central European crossroad."[19] Meanwhile, the closing scene of Sylwester Chęciński's 1991 film *Calls Controlled*, set during the martial-law winter of 1981, features the main protagonist, an accidental anti-regime

18 The "untypical" correspondence is elaborated on in Murawski, "Big Affects: Size, Sex and Stalinist 'Architectural Power' in Post-Socialist Warsaw," in *Elements of Architecture: Assembling Archaeology, Atmosphere and the Performance of Building Spaces*, eds. Mikkel Bille and Tim Flohr Sorensen (London: Routledge, 2016).

19 Tadeusz Konwicki, *A Minor Apocalypse*, trans. Richard Lourie (New York: Farrar, Straus and Giroux, 1983), 4.

conspirator, fleeing from pursuit by the Citizens' Militia into the Palace of Culture where, at the same time, a New Year's Eve banquet for the communist top brass is being held. Hiding in a toilet cubicle, the escapee pulls the flush to escape the suspicions of prying toilet users. Immediately the entire Palace crumbles and topples over, an unambiguous allegory for the fragility of the repressive, conflicted, and unsustainable system that the building represented. The culprit crawls out of the rubble, hopelessly muttering, "We'll rebuild it..."

Moreover, the scenography of Kulik's *Letter from Milan* provides an anticipatory staging of the many planned—but failed—architectural reconfigurations of the Palace's surroundings during the post-socialist period. The clay figures, which "grow larger and turn monstrous as they try to reach the building as it moves away [...] turn[ing] into a tyrant"[20] are suggestive of the multiple attempts to build a high-rise city center (whether symmetrical or consciously anti-symmetrical) in the vicinity of the Palace from the 1980s onwards—successful on the outer peripheries of the Palace's surroundings, beyond the perimeter of Parade Square (beyond the suitcase, as it were), but unsuccessful, so far, on the Square itself. The affect—the "madness" with which Kulik fills this scenography—is mirrored by the affection, fixation and obsession, anger and love that Warsaw and Varsovians attach to the Palace (and its surroundings). All of this, as Nader observes, "manifests itself as a force with both a positive as well as a negative influence on the world."[21]

After 1989: To Disperse, to Converge

Kulik's treatment of the Palace in her 1970s works was already characterized by an extremely high level of complexity and dialectical probing of the contradictions invested in the Palace's Closed (and Complex) Form—encompassing, to paraphrase Nader's analysis, both the positive and negative consequences of the Palace Complex. Nevertheless, it appears, on the strength of *Letter from Milan* and *Instead of Sculpture*, that Kulik, at this point, still considered the disappearance of the Palace to be a prerequisite for an "opening" of the form of the

20 Nader, "Materializing Conceptual Affects."
21 Nader, "Materializing Conceptual Affects."

city. However, despite the collapse of the Polish People's Republic in 1989, the Palace not only failed to disappear from Kulik's works—as her 1970s creations seemed to suggest that it might—but its presence actually increased, in terms of both frequency and intensity.

A preoccupation with centrality, symmetry, and their opposites—with the "geometry of power," in Izabela Kowalczyk's term,[22] and with the Palace's role as a pivot of this geometry—comes to the very foreground of Kulik's œuvre in 1989—at the very moment, in fact, that the Polish People's Republic collapsed. In *Human Motif* (1989), the Palace's mirror-image appears on either edge of the foreground as a focal point for an ultra-symmetrical mass spectacle. In *Monument I* (1989), however, the Palace's presence is already more ambiguous—it is a burden borne on the back of a naked, dog-like male figure (the artist Zbigniew Libera, Kulik's model in most of her photomontages) crouched on all fours—a pathetic, canine caricature of the stele-bearing turtles from Chinese mythology. Moreover, the spire of the Palace on Libera's back is transformed into a spear—pointed, with castrating, emasculating intent, directly between the legs of the druid-like male figure (also Libera), whose body and cape hover over the Palace-stele. This positioning seems especially subversive in light of the highly gendered and sexualized images of the Palace that began to appear in the 1990s, depicting the Palace as a phallus poised to penetrate female flesh.

1990's *Self-Portrait with the Palace I* shows an upside-down Palace dangling precariously over Kulik's head; it is unclear whether the robed male druid-clones whose arms reach towards the building on either side are dropping the Palace onto Kulik, with the aim

22 Izabela Kowalczyk, "The Geometry of Power in Zofia Kulik's Work," *n.paradoxa*, online issue no. 11 (October 1999): 19–25, https://www.ktpress.co.uk/pdf/nparadoxaissue11.pdf.

of killing her ("hammering" her, in her own phrase[23]); are protecting her against it (by holding it up); or have mounted the Palace on her head as a crown. If it is not an admission of naivety, then Kulik's confident gaze, and the spear she holds in her own hands, appears to suggest that the latter interpretation is the most accurate.

In *The Guardians of the Spire* from 1990, the guardians appear neither to be the May Day crowd gathered beneath the building, nor the communist apparatchiks greeting them from its honor tribune, but the twin, naked Liberas perched calmly on either side of the metallic structure—redolent of a window frame in a Gothic church—which Kulik erects around the Palace. Perhaps this frame is a cocoon to protect the now-vulnerable Palace (vulnerable like Libera's spindly male body) from the baying post-socialist throng; a frame to preserve its symmetry in the face of the chaos-causing centrifugal uncertainties of the incoming epoch; or a pyramid-like encasing, intended to contain the Palace's dangerous radiation within its immediate vicinity. The whirling kaleidoscope of (partially dismembered) male bodies at the center of the image, however, suggests that the task of the guardians is not as easy as the calmness exuded by the duplicate Libera figures makes it seem.

May Day Mass (also from 1990), makes clear, however, that the artist does not necessarily see the symbolism, rites, and symmetries of the two epochs (pre- and post-1989) as being at odds with each other. Here, the May Day crowds are replaced with the faithful, gathered at Pope John Paul II's open-air Mass on Parade Square during his historic 1987 pilgrimage to Poland (actually held on June 14 of that year). This Mass/spectacle was notable less for the words spoken by the pontiff than for the experiments with palatial symmetry, which the temporary altar—erected specially for the

23 Kulik, "Autokomentarz," *Magazyn Sztuki*, no. 15/16 (1997): 214. Ewa Lajer-Burcharth, Piotr Piotrowski, and Izabela Kowalczyk have written about Kulik's understanding of "hammering," and of Kulik's own working-through (and "subordination" to) the mechanisms of "hammering" to which communist, totalitarian, patriarchal, and capitalist regimes submit artists and women. See Lajer-Burcharth's text, "Old Histories: Zofia Kulik's Ironic Recollections," reprinted in this volume; Piotrowski, "Between Siberia and Cyberia: On the Art of Zofia Kulik and on Museums," in *Zofia Kulik: From Siberia to Cyberia*, eds. Kulik and Piotrowski (Poznań: National Museum, 1999); and Kowalczyk, "The Geometry of Power."

occasion—was itself deployed to carry out. Plans were initially made to hang a 70-meter crystalline crucifix from the Palace's main facade in the spot ordinarily occupied by Lenin, crownless eagles, or other elements of the socialist state's symbology during May Day parades, but these came to nothing, apparently in the face of objections from the Soviet embassy, who did not want "any holy trinkets hung from our gift."[24] The Palace's facade remained bare, but an enormous altar, styled after organ pipes and centered on a crucifix wrapped in aluminum foil, was erected on top of the tribune, directly in front of the Palace's main entrance. As several hundred thousand people crowded into the Square and surrounding streets, all eyes were focused on the altar. Although its pyramidal symmetry directly corresponded with (and was therefore subordinate to) the form of the Palace, the weight of the occasion was such that the hierarchy was reversed: the Palace either seemed to become "part of" the altar or to be displaced by it—even cosmically banished, as in Julian Bohdanowicz's 1987 cartoon—in an act redolent of the Palace's disappearance in Kulik's 1972 *Letter from Milan*. There is no suggestion of banishment, movement, or flight on the Palace's part in Kulik's image, but the Libera-males seem to float into the ether—either in a dream-state (dreaming of the Palace, no less, as the central image of Palaces circulating around Libera's sleeping head suggests), or ascending into heaven.

The Palace appears again in 1991's *Favorite Balance* —a monumental image of daunting intricacy and complexity; and in 1992's *All Things Converge in Time and Space; To Disperse, To Converge, To Disperse, and So on*—an explicit exploration of the relationship between center and periphery, symmetry and asymmetry, fission and fusion—the "ceaseless battle between centrifugal forces that seek to keep things apart, and centripetal forces that strive to make things cohere"—the former of which were in the ascendancy during the 1990s, years of center-irrupting, disorienting "wild capitalism."[25]

24 Irena Świerdzewska, "Krzyż na Pałacu Kultury," *Idziemy*, May 30, 2012, http://www.idziemy.com.pl/polityka/krzyz-na-palacu-kultury/2/.

25 As Michael Holquist puts it, with reference to Mikhail Bakhtin's philosophy of language. M. M. Bakhtin, *The Dialogic Imagination: Four Essays*, ed. Michael Holquist (Austin: University of Texas Press, 1981).

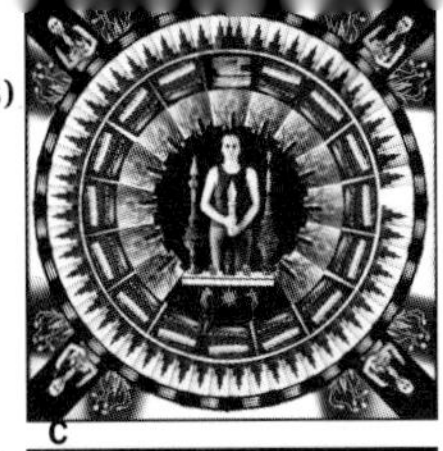

C

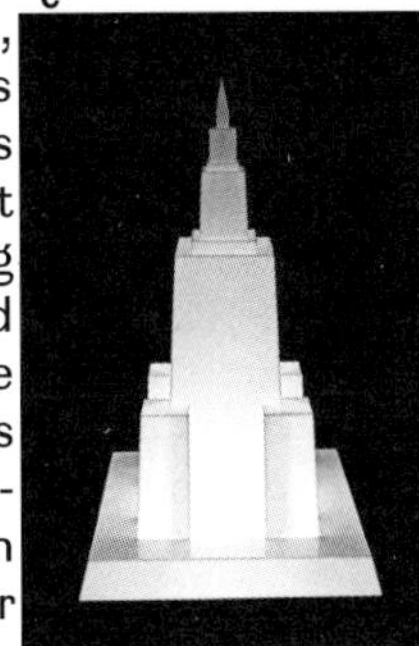

D / P. 36

Here, the Palace-bearing male dog/turtle reappears, and the spire of the Palace once again doubles up as a spear, pointing with violent intent—this time towards a woman's loins. Not a living person, however, but a monumental sculpture (an allegory of music, holding a violin), whose exaggerated musculature is contrasted with the lanky frame of the young Libera—one of the dozens of sculptural figures positioned in niches around the ground-floor facade of the Palace of Culture. Above looms the figure of warrior-craftswoman Kulik, clutching another spire as if it was a spear (repeating the pose from 1990's *The Guardians of the Spire*), flanked by two enormous assemblages of drill bits fashioned into spires (or spears). The usual collection of cloned Liberas dance, in Chaplinesque fashion, around the composition, endowing the whole with movement, comedy, and gravitas. The same image of the spear-brandishing Kulik constitutes the centerpiece of **MYSELF, POPPIES, AND THE JOKE** C (1992), in which dozens of dark Palace silhouettes, projecting from the edge of a circular halo surrounding Kulik, perform the functional, tireless, and un-singular role of a cog in a greater structure.

In Kulik's "geometry of power," then, the Palace's role is hardly unambivalent or unidirectional. It performs a number of seemingly contradictory functions and adopts an array of different directionalities, both centripetal and centrifugal: it is a heavy burden, borne by an emasculated male (a gift that demands reciprocity); a stele (a bearer of signs and symbolic meaning); a weapon (a "spire" or a "hammer") of both symbolic and sexual violence; and a spatial, structural, or symbolic center, holding the whole together and providing it with meaning; as well as a periphery, a cog doing the bidding of a system or cosmos, whose real core is located elsewhere.

Beyond the photomontages, the Palace plays an important role in Kulik's sculptural/archival installation **KURGANS OF FAME AND INFAMY** D (1993), exhibited at Warsaw's Zachęta National Gallery of Art; here, a Palace-like shape is one of a series of illuminated Plexiglas maquettes, accompanied by figures resembling

Alexey Shchusev's Lenin's Mausoleum on Red Square, a Mesoamerican pyramid, and a series of other obelisks, ziggurats, and plinths. The reference to kurgans in the title of the work—ancient burial mounds found throughout Central Asia and Eastern Europe, which were appropriated into Polish national memorial culture in the 19th century—appears to suggest a sort of Eurasianist dimension to Kulik's work here, further hinted at in her invocations of the symmetry of oriental carpets, mandalas, and Chinese mythology. The *Kurgans* series brings home the aesthetic and morphological kinship of Kulik's art with the late-Soviet and post-Soviet Russian artistic avant-gardes, as well as with the decorative and applied Soviet arts of the 1920s to 1940s—the agit-carpets and agit-fabrics that Kulik may have come across during her 1971 student trip to Moscow.[26] The Moscow Conceptualists (Andrei Monastyrski, Vitaly Komar, Alexander Melamid, and others)—famously analyzed by Boris Groys[27]—devoted their practice during this time to a fixation on and (ironic) exploration of the symmetries and monumentalities of high-Soviet civilization and its material and mnemonic legacies, such as Lenin's Mausoleum or the Exhibition of Achievements of the People's Economy (VDNKh) in the northern suburbs of Moscow. Similarly but distinctly, the New Academists (Timur Novikov, Alexey Belyaev-Gintovt, Georgy Guryanov, and others) explored the aesthetics of Stalinism, fascism, and—most markedly in the case of Belyaev-Gintovt, a self-avowed Russian nationalist and Eurasian Romanticist—Russo-centric Eurasianism. The New Academists' aesthetic is, like that of the concept band Laibach and the Neue Slowenische Kunst (NSK), much more openly queer and camp than that of the Moscow Conceptualists, but unlike the NSK, who are unmistakably ironic, and unlike the Moscow Conceptualists, who are quite safely left-liberal and postmodern, the

26 See also Sarah Wilson's reflections on the relationship between Kulik's work and the broader genre of East European "Soc-art" postmodernism, with which the works of the Moscow Conceptualists and New Academists are sometimes associated. Sarah G. Wilson, "Zofia Kulik: From Warsaw to Cyberia," *Centropa* 1, no. 3 (September 2001): 233. Reprinted in this volume.

27 Boris Groys, *The Total Art of Stalinism: Avant-Garde, Aesthetic Dictatorship, and Beyond*, trans. Charles Rougle (Princeton: Princeton University Press, 1992).

New Academists flirt on a meta-ironic level not only with Stalinist, far-right, conservative, and fascist aesthetics, but also with the corollary political ideologies and movements.

Zofia Kulik is a strange bedfellow to Moscow Conceptualism, New Academism, and the NSK, but she is probably the only major Polish artist of the late- and post-socialist period whose œuvre is fixated—like them—on the symmetries and centripetal-centrifugal geometries at the core of state socialism's aesthetic makeup, legacy, and unraveling. She is also, unlike the (largely but not exclusively) male and woman-blind Moscow Conceptualists and New Academists (for all their exploration of male sexuality, Novikov and Belyaev-Gintovt were not particularly concerned with gender), consistently concerned with exploring the intersection between gender, aesthetics, and politics: Kulik's art, in Sarah Wilson's phrase, has been "from the outset [...] resolutely antipatriarchal."[28]

In her analysis of the work of Guryanov, Novikov, Belyaev-Gintovt, and the New Academists after 1990, Maria Engström argues that these artists carried out a "queering" of socialist realisms in the political-aesthetic context of late-Soviet and post-Soviet Russia.[29] Following David J. Getsy,[30] Engström uses the phrase "queer" to refer to a "strategic undercutting of the stability of identity and the dispensation of power that shadows the assignment of categories and taxonomies." The New Academists, says Engström, queered the aesthetics of Stalinist socialist realism by exploring its sublimated sexual and homoerotic content, but also by retaining its heroism and monumentality, in a "metamodernist" move, which differs in its sincerity from the irony-laden postmodernism of the Moscow Conceptualists. In a not-unrelated gesture, I would argue, Kulik queers Closed Form—and especially its epitome, the Palace of Culture—by undermining the stability of the binary taxonomies (aesthetic, political, sexual, geometric) through which Closed Form/the

28 Wilson, "Zofia Kulik: From Warsaw to Cyberia," 235.
29 Maria Engström, "Queering Socialist Realism: Timur Novikov's New Academy," conference paper presented at "1917–2017: Russian Revolution in Arts and Aesthetics," Stockholm, October 19–21, 2017.
30 David J. Getsy, ed., *Queer (Whitechapel Documents of Contemporary Art)* (Cambridge, MA: MIT Press, 2016).

Palace are habitually made sense of by the Polish intellectuals of the late-socialist period (whether Konwicki, Chęciński, Hansen, or even—to some extent—the Kulik of *Letter from Milan*).

Queering the Palace Complex: Towards a New Red Palace

Kulik's exploration of the Palace's multiple symmetries, centricities, aesthetics—and sexualities—runs alongside, I would like to suggest, the "queering" of the Palace, which has intensified during the past several years in Warsaw, especially in the context of the ultra-Catholic, homophobic, misogynistic, and xenophobic ideological climate created in Poland since 2015. In the context of Law and Justice's combined assault on women's rights and contraception, and on what it perceives to be Poland's "postcommunist" condition, could it be that the seemingly ultra-phallic, domineering Palace could even be made to take on some symbolic feminist attributes?

Among the relatively few people I met in Warsaw who virulently disliked the Palace or who wanted to see it knocked down, I mostly remembered encounters with young or youngish boys and men—patriotically minded, politically conservative activists in their teens or twenties handing out fliers on the street or attending public discussions about the history of Warsaw, fueled by varying degrees of anger and nationalistic zeal; indeed, the data I collected in my Palaceological survey (conducted in October 2010) backs up this impression. Among the most striking figures revealed in the respondents' answers was the disparity between male and female attitudes towards the Palace of Culture. 73 percent of women, but only 57 percent of men, described themselves as "positively disposed" towards the Palace (64 percent overall). More strikingly, just 21 percent of female, but over half (51 percent) of male respondents thought that "Warsaw needs to have a skyscraper taller than the Palace of Culture," and almost three times more men (23 percent) than women (8 percent) expressed their desire for the Palace to be demolished.

During a public meeting at the Museum of Modern Art in Warsaw in the autumn of 2010 at which I presented my survey results, audience members were unanimous in their psychosexual etiology of these figures: Warsaw's men are more aggressively disposed towards the Palace than its women are, because its vast dimensions—and perhaps its architectural power—leave them feeling belittled and intimidated. In other words, Warsaw's men are uniquely afflicted by the Palace Complex. A Facebook discussion that emerged following my presentation of these statistics during a lecture at Warsaw's Academy of Fine Arts in March 2017 also gave rise to a conversation about the relation between gender and the Palace Complex, and about belligerent versus nonbelligerent attitudes towards the Palace itself and Poland's communist past in general. The conversation started lightheartedly: feminist philosopher and artist Ewa Majewska posted a photograph of my slide presenting the survey figures, accompanied by the comment, "It would seem that men are dangerous." "Rather, it seems that they have complexes," responded sociologist Katarzyna Kasia. Soon, however, the conversation was joined by a male Facebook friend of one of the participants (who hadn't been present at the lecture). He expressed outrage at the idea that the Palace was being considered in a positive light at all: it was a terrible imposition on Warsaw; it ripped apart the whole prewar layout of the city, separating the western Wola district from the center! And he expressed even more consternation at the idea that gender was a relevant factor in attitudes towards the Palace, towards Poland's history, or towards everyday life in general.

The paradoxically belligerent manner in which this protest against the belligerent nature of the Palace—and of the political system that stood behind it—was delivered also reminded me of the competitive, macho turn taken by a discussion about the Palace that I organized in the context of my fieldwork in July 2010: several male members of the panel and audience began accusing each other of "impotence" or "dwarfishness" for their perceived inability to deal with the Palace Complex. Right-wing architect and Law and Justice mayoral candidate Czesław Bielecki even went so far as to claim that he is in possession of the "legislative Viagra" (a phrase that Bielecki, as he emphasized, actually trademarked) to break through the so-called "administrative impotence" hampering the city's plans to overcome the Palace's domination over the city.[31]

31 This interaction is described in more detail in Murawski, "Big Affects" (2016).

The character of Warsaw's Palace Complex—although ultimately rooted in the political-economic parameters underlying the building's ability to continue to function publicly—affects, afflicts, and enriches the life of Warsaw on numerous uneven, contradictory, and complementary levels. Various working generalizations can be made in order to try to make sense of—to "reveal" rather than to obscure—some of this complexity and contradiction. On a comparative, global scale, the Palace Complex does appear to be highly unusual in terms of the extent to which the attention of an entire city is concentrated—to Oskar Hansen's dismay—on one architectural object. However, even if the Palace Complex is not exactly "normal," it is not pathological either; rather than being an affliction that only "the other Varsovian" has, the Palace Complex permeates pervasively, if asymmetrically, throughout the whole social existence of 21st-century Warsaw.

To dwell a little more on belligerent versus nonbelligerent attitudes towards the Palace, it is also clear that—contrary to an opinion I often heard expressed while in Warsaw—these are not distributed linearly according to age: older people are no more likely to dislike the Palace than younger ones. Apart from gender, few demographic categories underlie substantial divergences in disposition towards the Palace, with political opinions and attitudes towards Poland's communist past being among the few exceptions: unsurprisingly enough, 79 percent of self-described left-wingers were positively disposed towards the Palace (only 5 percent negatively), while the corresponding figures for right-wingers were 45 percent versus 34 percent (57 percent versus 17 percent for political centrists). All respondents who evaluated the communist past in positive terms were fond of the Palace, while less than half of those whose attitude towards the socialist period was negative thought likewise. Even among this anti-communist demographic, however, it is interesting to note that the Palace had more admirers (47 percent) than detractors (30 percent).

For all its phallicness, then, the Palace—in its awesome capacity to provoke male belligerence—may, perhaps, be able to play an anti-patriarchal role in Warsaw's symbolic-political landscape.

For all its morphological centrality and symmetry, it veers distinctly closer towards Warsaw's political left side than to its right. As the meeting place for Warsaw's annual feminist Manifa marches, and a focal point for the city's LGBTQ Pride parades; as an object of hatred and symbolic censorship for Poland's currently reigning nationalist right; as a powerful container and radiator of public spirit in a city of wild restitution and resurgent deprivation; as a vivid reminder of the extent to which Poland's socialist regime was as invested in the provision of new kinds of public culture and opportunity to previously dispossessed classes as it was in the withdrawal of old kinds of privilege from the feudal and bourgeois elites; and as a near-universal object of affection and fascination—even for the greater share of Warsaw's belligerent males, right-wingers, and anti-communists—the still-socialist Palace may, so long as its publicness remains intact, serve as a powerful agent and device for the reconfiguration of the left-less, patriarchal, and privationary economic, aesthetic, social, and ideological landscape of 21st-century Warsaw.

The Palace, then, has queered itself, but it has also been queered by circumstance. Zofia Kulik—who sought to "fill the Palace with her own madness"—is a witness, an archivist, and an activator of this process of queering the Palace and of switching on its radical potential—of reactivating the Palace's public spirit, and thereby of building a New Red Palace. This is especially true in the context of the recent right-wing upsurge in Polish politics, and of reactionary politicians' calls to demolish the Palace in time for the celebration of the centenary of Polish independence in November 2018.

Suzana Milevska, PhD, is a curator and a visual culture theorist based in Skopje. Her theoretical and curatorial interests include postcolonial and feminist critique of representational regimes of hegemonic power in the arts and visual culture, and collaborative and participatory art practices in marginalized communities. She was principal investigator for the Horizon 2020 project Transmitting Contentious Cultural Heritages with the Arts (TRACES), and curated the exhibition *Contentious Objects/Ashamed Subjects* (Politecnico di Milano, 2019). She was the Endowed Professor of Central and South Eastern European Art Histories (Academy of Fine Arts Vienna, 2013–15) and taught history and theory of visual art (Faculty of Fine Arts, Skopje, 2010–12). She initiated and directed the Center for Visual and Cultural Research Skopje (2006–08). She holds a PhD in Visual Cultures from Goldsmiths, University of London, and was a Fulbright Senior Research Scholar at the Library of Congress in Washington, D.C. She curated *The Renaming Machine* (Ljubljana, Zagreb, Vienna, 2009–11), *Roma Protocol* (the Austrian Parliament, Wiener Festwochen), and *Call the Witness* (BAK, Utrecht, 2011), and was the initiator of *Call the Witness* (Roma Pavilion, Venice Biennale, 2011). She authored *Gender Difference in the Balkans* (2010), and edited *The Renaming Machine: The Book* (2010) and *On Productive Shame, Reconciliation, and Agency* (2016). She is the recipient of the Igor Zabel Award for Culture and Theory (2012).

CALL OF DUTY: ON INFINITE WARFARE AND PATRIARCHY IN ZOFIA KULIK'S WORK

This essay is envisaged as an attempt to look closely at the use of repetition, difference, and temporality in Zofia Kulik's works from a feminist perspective. In particular I will look at her work *All the Missiles Are One Missile*, a huge photomontage that has been exhibited widely, along with several other related works.[1] When composing the work, the artist used multiple images including TV stills. In other works in which Kulik critically addressed various "militant" imagery of warfare and the casualties of ethnic conflicts she mostly referred to those that dominated TV screens in the 1990s, but more recently the artist has returned to those works as a kind of metaphoric reference to more recent conflicts and casualties of war.

In her photo-collage-like works Kulik mostly experiments with compositions made through the repeated imprinting of one or more negatives on carefully masked photographic paper, which, in a way, turns technological means into a metaphorical

1 Also translated as *All Bullets Are One Bullet*, in Paweł Leszkowicz, "War (!!!) and Peace (?): Fascination with Militarism in Contemporary Polish Art," *War and Peace*, ex. cat. (Lublin: Galeria Labirynt, 2015), wystawy.labirynt.com/wp-content/uploads/2015/10/Paweł-Leszkowicz_en.pdf.

device for pointing out the potentials and dangers of the *return of the different*, not the *return of the same*, in Deleuzian terms.[2] The Deleuzian concept of time is cracked, and open to the potentialities generated by a return of difference: "It is not the same which returns, it is not the similar which returns; rather, the Same is the returning of that which returns,—in other words, of the Different; the similar is the returning of that which returns,—in other words, of the Dissimilar."[3] Deleuze's warning is about the danger of an oversimplified interpretation of eternal recurrence, insofar as it designates a certain metaphysical understanding of the return as *more-than-historical*.[4]

I wish to argue that Kulik's works contemplate both the intrinsic structure of the imageries that have been accumulated, circulated, and proliferated via the media, and also the effects that the perpetuation and spectacularization of images of war have on reciprocal relations between femininity and masculinity, both in the East and West.

Nevertheless, the perspective from which this essay developed has been heavily swayed by the current, widespread, and strengthened patriarchal and sexist oppression of women in Eastern Europe that has been imposed by the state, church, family, and other institutions.

> It seems that artists are looking for effigies and metaphors, which link the iconography of a soldier with the context of military past and current wars as well as the contemporary discussion about masculinity and its metamorphoses. This intensified gender awareness, though nowadays articulated openly, from a visual perspective is nothing new in Polish art.[5]

2 Gilles Deleuze, *Difference and Repetition*, trans. Paul Patton (London: Continuum, 2004), 374.

3 Deleuze, *Difference and Repetition*, 374.

4 As Lee Spinks explains further, in Deleuze's view, one should explicitly repudiate the naive reading of Nietzsche that envisages eternal return as a doctrine proclaiming the infinite recurrence of every historical moment in exactly the same order throughout eternity. Spinks, "Eternal Return," in *The Deleuze Dictionary*, ed. Adrian Parr (New York: Columbia University Press, 2006), 84.

5 Leszkowicz, "War (!!!) and Peace (?)."

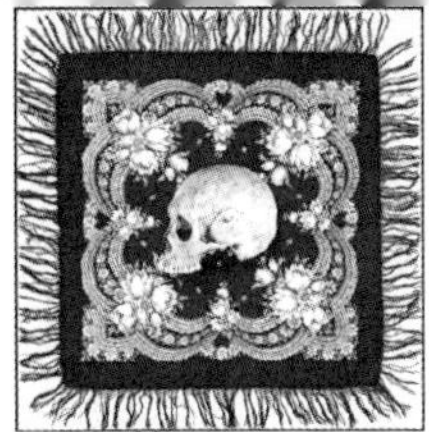

A / P. 44

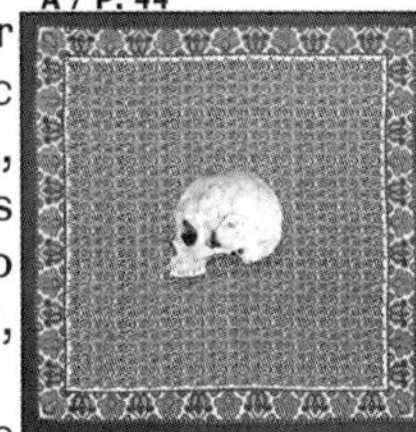

B / P. 44

While socialist ideals at least aimed towards gender and social equality, and claimed programmatic improvement of production relations in the future, nowadays it feels as if even the "map" of ideals has changed, and as if the clock has been turned back to premodern times when patriarchy used to be the norm, not the target to fight.

The racism and conflicts from the 1990s originally motivated Kulik's work **ETHNIC WARS. LARGE VANITAS STILL LIFE** A + B (1997–2017)[6] via Luc Delahaye's photo "UN Soldiers and Refugees, Tuzla, July 1995" (Magnum Photos for *Newsweek*), which was shown at the World Press Photo exhibition in 1995 [FIG. 1]. Since then the reporter's "spectacularized" images of atrocities, horror, and sorrow have been replaced by images from new battlefields, conflicts, camps, and racial outbursts. However, Kulik's ethnographic and anthropological collection of juxtaposed skulls[7] over shawls with different patterns foresee, in a way, the newly raised racism across Europe, the frequent anti-Semitic or anti-Roma slurs, and the Islamophobic attacks that undeniably link the current humanitarian refugee crisis with historical Islamophobia in Europe.[8] Whilst the reality captured by the reporter's lenses could not address the prospect of recurring and future conflicts that are ever more frightening—because the missiles became more advanced, and thus ever more lethal—Kulik's frieze-like installations of scarves and skulls point to the never-ending archives of memento mori that grow in piles on humanity's graveyards worldwide as I am writing this text.

6 There are two versions of the work: a slideshow from 1997 and a printed version from 2017 (Museum Susch collection).

7 "A skull borrowed from Jasio Rasiński. I don't know where he got it from, photo 1994." Kulik, quoted in *Zofia Kulik—The Splendor of Myself V (Mother, Daughter, Partner)*, trans. Weronika Bachman and Ron Rocco, ex. cat. (Berlin: ŻAK BRANICKA, 2008).

8 Suzana Milevska, "53 Wounds in Solidarity: Appropriation and 'Hostipitality' in the Slogan 'We Refugees,'" *Eurozine*, January 21, 2017, https://www.eurozine.com/53-wounds-in-solidarity-appropriation-and-hostipitality-in-the-slogan-we-refugees/.

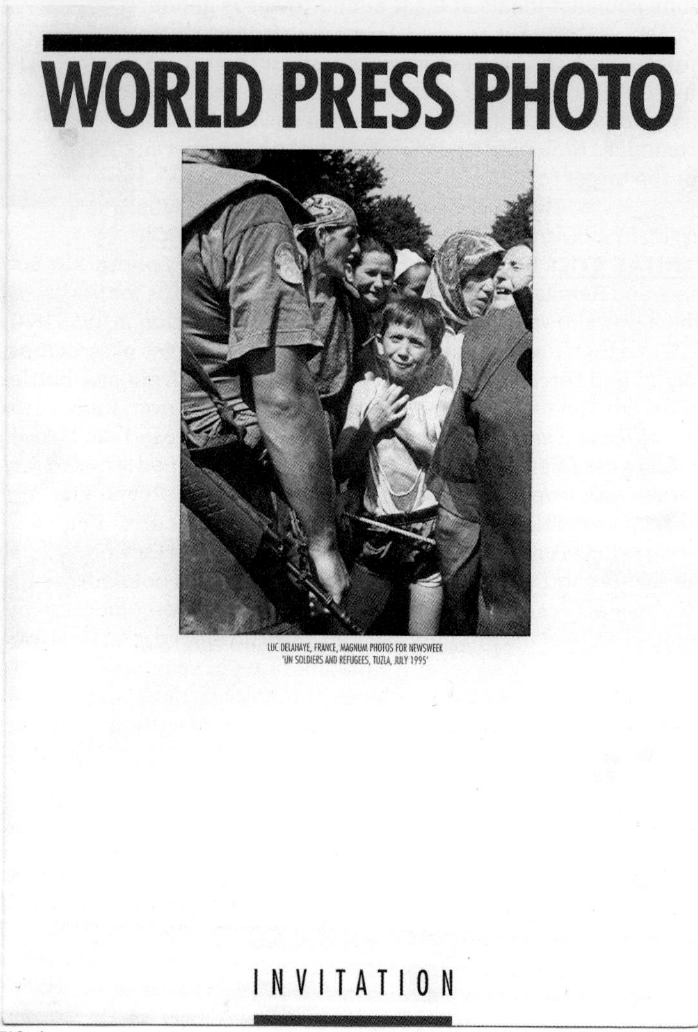

FIG. 1
INVITATION TO THE WORLD PRESS PHOTO EXHIBITION HELD AT ZACHĘTA NATIONAL GALLERY OF ART, WARSAW, 1996; LUC DELAHAYE'S *UN SOLDIERS AND REFUGEES* PICTURED

About Repetition, Difference, and the Terror of the Eternal Return

Gilles Deleuze's unorthodox emphasis on eternal recurrence as contaminated by inevitable difference leads to an entirely different understanding of temporality. It is productive, and history is ultimately unrepresentable in consciousness or language. In *Difference and Repetition* Deleuze addressed in detail the Nietzschean problematic of the "eternal return of the same."[9] According to his pivotal earlier book *Nietzsche and Philosophy* (1962), he had already announced that it is not the empirically same, but difference, multiplicity, and becoming that return. What remains eternal and "the same" is the movement of recurring itself: "It is not the 'same' or the 'one' which comes back in the eternal return but return is itself the one which ought to belong to diversity and to that which differs."[10]

For Deleuze, eternal return implies that difference and becoming, as basic ontological principles, split the very heart of being from the beginning. Thus diversity and multiplicity must fundamentally *occur*, which is to recur.[11] Moreover, Deleuze argued that there are two aspects of the eternal return in Nietzsche. The first is its cosmological aspect, under which Nietzsche attacks the thermodynamic notion of entropy prevalent during his day. This may be closely related to and reflected by the universal and all-encompassing aspects of *All the Missiles Are One Missile*. The second aspect is the ethical one, through which one *selects* the past that has to return to one's present *as if* this present were perpetually repeated (e.g. the concrete and recognizable images from different historical events included from journalistic reports in the same work).[12] One may also

9 Deleuze, *Difference and Repetition*, 374–75.
10 Deleuze, *Nietzsche and Philosophy*, trans. Hugh Tomlinson (London: Athlone Press, 1983), 46.
11 Deleuze, *Difference and Repetition*, 372–74.
12 Suzana Milevska and Arun Saldanha, "The Eternal Return of Race: Reflections on East European Racism," in *Deleuze and Race*, eds. Arun Saldanha and Jason M. Adams (Edinburgh: Edinburgh University Press, 2013), 225–47: 227.

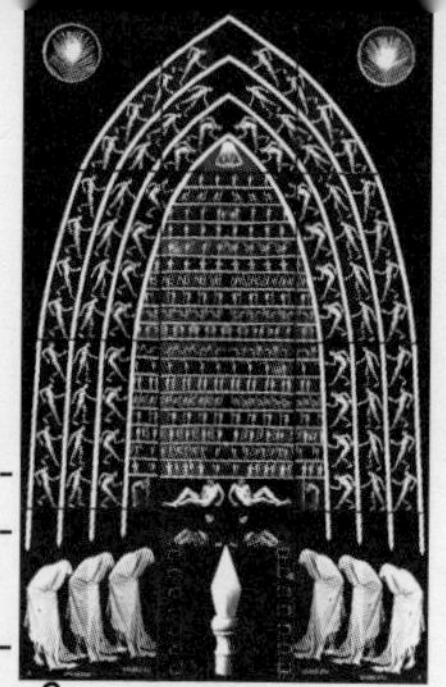

recognize both aspects in Kulik's mandalas, in her mirroring reflections, and the other symbolic representations of the *selective eternal return*.[13]

In order to understand the recent organized amnesia in Central, Eastern, and Southeastern Europe, and the rise of conservative, nationalist, patriarchal, and racist sentiments and policies in the politically and economically emergent European states at this point in history, it is necessary to emphasize the danger of misunderstanding what it is that returns and what exactly repetition does to memory. Kulik's works serve as a guide towards such a critical reflection of both the past and present.

Starting from the current sociopolitical context in Poland and other post-socialist countries, this essay aims to examine the potentiality to interpret the structure and visual language of several seminal works created by Kulik in the 1990s as a feminist critique of repetitive militant and phallocentric power. This is not solely imposed by the vocabulary used in their titles, which refer to phenomena and rituals from the socialist past: e.g. **MARCH, MARCH, MARCH** C (1990), and *The Guardians of the Spire* (1990) (an obvious reference to the Palace of Culture and Science in Warsaw—Stalin's gift to Poland—which is adorned by a spire), but also represented through the link between the words' meanings and the rigid visual order and symmetric, mirrorlike compositions.

The designs typical for (or merely resembling) various artistic and architectural media, genres, objects, and patterns from the treasury of national or international cultural heritage (e.g. triptychs, altars, mosaics, tapestries, carpets, patterned headscarves, mandalas, or Gothic windows) have not been applied by accident: they form both the systemic bases and superstructure that frame

13 Deleuze, *Nietzsche and Philosophy*, 47.

the subject, or more precisely to which the subject is conformed and subordinated—even crucified (or, in Kulik's words "hammered": "I have been hammered, we all have been hammered").[14]

In these works, accumulation, mirroring symmetry, repetition with difference, and processual iconography accentuate the images that serve the metaphoric pointing towards dismantling of the recurrent, stereotypical national and political myths. And not only by revealing patriarchal myths about femininity, but also by deconstructing the stereotypical myths of masculinity.[15] Because of the ways in which Kulik presented male protagonists, the "guardians of the spire" represent "a system of cultural signification defined as a repertory of specific signs and poses," which has often been interpreted in psychoanalytical terms:

> Not only are its motifs conspicuously phallic (not by chance is Warsaw's spired Palace of Culture the artist's favorite architectural motif) but its formal structure insistently aligns the idea of composition with the symbolic order defined as the invisible but omnipresent Law governed by the phallic signifier.[16]

I wish to argue that Kulik's works can be interpreted as a certain warning, or even an anticipation, of the evident recent recurrence or strengthening of patriarchy, the organized amnesia around fascist atrocities from the past, and the growing racism in contempo-

14 Kulik, "Na temat repetycji," in *Obecność III / Presence III*, Poznań, 1992, quoted in Piotr Piotrowski, "The Old Attitude and the New Faith," in *Beyond Belief: Contemporary Art from East Central Europe*, ed. Laura J. Hoptman (Chicago: Museum of Contemporary Art, 1995), 43.

15 The frail and vulnerable body, often doubled, split in half, or wrapped in bandages like a mummy, of the male model (Polish artist Zbigniew Libera, Kulik's model while her student in the 1990s), was turned into a symmetrical compositional grid. His figure becomes a reverse reflection of the patriarchal "world order," a kind of metaphoric framework for understanding the subordinating representational regimes, and the stereotypical divisions and distribution of power between masculinity and femininity.

16 Ewa Lajer-Burcharth, "Old Histories: Zofia Kulik's Ironic Recollections," in *New Histories*, ex. cat. (Boston: Institute of Contemporary Art, 1996), 119–36: 124. Reprinted in this volume. Psychological and psychoanalytical references have frequently been used in the interpretation of Zofia Kulik's work, e.g. by Izabela Kowalczyk in her early essay "The Geometry of Power in Zofia Kulik's Work," *n.paradoxa*, online issue no.11 (October 1999), 19–25, https://www.ktpress.co.uk/pdf/nparadoxaissue11.pdf.

rary Poland that was recently underlined by the new anti-defamation bill. Not only can her works created in the 1990s—the period of transition, and before May 1, 2004, when Poland was officially accessioned to the EU—be interpreted as a kind of "artistic revenge" (in Kulik's own words), a type of poignant critique of the biopolitical control of socialist regimes over the body and subjectivity, but they can also serve as anticipatory visualized announcements of the currently prevailing, hegemonic neoliberal powers and their rampant violation of human rights, gender and sexual equality, along with accumulation and dispossession, in David Harvey's terms.[17]

For example, the controversy surrounding an amendment to the IPN Act (the Act on the Institute of National Remembrance signed by Polish President Andrzej Duda on February 6, 2018) is just one of a recent unprecedented series of controversial political initiatives that prove the attempts of the current Polish state to control and overwrite historical narratives. The proposed revision of the IPN Act would have imposed a fine or imprisonment of up to three years for anyone who publicly or "against the facts" stated that the Polish nation or state are responsible (or co-responsible) for crimes committed by Nazi Germany or other crimes against humanity.[18] However, after intense public disputes that were particularly prompted by Israel, the United States, and Ukraine regarding the new regulations (which came into effect in March 2018), the Polish

17 A similar anticipatory critique can be recognized in several early performances, documented as video works or photographs, which Kulik realized in the 1980s and early 1990s (as part of KwieKulik, with Przemysław Kwiek, her partner at the time), e.g. the complex political links between the national and international regimes of the control of movement (*The Monument without a Passport*, 1978), or the Debordian links between consumerism, media, and advertisement (e.g. the video *Supermarket*, Stuttgart, 1981) [FIGS. 2–3].

18 Barbara Bodalska, "Polish President signs anti-defamation bill, causing international protests," EURACTIV Poland, February 7, 2018, https://www.euractiv.com/section/central-europe/news/polish-president-signs-anti-defamation-bill-causing-international-protests/.

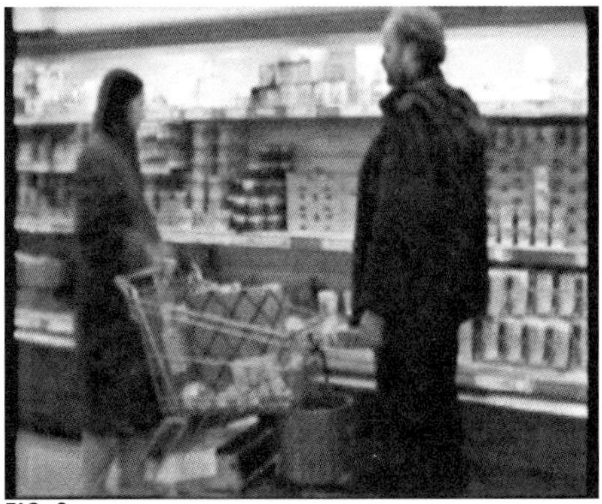

FIG. 2
KWIEKULIK, *SUPERMARKET*, 1981

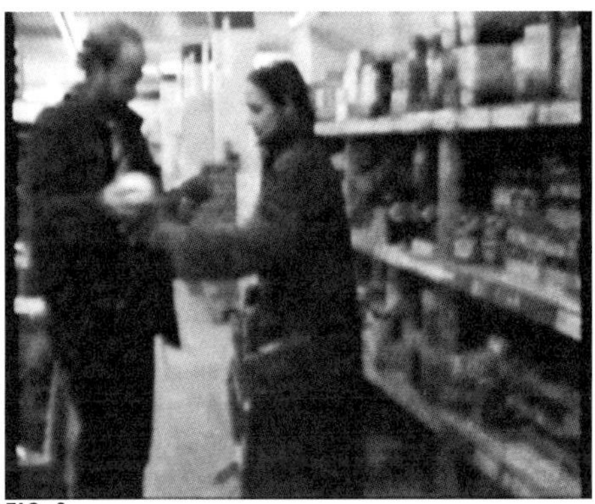

FIG. 3
KWIEKULIK, *SUPERMARKET*, 1981

Senate, in June 2018, abolished "the clause that assumed criminal responsibility for attributing Nazi crimes to Poland," although it approved the majority of the other changes.[19]

Such acts and protocols, mostly introduced by right-wing powers, resonate awkwardly with socialist regimes' control over memory. The question here is whether there are any positions available to discuss and deal with the embedded and inherited aggression of dispossessions from the premodern and modern past without inducing new aggression and without enhancing the vulnerability of newly constructed subjectivity. Wendy Brown, by comparing Marxist and Foucauldian interpretations of economic, societal, and political structures and relations, warned of a whole new level of surveillance, control, exploitation, and aggression that emerged with neoliberalism, and that surpasses the human and class hierarchies known from late capitalism. Moreover, according to Brown's observation, the relations produced by anti-capitalist movements and struggles are themselves not immune to producing new hierarchies and violent and aggressive instruments for controlling the body through imagery and human relations.[20]

Yet one could argue, as with Deleuze's arguments about racism, that such distinctions between the patriarchy in various countries and historical periods can be made on an empirical level, but not on the transcendental, immanently conceptual level that resonates with Kulik's works. There are links between various sexisms and racisms that point to the role of the reactive, herdlike mechanisms of the state, of moralism, and of right-wing populism (which Nietzsche so abhorred, although he himself internalized patriarchy and misogyny).[21] Patriarchy as a systemic mechanism connected to private property and to domination in the name of the

19 "Polish Senate approves changes to the Law on the Institute of National Remembrance," *UAWire*, June 28, 2018, https://uawire.org/the-polish-senate-approved-the-changes-to-the-law-on-the-institute-of-national-remembrance.

20 For an in-depth comparative analysis of the Marxist critique of bodily exploitation in capitalist societies and the Foucauldian critique of the biopolitical regime of control and surveillance developed under liberal capitalism, see Wendy Brown, *States of Injury: Power and Freedom in Late Modernity* (Princeton: Princeton University Press, 1995), 10.

21 Milevska and Saldanha, "The Eternal Return," 229.

state; the origins of patriarchy; and the interconnections between patriarchy and the control of female sexuality, violence, war, conquest, and rape in war, can all be read in Kulik's work.

Relatedly, there is a continuing problem of whether and how to make distinctions between historical Western patriarchy, the historical patriarchy in socialist countries, and the current escalating patriarchy among white Eastern Europeans that also increases against women of Romani and other ethnic minority backgrounds. Therefore, the present day provides for yet another point on the indexical grid to conceptualize a triangulated, back-and-forth reading between the socialist past, the neoliberal present, and Kulik's complex work, which also provides a kind of coordinate system that can assist with determining the points of intersection between these different registers and levels.[22] Hence it is worth pointing out the overall rise of the different (yet generally controlling) state-run neoliberal policies of the present, which strongly resonate with the authoritarian regimes of the modern past—the target of most of Kulik's works analyzed here.

The scope of Kulik's works is therefore not limited to the usual feminist slogan "the personal is political," or to any one-sided critique, because they serve as warnings and calls for the dismantling of biopower and ideology based on military and colonial conquest and dispossession.[23] There have already been a great number of relevant essays written about Kulik's art practice that targeted similar issues of the ideological and biopolitical apparatuses

22 Kulik, *An Iconographic Guide to* All the Missiles Are One Missile (Warsaw: Zachęta National Gallery of Art, 1997).

23 For a general comparison between the concerns of feminist artists from the East and West, see Ewa Grigar, "The Gendered Body as Raw Material for Women Artists in Central Eastern Europe after Communism," in *Living Gender after Communism*, eds. Janet Elise Johnson and Jean C. Robinson (Bloomington: Indiana University Press, 2006), 80–104.

overwriting female and male bodies and subjectivity, the spectacularization of body image, and other repressive and representational regimes.[24]

I wish to argue that the current, rapid change of socio-political conditions in post-socialist countries not only reiterates the relevance of Kulik's work, but also confirms the relevance of the numerous texts that have stressed Kulik's critique of iconography, ideology, and the spatiality of power. Nevertheless, the texts written about similar aspects of Kulik's work in the late 1990s and early 2000s generally used the past perfect tense; these texts may be revisited and perceived from both directions of the historical axes because of their resonance with the present.

I am referring to the alleged return of general patriarchal "values" and the militant aggressivity usually linked to masculinity. "Alleged," because one could argue that either the patriarchy never disappeared, or that what humanity experiences today is a return of patriarchal rules—but of a slightly modified set. The loss of many equal rights at work, and at home, within the family, that in previous socialist contexts were wrongly assumed to be completely accomplished and irreversible, begs several urgent questions.

I want therefore to address some of the main questions that continue to puzzle feminist theorists today: whether the patriarchy was dismantled during socialism, whether it returned (and how), or whether it never "left" and was cunningly concealed

24 Sarah G. Wilson, "Discovering the Psyche: Zofia Kulik," *n.paradoxa* 4 (July 1999): 55–64; Piotr Piotrowski, "Between Siberia and Cyberia: On the Art of Zofia Kulik and on Museums," in *Zofia Kulik: Od Syberii do Cyberii / From Siberia to Cyberia*, eds. Kulik and Piotrowski (Poznań: National Museum, 1999), 7–33; Sarah G. Wilson, "Zofia Kulik: From Warsaw to Cyberia," *Centropa* 1, no. 3 (September 2001): 233–44 (reprinted in this volume); Gregory Volk, "Sculpting with Images: On the Early Photomontages of Zofia Kulik," in *Zofia Kulik*, ex. cat. (Berlin: ŻAK BRANICKA, 2016).

during the limited span of (alleged) socialist emancipation and equality.[25] Or, to put it even more precisely, how was it possible that the reversal took place so quickly if equality had really been achieved?

Piotr Piotrowski already tried to answer some of these questions in his essay "The Old Attitude and the New Faith" (1995), particularly the issue of the disguise of patriarchy during socialist times or, as he put it, that the emancipation of women was merely one more "fraud" or "camouflage," typical of Poland's socialist past.[26]

> On the surface, women seemed to play a significant role in the political, cultural, and national arenas during the heroic years of communism, and women's lives were ostensibly shaped by the ideology of liberation and equal rights, as the phrase went in Poland. But fraud was a characteristic feature of real socialism, and the appointment of seamstresses to the politburo, the meetings between the League of Women and the first secretary, and the annual celebrations of Women's Day were incapable of concealing the true situation of women in those years.[27]

According to Piotrowski, after the fall of the Berlin Wall the authorities even gave up on trying to obscure the prevailing, systemic, repressive, and sexist attitudes towards women, and for him there were two factors that contributed to this: the political, to be recognized in "the vehement eruption of right-wing rhetoric" towards family, childcare, and motherhood that was easily accepted as a counterreaction to the communist indoctrination of the "past era," and

25 Sławomir Sierakowski, "The Polish Church's Gender Problem," *New York Times* online, January 26, 2014, https://www.nytimes.com/2014/01/27/opinion/sierakowski-the-polish-churchs-gender-problem.html; Katheryn Detwiler and Ann Snitow, "Gender Trouble in Poland," *Dissent*, Fall 2016, https://www.dissentmagazine.org/article/gender-trouble-poland-pis-abortion-ban.

26 Piotrowski, "The Old Attitude," 41.

27 Piotrowski, "The Old Attitude," 41.

the economic, to be recognized in the uneven and unequal competition in the labor market after the transition from a centralized to a free-market economy.[28]

Although Polish society now functions on entirely different sociopolitical and economic parameters than in the past, during socialism, the evident, more recently proposed and still-deliberated stringent control over the female (and male) body and sexuality resonates with the surveillance and control that regimes in the past exercised in parallel with the equality they proclaimed. Particularly relevant is the affected freedom to make important decisions and choices that directly determine women's lives in a situation where the state and church make advancements towards gaining increasing control over natalist politics, e.g. the rights to abortion and contraception, or the right to work, the right to remain single, etc.

In Zofia Kulik's works, repetition is used to evoke temporality, due to the spatial and visual way in which the repetition is presented. It is not just an impromptu interpretation if one recognizes exactly the resonance of these images with the return of patriarchy with difference. The question of whether patriarchy was ever unified and homogenous is even more compelling, because if the cracked structure was always there, it becomes clearer that not only was the return (as different) inevitable, but also that patriarchy was never isotopic to itself. One could easily apply this assertion to patriarchy in order to consider whether the patriarchy that returned is the same patriarchy from the past, or is rather a kind of updated version 2.0 of patriarchy that is ever more resilient to any criticism and overwrites resistance to its rules. Although patriarchy was under scrutiny during the socialist period, it never completely disappeared. Yet it was somehow weakened and fragmented between the faithless state, dormant church, and family. Its continuity, however,

28 Piotrowski offered gruesome statistics regarding the structure of employment in Poland in 1995: "80 percent of women are employed in jobs which require absolutely no skills, and their pay is 30 percent lower than that of men [in the same jobs] [...] There are only 30 women among the 360 managers of light industrial plants (where 70 percent of the workers are women)." Piotrowski, "The Old Attitude," 42.

persisted and has been maintained in various societal cells, so its contemporary repetition and mirroring happens with differences almost invisible to the naked eye.

Archive of Monuments and Movements

Kulik dealt with the historical past, with personal and collective memory, and with the indentations and incisions that societies of control leave behind on the epidermis of (and deeper into) societal tissue. The versatile and vast body of her work has often been referred to as to an archive, both personal and historical. For example, in some larger installations, the museum vitrines that accumulate various socialist "memorabilia" (medals, souvenirs, photographs, postcards, etc.) provide the contextual background for viewers.[29]

As in any archive, though, in Kulik's collection of appropriated forms, shapes, and images there are a lot of duplicates, with asymmetrical mirroring images that are not completely the same but include subtle differences and motions by proxy, resulting from technology and production, not always in the realm of the visible. The intersections between nation, church, power regime, and other patriarchal authorities, on the one hand, and the body, subjectivity, gender, and sexuality, on the other, are so perplexing that they encompass women's lives—from giving birth until death. However, the usual (but complex) cycle of life (to which Kulik referred in, for example, *From Siberia to Cyberia*) and whatever happens between birth and death is heavily disturbed, interrupted, and deconstructed: it is turned in a closed circuit, reciprocally influenced by representation and the visual field, so that the virtual world of images and the real world are both equally confining.

The artist has provided us with a valuable, cross-referential iconographic guide for the interpretation of her complex and multilayered artworks, particularly for understanding *All the Mis-*

29 Vitrines were used by Kulik on various occasions; as an autonomous work they were presented at her solo exhibition *Symbolic Weapon* in 1993 (BWA Gallery, Sopot; Zachęta National Gallery of Art, Warsaw) as *Private, Common, Soft, Metal, Faded Propaganda, Retrospective—Things*.

siles Are One Missile (1993), which she exhibited in the frame of the Polish National Pavilion when she represented Poland at the Venice Biennale in 1997.[30] The *Guide* (1997) pointed out many resourceful influences and possible readings of the work, with plenty of textual and visual references. The unusually precise analysis of forms and contents from diverse geographical and geopolitical resources points to the complex and painstaking research that preceded the execution of Kulik's work. Historical visual imagery is compared, cross-referenced, and staged (by Zbigniew Libera) side by side with contemporaneous references, thus building an archive "of visual tricks and references" that stands as a work on its own. In the *Guide*, diverse drawings and photographic reproductions from books, newspapers, and postcards, referring to images of events and objects from different regions and periods (e.g. the Italian Renaissance, the Austro-Hungarian Empire, communist China and Russia, and contemporary Poland) are carefully assembled, so that no additional commentaries are necessary. The Freedom Monument (from a cemetery in Riga), along with images from processions and Communions in Poland, point to the artist's interest in the uses of imagery of women and children for the representation of the nation and state, as if a beautiful woman or an innocent child could make gruesome reality and war atrocities more bearable.

However, some of Kulik's obvious inspiration for representing movement with static images comes from the more distant past: from the obsessive photo-experiments of British photographer Eadweard Muybridge and French scientist Étienne-Jules Marey, who both dedicated their careers to recording several phases of a movement on one photographic surface.[31] Some direct or indi-

30 Kulik, *An Iconographic Guide*.

31 Eadweard Muybridge (1830–1904) is important for his pioneering work in the photographic studies of human and animal locomotion (by using multiple cameras), and his early work in motion-picture projection (e.g. the zoopraxiscope, the predecessor of the film strip used in cinematography). Simultaneously, in the 1880s, the French scientist and chronophotographer Étienne-Jules Marey (also 1830–1904) invented a photographic gun that used a rotating glass plate to take twelve consecutive pictures per second in order to learn how birds fly.

rect links between military technology, repetitive iconography, and representational regimes are relevant to Kulik's work, although they are not necessarily closely related in thematic terms.[32]

In fairness, many of the systemic relations between hegemonic representational regimes, knowledge-production based on the developments (and limitations) of representational technological means, and the unstable nature of perception have been thoroughly discussed by Jonathan Crary, the renowned American art historian and theorist of photography.[33] However, in Crary's acclaimed books there is no in-depth analysis of the links between different technological inputs in the creation of the dominant representational regimes of gender stereotypes.

Kulik, on the contrary, applied repetitive iconography in order to evoke and attack the patriarchal macro-narrative of the reiteration and internalization of power, and offered a kind of fragmenting and dismantling of the monumentalizing iconography of the "world order," turned into images and objects as her imagined "revenge," in order to fight amnesia and the return of unwanted history. Despite the desire to freeze time, the organized suppression and forgetting of visual memory often prevails, and one of the many compelling elements of her work is the disclosure of the camouflage of the contrast between such patriarchal mechanisms. However, patriarchy is a system that was invented and developed historically rather than naturally, which means that it is neither pre-given nor inevitable, and some women and men have resisted its rule throughout its history. Zofia Kulik is not only one of them, but in her works she also aims towards the unraveling and dismantling of the ongoing and omnipresent patriarchal rules of representation, regardless of the historical, geopolitical, cultural, or religious context.

32 For example, Marey's gun was constructed with knowledge of the mechanism of the Henry repeating rifle (a lever-action, breech-loading, tubular magazine rifle), designed by Benjamin Tyler Henry just a couple of decades earlier, in the early 1860s.

33 Jonathan Crary, *Techniques of the Observer: On Vision and Modernity in the Nineteenth Century* (Cambridge, MA: MIT Press, 1999); Crary, *Suspensions of Perception: Attention, Spectacle, and Modern Culture* (Cambridge, MA: MIT Press, 2001).

Luiza Nader, PhD, is an art historian. Her research is dedicated to avant-garde, neo-avant-garde, modern, and contemporary art, with a strong focus on the art of the 1940s, 1960s, and 1970s, inspired by theories linked to affect, emotion, memory, archive, and trauma. Nader is the author of the book *Konceptualizm w PRL / Conceptual Art in the Polish People's Republic* (2009). In her recent studies she has concentrated on the relations between art practices and limit events, and on works both from and after the Holocaust. She has published texts in *Zagłada Żydów: Studia i materiały*, *Teksty Drugie*, *Konteksty*, and *RIHA Journal*. Her latest book, *Afekt Strzemińskiego: Teoria widzenia, rysunki wojenne, Pamięci przyjaciół—Żydów* (Strzemiński's Affect: Theory of Seeing, War Drawings, In Memory of Friends—Jews), was published in 2018. She is president of the Polish Section of the International Association of Art Critics (AICA).

WHAT DO ARCHIVES FORGET? MEMORY AND HISTORIES, *FROM THE KWIEKULIK ARCHIVE*

Many artworks from East-Central Europe have struggled with the mode of history writing that Piotr Piotrowski defined as vertical. About this mode he wrote:

> [The] vertical narrative implies a certain hierarchy. The heart of modern art is the center—a city or cities—where the paradigms of the main artistic trends came into being: Berlin, Paris, Vienna, London, New York. From those centers particular models come to the periphery, radiating all over the world. [...] Hence, the art of the center determines a specific paradigm, while the art of the periphery is supposed to adopt the models established in the centers. The center provides canons, hierarchy of values, and stylistic norms—it is the role of the periphery to adopt them in a process of reception. It may happen, of course, that the periphery has its own outstanding artists, but their recogni-

> tion, or art-historical consecration, depends on the center: on exhibitions organized in the West and books published in Western countries.[1]

Most of the art projects that have fought to develop a different type of narration and alternative languages of thinking, speaking, and writing about the artistic past in East-Central Europe focus on the archive, information, and knowledge production. One such project was the exhibition curated by Zdenka Badovinac—*Interrupted Histories*, which took place in 2006 at the Moderna galerija in Ljubljana.[2] The exhibition focused on the phenomena of artistic practices and art history that—together with their specific problems—were pushed out, for political or economic reasons, from the mainstream of contemporary historiography. As Badovinac observes in the exhibition catalog (in the form of a binder that can be filled with additional materials), Eastern Bloc countries, with their histories of wars, totalitarian regimes, and ideological repressions, experienced a lack of continuity in the historical course of events, while the dominant method of building both historical narration, as well as the perception of the past in the West was—due to economic dominance, dissemination, and the growth of capitalism—somewhat linear.[3] Badovinac believes that the Western art history represented by museum institutions constructs a narration that is uninterrupted and at the same time hegemonic. In the countries of East-Central Europe, conversely, we are dealing with defragmented collective histories, or spaces of "small historiographies." *Interrupted Histories* undermined not only the phenomenon of historical exclusion and repression, but also revealed

1 Piotr Piotrowski, "Toward a Horizontal History of the European Avant-Garde," trans. Marek Wilczyński, in *European Avant-Garde and Modernism Studies*, eds. Sascha Bru and Peter Nicholls (Berlin: De Gruyter, 2009), 50–51. For more see Piotrowski, "O dwóch głosach historii sztuki," *Artium Quaestiones* XVII (Poznań: Wydawnictwo Naukowe, 2006), 195–214. Piotrowski is the author of the book *In the Shadow of Yalta: Art and the Avant-Garde in Eastern Europe* (London: Reaktion Books, 2009), which focuses on the art of East-Central Europe from the perspective of critical geography and implements a geopolitical "framing." The book is without doubt an outstanding example of constructing a "horizontal history."

2 For more on the exhibition, see Agnieszka Szewczyk, "Sztuka z historii, historia ze sztuki: *Interrupted Histories* w Moderna Galerija w Lublanie," *Obieg*, May 15, 2006, http://archiwum-obieg.u-jazdowski.pl/recenzje/2944.

3 Zdenka Badovinac, "Interrupted Histories," in *Interrupted Histories*, ex. cat. (Ljubljana: Moderna galerija, 2006).

the rich variety, heterogeneity, and lack of claims for any collective treatment of the histories created by artists from East-Central Europe who, from the 1970s onwards, were subject to a double marginalization of sorts—both in the local discourse, and more broadly in the functioning Western idiom of art history.

Badovinac's exhibition included one other project—*East Art Map*[4]—initiated by artists associated with the IRWIN collective, which is important for the historiography of East-Central Europe aimed at "horizontalization." *East Art Map*, whether appearing in the form of a book publication, an exhibition, or a website is, in the words of Marina Gržinić, a type of discourse-based platform.[5] The artists invited art historians from different regions of East-Central Europe to participate. Their task was to propose a narration that described the cultural history of the region they came from. The objective of *East Art Map* was to remove the artists from national frameworks, and simultaneously deprive them of the context of the local mythologies accompanying them. At the same time, there were efforts to represent the art of artists "from this place" according to a somewhat uniform scheme that made it possible to apply an order to and interpret the art made behind the Iron Curtain, to create a system of references respected beyond the borders of East-Central Europe, undermining the foundations of the Grand Narration of art history created in the West. The proposals of the historians who delineated the map (or rather the constellation) of art history in East-Central Europe were subjected to permanent negotiation: upon giving an appropriate justification via the website, one could offer to supplement, add, delete, or replace the suggested artists with others. The motto on the website: "History is not given. Please help to construct it," underlines the provisional character of any historical narration, unmasking the mechanisms of its creation.[6] Not only does *East Art Map*

4 IRWIN, eds., *East Art Map: Contemporary Art and Eastern Europe* (London: Afterall; Cambridge, MA: MIT Press, 2006).

5 A corresponding project, also initiated by IRWIN, is *Mind the Map! History Is Not Given*. For more see Marina Gržinić, "Recenzja dwóch projektów książkowych: *East Art Map* i *Mind the Map! History Is Not Given*," *Obieg* 75–76, nos. 1-2 (2007), suppl. *Gazet'art*, no. 4, xxx–xxxiii.

6 *East Art Map*, last modified 2004, accessed September 12, 2018, http://www.eastartmap.org/.

create an alternative geography vis-a-vis the established map of Western art history but, first and foremost, it offers a history of art that is nonidentical—one that refutes a homogenous and linear vision of the past.

Interrupted Histories and *East Art Map* are just two examples of endeavors that synthesize the issues of documentation, narration, and historical repression in reference to art and the history of art in East-Central Europe. A similar type of opposition to the coherence, linearity, and smoothness of narrations created by either Western or local historiography is represented in Zofia Kulik's *From the KwieKulik Archive*. It was commissioned by Zdenka Badovinac, created in 2006, and presented for the first time at the *Interrupted Histories* exhibition; however, it was not the first of the artist's activities to focus on the problems of the archive, visibility, and art-history writing. It must be emphasized that Zofia Kulik, together with her then-life-and-art-partner Przemysław Kwiek—as the KwieKulik duo—began the Studio of Activities, Documentation and Propagation (Pracownia Działań, Dokumentacji i Upowszechniania, PDDiU) in the early 1970s. The artist, either in tandem with Kwiek or later, independently, used parts of the KwieKulik Archive several times as the fabric in her works.[7]

7 The subject of the usage of "an archive," or more specifically the "KwieKulik Archive" in KwieKulik and/or Kulik's artistic practice, shall be the topic of a separate text and requires detailed studies. I would just like to mention that before 2006 Kulik showed constellations of materials from the KwieKulik Archive under the title "Od sztuki obiektu do sztuki procesu" during the exhibition *Szare w kolorze* (Zachęta National Gallery of Art, Warsaw, 2000); KwieKulik showed documents and materials from their archive in the complex work *The Light of a Dead Star* during the exhibition *Works and Words* in De Appel, Amsterdam (1979); they also attempted to publish another set of documents from the PDDiU in the art periodical *Sztuka* (the materials were published in 1981, but due to the political circumstances—martial law in Poland—this issue of the periodical was censored once more and not distributed; after an intervention KwieKulik gained permission to receive and distribute one hundred and fifty copies of the periodical); parts of the KwieKulik Archive were also exhibited at the Walter Philips Gallery during the *Contemporary Art from Poland* exhibition (Banff, 1985). For more information see Łukasz Ronduda and Georg Schöllhammer, eds., *KwieKulik: Zofia Kulik & Przemysław Kwiek* (Warsaw: Museum of Modern Art in Warsaw and KwieKulik Archive; Wrocław: BWA Wrocław Galleries of Contemporary Art, Awangarda Gallery; Vienna: Kontakt. The Art Collection of Erste Group and ERSTE Foundation, 2012), 150, 163, 190.

In 2006, using the KwieKulik Archive, as well as the power of the affective associations of memory, Kulik made an effort to disturb and bifurcate standard forms of historical narration, with reference both to art in Poland and East-Central Europe, as well as to the Western idiom. Most importantly, however, Kulik formulated the intriguing proposal of constructing history in the crevices between the reading of the archive and the efforts of memory, revealing the issue of histories unwritten and stifled, although remembered and archived in local contexts. Hence she brought up the issue of the symbolic violence of official archives and their affiliated narrations, which dominate in the area of East-Central Europe (Poland, in this case), as well as the need not so much for an indispensable complementation, but rather for reworking and rethinking history anew in its micro-streams.

As mentioned above, the material of Kulik's work, which in this case can be understood both in the sense of a verb or a noun, was the KwieKulik Archive—namely the archive of the PDDiU. This archive, managed by the KwieKulik duo, was collected and maintained in their private two-room flat on Wójcika Street (currently Kłopotowskiego Street) in Warsaw, and later in their house in Łomianki. The PDDiU was "the venue where the artists lived, worked, exhibited, and received guests."[8] KwieKulik not only collected the documentation of their own activities and of other artists, who transgressed the established idioms of art-working and were excluded from the official discourse, but also developed modes of documentation adequate for process-based artistic actions and events. The activities of the PDDiU were aimed in particular at documenting the artists' ephemeral projects of the 1970s, so as to protect them from obscurity and disappearance. "The motive of our documentation efforts in the 1970s was the following: we have to save [...]. We have to act as if we were providing first aid to a wounded one. [...] We did not want to do the work of scientists, to analyze anything, but rather to systematically create a live collection. We were first of all keen on the formula of an emergency service. And needed money for that.

8 Ronduda and Schöllhammer, "Editors' Note," *KwieKulik: Zofia Kulik & Przemysław Kwiek*, 4.

[...] In 1974 we filed an application to the Ministry of Culture and Art asking for a subsidy for the PDDiU, however the only result was the systematically growing binder with documents related to this proposal, nothing more," said Kulik when discussing the issue.[9] Understanding the vital importance of the protection of the vulnerable, ephemeral works, as well as the distribution of information, KwieKulik documented, stored, and exhibited selected materials from the PDDiU, along with exchanged materials from other art archives around the world. In the mid-1980s the KwieKulik duo ceased to exist: Zofia Kulik and Przemysław Kwiek continued their careers as individual artists. Despite the artists' efforts, any attempts to institutionalize the collection failed, whether in 1970, 1990, or 2001.

The location of the documentation collected by the PDDiU had not changed the status of privacy; however, it transformed the inconvenient domestification into a kind of house arrest. In this sense, the KwieKulik Archive is similar to Jacques Derrida's *arkheion*, as described in the famous *Archive Fever*.[10] Derrida claimed that the Greek work *arkheion*, which signified the house of the highest-ranked public officer—the *Archon*—was the root of the Latin words *archivum* and *archium*. Archons, citizens with the highest political authority in ancient Greece, were also seen as those who created and/or represented the law; they became the first guardians of the law's documentation. They not only made sure that the documents were physically safe, but also had the hermeneutical competence to interpret the archives. As Derrida remarked, the documents with which Archons were entrusted constituted the law, required the law, and imposed the law.[11]

The Archonic dimension of authority over interpretation of the PDDiU was ironically underlined and complemented by Kulik's exhibition *From the KwieKulik Archive* and her photographic work *Ambassadors of the Past* (2006), exhibited at Galeria Le Guern in

9 "KwieKulik—sztuka i teoria ilustrowana przypadkami życiowymi czyli sztuka z nerwów, wywiad z Zofią Kulik i Przemysławem Kwiekiem, rozmawiała Maryla Sitkowska, Warszawa 1986–1995," *Kulik-KwieKulik Foundation*, accessed April 21, 2008, http://www.kulikzofia.pl/wywiad.html.

10 Jacques Derrida, "Archive Fever: A Freudian Impression," *Diacritics* 25, no. 2 (Summer 1995): 9–63.

11 Derrida, "Archive Fever," 9–10.

Warsaw in 2006, which followed the model of the famous double allegorical portrait by Hans Holbein.[12] As Kaja Pawełek noted in her analysis of *Ambassadors*:

> In Zofia Kulik's composition, the French diplomats at the English court of King Henry VIII portrayed by Holbein are replaced by the artist herself and Przemysław Kwiek, while the Renaissance allegorical tool-kit has changed into an arsenal of neo-avant-garde transformations of the 1970s—camcorders, cameras, and tape recorders made in Czechoslovakia, the GDR, the USSR, and Poland. It would be difficult to find a more ironic, and at the same time a more metaphorical image of the two artists than as ambassadors—taking into consideration the fact that in the years 1975–79 Kulik and Kwiek were banned from leaving the country, which was a repercussion of the use of their famous term "art barracks" for the state institution of the Visual Arts Studios [Pracownie Sztuk Plastycznych, PSP] published in the 1975 catalog to an exhibition at Malmö Konsthall, as well as their presentation of a sculpture entitled *Man-Dick*. [...] It was the passport photos taken in the hope of leaving the country and participating in Arnhem, attended by [Joseph] Beuys, among others, that Kulik used as portraits for Ambassadors...[13]

In the context of *From the KwieKulik Archive*, it could be suggested that the artist ironically portrayed KwieKulik as clerks, archivists, and at the same time as guardians of the historical narration, never fully expressed, or of identity, never closed. However, the ambassadors—Kwiek and Kulik—who had been locked up in both the "house arrest" of bureaucratic and authoritarian Poland of the late 1970s and their own home archive, returned with their own history, which had the

12 *Made in GDR, USSR, Czechoslovakia and Poland*, Galeria Le Guern, Warsaw, September–November 2006. In the second edition of the exhibition at the Polish Institute in Berlin (June–July 2007), the work was titled *Ambassadors of the Past*, with the additional subtitle *Made in GDR, USSR, Czechoslovakia and Poland*.

13 Kaja Pawełek, "Z archiwum ambasadorów," *Obieg*, November 7, 2006, http://archiwum-obieg.u-jazdowski.pl/recenzje/4020.

power of the excluded. At the same time, Kulik, the creator of *Ambassadors*, gave herself the hermeneutical right or competence to interpret this domesticated archive in its present form, and stressed the exclusion that the PDDiU materials had been subjected to. Kulik changed the symbolic representation of death in Holbein's painting—the anamorphic image of a skull—into a clear representation of the premises of the Center for Contemporary Art (CCA) in Warsaw, one of the few Polish public institutions dedicated to exhibiting and documenting contemporary art (founded in 1981, opened in 1988). The gesture of portraying the CCA in the position of the skull from Holbein's work can be interpreted as both a secret private vendetta, as well as the representation of the phenomenon of the indifference of public artistic institutions in Poland, prior to 2006, towards existing artistic archives and collections of documents of the neo-avant-garde art of the 1960s and 1970s; an indifference that had truly destructive effects both on the vulnerable archival fabric as well as on the galaxies of unwritten histories. Kulik's comments on historical scenarios were not in search of a consensus, but stem from the symbolic antagonism between the history written "in" the archive, and the history developed both "with the help" of and "against" the archive, underlining the one thing that archives forget—namely memory.

From the KwieKulik Archive had an open structure. It was composed of nine tableaux (with the possibility of adding more), tightly filled with copies of prints and photos in most cases (only a few original documents could be found), as well as with descriptions of selected PDDiU documents, which created a sort of a thin gray margin on each tableau. The work was preceded by a text, where the artist explained her understanding of the project. Most of the archival materials had been systematically scanned and reduced in size. The documents and their copies were inscribed in the rectangular frames of the panels, creating colorful, almost ornamental compositions placed in a linear chronological sequence—from 1968 until the mid-1980s. The last photograph, from 2006, which shows the process of preparing one of the pieces for *Interrupted Histories*, could be treated as the full stop at the end of a sentence. This order, however, was distorted within each of the sets of perfect document copies, thus creating temporal whirlpools and either running forward or retrospectively reading past events in a new constellation of meanings. The selection, the chronology, and the mutual relations of documents seemed to be determined by three vectors: excluded histories, the metonymy of experience (Kulik's memory), and the rules of composition that Kulik had developed over the period following the breakup of the KwieKulik duo.

The status of the events and figures represented by the documents, along with their layout (neighborhood, relations), underlined their location in the footnotes of art history in Poland, if not on its margins. Kulik empathically extracted the "weak" narration—all those who had never been part of strong definitions or the categorical divisions, dominant traditions, and institutional-ranking lists: Andrzej Partum, Anastazy B. Wiśniewski, Włodzimierz Borowski, Jerzy Ludwiński, the KwieKulik duo, and Paweł Kwiek.[14] Kulik—the creator of *From the KwieKulik Archive*—did not respect the developed hierarchies and divisions, emphasizing the historical dividing lines rather than making an attempt to eliminate them. She was not interested in sources, but in faded traces and unfinished projects—in all that has been crossed out as not sufficiently important during the editing process of neo-avant-garde art history in Poland (e.g. the project of the Museum of Current Art, the attempts at establishing an Association of Other Media, or Anastazy B. Wiśniewski's Yes-No Gallery). All the facts and events that she found important, such as Oskar Hansen's theory of Open Form and the projects that were based on it (such as the film *Open Form*), as well as games and participations (e.g. *Game on an Actress's Face*, *Game on Morel's Hill*); all the modi operandi developed by KwieKulik (*For-Camera Activities*, *Parasite Art*, *The Art of Commentary*; all the neo-avant-garde artists' meetings (such as the Dreamers' Congress, the meeting in Nowa Ruda, meetings in Osetnica); and places (e.g. the PDDiU, Andrzej Partum's Poetry Office, Galeria EL), form a type of micro-

14 Since 2006 this situation has changed considerably. Some of the abovementioned artists, critics, galleries, and institutions (just to mention Oskar Hansen's theory of Open Form, Jerzy Ludwiński's art criticism, or KwieKulik's art practices) have become important subjects of art-historical inquiries and studies. The art history of the 1960s and 1970s has been systematically opened, written, and rewritten. However, many artistic practices and works still await basic art-historical and curatorial recognition and work.

history. By including in these projects the collected publications (such as *Notatnik Robotnika Sztuki*, *Tango*), exhibition invitations, outdoor art workshops, lectures, or seminars, Kulik reconstructed the map of intellectual references—a circulation of information, contacts, and meeting points of different undertakings—as well as the peculiar Weltanschauung of the artistic environment in which she functioned. Another group of micro-histories was clearly focused on the material living and working conditions of Kwiek and Kulik, illustrating the whole sphere of privacy, politics, and politicality. By reconstructing the whole issue of the so-called *chałtura*,[15] reluctantly recalled by avant-garde artists, Kulik pointed to the artists' humiliating dependence on the state enterprise—the PSP, which was the bestower of commissions for the visual ornamentation of different ideological festivities and celebrations. Paradoxically enough, this institution was also the patron of the avant-garde Galeria Foksal, hermetically sealed to the projects, initiatives, and practices referred to by Kulik. *From the KwieKulik Archive*'s collage of micro-histories functioned as avant-garde shock therapy: it indicated marginalized reasons by fragmenting narration and, at the same time, by omitting the events consecrated by art history in Poland, in the discipline's state of knowledge of neo-avant-garde art circa 2006. Furthermore, Kulik ostentatiously excluded well-established artists, well-known galleries, famous artistic events, etc., as if mocking the logic of the archive described by Derrida. She illustrated the neo-avant-garde ethos as filtered by the requirements of the empty, official language of ideology, the shortcomings of everyday life, as well as all of the red tape. Her history was one of processes and actions, ephemeral projects and vanishing galleries, short-lived printings and publications—limited in copies and published at her own expense, un-granted fellowships, withdrawn passports, isolation and a shortage of information. The constellations of meanings

15 *Chałtura* is a word with an unquestionably negative meaning, difficult to translate [most commonly translated as hackwork. —Ed.]. In Polish it was adopted from the Russian language. It suggests an artistic activity, somewhat embarrassing, undertaken for financial reasons only, which could in some respect negatively affect the "image" of the artist. In the Poland of the 1960s and 1970s the *chałtury* consisted, for example, of the creation (sketching, painting, sculpting, etc.) of the visual frame of official, political, communist ceremonies.

appearing in *From the KwieKulik Archive* revealed, at the same time, facts that had been, in a way, pushed into the realm of the repressed in the spaces of famous Polish art archives. In the case of the archives of Galeria Foksal, this would be their connections with the state-run PSP, or in the broader sense—a dimension of micro-authority permeating the structure of meanings and the dimension of the artistic praxis of the neo-avant-garde in Poland.

These events also performed the function of a metonymy of memory, and delineated the map of Kulik's subjective references in her work. The activities of KwieKulik, and hence the experience of Kulik herself, served as an axis that integrated the narrations emerging from the constellation of documents. The montage of colorful images was not limited to a mosaic of the archived pieces, but also included different traces of memory and the stories told. In the introduction to the colorful tableaux, Kulik even revealed her perspective or role in constructing this history: it was her memory and experience that had been incorporated into the rectangular frames. The reflection emerging from scraps of documents was clear but broken, and identity could not have been restored, as the crevices in the emerging Self are too deep to be able to forget its provisional character. The documents, locked under a glass surface, somewhat resembled another of the artist's works, *From Siberia to Cyberia* (1998–2004). In this case, the archive of television images referred to the issue of a crisis of experience; to a peculiar state of abulia of the subject in a mediatized reality; to the lack of memory; and, as Bożena Czubak notes, to the impotence of history against the overgrowth of visual messages and the mania of historicizing.[16] In the case of *From the KwieKulik Archive* we were presented with a specific "turn towards experience," which meant representations of events that the artist had witnessed, and in which she participated "then." This "then," however, was ever more effective in underlining its absence "now." The image of the archive did not, in this case, contradict memory, but rather played the role of a prosthesis or supplement. In many cases this memory had traces of the memory of trauma; it was related

16 Bożena Czubak, "Od Syberii do Cyberii 1998–2004," in *Zofia Kulik: Od Syberii do Cyberii*, eds. Bożena Czubak and Zofia Kulik (Warsaw: Zachęta National Gallery of Art, 2004), 65.

to the experience of long-term exclusion and the marginalization of politicized artistic activities—in art history, as well as in local artistic circles—which both used and were a parasite on the language of political power. There was a certain aura of nostalgia that accompanied the narrative streams initiated by Kulik; at the same time, there was a feeling of peculiar claustrophobic anxiety reevoked, which emerged from the recollected events, projects, and endeavors, often stigmatized by either lack of fulfillment or abandonment. Kulik's attitude towards the past was ambiguous. The artist herself commented on her joint ventures as part of KwieKulik in the 1970s, referring to the period as a time when she had no say—she had experienced something of a block as an individual.[17] In a few cases she refrained from illustrating events that she (or her circle of friends) saw in traumatic terms. One such event was the publication of Wiesław Borowski's article "Pseudoawangarda" (Pseudo-Avant-Garde, 1975) in the important and influential periodical *Kultura*, where the well-known author, connected to Galeria Foksal, openly condemned art practices focused mostly on the body, sexuality, and everydayness, as practiced by KwieKulik and many other artists of their milieu.[18] The omission of this, however, still played a part: it was an active silence, significant in its meaning. *From the KwieKulik Archive* was a fragmented representation of both awareness and the lack thereof, recalling facts that had been remembered and edited, alongside absent ones, which filled the crevices of the narrations Kulik built. Memory, as proposed by Kulik, resembled the type of narrative memory described by Mieke Bal: it was emotionally colored; it resembled a collection of stories; it was "active and situated in the present."[19] Its social dimension was revealed in the demand for critical reception, in provoking reaction.

17 "The Rebellion of a Neo-Avant-Garde Artist: An Interview with Zofia Kulik Conducted by Joanna Turowicz," *Kulik-KwieKulik Foundation*, accessed June 9, 2018, http://kulikzofia.pl/en/archiwum/bunt-neoawangardowej-artystki/. First published as "Bunt neoawangardowej artystki," in *Artmix*, no. 9 (March 2005).

18 Wiesław Borowski, "Pseudoawangarda," *Kultura*, no. 11 (1975).

19 Mieke Bal, "Introduction," in *Acts of Memory*, eds. Mieke Bal, Jonathan Crewe, and Leo Spitzer (Hanover: University Press of New England, 1999), vii.

The documents integrated within the tableaux were not composed in line with archival procedures, but rather with the use of the visual knowledge present in the works created by Kulik since the late 1980s. Pieces such as *The Guardians of the Spire* (1990), *Square of the Palaces* (1990), *All the Missiles Are One Missile* (1993), and *Who Conquered the World?* (1994) were characterized by the closed structure of an architectural facade or a carpet, an almost obsessive symmetry, and a multiplication of detail, meticulously dissected from the context. *From the KwieKulik Archive* is governed first of all by the principle of accumulation and collation; symmetry appeared only in the documentary micro-courses. The artist did not compare the structure of *From the KwieKulik Archive* to a carpet, which had a closed composition that enabled a symmetrical layout, but to unrolling a "floorcloth" or a runner.[20] The margins, with their descriptions of documents, imposed a unified rhythm, while the archived elements were not sequenced according to the logic of an architectural exterior, but to the interior—the successive cells, rooms, corridors, and compartments. The tableaux were constructed as a collage of sorts, giving order to selected digital copies by means of the procedure of collation. The surface of the documents was exposed, rather than their contents. By integrating them into the rectangles of the tableaux and covering them with glass, a certain discipline was suggested, which was imposed not only on the archived elements but, first and foremost, on the viewer—who was forced to see the entirety of the material and the logic behind the work. The PDDiU was transformed-absorbed by Kulik's then-current artistic practice. The documentation, which was still "telling in itself" when presented at the *Contemporary Art from Poland* exhibition in 1985 in Banff (Walter Philips Gallery [FIG. 1]), was transformed here into a silent (thereby requiring a narrator) ornamental composition. Whilst in Banff KwieKulik's documents were exhibited on tables, inviting the visitor to see their contents, here Kulik barred the viewer from them, thus inciting curiosity about their hidden histories. By doing so, the artist dispelled the illusion of a document as a transparent source, and an archive as a beginning and a space of historical truth; she rather revealed her

20 Kulik, e-mail to the author, April 22, 2008.

story as a narrative construct. Hayden White made the distinction between narration and narrativization in historical discourse: the first notion means opening up to the world and reporting on it; the second pretends that the world speaks for itself.[21] The value of the latter in representing actual events stems from the desire for those events, embedded in the causal sequence, to be marked with cohesion, integrality, fullness, and a certain complete vision of life. White claimed that this value can only be imaginary. In reference to these claims, Kulik's world did not take the form of a tailor-made story; the artist did not create an illusion of reality that would speak for itself (as was the case in Banff in 1985). By composing the copied documents of her archive into a certain visual and narrative form, she rather attempted to take the place of the narrating subject in the discourse of history, intervening at a lower level—namely that of archaeology. Kulik referred to the process of forming and transforming the narration, yet the discourse to which she referred was no longer her own but—to follow Foucault—it delineated the externality of her own language.[22] At the same time, Kulik did not construct an archive that could be measured by means of an authoritarian adequacy of reality; instead, she rather tried to negotiate the space of knowledge between the KwieKulik Archive and other archives (and the histories that they constructed), such as the archives of the Center for Contemporary Art, or of Galeria Foksal. Kulik also made sure to indicate the antagonism that founded these alternative histories.

Like Silvia Kolbowski's *An Inadequate History of Conceptual Art* (1998–99) and Santiago Sierra's *The History of the Foksal Gallery Taught to an Unemployed Ukrainian* (2002), *From the KwieKulik Archive* can be treated as both an artistic and a historical work.[23] Kolbowski's work was

21 Hayden White, "The Value of Narrativity in the Representation of Reality," *Critical Inquiry* 7, no. 1 (Autumn 1980): 5–27.

22 Michel Foucault, *The Archaeology of Knowledge*, trans. A. M. Sheridan Smith (London: Routledge, 1972), 130.

23 I am using this phrase following Mignon Nixon, who used it in reference to the mentioned work by Silvia Kolbowski; see Mignon Nixon, "Oral Histories: Silvia Kolbowski and the Dynamics of Transference," in *Silvia Kolbowski: Inadequate... Like... Power*, ex. cat. (Vienna: Secession, 2003), 93–102.

based on interviews with artists.[24] In the gallery space one could have seen the projection of artists' gesticulating hands, supplemented by their (inadequately adjusted) voices. The work triggered oral histories of conceptual art that were neither previously written nor told, and which engaged anxiety, desire, the question of subjectivity, memory, and loss. Sierra's work utilized four art historians, who explained in detail, and with the mediation of a translator, Galeria Foksal's past to Wiktor, the unemployed Ukrainian.[25] The work can be interpreted as being focused both on historical fissures and the process of memorization, on power and knowledge tensions, and on literal and symbolic exclusion. All three works—Kolbowski's, Sierra's, and Kulik's—refer to the issue of historical repression, the relation of memory and history, and the role of transference in the writing of history; however, the element that makes Kulik's project different from the others is the powerfully emphasized archival impulse that accompanies the artist in her work. As Hal Foster notes in "An Archival Impulse," practices that have an archival impulse not only use, but also establish archives, revealing their elements as simultaneously found and constructed—referring to facts, but at the same time being fictitious.[26] Artists who follow an archival impulse try to construct historical narrations, which have been subject to either denial or displacement. Such an impulse stems from the feeling of emptiness—the absence of significance, of which reality is so disturbingly deprived. Despite the fact that the archival practice of Zofia Kulik was often in line with Foster's abovementioned comments, it was distinctly different from the works analyzed by the author. The

24 Silvia Kolbowski sent the following instruction to sixty selected artists: "Briefly describe a conceptual art work, not your own, of the period between 1965 and 1975, which you personally witnessed/experienced at the time. For the sake of this project, the definition of conceptual art would be broad enough to encompass such phenomena of that period as actions documented through drawings, photographs, film, and video; concepts executed in the form of drawings or photographs; objects where the end product is primarily a record of the precipitant concept, and performative activities which sought to question the conventions of dance and theater." Citation after Rosalyn Deutsche, "Inadequacy," in *Inadequate... Like... Power*, 72.

25 Santiago Sierra, *The History of the Foksal Gallery Taught to an Unemployed Ukrainian* (Warsaw: Galeria Foksal, 2001).

26 Hal Foster, "An Archival Impulse" [abridged ed.], in *The Archive*, ed. Charles Merewether (Cambridge, MA: MIT Press, 2006), 143–48.

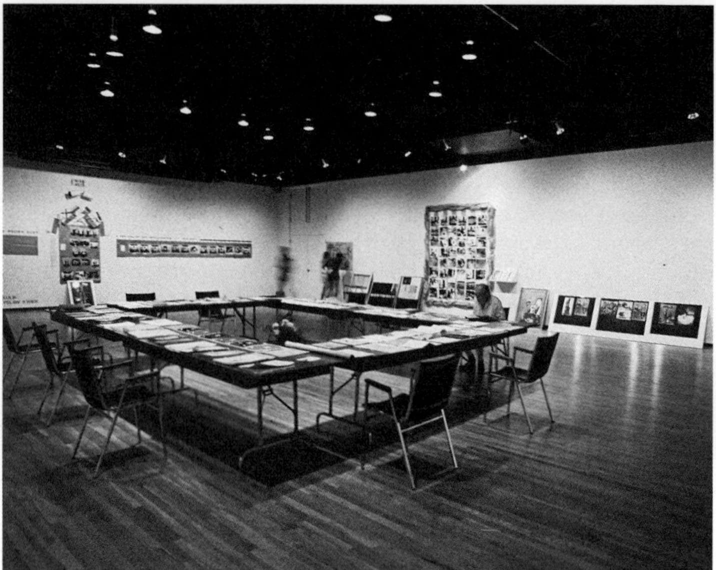

FIG. 1
KWIEKULIK, *ARTISTS' BOOKS, POSTERS, PRINTS, AND CATALOGS*, 1985, EXHIBITION VIEW, *CONTEMPORARY ART FROM POLAND*, WALTER PHILIPS GALLERY, BANFF

archive used in the project was one that actually existed and belonged to the author, but it was also its synecdoche: part of it was speaking on behalf of its entirety. Hence Kulik not so much presented, but rather represented the archive; she constructed her expression using the archive as if it was a sharp tool. However, an archive, as Foucault claims, "cannot be described in its totality; and in its presence it is unavoidable. It emerges in fragments, regions, and levels, more fully, no doubt, and with greater sharpness, the greater the time that separates us from it."[27] By constructing these fragments in some areas and levels of the PDDiU, and by composing constellations of micro-histories (hence making ever new decisions of selection, reduction, and exclusion), the artist became more remote from the KwieKulik Archive, gaining the necessary distance.

From the KwieKulik Archive is a reflection on the peculiar compulsion to collect and archive, articulating the works of the artist created since the late 1980s, which Kulik usually sets against the processual and documentary practice of the 1970s. In that sense *From the KwieKulik Archive* can be seen as an attempt at mediation between the elements of one's own broken history and identity: the remembering, forgetting, and denying. This attempt coincided with the process taking place in art history, which dealt with this period. *From the KwieKulik Archive* does not so much reveal the fictitious character of archival structures and the anomies in archival conditions, but rather indicates the provisional nature and tokenism of the archive, as well as the involvement and enthusiasm once invested in its existence. Kulik emerges as a participant of the history she created, without hiding her empathy for the other participants she presents. As an artist, she also refutes the seemingly objective position of a historian, instead presenting history as an element that is important in creating and transforming current collective and individual identities. As with the practices described by Hal Foster, a certain change in the understanding of an archive took place in *From the KwieKulik Archive*: it was not an "excavation site," but rather a "construction of the meaning" taking place within culture.[28] The sources of

27 Foucault, *The Archaeology of Knowledge*, 130.
28 Foster, "An Archival Impulse," 146.

such artistic projects and undertakings, however, should not be sought in the feeling of the failure of cultural memory and the lack of tradition to which one could refer; on the contrary: as Kulik did not trust the concept of tradition, she used the prosthesis of her archive to return memory to history, to point to their possible affective ties and critical relations.

From the KwieKulik Archive was an aporetic structure par excellence, where the photograph, the document, memory, death, and archival fever were tightly intertwined. This work, unlike the archive described by Derrida, did not forget about memory. It also returned the status of a promise of the future to the archival elements. Constellations of micro-histories gravitated in their disciplining arrangements around the notion of history as a discourse of authority. This aporetic representation of the KwieKulik Archive was a stage for narrative constructions, as well as an arena of the cultural reprocessing of a memory whose fragments had not yet been subject to integration. As Mieke Bal claims, cultural memory is an activity taking place in the present where the past is constantly modified and rewritten.[29] Bal writes that cultural memory is not just anything that "befalls," but something that is actively replayed. The cultural recall proposed by Kulik in 2006 in Ljubljana was mobile, underlining the retroactive order of temporality in which history is submerged, and the constant haunting of the image of the "then" by the "now." This cultural recall gave order both to the memory and to the history of the subject, and made it possible to recapture the subject's experience. By means of projection it also revitalized the vanishing memory, helping to uncover the contours of faded inscriptions. Such a history, filtered through memory and horizontally bifurcating its branches and announcements, created a type of therapy. It was a therapy that, by means of reprocessing, testifying, constructing narrations, provoking reception, and reentering the readings of the past, could have helped not to stabilize, but to open the identity, history, and memory of the "then"—for the future.

Since 2006 the KwieKulik Archive has changed the history of the neo-avant-garde in Poland for good. Considering the recognition of the KwieKulik œuvre, it might even be claimed that it also

29 Bal, "Introduction," in *Acts of Memory*, vii–x.

reached transregional and transnational levels. However, one cannot forget about its nucleus—the never-ending work on the excluded, repressed parts of history, on the historical margins and peripheries defined by its centers. This rich rhizomatic archive, proliferating with knowledge and affect—an archive of actions, processes, activities, performances, and an archive that is in itself performative—still awaits recognition, among other things as a hidden form of historical writing not only about art in Poland or East-Central Europe, but also, perhaps, about art practices in the globalized world. An intuition on how to write about the promise of the KwieKulik Archive in the larger perspective—what it might be, the trace of a potential method or matrix of history buried under the document files and traces of vulnerable artworks stored there, was suggested by Piotr Piotrowski in his text "From Global to Alter-Globalist Art History":

> This method would involve two moves: firstly, horizontal historical cuts of the selected moments in global history and art history and, secondly, comparisons drawn in this perspective. It could be done in various areas—on the transnational, transregional and finally, global level. [...] Art history which would handle such undertaking in the horizontal and comparative perspective [...]—the global undertaking which would involve exposing repressive practices directed towards margins, peripheries both geographically and topographically [...]—I would call alter-globalist art history. [...] Its key feature should be criticism and resistance to centralistic and exclusive art-historical activities and ability to reveal mechanisms of building hierarchy and hegemony as well as repression and denial in the global scale.[30]

Translated by Ewa Kanigowska-Gedroyć

This text was originally published in A Story Differently Told, *ex. cat., Gdańsk: Łaźnia Center for Contemporary Art, 2008; it is published here in a revised version.*

30 Piotrowski, "From Global to Alter-Globalist Art History," trans. Marta Skotnicka, *Teksty Drugie* 1 (2015): 125.

Katarzyna Ruchel-Stockmans teaches contemporary art, photography, and new media at the Vrije Universiteit Brussel (VUB) and at the KASK School of Arts, Ghent. Her research interests include photography and art theory, media archeology, documentary practices, postcolonial theories, Eastern European cultures, history, and representation. She is a member of the Network for Research on Drones and Aesthetics. Her book *Images Performing History* was published in 2015 by the Leuven University Press.

KATARZYNA RUCHEL-STOCKMANS

ZOFIA KULIK'S PERFORMED ARCHIVES

Frequently the best commentator on her own enterprise, Zofia Kulik once described herself as a collector of all sorts of objects: "all my works consist of endless gathering and archivization of the images of this world."[1] As an artist, she incessantly archives the material traces of things, not only of her own and other artists' work, but of virtually everything around her: she photographs objects, situations, television images, staged performances, and compositions. The archetypal collector in the age of technological reproducibility, she concedes to mere reproductions of things she cannot afford to possess.[2] This insatiable archiving process will be analyzed here in its two apparently discrepant aspects. On the one hand, the artist stages a seemingly endless number of well-rehearsed poses in her *Archive of Gestures*. In the playful reversal of gender roles, the gestures performed by the male model question notions of nature, history, femininity, and agency. On the other hand, Kulik accumulates, seem-

1 Katarzyna Kosmala, "The Identity Paradox? Reflections on Fluid Identity of Female Artist," *Culture & Organization* 13, no. 1 (2007): 44.

2 Adam Szymczyk and Andrzej Przywara, "Let the Archeologist Not Put His Shovel Away" (1998), *Kulik-KwieKulik Foundation*, accessed August 16, 2018, http://kulikzofia.pl/en/archiwum/niech-archeolog-nie-odklada-lopaty/.

ingly indiscriminately, large numbers of television screenshots in *From Siberia to Cyberia*. Images of mass gatherings, dances, and military parades trigger reflections on historical representations of collectivity. While different in method and formal result, these extensive cycles reveal the entanglement of the artist's practice with her private life and the collective history she is part of. Ultimately, it appears that the various formats and approaches in these cycles are intertwined, so that, in a sense, all of Kulik's work is about archiving, and all archives eventually lead to self-representation, juxtaposing the private perspective with the grand narrative of history.

It should be noted that the artistic practice discussed in this contribution is marked by a departure from the activities of the artistic duo KwieKulik, which the artist constituted, together with Przemysław Kwiek, in the period from the late 1960s through to the 1980s. Around 1987, just before the collapse of the communist governments in Eastern Europe, Kulik broke with her life and work heretofore. She parted with Kwiek and redirected her artistic force by 180 degrees, embarking on the making of that which KwieKulik both despised and tried to eschew; namely, large-scale tableaux. Much of her work after 1987 is seen as a reaction to her former self, both in the private and public spheres. The clearing of accounts with Kwiek—as partners, as performers, and communist citizens—is central to that approach, sometimes leading to a reductive view of her activity. Apart from that ineluctable element of revenge, however, her work is a confrontation with the artistic principles of modernism and its claims. Through her reckoning with the theory of Open Form developed by Oskar Hansen, Kulik's work examines the contradictions intrinsic to the modernist project. By exposing the aporias of gender roles, she offers a valuable reconsideration of the status of history within modernism. She achieves this by confronting different strands within modernism with the traditions of the "other" Europe, which leads her historiographic endeavor close to the redefinitions of modernism conducted, for example, by Boris Groys and Vladislav Todorov.[3]

3 Boris Groys, *The Total Art of Stalinism: Avant-Garde, Aesthetic Dictatorship, and Beyond*, trans. Charles Rougle (Princeton: Princeton University Press, 1992); Vladislav Todorov, *Red Square, Black Square: Organon for Revolutionary Imagination* (New York: State University of New York Press, 1995).

Recognizing that her work often functions as a "quotation from the East" inserted into the international narratives of art—as was the case with the *Wanderlieder* exhibition in 1991, *New Histories* in 1996, or even *Documenta 12* in 2007—Kulik attempts to question the label and investigates her own conditioning by historical circumstances.[4] She takes on the role of a mediator of the Eastern European mindset, who carefully observes globalized culture in order to find the right angle from which to expose local issues. When seen in the Polish context, however, she should equally be viewed as an artist straddling two distinct worlds, which are separated by both a historical and a generational gap. Belonging to the generation that emerged before 1989, she has nevertheless turned towards the artistic language and concerns of the younger generation that came after that date. This duality is visible in her double biography. In its first stage she embraced the principles distinctive for the artistic generation which came of age in the 1970s, such as processual, ephemeral, and collaborative work, although she always struggled with her own propensity for art centered on an object. Simultaneously, with her activity in the KwieKulik duo, she engaged in a process of writing the art history of her generation by amassing an extensive archive of ephemeral actions and documentation of other artists' work.[5] When, in 1987, her work underwent a radical turn, her decision was precipitated by, among other factors, the influence of the younger generation of artists. Kulik has admitted to being persuaded by artists such as Andrzej Partum, Zbigniew Libera, and Jerzy Truszkowski to revisit the traditional notion of the artwork.[6]

4 "Bądź tylko posłusznym psychofizycznym instrumentem: Wywiad z Zofią Kulik; Rozmawiał Ryszard Ziarkiewicz," *Magazyn Sztuki*, no. 1 (1993): 12–21; Anna Zielińska and Anna Rosińska, "I Wish to Be in a Museum" (1999), *Kulik-KwieKulik Foundation*, accessed August 16, 2018, http://kulikzofia.pl/en/archiwum/chce-byc-w-muzeum/.

5 It has been repeatedly stressed that Kulik's archive, collected as the Studio of Activities, Documentation and Propagation (Pracownia Działań, Dokumentacji i Upowszechniania, PDDiU), forms a unique source for the study of the art of the period. See "An E-Mail Conversation between Zofia Kulik and Marek Bartelik," *Kulik-KwieKulik Foundation*, accessed June 9, 2018, http://kulikzofia.pl/en/archiwum/rozmowa-internetowa-z-zofia-kulik-rozmawial-marek-bartelik; Karol Sienkiewicz, "Zofia Kulik oraz KwieKulik—Duet z Przemysławem Kwiekiem," *Culture.pl*, June 2008, http://www.culture.pl/pl/culture/artykuly/os_kulik_zofia. See also Luiza Nader's essay in this volume.

6 "Bądź tylko posłusznym psychofizycznym instrumentem."

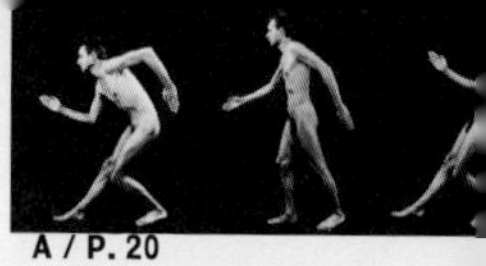

A / P. 20

Archivizing Past Bodies

The first such reassessment of the art object and the artistic representation of the human body can be found in Zofia Kulik's **ARCHIVE OF GESTURES** A (1987–91). The work consists of series of black-and-white photographs showing a single male model performing various gestures and figures. The model's poses, derived from rhetoric, antique sculpture, and different iconographic traditions or ornamental patterns, come together in one vast repertory of images. As the result of a chance encounter, younger artist Zbigniew Libera—the model in all the photographs—became the voiceless substitute for Kulik's previous companion, Przemysław Kwiek. Far from being another form of artistic collaboration, this project of photographed "bodily motifs" is Kulik's individual enterprise. While it bears many signs of an active reworking of her private experiences, it implicitly revisits the collective past she is part of. Libera's role is passive, his contribution to the project consisting of possessing the right kind of body (slender and lean) and dutifully performing the prescribed figures.[7]

The extensive *Archive of Gestures* comprises approximately seven hundred photographs showing the same male model, often assuming the most demanding poses. Some of the frames resemble the experiments with movement undertaken by Muybridge, such as, for example, the sequence of Libera marching. Yet they are staged and photographed in motionless positions, ostensibly imitating movements predesigned by the artist. Other poses are shaped in geometric patterns, echoing the 16th-century anthropomorphic alphabet of Peter Flötner. But most compelling of all are the poses drawn from commonly identified images, artworks, monuments, or emblems. Kulik rehearses representations of the body that are firmly embedded in collective memory, among them those stemming from paintings by Jacques-Louis David, Hans Memling, Wil-

7 "An E-Mail Conversation between Zofia Kulik and Marek Bartelik."

liam Blake, Artur Grottger, or Lucas Cranach and El Greco.[8] Delving into this immense depository, one can recognize some of the sources more easily than others. For example, the figure with spread arms and legs resembles Leonardo da Vinci's Vitruvian Man, whereas a similar figure invokes Blake's Albion. There are also several versions of a well-known pose of the dead Christ. The fact that these are more recognizable is due to the closeness of Kulik's imitations to the original depictions; they are also images of a nude man, and therefore come as no surprise in this collection. But there are many other gestures imitated from paintings or monuments that were not originally shown as nudes and can therefore appear surprisingly incongruous. A disrobed politician or a warrior evokes new, contradictory meanings. This is also the case with various military poses, where the male nude holds a spear. One of the most notorious images imitates the Hitler salute (or *Heil Hitler*), giving it a particularly comic twist. The imitation of powerful, authoritative, and ballistic gestures turns them into farce.

Drawing extensively on Nazi iconography, Kulik makes her model appear as a swastika. At other times, she chooses less specific, but primarily heroic, military, or political gestures. One of these derives from the omnipresent figure of Lenin, as known from the monument by G. D. Alekseev, *Calling Leader*.[9] This in fact depicts an ancient posture, identified in rhetorical vocabulary as "the orator" and demonstrated in the *Aulus Metellus* sculpture. Both the Roman

8 Lesser-known outside Poland, Artur Grottger (1837–67) was one of the key figures of Polish Romanticism. Although, conforming to the "Romantic Ideal," Grottger died very young, he nevertheless furnished the most influential images of the Polish uprising movement in the 19th century. His cycles of chalk drawings on cardboard entitled *Polonia* and *Lithuania* comprised allegorical and idealized representations that fed into the Polish nationalist movement in the difficult period of partitions, and remained exemplary depictions of civil and moral virtues. Kulik's reference to the artist attests to her interest in reassessing the Polish Romantic, nationalist imagination. On the female allegories of Poland, see Maria Janion, "Polonia powielona," in *Niesamowita Słowiańszczyzna: Fantazmaty literatury* (Kraków: Wydawnictwo Literackie, 2006), 257–99.

9 The characteristic pose of Lenin in this monument was endlessly reproduced and transposed in various Soviet photomontages. See, for example, Aleksander Rodchenko's posters reproduced in Piotr Piotrowski, *Artysta między rewolucją i reakcją: Studium z zakresu etycznej historii sztuki awangardy rosyjskiej* (Poznań: Wydawnictwo Naukowe UAM, 1993), 76–77.

orator and Lenin are dressed in a way that speaks of their relative epochs and positions; Libera, however, is completely naked, which renders his act ambiguous. Not only does his nakedness pervert the meaning of the gesture, but it is also no longer clear who exactly he is imitating: the ancient *Aulus Metellus*, a protagonist from the imagery of the French Revolution, a 20th-century demagogue such as Lenin, or maybe... Walt Disney?[10] The neutral presentation of *Archive of Gestures*, limited to an act of imitating a bodily disposition, is further intensified by Libera's deadpan facial expression. His impassivity is totally inconsistent with the often agitated or dramatic gestures. Libera is obediently acting out prescribed poses without engaging in them emotionally; Kulik sees him as an object of scientific study who meticulously (but impassively) fulfils his duties. His deadpan attitude gives the whole *Archive* a unifying quality, being one of the "constant" elements next to the neutral background and uniform size of the photographs. It is his body that obeys and conforms to the rules and orders of the artist, and which therefore carries all of the meaning.

It has been noted that in *Archive of Gestures* Kulik reverses canons and conventions in depicting the male body.[11] The relationship between the male artist and the female model, established especially in the context of 19th-century academic art production, entailed well-defined divisions between gender roles, artistic activity, gaze, and subjectivity. In order to see Kulik's complex reworking of that tradition, it is necessary to look at the practice of studio artists in the classic period of monumental academic painting. The epic scale of Kulik's endeavor brings her paradoxically close to that tradition, exposing its tacit assumptions about gender difference. The archival mode of collecting gestures reveals itself as a vehicle for her relentless critique.

10 I'm referring here to the *Partners* statue in Magic Kingdom Park, Walt Disney World Resort, sculpted by Blaine Gibson in 1995. An allusion to Disney will return below in the discussion of Kulik's photomontage *From Siberia to Cyberia*.

11 Izabela Kowalczyk, "The Geometry of Power in Zofia Kulik's Work," *n.paradoxa*, online issue no. 11 (October 1999): 19–25, https://www.ktpress.co.uk/pdf/nparadoxaissue11.pdf; Izabela Kowalczyk, *Ciało i władza: Polska sztuka krytyczna lat 90.* (Warsaw: Wydawnictwo Sic!, 2002).

The Painter's Studio and Kulik's Studio

Early modern painting was based on detailed anatomical studies of the human body; the male nude, especially, was thoroughly scrutinized before it was represented. Even if the female nude was predominant throughout Western art from the 17th century onwards, for a long time it was both more acceptable in moral terms and more widely practiced to work from a male model.[12] As a result, Abigail Solomon-Godeau notes, the male figure was depicted with more empirical attention than the female nude, for the simple reason that male models were more accessible than female ones.[13] As classical academic teaching prescribed assiduous drawn studies of the body before the final composition could be realized, the presence of a naked male model in the academy or the artist's studio was a common occurrence.[14]

A significant change in this practice was made possible by the invention of photographic technique. Since its introduction in studio practice, the mechanically precise image could be used in the study of poses and physical features—as an addition to, or even instead of, life drawing. Some late-19th-century painters staged and photographed whole compositions with models and props in order to facilitate the process of painting. It is important to note, however, that photography itself served as an auxiliary medium. The making of a grand historical scene in the academic style of the late 19th century could therefore proceed as follows. First, life models in various poses were studied in order to improve drawing skills. Painters often worked directly from photographs, either created especially for that purpose or prefabricated in one of the flourishing photographic ate-

12 Kenneth Clark, *The Nude: A Study of Ideal Art* (Harmondsworth: Penguin, 1960), 343.

13 Abigail Solomon-Godeau, "The Other Side of Vertu: Alternative Masculinities in the Crucible of Revolution," *Art Journal* 56, no. 2 (1997): 55. On the traditional discourse of art history favoring the scheme of male artist and female model, see Susan Waller, "Professional Poseurs: The Male Model in the Ecole des Beaux-Arts and the Popular Imagination," *Oxford Art Journal* 25, no. 2 (2002): 43–64.

14 Kenneth Clark speaks of the difference between the naked and the nude as a shift from the actual to the ideal. Kulik reverses that as well—her model is an actual body assuming ideal poses. Lynda Nead, *The Female Nude: Art, Obscenity and Sexuality* (London: Routledge, 1992), 14.

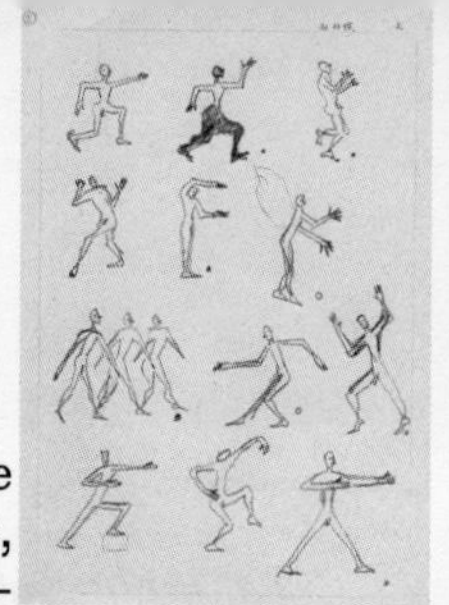

B

liers of the time. Further, the artist staged the whole composition and had it photographed with life models, mannequins, and props. On the basis of these preliminary studies, he could begin working on the canvas.

In her vast photographic murals, Kulik reverses this process. She also uses drawing, studies traditional poses, works with a model, and uses photography; yet she is not a painter, and her final work consists not of paintings, but of vast photographic compositions made with the technique of combination printing. Interestingly enough, she follows a working method that is as complex as that of the traditional history painter, although she changes its order and subverts its goals. She first designs the various poses and gestures of the male body, making numerous **DRAWINGS** B (1987–ONWARDS) and studies. Some of the compositions come directly from art-history textbooks, while others are invented by her or transposed from her individual experience.

Only at a subsequent stage does she require her model, Libera, to imitate the drawings, often forcing the real body to take on near-impossible physical poses.[15] She photographs the staged model against a neutral background, usually without props or clothing, relying only on the body to convey meaningful gestures. Her relationship to the grand academic tradition is ambiguous. When she draws her examples from artworks, she actually remains very close to the prescriptions of French academia, where students were taught to imitate the Old Masters before they were allowed to make studies from life models.[16] Nevertheless, unlike the conven-

15 Zbigniew Libera's submissiveness to Kulik's goals reappears in his own artistic projects, where the disciplining of the body is one of the main themes. Moreover, the fact that he is an artist lends a resemblance to Kulik's earlier artistic activity in the KwieKulik duo. Especially in the performances of the 1970s, Kulik was the passive, voiceless partner. In her work with Libera, the roles are drastically reversed, and the male collaborator is a mere executor of her ideas.

16 Waller, "Professional Poseurs," 46.

tion of the grand style in painting, her subsequent infliction of the desired bodily gesture on the model is final—she takes a photograph of the posing nude as if it were a document of a performance.[17]

Therefore, what connects Kulik to the academic tradition is her studious repetition of classical gestures and poses. The difference between the two approaches, however, is decisive: on one side is the traditional method of studying the life model in order to transpose the image of the body into an idealized artistic representation; on the other, the method that Kulik applies is based on the treatment of a real body as raw material that is compounded and framed according to a predesigned image. Only when the composition is ready is the "docile" body photographed. This reversal of the artistic process in Kulik's practice means not only the recognition of photography as an equal medium, but is also an allusion to the effect that art—or rather visual representation in general—has on the real world, and on the physical body in particular. Past images of bodies—whether they are frozen in poses from history paintings, monuments, or photographs—provide the mold in which the model's body has to fit. By exercising similar studiousness in learning from tradition, Kulik imposes her subversive commentary on this bodily "inheritance."[18]

The Language of Gesture

The ambiguity arising from such transformations of "borrowed" gestures hints at the subversive character of Kulik's archival enterprise. The gestures that she took from history painting or monumental sculpture are conventionally recognized as

17 As noted earlier, Kulik's work evolved from her earlier practice in KwieKulik, e.g. *Documented Activities* or *Activities for a Camera*, in which similar motives and gestures appeared. For a definition of these actions see Łukasz Ronduda and Georg Schöllhammer, eds., *KwieKulik: Zofia Kulik & Przemysław Kwiek* (Warsaw: Museum of Modern Art in Warsaw and KwieKulik Archive; Wrocław: BWA Wrocław Galleries of Contemporary Art, Awangarda Gallery; Vienna: Kontakt. The Art Collection of Erste Group and ERSTE Foundation, 2012), 465. Kulik's transition to still images and minute compositions bears a clear resemblance to her earlier preoccupation with documenting ephemeral actions.

18 A similar idea of a critique was developed by Roland Barthes in "Encore Le Corps," *Critique: Revue Générale des Publications Françaises et Étrangère* 38, no. 423–24 (1982): 645–54.

meaningful rhetorical signs. They already functioned as such in antiquity and constituted an archaic—some even say primordial—form of language from which spoken languages developed.[19] As such, they were employed in the visual arts, especially in periods when the narrative aspect of the image was a particularly sought-after quality. Therefore, when the academy artists of the 18th and 19th centuries studied various poses from the Old Masters, they learned not only the techniques of draughtsmanship, but also acquired suitable pictorial conventions and visual codes. For that reason, life models were often posed "in the manner of Antique sculptures."[20] The body, in this tradition, conveyed social meaning, which was provided by a generally accepted convention. W. J. T. Mitchell says that "'gesturality' as such [...] captures one of the central features of Western history painting, the language of the human body as a vehicle for narrative, dramatic, and allegorical signification."[21] Mitchell refers to this tradition in order to criticize it, suggesting the superficial literalness of putting words into gestures. Yet Kulik seems to be consciously reviving this denigrated understanding of the visual arts, where the language of gesture is stereotypical and derivative. By employing the flatness of expression in her model she reduces the possibility of individual meaning behind the convention. She literally employs the same body, always photographing one model, to convey the very different "meanings" traditionally bound to certain poses.

When comparing Kulik's artistic strategy to the academic tradition, one can notice a similar constancy of models. James H. Rubin remarks that, at a certain moment in the history of the

19 An interesting theory of gesture as the universal language of man can be found in the 17th-century treatises by John Bulwer entitled *Chirologia, Or, the Natural Language of the Hand Whereunto Is Added Chironomia, Or the Art of Manual Rhetoric* (New York: AMS Press, 1975) and *Pathomyotomia, Or a Dissection of the Significative Muscles of the Affections of the Minde*, published in London in 1649. Stephen Greenblatt, "Toward a Universal Language of Motion: Reflections on a Seventeenth-Century Muscle Man," in *Choreographing History*, ed. Susan Leigh Foster (Bloomington: Indiana University Press, 1995), 25–31.

20 Richard Thomson, "The Creative Copy in Late Nineteenth-Century French Art," in *Drawing: Masters and Methods: Raphael to Redon: Papers Presented to the Ian Woodner Master Drawings Symposium at the Royal Academy of Arts, London*, ed. Diana Dethloff (London: Harry N. Abrams Inc., 1992), 23.

21 W. J. T. Mitchell, *Picture Theory: Essays on Verbal and Visual Representation* (Chicago: University of Chicago Press, 1995), 26.

French Academy, a particularly suitable model named Descamps was employed for a very long time. As a result, he was studied for "almost all the figures of painting of the French school." One can ask how this was possible and why it is not visible when looking at the paintings produced by the members of the academy. "Given the variety of life drawings it is amazing to learn that for more than forty years the same model was employed," states Rubin.[22] The answer lies in the fact that what was studied from the life model was still very distanced from the final goal, which was an idealized composition: the model Descamps could be used to practice the gestures of female characters, but eventually a woman would be placed in the picture. The similar suitability of a single model leads Kulik to expose this practice of exercising figures with one and the same male body, yet, unlike her 19th-century predecessors, she does so without concealing her working process. Kulik allows the repetitive use of the model to play an important part in her endeavor. Her project of gathering all meaningful gestures, supplemented by purely ornamental, geometric poses, resembles a visual dictionary of theatrical tricks or a manual of decorum. She isolates the gestures from their contexts and brings them together in a peculiar taxonomy of poses. Once-meaningful signs lose their connotations and become mere ornamental motifs, ready to be redeployed in different configurations. The sheer quantity and repetitiveness of this collection of gestures, poses, and ornamental patterns performed by a male model reminds one of the inevitable tensions in representing the human body. As James Elkins demonstrates, images of bodies gravitate towards either embodiment and materiality, or geometry and formality. When the bias towards geometry dominates, the bodies turn into an alphabet.[23] Kulik's use of photography reasserts the anti-idealizing, flattening effect of the archive, as her photographs demonstrate—paraphrasing Rubin—the "meanness of the naked rather than the nude."[24]

22 James H. Rubin, "Concepts and Consequences in Eighteenth-Century French Life-Drawing," in *Drawing: Masters and Methods*.

23 James Elkins, *Pictures of the Body: Pain and Metamorphosis* (Stanford: Stanford University Press, 1999), 245–84.

24 Rubin, "Concepts and Consequences," 18.

Gender Trouble

The nudity and neutrality of this still-image theater allows Kulik to smuggle in peculiar incongruities. Under closer scrutiny, on several occasions it appears that Libera is—like the French model Descamps—assuming female roles. In one of the early frames, an etching of Polish Romantic artist Artur Grottger is staged, with Libera and Kulik herself playing out a tableau vivant. However, the original roles of the patriotic artist and the angelic muse who encourages him to revisit images of war are reversed, since Kulik assumes the pose of the man and the half-naked Libera embodies the muse.

Even when Libera is not imitating a female protagonist, his renditions of the dead body of Christ or a martyr bear some feminine qualities. This is visible in his representations of conventionally male protagonists, which reveal the deficiencies of the model. His body is entirely vulnerable and exposed, which turns his bellicose and heroic poses into farce. If the 20th-century iconography of war (be it fascist or communist) propagated the masculine body as armor, thus idealizing the figure of the warrior or soldier, then Libera's body appears utterly defenseless and weak.[25] Following Kenneth Clark, one could say that this archive of motifs irritates or even embarrasses the viewer because of its "unresolved mixture of conventions," as was the case with 16th-century painter Jan Gossaert, who, according to Clark, carelessly mixed Flemish realism with Italian composition. On yet another level, this archive of gestures exposes the constructed nature of gender that lies at the heart of the European tradition. The manifest incongruities in the representation of "male" and "female" make it possible to experience how certain postures are bound to one and excluded from the other. Here, Kulik uses a similar strategy to Anthony Gormley's sculptural work, in which, quoting W. J. T. Mitchell's interpretation, "figures

25 Compare Walter Benjamin's discussion of fascism based on Marinetti's quotation about the dreamt-of metallization of the human body during war, in Benjamin, "The Work of Art in the Age of Mechanical Reproduction," in *Illuminations*, ed. Hannah Arendt, rev. ed. (1969; repr., New York: Schocken Books, 2007), 241. For another interesting discussion of these issues, see Hal Foster, "Armor Fou," *October* 56 (Spring 1991): 65–97.

express mixed messages about the relation of sex and gender, the 'intractable' facts of the material, biological body and its 'constructed' cultural form."[26]

The reversal of traditional artistic procedures from the 19th-century studio painter runs in parallel with the supposed reversal of gender roles noted by Ewa Lajer-Burcharth, Izabela Kowalczyk, and Piotr Piotrowski, among others.[27] In an obvious way, a female artist photographing a male model undoes the classical division between the artistic genius and his (passive) muse. Yet Kulik's work cannot be fully explained by pointing to this reversed opposition. Admittedly, her childhood experience must have instilled in her the dualism of her father's military discipline and her mother's "soft" and sensuous craft as a seamstress.[28] Because her father was an army officer, her family lived in military quarters for some time, surrounded by drill and discipline. Simultaneously, her mother worked at home, constantly receiving female customers in a house filled with scraps of cloth, unfinished models, and stencils. The neat oppositionality of these two worlds crossing each other at the heart of the artist's home is a curious coincidence that must have left its mark on the way Kulik interacted with the outside world as a mature artist.[29] She summarizes this double influence by saying that she started to depict the content of her father using the form of her mother.[30] Some commentators hastily project this oppositionality onto the artist's attitude towards her own past in the KwieKulik duo, finding yet another confirmation for a feminist reading of her post-1987 work. Admittedly, this interpretation remains valid, especially

26 W. J. T. Mitchell, *What Do Pictures Want? The Lives and Loves of Images* (Chicago: University of Chicago Press, 2005), 225.

27 Kowalczyk, *Ciało i władza*, 118–28; Ewa Lajer-Burcharth, "Old Histories: Zofia Kulik's Ironic Recollections," in *New Histories*, ex. cat. (Boston: Institute of Contemporary Art, 1996), 119–36 (reprinted in this volume); Piotr Piotrowski, "Between Siberia and Cyberia: On the Art of Zofia Kulik and on Museums," in *Zofia Kulik: Od Syberii do Cyberii / From Siberia to Cyberia*, eds. Kulik and Piotrowski (Poznań: National Museum, 1999), 7–33.

28 Izabela Kowalczyk and Zofia Kulik, "Zofia Kulik: Authority Also Has a Body" (2002), *Kulik-KwieKulik Foundation*, accessed August 16, 2018, http://kulikzofia.pl/en/archiwum/wladza-tez-ma-cialo/.

29 Kowalczyk and Kulik, "Zofia Kulik: Authority Also Has a Body."

30 Sarah C. Wilson, " Discovering the Psyche: Zofia Kulik," in *Zofia Kulik: Od Syberii do Cyberii*, 53–73.

since it is confirmed by the early statements of the artist, who remarked that she wanted to take revenge with "every weapon (symbolic and formal)" that had been used against her.[31] Nevertheless, my contention is that this does not exhaust the meanings of Kulik's engagement with the past. Her seeming reversal of oppositions such as male/female often proves to be their disguised repetition, thus exposing the limits of binary modes of thinking. The play and interchangeability of male and female gestures in the *Archive of Gestures* appears, using Louis Adrian Montrose's words, to "counter the logic of inversion in European categories of thought."[32]

In his peculiar intellectual biography of Jules Michelet, Roland Barthes describes the dualist thinking of the 19th-century historian in terms of the opposition of male and female: "Woman begins where History ends," he states.[33] In this account of the 19th-century worldview, the juxtaposition of history and nature, and of public and private life, are concomitant with the gender division of roles, statuses, and—importantly for this analysis—temporalities. The male is associated with the office, the public sphere, and linear history, and the female is relegated to the home, the nourishing of children, and the cyclical idea of time. In parallel fashion, the male is the maker and the artist, while the female is the object of his gaze—his model and muse. The passive woman is thus an inversion of the active man, and any possible progress in society or development of history entails suppressing nature, materiality, and the feminine.[34] Kulik's *Archive of Gestures* appears to enter into a playful dialogue with this tradition of thinking, revisiting its effects in the artist's studio, and continuing through the statesman's office to the warrior's armaments and the historian's notion of time.

31 Kowalczyk, "The Geometry of Power in the Zofia Kulik's Work," 19.

32 Louis Adrian Montrose, "'Shaping Fantasies': Figurations of Gender and Power in Elizabethan Culture," *Representations*, no. 2 (1983): 88.

33 Roland Barthes, *Michelet*, trans. Richard Howard, rev. ed. (1954; repr., Oxford: Blackwell, 1987), 148.

34 Bonnie G. Smith, *The Gender of History: Men, Women, and Historical Practice* (Cambridge, MA: Harvard University Press, 1998), 149–50.

As a result, Kulik's archive exposes the constructed nature of gender roles. The confusion generated by her strategy of mixing historical traditions and registers is exacerbated by the neutral, inconspicuous presentation of poses, making it difficult at first sight to trace their origins. Compared to Aby Warburg's *Atlas*, this taxonomy of gestures extracts the bodily disposition from any historically specific details, thus leaving the original image and the iconographic genealogy of gesture behind. Using concepts developed by Giorgio Agamben, it could be said that this archive pertains to the recollection not so much of images, but of forgotten gestures, as a sheer communication of communicability.[35] An archaic sign language brought into this particular archive confuses the established representations of the male—immersed in history—and the female, linked to nurture and nature. In this playful reversal, new divisions are established between the female artist-spectator directing the male model to reenact history.

The Carpet of Visual History

If *Archive of Gestures* is a potentially endless lexicon of borrowed or invented poses imposed on a docile model, *From Siberia to Cyberia* is a monumental photomural that assumes an open-ended form, amenable to being continuously expanded in a horizontal sequence. This piece also ingeniously demonstrates how archival practice—a steady undercurrent throughout all of Kulik's activities—may at some point result in an accomplished work. The monumental grid of small, identical black-and-white frames that make up the montage have been continuously collected by the artist since the 1970s, possibly without any definitive idea of how and when they would fit into a concrete artwork. Some of the images have been used in various other compositions, such as *May Day Mass* (1990).

From Siberia to Cyberia consists of screenshots of the artist's television set at home. The frames are arranged chronologically, beginning in 1978 and ending in 2004, shortly before the first

35 Giorgio Agamben, "Notes on Gesture," in *Means without End: Notes on Politics* (Minneapolis: University of Minnesota Press, 2000), 59.

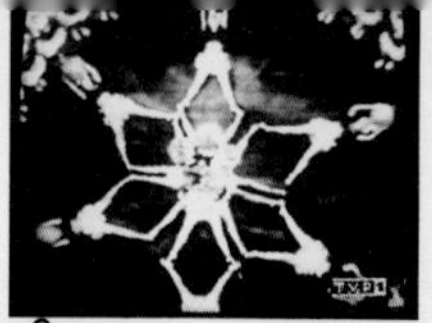

C

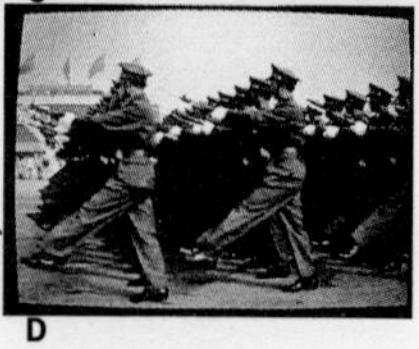

D

presentation of the work.[36] They are arranged in monumental panels that can be extended horizontally and which, when seen from a distance, reveal a pattern of white (empty) frames arranged in a zigzag, underscoring the horizontal flow of the sequences. This macroperspective gives the impression of an overwhelming mass of undifferentiated small pictures, which lose their specific content and become building blocks in the endless, monumental carpet. Nevertheless, on closer inspection, the panels make it possible to view each frame clearly and distinctly, revealing a complex web of parallel stories. The extensive catalog accompanying the work contains captions for each frame or sequence of frames, detailing quotations, the titles of programs, and, sometimes, the artist's comments on the content of the broadcasts.[37] The mural can thus be read and analyzed as if it was a visual book of a televised reality. It is the world as "edutainment," available to the housewife spending long hours in the kitchen. Belonging initially to the artists' ménage, and later to Kulik alone, this kitchen became the locale for cultural analysis and archivization through ongoing recording. This practice can thus be seen as a compromise—a diversion that could be perfectly combined with the female artist's household chores. Initially, Kulik photographed the broadcasted programs directly; later, she recorded sections of programs, which she then photographed more precisely from the video recordings.

Although virtually any theme can be found in this seemingly all-encompassing collection of images, several types of scene stand out. Dancers, gymnasts, and acrobats return almost as frequently as military parades and marches, alternating with scientific, ethnographic, and natural science programs. However, a single theme seems to dominate the collection—namely the political history of the

36 There are two versions of *From Siberia to Cyberia*. The first, smaller one was presented in 1999 at the National Museum in Poznań and at the exhibition *After the Wall* in Stockholm and Berlin. The second, larger version, which was made for solo exhibitions in Warsaw and Kraków in 2004, included newer images and was accompanied by a catalog. Kulik, personal communication with the author, 2014.

37 Bożena Czubak and Zofia Kulik, eds., *Zofia Kulik: Od Syberii do Cyberii* (Warsaw: Zachęta National Gallery of Art, 2004).

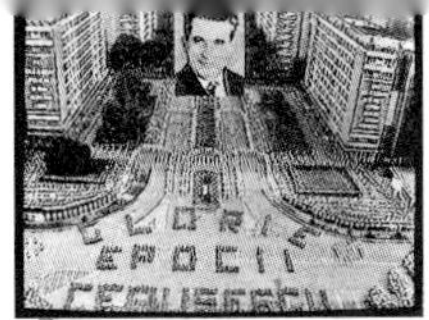

E

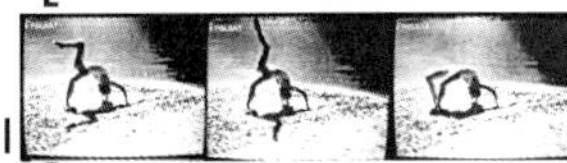

F

20th century. Many images of war, political oppression, and the spectacle of power and mass death evoke what Didi-Huberman described as "the night of history."[38] Panel 12, for example, shows several frames featuring geometrical figures performed by female gymnasts, either in a water ballet from the 1930s or in top-down views of dancers' legs arranged in a star shape (**PANEL 12, J2** [C]). The subsequent rows of frames are devoted to a radically different subject—that of the Second World War and other military conflicts, illustrated on panels filled with endless images of soldiers, artillery, and military actions. The themes of dance and entertainment seem distant from those of war and militarism; perhaps they appear next to each other only because this was the sequence of programs viewed by the artist during a particular period. However, two scenes on Panel 12 indicate that they are, to some extent, connected. Frames I2–3 show the Hollywood-style dancing girls in rows, each holding a large rifle this time, imitating a military parade or perhaps entertaining an army audience.

Continuing this conjunction of the two disparate themes of entertainment and militarism, the geometric figures of gymnasts or dancers are often shown next to mass rallies such as those held in communist China (**PANEL 18, K1** [D]), Ceauşescu's Romania (**PANEL 02, F4** [E]), or at the 10th-Anniversary Stadium in Warsaw. The gymnastic figures of Eva Braun (**PANEL 79, G4–6** [F]) seem to be reflected in the pre-cinematic visual experiments of Marey (Panel 31), and, in a perverse manner, in the emaciated and mutilated bodies of the victims of Stalin and Hitler. On the other hand, the geometric arrangements of dancers are echoed by the scientific images of microscopic genetic structures or the fractal models on **PANELS 163, I1, F5, G5**.[G]

On closer scrutiny, it becomes clear that the gesture of Libera the model, described above as the orator or as Lenin, has many incongruent sources. Countless images of political leaders, including Stalin, Mao, Hitler, Castro, and Ceauşescu, reappear on the grid,

38 Georges Didi-Huberman, "Image, Histoire, Désastre," in *L'image et les traversées de L'histoire: Figures de L'art; Revue d'etudes Esthétiques*, ed. Isabelle Alzieu and Dominique Clévenot (Pau: PUP, 2008), 29.

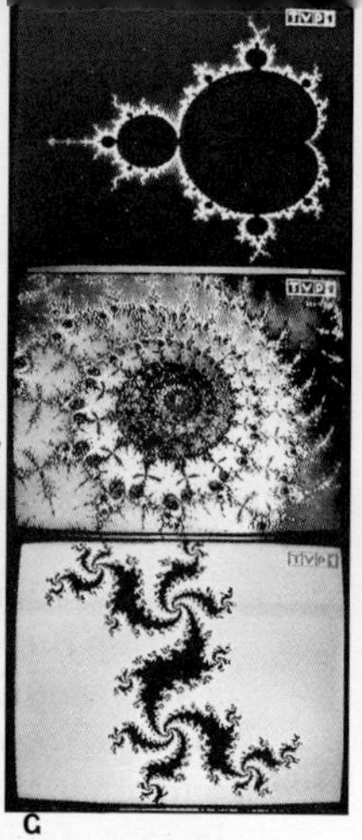

G

but are also imitated within this vast visual repertory in an apolitical context by the monument to Walt Disney and Mickey Mouse (**PANEL 14, K3** H). The pathos implied by that gesture slips easily into trivial imitation.

Some frames selected by the artist seem to condense a whole section or broadcast into a single picture; others show the stop-motion of an action in a number of frames, such as with the execution of a soldier on **PANEL 33, F3** .I[39] The formally open-ended mural offers a particular image of history; as a representation of past events, it is the result of a twofold process of selection: firstly, by the television broadcasting team, and secondly, by the spectator-photographer, who selected and rephotographed particular frames, positioning them on an all-leveling grid. However, it is also a private archive, from which images are transposed and reused for other compositions, or, in the case of the performed archives of gestures, staged and remade in the photography studio. History appears here as an afterlife of motifs, figures, and configurations that accrue meaning only in relationship to one another.

The continuous practice of archiving is transformed here into an image—almost a Benjaminian standstill—of an ongoing process parallel to that of the flow of history. As in historical reality, the process itself has no narrative beginning or end, and hence also no definite closure. Unlike historical reality, though, this is not a mosaic of disparate events, but of their representations on television. This double relay from real-life events suggests that the work is a reflection on the already-mediatized reality of image production, more than on the past itself. Because of its break with Closed Forms, *From Siberia to Cyberia* has been seen as a further step in Kulik's artistic development.[40] However, the work is in fact a retrospective exposure of what was going on in the artist's studio, and in that way is similar to *Archive of Gestures*. The presentation of the material comes after

39 This series of images reappears in Kulik's *All the Missiles Are One Missile* (1997). See my analysis of this photomural in Ruchel-Stockmans, *Images Performing History*, 144–47.

40 Maria Anna Potocka, "Ideologie i postideologia," in *Archiwum gestów*, ed. Zofia Kulik (Kraków: Starmach Gallery, 2004), 18–31.

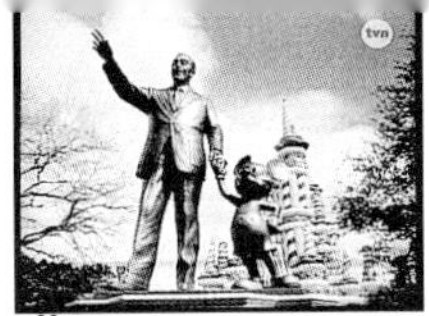

H

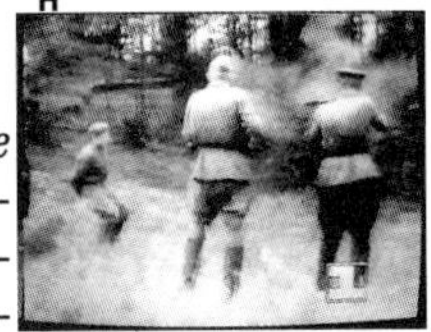

I

the "closed" compositions, such as *All the Missiles Are One Missile* or the various self-portraits, but the work process itself precedes and accompanies earlier projects.[41] The horizontal progression of the images suggests the linear model of history, but the timeline of the frames is the timeline of the television sequence, and not of the actual content of the images. The steady return of certain particular motifs and sequences—such as the dancers, or violence and war—endows this linear display with the circularity of recurrence.

Following modernism's divisions into high and low, television continues to be seen as the epitome of the post-ideological age and the chief instrument of the culture industry.[42] In other words, television is the main object of critique within modernism, being a dulling ersatz of real life (in soap operas), the false appearance of reliable information (in the news), or the empty promise of knowledge (in edutainment channels), standing for passive reception of the undifferentiated mass of images produced by consumer society. This point features prominently in the cultural critique of Oskar Hansen, for whom television epitomizes the mechanisms of the Closed Form. According to Hansen, television increases the psychological enslavement of its viewers, turning them into passive consumers of the endlessly repetitive commercials. As an instrument of domination, television can therefore be equated with the Gothic cathedrals of the Middle Ages, or the fascist and socialist-realist architecture of the 20th century, all of which belong to the closed, patriarchal, dominant model of society.[43]

Kulik's presentation of television images in screenshots does not fit into this view. Although she seems to underscore the principle of art as the Flusserian "dam" blocking the incessant flow of images, her work can equally be seen as embracing (or at least

41 For an analysis of Kulik's "closed" compositions, see Ruchel-Stockmans, *Images Performing History*, 140–47.

42 Theodor W. Adorno, "How to Look at Television," *The Quarterly of Film Radio and Television* 8, no. 3 (1954): 213–35; Theodor W. Adorno, *The Culture Industry: Selected Essays on Mass Culture*, trans. J. M. Bernstein (London: Brunner-Routledge, 2001); Potocka, "Ideologie i postideologia."

43 Oskar Hansen, *Zobaczyć świat* (Warsaw: Zachęta National Gallery of Art, 2005), 71.

mirroring) this interminable flood of undifferentiated visual information. Thus, *From Siberia to Cyberia* can be interpreted as the convergence point in which the endless flow of television images is sieved through the camera lens, only to explode again into an equally endless and inchoate grid of stop-frames. The camera uniformizes the pictures, rendering them black-and-white and motionless, making it possible to see hundreds of discrete frames at a single glance. The work thus allows for two different ways of viewing, furnishing different experiences from the macro- and the micro-perspectives. If the total view reveals the discrete zigzag pattern, the close reading discloses particular propensities—either in the selection of broadcasts or in the types of visual materials.

In *Archive of Gestures* and *From Siberia to Cyberia*, images are serialized and inserted into a grid of identical frames, defying the model of the definite, accomplished composition. The kaleidoscopic succession of these varied-but-serialized frames precludes any one-sided interpretation. Surprisingly, these cycles reveal the same repetitive themes and patterns known from Kulik's "closed" compositions, thus troubling the linear chronology of her œuvre. Although vaguely suggesting a critique of the subordination and oppression present in closed structures, *Archive of Gestures* and *From Siberia to Cyberia* playfully expose their forms and implicit dangers in order to disarm them.

These are excerpts originally published in Katarzyna Ruchel-Stockmans, Images Performing History: Photography and Representations of the Past in European Art after 1989, *Leuven: Leuven University Press, 2015.*

Dorota Łuczak, PhD, is an assistant professor in the Department of Art History at Adam Mickiewicz University in Poznań, Poland. Her professional interests concern modern art, the history of and the theory of photography, artistic and photographic historical methodologies, and modes of photographic and filmic representations of art. Łuczak has been a fellow of the French Government (2009), the Lanckoronski Foundation (2010), the Corbrdige Trust (Cambridge University, 2010), and the Stiftung Preußischer Kulturbesitz (2012). She is the author of the book *Foto-oko: Wizja fotograficzna wobec okularocentryzmu w sztuce I połowy XX wieku* (Photo-Eye: Photographic Vision in the Context of Ocularcentrism in the Art of the First Half of the 20th Century) (2018). The book is based on her PhD thesis, which was awarded by the Polish Society of Art Historians in 2016. She has published critical and academic articles in journals such as *Artium Quaestiones*, *Sztuka i Dokumentacja*, and *Kwartalnik Fotografia*, and chapters in monographies, mostly on the history of photography. Since 2015 she has been involved in the scholarly project "Polish Photographers, Critics, and Theorists on Photography, 1839–1989," funded by the Polish Ministry of Science and Higher Education. She is a member of the International Association of Art Critics, the Polish Society of Art Historians, and the Polish Photographic Society of Scholars.

SEWING IMAGE-BODIES TOGETHER: PHOTOGRAPHIC COLLAGE AS A SCULPTING STRATEGY OF ZOFIA KULIK

The work of Zofia Kulik, a graduate of the Department of Sculpture at the Academy of Fine Arts in Warsaw, is usually discussed in the context of photography. But this wasn't always so. Even though the camera has been one of her favorite tools since her art-school days, it is only since 1987 that she has been called a photographer, despite the fact that—as she declares herself—she has never been one.[1] This change, forced by art discourse, is noteworthy. Firstly, it points to a shift of Kulik's practice as perceived by Polish art-historical and critical narratives, and secondly, to changes in the institutional conditions of their definition of photography in the field of art. The purpose of this essay is neither to prove nor disprove that Zofia Kulik is

1 Kulik's first solo exhibition was held in 1989 at the Association of Polish Art Photographers' ZPAF Small Gallery, where art photography and photography-related art had been presented since the 1970s. It should be noted that, while the Small Gallery was geared mainly towards the exhibition of works informed by the conceptual turn in photography, the institution's status remained strictly inscribed in photographic discourse. Moreover, Kulik was featured in the first post-1989 lexicon of contemporary Polish photographers: Adam Mazur, *Decydujący moment: Nowe zjawiska w fotografii polskiej po 2000 roku* (Kraków: Wydawnictwo Karakter, 2012). Kulik's comment on never having been a photographer from a conversation with the author, May 30, 2018.

a photographer, but rather to show the intermedia nature of her practice as a kind of critical strategy.[2] Kulik often makes monumental photo-collages that can be ascribed the status of photo-objects. In light of their material aspect, as well as the way they are composed, my purpose is to demonstrate that they should rather be defined as photo-sculptures, thus returning to sculpture—Kulik's artistic point of departure, even though she has stuck to the field of images since 1987. I will also argue that the critical aspect of her practice consists largely of working on the "body of the image." This work is not about manipulating representations of a totalitarian order, but rather about endowing them with a material aspect, and therefore giving an account of their realness—the realness of their influence, their power to shape and regulate social relations. Kulik furnishes images with bodies and sews them together, trying to deal with their power and the power they represent.

The Body of the Image

Kulik "is and has been a political artist, interested in the problematics of power and in dominance of the system over individuals,"[3] Piotr Piotrowski wrote in the catalog of the artist's solo exhibition *From Siberia to Cyberia*, shown at the National Museum in Poznań in 1999. There is no doubt that politics and power—the history and aestheticization of terror—define the field of her practice. In the photographic works that she has been making since the breakup of KwieKulik in 1987, Kulik explores the visual structures of supervision and domination. In the monumental project *From Siberia to Cyberia*, the photographic tableau consisted of about 10,000 pic-

2 Gregory Volk writes that Kulik was and is a sculptor, and her photographic compositions are "sculpture transmuted into photographs and collage." In his analysis of *All the Missiles Are One Missile*, Volk stresses: "All the teeming ideas, historical references, and connections between diverse objects and scenes are important in *All the Missiles Are One Missile*, but so too are really sculptural things like shape, texture, materiality, volume, density, surface, and depth." Volk, "Sculpting with Images: On the Early Photomontages of Zofia Kulik," in *Zofia Kulik*, ex. cat. (Berlin: ŻAK BRANICKA, 2016).

3 Piotr Piotrowski, "Between Siberia and Cyberia: On the Art of Zofia Kulik and on Museums," in *Zofia Kulik: Od Syberii do Cyberii / From Siberia to Cyberia*, eds. Zofia Kulik and Piotr Piotrowski (Poznań: National Museum, 1999), 10.

tures[4]—photographs of television images that the artist had been taking since the 1970s. Kulik exposes the image as an instrument of an ocular-centric system of power, where images—the Baudrillardian simulacrum—do not represent reality, but rather produce an environment of ideologized phantasmagoria.[5] This is true as much for the cybernetic world as it is for the press, television, or art, which are always ideological, like the seemingly neutral, white landscapes of Siberia, with its sites of great terror. Kulik reveals the "mechanics of the influence of the image, or of its terrorist function."[6]

The number of micro-photographs arranged into the huge tableau induces a sense of near-physical violence in the viewer, a confusion and impotency caused by our inability to recognize and visually control all of the images. A vivisection of the work, a precise inspection of the individual images, becomes possible only with the help of a photo-book, where each picture has been reproduced and annotated for subject and source.[7] In the exhibition space, however, one feels overwhelmed by the work's scale and physical dimensions, succumbing, as it were, to a horizontal zigzag—a wave running through the visual collection. One of the project's strengths is that the flood of images that we experience every day ceases here to be merely virtual; it gains a physical, corporeal dimension, and thus the way the pictures act on you seems more real. In other words, the hidden (yet actual) power of images—simulacrum—is exposed here by accumulating them and endowing them with material bodies. This in turn makes evident their being actors in a network in which, according to Bruno Latour's theory, nonhumans not only cause humans to act, but are themselves vested with the power to act and thus capable of participating in social life.[8] The premises that actor-network theory holds about social structures lead in consequence

4 The first version of *From Siberia to Cyberia*, shown in Poznań in 1999, consisted of about 10,000 images. The second, completed in 2004, consisted of about 18,000 images.

5 Piotrowski, "Between Siberia and Cyberia," 29.

6 Piotrowski, "Between Siberia and Cyberia," 29.

7 Bożena Czubak and Zofia Kulik, eds., *Zofia Kulik: Od Syberii do Cyberii* (Warsaw: Zachęta National Gallery of Art, 2004).

8 Bruno Latour, *Reassembling the Social: An Introduction to Actor-Network-Theory* (New York: Oxford University Press, 2005).

to a redefinition of the status of the human being—in this case, the artist. The latter, however, does not gain here a role clearly dominant over or subordinate to extant symbolic power; instead, it becomes interesting to note the interaction and inextricable entwinement of human and nonhuman agents, which are not only subjects of power, but in themselves (as material entities) constitute a network of social behavior-regulating relations, for they are endowed with agency.

As emphasized here, the material aspect of the photographic tableau *From Siberia to Cyberia* is one of the elements of Zofia Kulik's practice that allow us to speak of the role of materiality, and then of photographic materiality or photographic bodies. Photomateriality relates here to the works themselves—their physical form—but also to the represented and to the creative process, or rather the feedback between them. As I have written above, the way Kulik's works are embedded in the material or the sculptural is a foundation of her critical strategy. The artist does not confine herself to analyzing the symbolic meaning of images of power; she tries to cope with them, endowing symbolic power-forms with corporeal status, and thus making us aware of their material—"real"—dimension. This happens in the sense in which Hans Belting writes about the body of the image as one of the elements—besides the image and the viewer—of the triad that defines the anthropology of the image. The body of the image is the medium here, the technical conditions through which an image gains the status of an entity. Media are construed as carriers or "host media," necessary for us to be able to see the images.[9] Thanks to the medium, images appear in social space, constituting their own place, and thus their being, in the world of bodies.[10] Images themselves are not only what is seen, what appears before the gaze, but they also belong to our body, memory, and imag-

9 Hans Belting, "Obraz i jego media: Próba antropologiczna," in *Perspektywy współczesnej historii sztuki: Antologia przekładów "Artium Quaestiones,"* eds. Mariusz Bryl, Piotr Juszkiewicz, Piotr Piotrowski, and Wojciech Suchocki (Poznań: UAM Wydawnictwo Naukowe, 2009), 1031; and Belting, *An Anthropology of Images: Picture, Medium, Body*, trans. Thomas Dunlap (Princeton: Princeton University Press, 2011).

10 Belting, "Obraz i jego media," 1043.

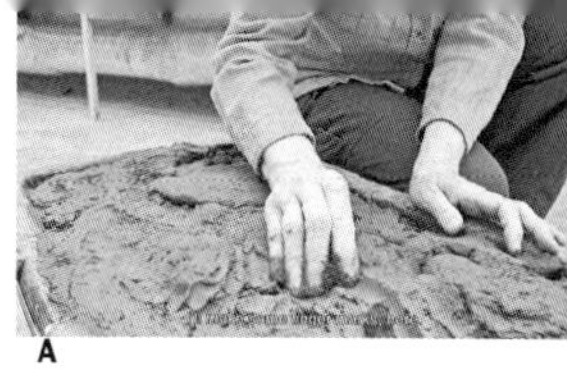

A

ination.[11] Hence the third element that defines the phenomenon of the image—the viewer, whose gaze co-constitutes images, and who in his or her memory carries images "from nature," but also fantasies.[12] The work performed by Kulik during the making of *From Siberia to Cyberia* seems to be an operation carried out in full awareness of the relationship between the image—the body of the image—and the viewer. The artist appropriates the bodies of images (in the Beltingian sense), aggregating them and investing them with a new material dimension. For it seems that only by working with their bodies can she confront them. Kulik furnishes these images with new bodies, creating new material entities in order to cope with the legacy of images in our history, culture, and, above all, memory.

Clay/Photographic Substance

Kulik reveals the significance of materiality in her commentaries, like those featured in the film **THE LOST SCULPTURE AND RETURN TO SCULPTING** A (2017) (which I will discuss later), where, with fetishistic fascination, she speaks of the pleasure of touching clay. It is precisely the artist's sculpting experience that allows her to grasp the material aspect of photographic works. As mentioned above, Kulik has noted on numerous occasions that she is not a photographer, stressing instead her background in sculpture. She used photography to explore sculpture beyond the traditional discipline. Her graduation project, *Instead of Sculpture* (1968–71), comprised of a slide show divided into five parts, was already radical.[13] Kulik not only annulled the finiteness of the work, making

11 Belting, *An Anthropology of Images*.

12 Mariusz Bryl, *Suwerenność dyscypliny: Polemiczna historia historii sztuki od 1970 roku* (Poznań: Wydawnictwo Naukowe Uniwersytetu im. Adama Mickiewicza, 2008), 555.

13 The original concept, explained in the theoretical part of the graduation project, provided for making a film that would show various ways of looking at sculpture, thus offering an analysis of the viewer-sculpture relationship. See Łukasz Ronduda and Georg Schöllhammer, eds., *KwieKulik: Zofia Kulik & Przemysław Kwiek* (Warsaw: Museum of Modern Art in Warsaw and KwieKulik Archive; Wrocław: BWA Wrocław Galleries of Contemporary Art, Awangarda Gallery; Vienna: Kontakt. The Art Collection of Erste Group and ERSTE Foundation, 2012), 72. The presentation of five hundred slides was accompanied by a rag copy of the Warsaw Academy of Fine Arts' marble copy of Michelangelo's *Moses*. In 2015, Kulik produced a digital reconstruction of the show.

the parts rearrangeable, but also dematerialized sculpture defined as a three-dimensional object, deconstructing the modernist purity of the medium. *Instead of Sculpture* can be considered as a manifesto of Kulik's artistic strategy, although it needs to be remembered that some of the images were from projects carried out with Przemysław Kwiek or others. Kulik assumed here the role of a magic-lantern showperson who conjures up a spectacle and builds narratives using slides—photographs from 1968–71. This modus operandi also underpins her work after 1987, but on entirely different terms: previously collected images are sewn together into larger heterogeneous bodies.

Each of the five parts of *Instead of Sculpture* is an enunciation in a polyphonic statement. Their objectives are as follows: to demonstrate the potentialities of forming and transforming the photographic image (images from London); to present activities and their (photographic) traces (images from 1970, including a documentation of the *Horizontal Composition* by Przemysław Kwiek and Grzegorz Kowalski); to define intervention as a new sculptural material (images taken at a cemetery and in front of the Palace of Culture during a performance featuring Zofia Kulik, Przemysław Kwiek, his sister Urszula Kwiek, Jan S. Wojciechowski, and Bartłomiej Zdrojewski); defining film as the result of a sculptural process (a nude study); and recognizing, in line with the idea of Open Form, the processuality of the sculptural object. It is not my aim to conduct a detailed analysis of this important work, but I wish to stress those of its aspects that evince an affinity between the forming of photographic material and the sculptural process.

In a video reconstruction completed by the artist in 2015, the first part of the show consists of the images from London. They have been taken through various manual operations meant to improve their "legibility." In practice, this meant interacting with photographic film and prints, as with a picture of a mother holding a child, which appears in the following forms: as a negative, a

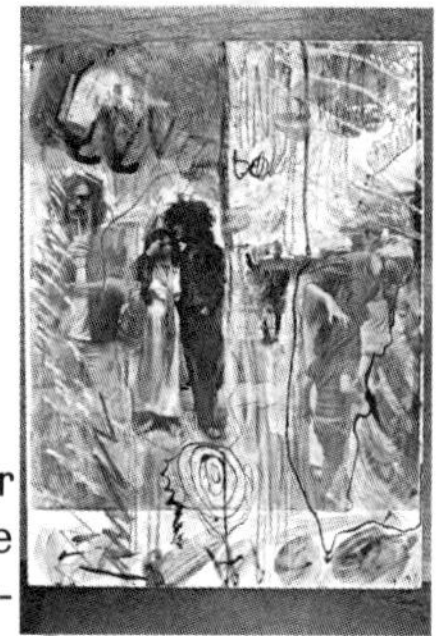
B

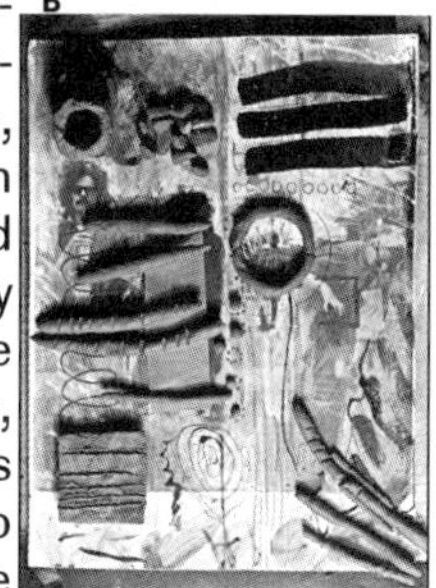
C

black-and-white print, and a print covered with color paints.[14] The body of each of those images modifies the image of the figure; framing is another form of intervention, which Kulik suggests with a series of photographs showing buildings seen from street level at various angles. In the closing slides of the first part, a picture of people on a public lawn is shown as an object (lying on a visible surface rather than cropped to fit the frame), then covered with paint, until finally clay and the sculptor's hands can be seen. Simple forms made of clay also appear in the second part, placed on photographs or next to them. It becomes clear that the photographic image is susceptible to being shaped, much like clay. What is meant here are not merely photographic manipulations, but the notion of photography as a new sculptural material; not so much a media transfer as an expansion of the boundaries of sculpture. Photographing, and operating on photographs, become new forms of the artist's sculptural practice.

This is also evident in *Activities on Moses* (1970), the photographic documentation of which was included in the final part of *Instead of Sculpture*. Here, the artist performed various operations on a marble copy of Michelangelo's statue *Moses* that is housed in the lobby of the main building of the Academy of Fine Arts in Warsaw. The artwork's coherence was subverted through direct intervention, but also—as in Kulik's slideshow—through the suggestive juxtaposition and formation of photographic representations.

14 At the same time, Kulik performed **INTERVENTIONS IN PHOTOGRAPHS** B + C (1969–71), operating directly on photographic material—scratching film, applying various substances to it, etc.—and photographing the effects. A different strategy is employed in works such as the photographs of the biblical-scene bas-reliefs from the door of Milan Cathedral (1972), onto which Kulik pasted captions with short excerpts from her intimate letters to Kwiek. The photographed objects are recontextualized here, their meaning altered. Captured in close-up, showing their details and textures, accompanied by private comments, they cease to belong to the public sphere and the great religious narrative; instead, they gain an intimate dimension. In other words, the public and prominent becomes private through photography.

Prior to 1987, the idiom of Kulik's solo practice was defined by the idea of transforming the field of sculpture with photography. After that date, the artist "unseals" photography through sculptural thinking. Among other places, Kulik reveals her strategies in films documenting her artistic practices, daily work, and conversations with Kwiek. In *The Lost Sculpture and Return to Sculpting*, subtitled *Or, in Other Words, Wet Clay in the Hands of the Archivist* (2017), the artist visits the sculpture workshop at the Academy of Fine Arts in Warsaw in order to recreate an early, student-era work—a male nude study, dating back to the turn of 1967–68.[15] Again, it is the process—the for-camera process of reproducing one's own work—that proves more important here than executing a three-dimensional copy of the artwork. Kulik not only comments on what she does, but at the same time instructs the camera operator on how to frame, thus modeling both a figure in clay and the image we see on-screen. This symbolic act of returning to the sculptural figure, abandoned at an earlier stage of artistic education, makes it possible to understand the artist's photographic strategy. When Kulik shows the interior of the piece—a wooden construction covered with the first layer of clay—she calls it a "rough shape" and compares it to the unprocessed, "untouched" digital image files she works with. A rough shape can be reworked and modified like a RAW image, Kulik says.[16] But work on raw photographic material does not end with digital processing—this "modeling," to use a term from the vocabulary of sculpture, also seems to continue during long hours in the darkroom; Kulik exposes her negatives multiple times, over the course of at least a couple of days. The first stage of work is to prepare stencils with the composition precisely traced out, including the placement of the figures and ornaments; the stencils are then cut up so that individual fields can be uncovered; and then the different elements are painstakingly exposed. The technique requires a lot of precision and resembles modeling with photographic material. Moreover, successive prints of the same work differ minimally, like multiple casts of the same sculpture.

15 After several years, the original object was removed from Academy storage and disposed of without the artist's knowledge

16 In the film *The Lost Sculpture and Return to Sculpting*.

Sewing Together

It takes some time to register the heterogeneity of Kulik's photomontages. At first sight, they seem to be a sewn-together whole. In other words, they camouflage their complexity. Working in the darkroom, Kulik sews the different elements together, producing what Belting calls the body of the image. The term "sewing together" is very significant here, highlighting the materiality of the works—their physical realness—but also indicating an attempt to deal with the symbolic order.[17] I have written above on the essence of the scale and material influence of the montage *From Siberia to Cyberia*. Piotrowski writes about it and *All the Missiles Are One Missile*: "They both are almost tangible, mainly due to the magnitude of both their size and the quantity of photographs used in them (in *From Siberia to Cyberia* there are—let us say again—over 10,000 photographs); they almost substantiate what constitutes the physical essence of the mass of information."[18] Kulik refers to both works as "carpets," which in the case of the latter is also true for the structure of the composition, based on the pattern of a Persian rug. Kulik applies the denomination of photo-carpets (repeating carpet patterns) to other works as well, for example *Human Motif (Carpet)* (1989), *Favorite Balance* (1991), and *Who Conquered the World?* (1994). This and other references to textiles recur throughout her work. By repeating the figure of Zbigniew Libera, she produced a montage she called *Libera—Lace*. In *Patterns*, she presented a portfolio of nine variations on decorative patterns, e.g. of textiles by William Morris, batik patterns, or the arabesque. *Patterns* bring to mind a product sampler offered to customers by upholstery, wallpaper, or carpet dealers.[19]

17 Sabine Kriebel writes about "suturing" in her analysis of the photomontages of John Heartfield, although the term does not have a material connotation for her. Kriebel refers to medical terminology and film theory (the way viewer experience is constructed in film or photomontage). Kriebel, "Manufacturing Discontent: John Heartfield's Mass Medium," *New German Critique* 36, no. 2 (Summer 2009): 53–88.

18 Piotrowski, "Between Siberia and Cyberia," 27.

19 "Zofia Kulik—Patterns," curatorial note, Galeria Le Guern, accessed February 18, 2019, https://www.leguern.pl/en/exhibitions/Zofia-Kulik-Patterns/.

Textile as fabric, as object, has always been important to Kulik. In *Instead of Sculpture*, rectangular sheets of patterned textiles comprise a frame for the central outline of what looks like the figure of a person who has been shot dead. Here, ornamental patterns compact the space in which an abstract human trace appears, doing so also by means of their material weight. In the part devoted to the nude study, a model presents textiles, but at the same time her body—assuming surprising positions—transformed into a sculptural substance that seems akin to the abstract clay forms shown in other images from the same set. The status of the woman also depends on the setting: she *models* when posing in a sculpture studio, and *exposes her intimacy* when we see her curled in bed, in a personal space. Last but not least, the materiality represented in the photographs interweaves here with the materiality of the prints themselves, which are often pasted onto other photographs or covered with paint. Again, an image (of a nude) is worked out by materiality, which complicates the simple division into the human and the inhuman, as well as into that which can be called sculptural material and that which cannot. Let us also remember that as part of Kulik's graduation project she made a rag copy of the *Moses*.

Calling Kulik's composing and montaging a work of sewing-together and inscribing it in the general concept of materiality become particularly meaningful in the context of the artist's comments about her childhood home and the roles of her mother and father. In an interview conducted by Izabela Kowalczyk, Kulik said: "I use the method of, say, my mother (embroidering by photography, with rows of hand-made 'negative confiture') and it is this *method* which makes me a feminist more than the content of the work itself."[20] She also stressed that: "I put my father's content into my mother's form,"[21] a reference to the symbolic power of her father, a career army officer, armed with a gun in peacetime and enacting the daily spectacle of military drill, defined by symbolic gestures and

20 Izabela Kowalczyk and Zofia Kulik, "Zofia Kulik: Authority Also Has a Body" (2002), *Kulik-KwieKulik Foundation*, accessed February 18, 2019, http://kulikzofia.pl/en/archiwum/wladza-tez-ma-cialo. Emphasis added.

21 Kowalczyk and Kulik, "Zofia Kulik: Authority Also Has a Body."

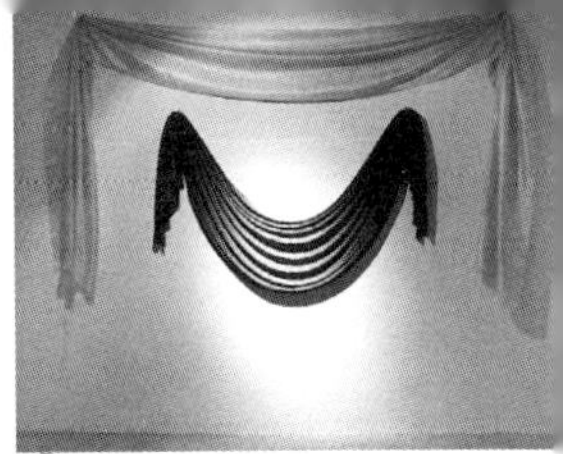

D

weapon-guaranteed power. Kulik confronted this spectacle—seen from the windows of her home, overlooking the military barracks where her father worked—with the work of her mother, a dressmaker. Her openly declared liking for draperies, fabrics, and her mother's working method becomes a strategy of dealing with, or working through, a world constituted by the symbolic power of images (**TWO DRAPERIES**) D (1993). A world identified with a father figure, subject to systemic (hierarchical, totalitarian) power. Like her mother, Helena, Zofia Kulik delineates an alternative, busying herself with the sewing-together of materials. She demonstrates this identification with her mother's work in the film *A Sum of Rags and an Archive Next Door, or, in Other Words, the Kingdom of Helena Kulik, Zofia's Mother, in Which the Archivist Grew Up*. In the first minutes of the film we see Helena Kulik in a room full of cloth pieces. She shuffles them around, presenting fragments of printed textiles—a deer in rut, a pair of ducks, a country cottage, a night-time scene with a cow. Then the frame freezes and a split-screen appears, showing Zofia working on archival materials. The message conveyed by this suggestive comparison recurs in Kulik's other filmic statements. In the first part of *Cultivating the Archive, or, in Other Words, a Performative Work*, we see her organizing documents, separating and filing negatives, and finally ironing archival materials.[22]

It is possible to speak of a material aspect of the "sewn-together" works, beginning with Kulik's first post-1987 projects: photographic collages that preceded the later multiple-exposure photomontages. In 1989, in her first solo exhibition, titled *Visual Idioms of the Soc-Ages* (ZPAF Small Gallery, Warsaw), the artist showed *Memorial I* (1989), *Black Tulle* (1987–89), *Self-Portrait with a Flag* (1989), the photo-carpet *Human Motif I* (1989), the collage *Master-Builder*, and presented a performance piece. The project reflected and expressed the course adopted by the artist: a fascination with structures that

22 Similarities between the work of Zofia Kulik and her mother, Helena, are discussed by Agata Jakubowska, who makes the idea of domestic "maintenance work" the binding agent of this comparison. Jakubowska, "Egzystencjalne i ekonomiczne wymiary 'czynnościowania' Zofii Kulik i jej matki Heleny," in *Miejsce: Studia nad sztuką i architekturą polską XX i XXI wieku*, no. 4 (2018): 12–24.

acquire symbolic significance, that in themselves and through their constituent parts evoke totalitarian systems. Here she contrasts two such kinds of power. Firstly, communism, represented by, among other things, the motif of a red flag, which is stuck on various photographic prints (the only color element in the works), or by agitprop-style images of human masses[23] and ideological architecture (e.g. the Palace of Science and Culture in Warsaw). Secondly, Christianity, with its promise of life eternal, alluded to through a repertoire of gestures drawn from Christian iconography. Kulik not only manipulated visual conventions here, but also endowed them with a material dimension. This materiality can be construed literally, as in *Human Motif I*, where photographic prints are pasted onto canvas and the whole thing is covered with rustling, crumpled yellow cellophane that forms a curtain for the images. Moreover, the distinction between the physicality of the cellophane, which is transparent and shows what is behind it, and the photographic facsimile of lace, an image gaining a corporeal dimension in a way, is erased. And finally, the images of a male model, taken from the so-called "archive of gestures," comprising a rectangular border or frame for the composition, introduce a dissonance characteristic of Kulik's works. These images are suspended between being an ornamental element, a visual vehicle of symbolic gestures, and their almost sculptural (or rather photo-sculptural) shape.

Photo-Sculptures of Gestures

The "archive of gestures" that Kulik produced from 1987 to 1991 can be referred to as a collection of photo-sculptures. The artist selected conventional poses and symbolic gestures, which were then enacted by her model, Zbigniew Libera. Even though some of the images are clearly rooted in Christian iconography (or sourced

23 Katarzyna Ruchel-Stockmans compares the repetition of the male figure (the image of Zbigniew Libera) in Kulik's works with the visual solutions found in the agitprop photomontages and photographs of Alexander Rodchenko and Gustav Klutsis. For all the differences, she nonetheless sees a similarity in their use of montage as a representation of bodily politics. See Ruchel-Stockmans, *Images Performing History: Photography and Representations of the Past in European Art after 1989* (Leuven: Leuven University Press, 2015), 155. Excerpts reprinted in this volume.

from specific works such as Cranach's *Crucifixion*, El Greco's *Resurrection*, or Memling's *The Last Judgement*), the lack of saintly attributes or obvious symbols "secularizes" them to a certain extent. Poses rendered after Passion-of-Christ representations or the iconography of saints are combined with images originating in ancient or totalitarian art. What becomes meaningful here are the gestures themselves and their emotive function, enhanced by the adopted photographic convention.[24] Kulik endows images of gestures with (in the Beltingian sense) bodies of a particular form—all the pictures were taken against a neutral black background, from which the pale, skinny, statue-like body of a white male stands out. Kulik evokes gestures—established and sanctioned by history and tradition—as virtual vehicles of significance, authority, and influential power. She removes them, however, from their original contexts and thus from the symbolic sphere of power, isolating them and conferring upon them a materiality, which allows us to see and understand them (and their function) in a completely different way. The convention adopted here brings to mind the classic convention, stretching back to the 19th century and still alive today, of reproducing sculptural works and three-dimensional objects. The sculptural dimension of the images comprising the "archive of gestures" was noticed by Bożena Czubak, who rightly compared them to the 19th-century practice of producing postcards showing representations of famous sculptural works as posed by live models.[25] The artist intensifies this objective character of the photographed gestures when she builds sets consisting of photographic prints, displayed in separate black frames as if in museum display cabinets, and also when she uses negatives to produce complex photomontages and combines them with images of spires, caverns, vases, or memorials and monumental architecture. Photographs of gestures become an element of woven patterns, but they also gain what is clearly a sculptural nature. This happens, for

24 See Bożena Czubak, "Archiwum gestów," in *Archiwum gestów*, ed. Zofia Kulik (Kraków: Starmach Gallery, 2004), 4–31. Ruchel-Stockmans considers Libera's posing as a token of his subordination and discipline, which express a strategy of political domination. See her *Images Performing History*, 152.

25 Czubak, "Archiwum gestów," 11.

example, in *Human Motif I*. Repeated in the border, the image of the model raising his hands in a gesture of victory, his silhouette standing out sharply from the black background, becomes monumental. It also resembles the photographs of sculptural objects used in other works (e.g. the memorials in *All the Missiles Are One Missile*). An objective dimension is also gained by elements of the *Columns* series, where arrangements of images on a black background are reminiscent of monuments, candelabra, or monstrances.

The idea of photographic sculpture is realized by Kulik in a special way in the collage *Black Tulle*, where she combines photographic representations with objects that actually possess substantial material bodies. In the center of the altar-like composition are two photo-sculptural images of a nude male model, showing him despairing (leaning over and covering his eyes) and lamenting (kneeling and raising his hands in a pleading gesture), separated by a perpendicular form with three despairing figures—corresponding with the predella of the altar. These photo-sculptural forms are flanked by four negative images, obtained through the tonal reversal of the positives, showing headless figures pointing at the objects in the main section of the "altar." The tonal inversion used here reminds us of the materiality of photography. In the finial there appear (visual representations of) implements: pliers, pincers, scissors, and a fork, which seem to be gaining the status of the *arma Christi*. This secular altar of suffering is capped by an arch with a frieze featuring images of a baroque putto playing a violin, the arch pierced in its central part by the fork, which looks like a lily—a symbol of purity, beauty, and innocence. The frieze is covered by a black tulle ribbon, which flows down the sides of the altar and encloses the whole structure, forming a frame for the piece. The distinction between the visual and the material is effaced.

Lens-Based Sculpture

Kulik works with photographic material in a manner close to sculptural experience. In her solo work, starting with the *Visual Idioms of the Soc-Ages* exhibition, she unseals photography, turning it into sculptural material. This strategy has become a contrariwise continuation of Kulik's pre-1987 use of photography in the field of sculpture. Her practices were part of a larger phenomenon, dating back to the 1960s, of the redefinition of sculpture, now construed as action and process, also realizable in public space and using all possible materials.[26] In the context of 1960s and 1970s American art, Rosalind Krauss called such projects "sculpture in the expanded field,"[27] where photography relocated objects, landscapes, buildings, and monuments, and the photo camera served as a means of neutral documentation.[28] Yet, as Herbert Molderings points out, the next generation of European artists placed greater emphasis on the discovery and construction—by means of the (photo and film) camera—of spatial and sculptural situations. According to Molderings, co-curator of the exhibition *Lens-Based Sculpture*, European artists conducted a kind of media analysis, turning projectors and cameras into a "sculptural playing field."[29] The use of photography as sculptural material led Kulik to work with and on the bodies of photographic images, which gain the status of photo-sculpture or lens-based sculpture.

Kulik wrestles with images representing totalitarian power—political, religious, and patriarchal. She does not do so, however, by going beyond the repertoire of familiar iconographic conventions and themes; rather, she decides to "tame" images and their symbolic power by working in the material dimension and endowing images with new bodies. Kulik complicates the visual order, shifting images into new bodily contexts and often altering their original meanings. The strategy of "sewing together" also

26 Herbert Molderings, "Introduction" and "Lens-Based Sculpture: The Contribution of Photography to Sculptural Experimentalization," in *Lens-Based Sculpture: The Transformation of Sculpture through Photography*, eds. Bogomir Ecker, Raimund Kummer, Friedemann Malsch, and Herbert Molderings (Berlin: Akademie der Künste Berlin; Vaduz: Kunstmuseum Liechtenstein, 2014), 10–20, 26–55.

27 Rosalind Krauss, "Sculpture in the Expanded Field" (1979), in *The Originality of the Avant-Garde and Other Modernist Myths* (Cambridge, MA: MIT Press, 1985), 276–91.

28 Molderings, "Introduction," 14–16.

29 Molderings, "Introduction," 15–16.

reveals the essence of the relations between what Latour calls the actants—in this case, images that interact with each other and form new material-semiotic systems.

Translated by Marcin Wawrzyńczak

Anna Kałuża is a literary critic. She lectures on contemporary Polish poetry in the Department of Contemporary Polish Literature, University of Silesia. She works on the intersections of contemporary poetry, art, and aesthetics. She has published books including *Pod grą: Jak dziś znaczą wiersze, poetki i poeci* (Underneath the Game: What Poems and Poets Mean Today) (2015), *Wielkie wygrane: Wspólne sprawy poezji, krytyki i estetyki* (Big Prizes: Common Affairs of Poetry, Criticism, and Aesthetics) (2011), and *Bumerang: Szkice o polskiej poezji przełomu XX i XXI wieku* (Boomerang: Essays on Polish Poetry at the Turn of the Twenty-First Century) (2010).

DÉTOURNEMENTS OF AESTHETICIZATION: ZOFIA KULIK'S *GARDEN (LIBERA AND FLOWERS)*

Polish neo-avant-garde women artists seldom represented the male body; rather, they focused on producing images of the female one. In doing so, they used various strategies of overidentification in reference to the cultural norms of body and gender. This has also been the modus operandi of most European and North American women artists. Since the recent surge in interest in feminist art, we have witnessed various games being played with the aesthetic ideologies of female representation, and a focus on presenting those aspects of female life that are shunned by "male" art history. This may seem an unavoidable course for women artists critical of the patriarchal system, and yet Zofia Kulik's works from the 1990s demonstrate otherwise, for here she frames the male body. In her best-known photomontages, such as *Inter-National Gothic* (1990), *Emblem* (1990), *May Day Mass* (1990), *The Guardians of the Spire* (1990), *All the Missiles Are One Missile* (1993), *March, March, March* (1990), and *Leaf I* (1998), as well as the photomontage series *Archive of Gestures* (1987–91), the model was Kulik's friend, the artist Zbigniew Libera. Kulik took some seven hundred photographs where the male body is typically associated with signs of power, violence, and

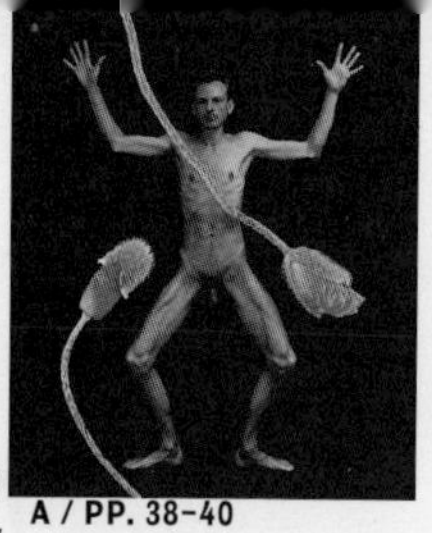
A / PP. 38–40

political or metaphorical terror: "The male body is both imprisoned in various ideological signs and actively co-creates them [here]."[1]

Kulik seldom references signifying systems other than those responsible for the figures of power, domination, and subjugation. There are, however, exceptions to this rule in her œuvre; one such exception is the series **GARDEN (LIBERA AND FLOWERS)** [A] (1996–2004). As Tomasz Fudala writes, "Kulik, long interested in the theme of the multiple reproduction of the work, based *Garden* on a single negative, using the same model's pose throughout the series."[2] The object of transformation here is a black-and-white photograph of a nude male body. Rather than being montaged into a complex arrangement of signs of power, it is associated instead with a biological-vegetable order. Kulik did likewise in the series *Human Motif: Libera—Christmas Tree* (1990) and the work *Libera—Lace* (1990).

The unique nature of the project outlined in the series of Kulik's plant-human photomontages with Libera can be seen not only against the historical background of the work of neo-avant-garde women artists, but also in the context of the development of the modern nude. This uniqueness is also evident in the way that Kulik uses the neo-avant-garde's characteristic technique of *détournement*.[3] She doesn't play with the male gaze, doesn't try to transform the dominant modes of defining women's role, situation, and function in patriarchal society, and doesn't try to undermine and challenge (through repetition) the normative rules of bodily representation; the photomontage series establishes alter-alternative rules of their own functioning. This means that—by hijacking the signs, symbols, or codes of the dominant, hegemonic structures of

1 Paweł Leszkowicz, *Nagi mężczyzna: Akt męski w sztuce polskiej po 1945 roku* (Poznań: Wydawnictwo Naukowe UAM, 2012), 447.

2 Tomasz Fudala, "Ogrody Zofii Kulik czyli Libera w królestwie flory" (2004), *Kulik-KwieKulik Foundation*, accessed September 3, 2018, http://kulikzofia.pl/archiwum/tomasz-fudala-ogrody-zofii-kulik-czyli-libera-w-krolestwie-flory.

3 After Guy Debord, I construe *détournement* above all as the hijacking, appropriation, and critical reuse of existing enunciative and discursive-visual cultural practices. See, for example, Debord, "A User's Guide to Détournement," in *Situationist International Anthology*, ed. Ken Knabb (December 2006), http://www.bopsecrets.org/SI/index.htm.

the power system in its historical courses—Kulik creates her own fields of context and meaning for the works. As a result, her works gain independence from the systems of reference that they draw their codes from, without, however, building an aesthetically autonomous, alternative narrative towards them about the production of genderized bodies. In this essay I will focus on the example of the *Garden (Libera and Flowers)* series and try, in its context, to describe the issue in greater detail.

The Kulik Garden

The photomontages—four at the Muzeum Sztuki in Łódź and five at the Zachęta in Wrocław, presented together as a series for the first time at Galeria Le Guern, Warsaw in 2004—are effects of operations on the medium: the enlargement of the negative and reproduction of one photograph, along with photographs of plants.[4] Kulik superimposed fragments of flowers/plants/stalks on a black-and-white picture of Zbigniew Libera's nude body (using the same negative for the whole series) and rephotographed the compositions in color; the image of Libera was taken from the *Archive of Gestures* series, where he reenacted bodily poses from various iconographic traditions. Kulik produced eleven images in this way. She excepted the photograph of Libera's gesture from the coding chain (that is, her vast photo archive), granting it the status of an "excluded object," and made the body featured in it an incomplete object. The photo-collages arrange themselves here, generally speaking, into a binary code-body, and the plants become signs, interconnected as in other communication systems.

Critics stress the contrast between the black-and-white photograph of Libera, familiar from Kulik's earlier works, and the intensely colorful, phallic-vaginal shapes of the flowers and stalks

4 "Flowers are photographed here while the figure is reproduced; one can say it is the image of an image." Bożena Czubak, ed., *Zofia Kulik—Self-Portraits and the Garden* (Warsaw: Galeria Le Guern, 2004), 72.

that partly cover the model's body.[5] Each configuration in *Garden* is different: within it, a division is made between the covered and the uncovered, and various operations are performed—of subordination, of cutting and disintegrating, and of connecting and filling. While we know that Libera's body has only been covered, the effect of Kulik's work nonetheless resembles the castrational marking of a material object by disciplining regimes. For example, in the photograph with a poppy flower, the model's body lacks the head and, partly, the shoulders; there is no reason why we shouldn't interpret the figure of the poppy in an order of addition (as an extra organ) rather than the photograph of the man in an order of subtraction (the headless body), yet the bodily figure that Libera presents here brings to mind a parceled-out, surface-spread, prepared body. This is a flat body that has begun to play the role of a surface to be marked. In another photograph, a rose blossom and stalk cut the object in half, covering the head as well; the genitals and part of the thighs are covered too. Moreover, montaging a flower onto an existing photograph of a male body produces the effect of inserting space between the objects and establishing three planes of signification: the black background; the male silhouette standing out against it; and the leaves, stalk, and rose blossom. The shape of the plant seems to emulate/paraphrase the shape of the human body here. Other operations on the human medium are performed by Kulik in the picture with the leaves arranged crosswise. The leaves hold the model's body at a sharp angle, and their crisscross pattern contrasts with his spread hands and legs. In turn, in the photograph with two poppy buds, the intersecting stalks trace a curve but don't cover the body—they adorn it as an added element. They do cut across the uniform surface of the skin, but they also outline it, establishing an ascending rhythm that keeps the flowers outside the body, whereas the stalks in the previous picture, which seemed sharpened, became an image of a repressive cut (in the middle of the figure).

5 See, for example, a discussion of *Garden* in the context of the sexual-erotic power of flowers: Monika Bakke, "Blossoming Sex: Floral Transpositions in the Works of Natalia LL and Zofia Kulik," accessed September 3, 2018, https://www.academia.edu/31387445/Blossoming_Sex._Floral_Transpositions_in_the_Works_of_Natalia_LL_and_Zofia_Kulik.

In the series, Kulik rather slyly paraphrases, I believe, her earlier works. The elements serially recurring in them, connecting Libera's nude body with signs of power and images of terror, can be interpreted as artistic notions of the formation of social objects-bodies within the political codes of power, generating fear-based subjection.[6] While floral motifs can also be found in other works by Kulik (for example, *From Siberia to Cyberia*), their use in *Garden* seems extraordinary, for here the floral and the human motifs are in 1:1 proportion. The plants don't differ in size from the human body, and, included in the "garden" as a whole, they highlight at least two important aspects of the series: firstly, they point to the absent artist, for it is her own garden that she took the flowers from,[7] and secondly, they activate the sensual, pleasure-related aspect of art, bound up with the philosophy of the garden as an artwork. As the Italian garden historian Francesco Fariello wrote in 1967:

> The garden can offer various forms of pleasure, depending on what is expected from it. What is needed to experience simple sensual or emotional pleasure is a basic sensitivity to shape, color, and natural elements. But to have intellectual and aesthetic pleasure, one needs an idea and a conception to turn the garden into a world to be contemplated; this implies a creative process, such as is present in every work of art.[8]

6 Kulik composes her series using a rich variety of symbolic, religious, and political signs that include the human body within the structures of rigorous patterns: carpets, wallpapers, monuments, mandalas, medals, columns, and gates. *The Guardians of the Spire* incorporated fragments of images of Warsaw's Palace of Science and Culture, while other works used ancient draperies, Soviet stars, Orthodox Christian symbols, etc. Critics (Leszkowicz, Piotrowski, Kowalczyk) have listed the signs/images/symbols employed by the artist, and Kulik herself even accompanied *All the Missiles Are One Missile* with an "iconographic guide" that explained the patterns used.

7 "I used fresh flowers, right after cutting them down in the *Garden* series but I have been collecting the images of flowers for a long time. I live several hundred meters from the Puszcza Kampinoska forest and a garden surrounds my house. [...] The floral-herbal elements built my works as much as the motifs of a naked body, architectural forms, and TV images." *Zofia Kulik—Self-Portraits and the Garden*, 56.

8 Francesco Fariello, quoted in Mateusz Salwa, *Estetyka ogrodu: Między sztuką a ekologią* (Łódź: Wydawnictwo Przypis, 2016), 93.

Without delving into various aesthetic theories, we can say that, at the point of departure of her work, Kulik confronts two formations: a semantic-symbolic one and a corporeal-material one. The garden is a sign of nature here (its cultural representation), and the body gets composed into an order of cultural gestures, which it surrenders to almost completely.

So, can we consider these floral and plant motifs—construed as tokens of something other than themselves as well as a visualized materiality[9]—as the kind of cultural-political motifs that are present in Kulik's other works? Is the order of the garden introduced here by the artist as repressive as the military-nationalist order? And on what basis does this order (re)produce the gender, corporeality, and visibility of the male/human body? Finally, is the form of the material here also a form of the articulation (formation) of the body in its universal horizons, and should the body be related to the motifs of power, and its elements seen as organic paraphrases of the signs of terror and fear?

Fields of Reference

The first imperative reference system for this particular series of works by Zofia Kulik is the tradition of the female and male nude, perceived in a more general perspective as a distinction of the ideological and political-aesthetic valuation of images of nude masculinity and nude femininity. As we know, this distinction is one that holds sway within the political hierarchy of the sexes: women's bodies have been subject to eroticization/fetishization in modern art since more or less the 19th century, which means, essentially,

9 "[In] the photograph which you took, similar to others, from the *Archive of Gestures*, Libera as a model is rather asexual. However, after you introduced flowers, a tension between the model and his body versus the shapes of flowers appears. [...] [In] one of the photographs this game becomes a little perverse with a penis touching a flower bud." *Zofia Kulik—Self-Portraits and the Garden*, 66.

that their representations are considered decorative, whereas representations of the male body are seen as a medium for important cultural topics.[10]

The domination of the female nude as based on the pleasure-related aesthetic values and procedures of emotional investment was challenged first by the counterculture of the 1960s, when the male body once again became an object of desire, rather than just a sign of power and violence.[11] New figurations of masculinity emerged—inspired, for example, by classical ideals,[12] and women with increasing regularity made male nudes. These became a groundbreaking phenomenon and a genre in their own right: "This role swap is a challenge for the gender structure of the Western visual system, where the woman was a passive object of the gaze and the man the looking subject of the action."[13] Of course, classical and classicizing homoeroticism developed different rules for presenting the male body than contemporary, postwar heterosexual patriarchal culture had,[14] but patriarchal representations in Western modernity still cast masculinity, rather than femininity, in the meaning-producing role.

Composed within this tradition, Kulik's *Garden* seems to differ doubly. Instead of the female body it presents the male one, but this presentation is not attuned to any normalizing principle of aesthetic visualization. The artist doesn't simply replace the female body with a male one without contesting traditional modes of presentation; she could reference homoerotic representations that associate the male body with eroticism and pleasure, as was the case in 1960s art, and although she herself suggests this interpretation by pointing to the erotic nature of flowers, such readings seem, to my mind, insufficient.[15] Kulik develops her own artistic analytical-

10 "The most important cultural contents were conveyed through the male body, which served as a medium of political, religious, and ethical values to a far greater extent than the female one. [...] The naked athlete mediates civilization, Venus decorates it." Leszkowicz, *Nagi mężczyzna*, 19.

11 See Leszkowicz, *Nagi mężczyzna*, 19; also Lynda Nead, *The Female Nude: Art, Obscenity and Sexuality* (New York: Routledge, 1992).

12 Leszkowicz, *Nagi mężczyzna*, 29.

13 Leszkowicz, *Nagi mężczyzna*, 168.

14 See David Freedberg, *The Power of Images: Studies in the History and Theory of Response* (Chicago: University of Chicago Press, 1989).

15 See *Zofia Kulik—Self-Portraits and the Garden*, 68.

presentational sets, where the body functions as an erotic symbol, but is, above all, a performed object, dependent on the context and code that form it. The body in Kulik's collages is never autonomous: because it is always part of a series, with shifts, chains, and structures, it evokes the system and code within which it operates as an object—we don't know whether it's the background here or the figure. Moreover, the use of materials customarily employed in decorative roles (flowers, plants) changes the conditions of the production of corporeality as a sign and as a body; in traditional aesthetics, flowers evoked elements of femininity or innocence, and neutralized gender, whereas in Kulik's works, being highlighted (by color, frontal positioning, or size), they rivet the attention and shift meanings. They cease to be supplementary background filler, and begin to operate in the field of corporeality, introducing their naturalizing, denaturalizing (etc.) laws to it. The different floral objects in this project become a synonym of nature, which refers us to a complex, multilevel field of references: the aesthetic contemplation of nature in art; the idea of nature as the greatest artist; the organic and inorganic materials used by (neo-)avant-garde artists; the naturalization of the human body through attempts to reintegrate it into the environment; the transformation of nature; and so on.[16] Unexpectedly, therefore, Kulik's project, included in Western art's nude tradition, seeks to redefine both the representation of the male body and the position of decorative-floral motifs in modernist art.

Another obvious context for Zofia Kulik's artistic practices is Polish neo-avant-garde art. From the 1970s onwards it experimented with nudity—with debatable results[17]—but it was then that the work of women artists such as Ewa Partum, Natalia LL, Teresa Murak, and Ewa Kuryluk initiated proto-feminist reflection in Polish

16 Fae Brauer, "Superevolution: Interspecies Modernism and the Naturization of Modernity," in *Superorganism: The Avant-Garde and the Experience of Nature*, eds. Aleksandra Jach and Paulina Kurc-Maj (Łódź: Muzeum Sztuki w Łodzi, 2017).

17 Leszkowicz, *Nagi mężczyzna*, 126. Citing Andrzej Matuszewski's performance *Postępowanie* (*The Procedure*) as well as the photographs of Zbigniew Dłubak and Zdzisław Sosnowski, Leszkowicz argues that Polish neo-avant-garde art never went beyond the patriarchal paradigm of gender roles.

art.[18] These experiments were continued by representatives of the "critical art" movement, with masculinity disenchanted in works such as Zbigniew Libera's *Body Master*, Dorota Nieznalska's *Passion*, Artur Żmijewski's performances, and Katarzyna Kozyra's *Men's Bathhouse* and *Dance Lesson*.[19] But even against the background of those works, Kulik's photo-collages[20] seem surprising and groundbreaking, as 1990s critical art was preoccupied mainly with issues of bodily and sexual repression, of repressed and taboo sexual behaviors, and highlighted the ways in which corporeality was involved in social and political contexts without canceling its somatic, biological nature. Yet with Kulik, the model's body becomes a serial reproduction, which, of course, is also a means of analyzing power and violence—as in the works of Kozyra, Żmijewski, Libera, and Grzegorz Klaman. But unlike those, it morphs, in Kulik's works, into an abstract sign, a non-biological construction, a hybrid plant-human form.

Gestures in the Garden

The focus on detail and the ornamentation traditionally and historically associated with it seem inherent to Kulik's works.[21] Variously functionalized, detail becomes a starting point for reflections on variationality, seriality, combinatorics, and framing.

Commenting on her series *Patterns*, which stands out from her other works due to the technique used, Kulik stresses that "every design is based on the principle of a repetitive segment [...] it has no beginning or end, nor center, but spills out all over the surface." She also mentions working on samples "like the ones from a

18 See, for example, Łukasz Ronduda, "In the Circle of Open Form: Visual Games, Interactions, Participation, Archives, Communities" in *Polish Art of the 70s*, editorial concept Piotr Uklański (Jelenia Góra: Polski Western; Warsaw: Centrum Sztuki Współczesnej Zamek Ujazdowski, 2009); Piotr Piotrowski, "Od Syberii do Cyberii," in *Sztuka według polityki: Od Melancholii do Pasji* (Kraków: TAiWPN Universitas, 2007); Agata Jakubowska, *Na marginesach lustra: Ciało kobiece w pracach polskich artystek* (Kraków: TAiWPN Universitas, 2004).

19 Izabela Kowalczyk, "Odczarowanie 'męskości' w sztuce krytycznej," in *Matki-Polki, Chłopcy i Cyborgi... Sztuka i feminizm w Polsce* (Poznań: Galeria Miejska "Arsenał," 2010), 117.

20 Zofia Kulik's primary medium is not collage but "multiple-exposure photography."

21 See Bożena Czubak, "Desenie" (2008), *Kulik-KwieKulik Foundation*, accessed March 3, 2018, http://kulikzofia.pl/archiwum/bozena-czubak-desenie/.

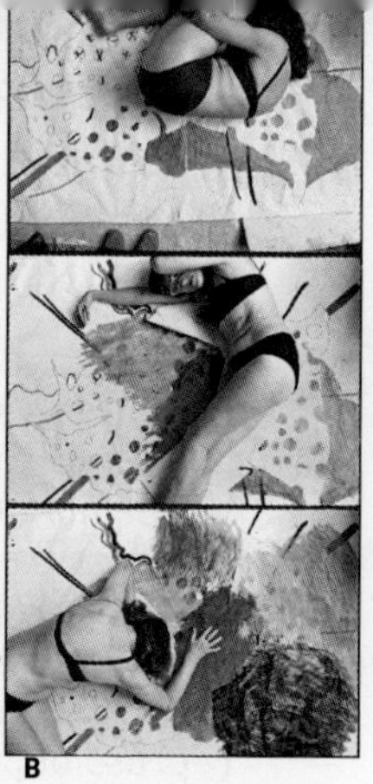

B

wallpaper or carpet store."[22] Such segment-based composition is a characteristic method of conceptual art: the artist uses repeatable series of elements that can enter into diverse relationships with each other, thus exposing the system that makes their production possible. In her serial works—even if they don't share their technique with *Patterns*—Kulik also draws attention to mechanisms, systems, or processes that have resulted in the constitution of various objects. Tomasz Załuski calls the photographic and diapositive images used by the KwieKulik duo indexed/indexable material, able to "engage in diverse, infinite relationships."[23] This is very important: the different elements of Kulik's artistic works, produced using different techniques and methods, are potentially capable of reconfiguration.

In her art-school graduation project, the artist captured the "same pose, posture, sequence of movements—the same profiles—of the model against the background of various spatial and situational contexts (**INSTEAD OF SCULPTURE** B [1968–71]). There is clearly an interest in combinatorics and variationality here."[24] Kulik photographed a female model's successive poses against the backdrop of a color animation in such a way as to, moving from sequence to sequence, finally show an empty frame—the model eventually "falling out" of our field of vision. Watching the complex arrangement, we pay more attention to what happens to the space that the object moves in than we do to the object itself. The frame as a motif of the work also appears, for example, in *From Siberia to Cyberia*. There, Kulik featured a number of photographs showing selected phases of move-

22 With its use of digital technology, the *Patterns* series differs from Kulik's works produced with stencils and multiple-exposure photography. "Bzik kulturalny: Zofia Kulik" (2011), *culture.pl*, accessed March 3, 2018, http://culture.pl/pl/wideo/bzik-kulturalny-zofia-kulik-wideo.

23 Tomasz Załuski, "Procesualne archiwum jako materia sztuki: O działaniach duetu KwieKulik," in *Materia sztuki*, ed. Michał Ostrowicki (Kraków: TAiWPN Universitas, 2010), 142.

24 See Załuski, "Procesualne archiwum jako materia sztuki," 137; see also Joanna Turowicz, "Zofia Kulik," in *Artystki polskie* (Warsaw: Wydawnictwo Szkolne PWN, 2011); Bożena Czubak, "Archiwum gestów" (2004), *Fundacja Kulik-KwieKulik*, accessed March 3, 2018, http://kulikzofia.pl/archiwum/bozena-czubak-archiwum-gestow/.

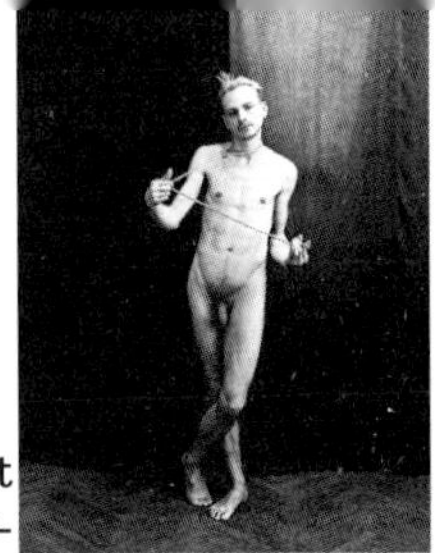

C / P. 20

ments performed by an athletic male (model) in front of Marey's "camera."[25] A similar technique was used earlier by British photographer Eadweard Muybridge, whereas in Poland in 1975 Wiktor Gutt and Waldemar Raniszewski made *Body Framing*, a series of photographs of a nude man performing gymnastic exercises. In Zofia Kulik's works, framing becomes an almost independent process that visualizes the work within the meaning of the space shown, on formatting and composing it, although this doesn't mean that the "visibility" of the frame is stressed in all of her projects. In **ARCHIVE OF GESTURES** C (1987–91), framing doesn't play an independent function, but it can still be associated with, for example, Gutt and Raniszewski's works. The affinity lies in accentuating specific bodily gestures as "effects" rather than in drawing attention to the process of framing per se. The artists' characteristic practice of marking the body or framing with the body means that one can hardly speak of decorativeness in the traditional sense here. These works produce codes of commands—bodily modules of gesture-orders and gesture-subjugations. In this way, they become politically meaningful material in which frames (as a means of spatial organization), in confrontation with the body's gestural mode of operation, direct us towards reflection on the methods of bio-disciplining societies and individuals.

The emphasis on gestures as singular projections of the prescriptive mode of human communication is not only found in the field of art. Philosophers Deleuze and Guattari argued that:

> The elementary unit of language—the statement—is the order-word. Rather than common sense, a faculty for the centralization of information, we must define an abominable faculty consisting in emitting, receiving, and transmitting order-words. Language is made not to be believed but to be obeyed, and to compel obedience.[26]

25 Bożena Czubak and Zofia Kulik, eds., *Zofia Kulik: Od Syberii do Cyberii* (Warsaw: Zachęta National Gallery of Art, 2004).

26 Gilles Deleuze and Félix Guattari, *A Thousand Plateaus: Capitalism and Schizophrenia*, trans. Brian Massumi (Minneapolis: University of Minnesota Press, 1987), 76.

Jonathan Crary, in turn, adds that the purpose of this kind of instrumentalization of language is to maintain or generate a social reality whose ultimate result is fear.[27] Similar contexts of the political notion of bodily communication are activated by the choreographic representations of Muybridge, Kulik, and Gutt. They introduce their own politics of the body: offering something that can be described as liminal forms of the body-sign, they are also an attempt to create an alphabet using the human body. References to pictograms, ideograms, and other systems of visual communication are an allusion to that attempt. Evident in all of these works is a fascination with bodily movement and gesture, which in the outlined perspective makes it clear that the notion of agency is not inherent to the subject, but that the subject is produced in a series of repeated cultural signs.

We can assume, of course, that *Garden...* is a continuation of these ways of showing the body, and say that what occurs in the work is a symmetrical reversal of the position of domination and power vested in men in patriarchal society. In Kulik's works, it is the man, the male model, who is subordinated to the actions of the woman who arranges his body. As Piotr Piotrowski puts it:

> However, what matters here are the employment relations; a woman not only is the one who accepts work, but in the first place shapes and accepts the picture. Then, if besides activity, action, and work, an optical molding of reality and subjugating it to a glance are the expressions of dominance, and consequently power, then the one who rules here is a woman, not a man.[28]

Critic Izabela Kowalczyk asks, along similar lines:

> [...] by ignoring the mechanisms of the control and subjugation of female bodies, does Kulik inscribe herself with her art in the meanings of universal culture, which

27 Jonathan Crary, *Suspensions of Perception: Attention, Spectacle, and Modern Culture* (Cambridge, MA: MIT Press, 1999).

28 Piotr Piotrowski, "Between Siberia and Cyberia: On the Art of Zofia Kulik and on Museums," in *Zofia Kulik: Od Syberii do Cyberii / From Siberia to Cyberia*, eds. Kulik and Piotrowski (Poznań: National Museum, 1999), 13–14.

> is above gender differences, or is it that she criticizes universalism as a smokescreen for an asymmetric and hierarchical gender system?[29]

But is it a reversed patriarchal logic that speaks, above all, in the construction of meaning in Kulik's works?[30] In these photo-collages, the male body, construed as an order of materiality, is susceptible to various radical transformations; turned into a gesture, an ornament, a pose, a sign, it loses and gains semanticity, somaticity, visuality, depth, and surface. In this context, Sarah Wilson writes of Kulik's "andrographies," her "writing with the male form."[31] We should remember that Kulik studied under Oskar Hansen, whose Open Form theory inevitably influenced her, and she must therefore have been critical of the universalistic categories of modernist culture.[32] We immediately recognize that the object of conceptualization, in works such as *All the Missiles Are One Missile* or *The Guardians of the Spire*, is masculinity defined by the military-nationalist discourse, so there are no gullibly construed "meanings of universal culture" here, although Kulik's works are not necessarily opposed to those either.

In *Garden* Kulik creates objects with ephemeral elements: compared to a national flag, a shroud, or a royal standard, flowers can be considered "weak" symbols. Moreover, the model's gesture is indeterminate: Libera represents neither a losing nor a winning gesture, and it is not entirely clear what his gesture would mean "autonomously." With such weak symbols and ambiguous gestures, it is easier for the artist to redirect our attention to series, sequences, and combinations, rather than focus it on an ephemeral

29 Izabela Kowalczyk, "Zofia Kulik: dekonstrukcja systemów władzy," in *Ciało i władza: Polska sztuka krytyczna lat 90.* (Warsaw: Wydawnictwo Sic!, 2002), 118.

30 The artist herself suggests this: "Do I, depicting 'subjection,' appreciate and praise it or mock and subvert it? Accepting 'subjection' as my problem and topic, filled with fear, but also with hatred against situations forcing me to submit, taking an artistic vengeance, taking up any weapon (symbolic or formal) used against me." Quoted in Piotr Piotrowski, *Znaczenia modernizmu: W stronę historii sztuki polskiej po 1945 roku* (Poznań: Dom Wydawniczy Rebis, 1999), 186.

31 Sarah G. Wilson, "Discovering the Psyche: Zofia Kulik" (1999), *Kulik-KwieKulik Foundation*, accessed September 3, 2018, http://kulikzofia.pl/en/archiwum/sarah-wilson-odkrywanie-psyche-zofia-kulik.

32 "[Open Form] was characterized by a departure from modernist anthropocentrism in architecture with its universalist idea of the 'mass individual.'" Ronduda, "In the Circle of Open Form," 172.

(though discrete) object. We can infer, therefore, that it is not Libera's gesture in itself that matters, but rather that which precedes it and has made it possible. As we recall, the civilization of gestures emerged in the Middle Ages, with *chansons de geste*—the epic "songs of heroic deeds"—as a popular literary genre. Gestures are codified and ritualized bodily actions: "Contracts and oaths are accompanied by gestures. [...] Prayer, blessings, incense, penance [...] a system of gestures spreads throughout all domains of liturgy and faith."[33] The regime of gestures is meant to restrain the body with morality, norms, and injunctions:

> Although reined in with morality or the rules of ritual, the body never surrenders; the stronger the pincers of norms and reason tighten on it and on gestures, the more pronounced other forms of gesturality become too—ludic ones (in jugglers), folkloristic and grotesque ones (in carnival), and finally mystic ones (in late-medieval pietists and flagellants).[34]

In order to arrange the body into the figure of a gesture, one needs to enact that gesture—to treat the body as artistic material, whereby art transforms the body into signs. But the body is not reduced to gesture here: in Kulik's work, Libera enacts the gesture of the muscular body, the body-as-edifice, the body inscribed in the structure of power.[35] Interestingly, the posture borrowed from *Archive of Gestures*, most likely expressing a gesture of surrender (although one that is not an image of a surrendering body), will not be shown to us in its entirety in *Garden*; as a result, the gesture, already "incomplete," is semantically reduced, with the plants adorning the different parts of the object becoming more important. Prior to being *détourned* it was a uniform gesture, a gesture-sign; now, in the new configuration of *Garden*, it reveals itself as divided. Plants outline/mark/perform the different parts—no longer of signs, but of the body. This is a cru-

33 Jacques Le Goff and Nicolas Truong, *Historia ciała w średniowieczu*, trans. Ireneusz Kania (Warsaw: Czytelnik, 2006), 126; originally published as *Une histoire du corps au Moyen âge* (Paris: Liana Levi, 2003).

34 Schmitt, quoted in Le Goff and Truong, *Historia ciała w średniowieczu*, 127.

35 For an interesting discussion of gestures, see Jeff Wall, "Gestus" in *Jeff Wall: Selected Essays and Interviews* (New York: Museum of Modern Art, 2007).

cial effect of the hijacking executed by Kulik: Libera's pose, originally from *Archive of Gestures*, is again embodied in *Garden*, for the plant elements introduce differentiating relationships within the (previously indivisible) body-sign. From the perspective of the culture of gestures, this means that Kulik again resignifies the male body, which was reduced in her previous works to a sign in the body-transgressing orders of forming and disciplining.

Détournements of Aestheticization

How does this resignification occur? The use of plant materials and the semantic context they convey matter a lot, of course, yet it is not only the attributes of naturalness or aesthetic-decorative organization that determine the intervention into cultural reifications of masculinity effected here; Kulik had accumulated a wealth of references, and she made sure that we remembered them. Based on material borrowed from earlier works, and on their ideological-aesthetic effect (masculinity exposed as submission in the military-nationalist order), *Garden détourns* the traditions of gestural culture, and when confronting these photo-collages, the viewer should bear in mind the structures that regulate the representation of male and female bodies in heterosexual and patriarchal culture. But the supreme "hijack," one that allows for a repetition responsible for the destabilization of the "performance" of gender in accord with phallocentric rules, consists of playing with the aestheticization of the male body.

Piotr Piotrowski discusses the issue of aestheticization in the context of Kulik's other works, referencing the traditional notion of aesthetics as beautification. "'Ennobling' a picture, aesthetics makes it less 'true,' yet far more enticing. It is aesthetics, as we know from Walter Benjamin, that makes politics attractive and propaganda more effective. [...] By aestheticizing politics, the authorities build up a screen, which, on the one hand, 'covers' the true face of reality, i.e. terror, while on the other hand, makes it useful."[36] Aestheticizing the signs of power, Kulik examines the ways in which

36 Piotrowski, "Between Siberia and Cyberia," 19.

power uses images to control society. In order to achieve its goal, aestheticization has to be based on various kinds of tension. In Kulik's *All the Missiles Are One Missile*, Piotrowski notes a tension "between the decorative, aesthetic structure of the *panneau* and the scene of execution shown in the 'stop-frame.'"[37] This is the tension that is most frequently enacted in Kulik's works: between decorativeness (ornamental function) of those elements that were usually the central object of the representation, and the brutality that detailed motif entails. It should be added that this brutality stems from the signs of violence, usually sampled from war-related and military iconography, which are evoked. In *From Siberia to Cyberia*, Kulik hijacked frames of TV footage (scenes of executions, monuments, leaders, flags, rallies, and religious and political festivals—next to porn, nature documentaries, and sports) and arranged them into panels, whereas in other works she has used the forms of mandalas, Gothic pointed arches, and oriental carpets.

This is not the case in *Garden*: the rich ornamentation familiar from Kulik's earlier works is gone; the artist achieves aesthetic tension in a different way. With their highly saturated hues, flowers are not a decorative element here: situated in the foreground, they are a meaning-producing figure, and the model's body becomes at best an equally important object. As critics stress, Kulik usually operates within two patriarchal systems: political (communist socialism) and religious (mainly Catholic), but they also point out the supra-historical nature of her photo-collage-marking system.[38] In this context, flowers do not separate us from historically situated signs so much as play a game with them—not directly, but via associations with Kulik's earlier works and through the aesthetic value of their decorativeness. Instead of historically meaningful objects, here we are dealing with objects of aesthetic contemplation, whose function is to adorn other objects. Libera is an adorned man—though uncostumed, without makeup, not campy at all, and yet with colorful flowers. Adornment seems to follow desire: the sign/gesture begins to function like the body—it "has" legs, arms, and gen-

37 Piotrowski, "Between Siberia and Cyberia," 21.
38 Piotrowski, "Od Syberii to Cyberii," 164.

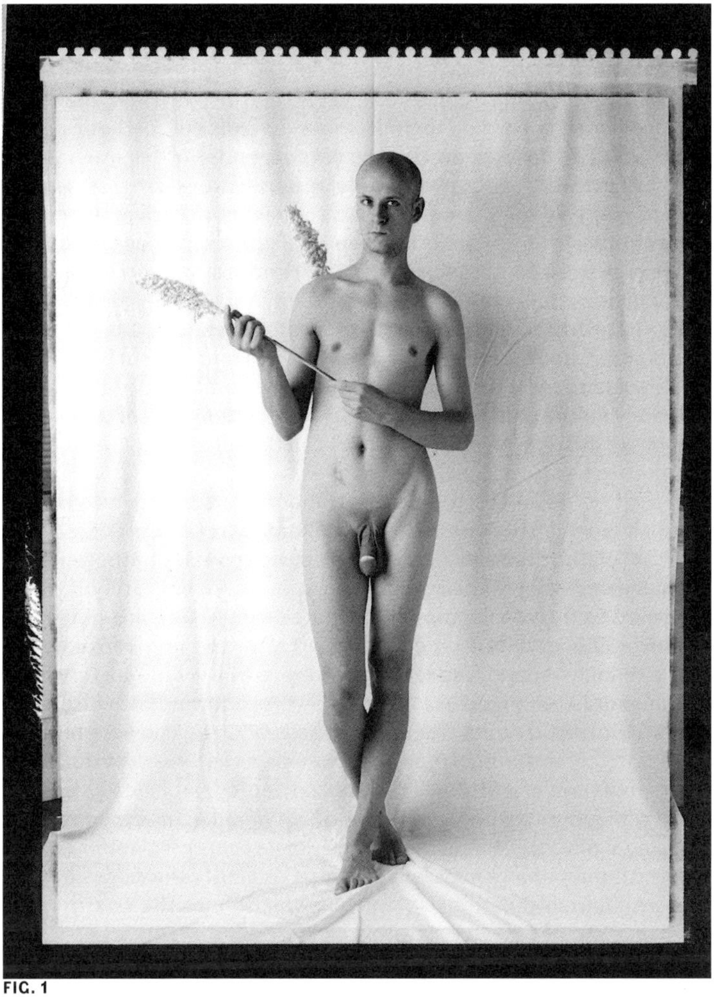

FIG. 1
KATARZYNA KOZYRA, *KARASKI*, 1992

itals; it loses transparency; it gains the weight of matter. Kulik hijacks the aesthetic modes used to stabilize gender identities, and shows their illusion: a nude male model is "adorned" with flowers—typically used to grace female bodies—and yet he neither turns feminine nor is represented according to the homosexual rules of aesthetic order. Kulik avoids being ensnared in the binary gender order; reenacting legitimate (traditional, gender-reifying and -naturalizing) strategies of representing the male body, she somewhat parodically *détourns* masculinity,[39] denying it both power and submissiveness, both heterosexuality and homosexuality. She renders incomprehensible those orders that seek to derive gender from an inner truth of the body. In *Garden* the body begins to resist both gestures and the plant forms signifying it, manifesting itself not as a uniform surface but as an object of recesses, cuts, and boundaries—in effect, of differences. The body as the sum total of differences—rather than of identification or identity—is an effect of what I call the hijacking of aestheticization processes by Kulik.

In order to explain the artist's strategy in greater detail, it is worth evoking the works of Katarzyna Kozyra: *Dance Lesson* and the related series *Boys*, consisting of videos and photographs. In both, the protagonists are dancing men (choreography again!), "adorned" only with vagina-imitating G-strings. Men are obviously feminized here, their bodies modelled after the homosexual aesthetic regime—something that is even more evident in *Karaski*, where a nude model, arranged in a "glamour" style, adorned with floral and plant elements, adopts "feminine" poses [FIG. 1]. The list could go on, but it's clear that the abovementioned works by Kozyra deal with masculinity by imitating the homosexual depiction of men as women (thus achieving a campy, glamour-y quality). Kulik, in turn, operates more speculatively, using the strategy of *détournement*, and does not reverse gender-hierarchy relationships or clarify the poses of gender-sexual identifications so much as she defines the coordinates

39 Judith Butler, *Gender Trouble: Feminism and the Subversion of Identity* (New York: Routledge, 1990).

(as it were) of the artistic modeling of the body, challenging the comprehensibility of the regulative practices responsible for the production of gender categories.

Translated by Marcin Wawrzyńczak

This text was originally published in Polish in Zagadnienia Rodzajów Literackich *61, no. 2 (126) (2018): 103–16.*

Agata Jakubowska is an associate professor and deputy director at the Department of Art History, Adam Mickiewicz University in Poznań. She runs—with Magdalena Radomska—the Piotr Piotrowski Center for Research on East-Central European Art (www.piotrpiotrowski-center.amu.edu.pl). She is the author of *Na marginesach lustra: Ciało kobiece w pracach polskich artystek* (On the Margins of the Mirror: The Female Body in Polish Women Artists' Works) (2004), *Portret wielokrotny dzieła Aliny Szapocznikow* (Multiple Portrait of Alina Szapocznikow's Œuvre) (2008), and editor of several books devoted to women artists: *Alina Szapocznikow: Awkward Objects* (2011), *Natalia LL: "Consumer Art" and Beyond* (2016), and *All-Women Art Spaces in Europe in the Long 1970s* (with Katy Deepwell, 2018). Over the last few years she has been working on a project devoted to the history of women-only exhibitions in Poland (www.wystawykobiet.amu.edu.pl). She is currently concentrating on a book devoted to the Polish sculptor Maria Pinińska-Bereś (1931–99).

PATTERNS: "IN A WAY, I BETRAY MYSELF"

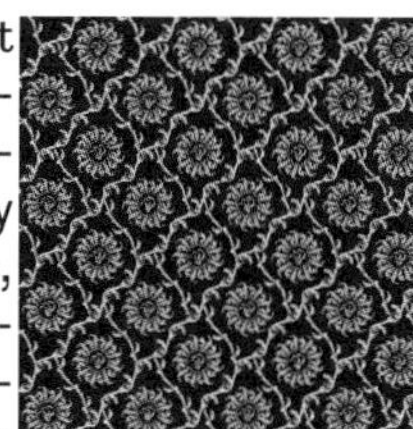
A

Zofia Kulik exhibited **PATTERNS** A (2007) for the first time at Galeria Le Guern in 2007. *Patterns* are—according to the simple and accurate description provided by the gallery—"her own variations of already existing designs, taken from various epochs, traditions, and cultural environments. She retains the basic structure of each pattern, making her own version of it, usually using the motifs which have appeared in her works before."[1] On the one hand, *Patterns* inscribe themselves well into Kulik's œuvre created after her split from KwieKulik, repeating its most characteristic features such as the medium of black-and-white photography; ornamental structure filled with a combination of human, floral, and other motifs; the multitude of elements; and the strict order in which they are arranged. One would easily attribute this work to Zofia Kulik. On the other hand, however, *Patterns* are significantly different. An interview conducted by Kamila Wielebska,

1 "Zofia Kulik—Patterns," curatorial note, Galeria Le Guern, accessed February 18, 2019, https://www.leguern.pl/en/exhibitions/Zofia-Kulik-Patterns/.

on the occasion of the abovementioned exhibition's opening, begins with a question that sounds as if it was expressing disappointment: "Why did you go in the direction of decorativeness? I can see here forms and motifs used in previous works, but the earlier content is missing."[2] This initial impression of disappointment disappears in the course of the interview, yet the artist herself says: "I did critical work, but at the moment I don't do it. In a way, I betray myself."

It is neither the ornamental character of the work nor its reference to craft that surprises in *Patterns*.[3] Ornament has been present in Kulik's work from the beginning of her solo practice. When, after having split from KwieKulik, she looked for new artistic forms, she focused her attention on mosaics, Gothic windows, altars, and—above all—carpets. She designed her works using these structures, and filled them with visual elements taken from the iconosphere of communist Poland and other totalitarian regimes. To underline the importance of the fact that her formal arrangements are based on traditional, ornamental structures, she included real carpets in her first solo shows. In *Visual Idioms of the Soc-Ages*, organized at the ZPAF Small Gallery in Warsaw in 1989 and at the Postmasters Gallery in New York City a year later, these hung next to the artist's collages [FIG. 1]. One could see the similarities, but also that Kulik's structures were filled with different content. Reviewers underlined that her works "developed as a protest against the rigid and dehumanizing aspects of communist rule."[4]

2 "W pewnym sensie zdradzam samą siebie: Z Zofią Kulik rozmawia Kamila Wielebska," unpublished, sent to me by the artist.

3 Kulik prefers to talk about ornamental character, not decorativeness. She explains: "I would rather not use the word decoration, because decoration is something that does not have order in it. Ornament, on the other hand, has a certain order, rules. If someone starts to make an ornamental pattern, he or she must first establish these geometric-composition rules." "W pewnym sensie zdradzam."

4 Catherine Maclay, "Patterns with Purpose: Decorative Works Hold Serious Messages," *Mercury News*, San Jose, California, October 1992. This is a review of the exhibition *Dark Decor*, organized by Independent Curators International (ICI), New York City; cooperation: Postmasters Gallery, New York City, 1992.

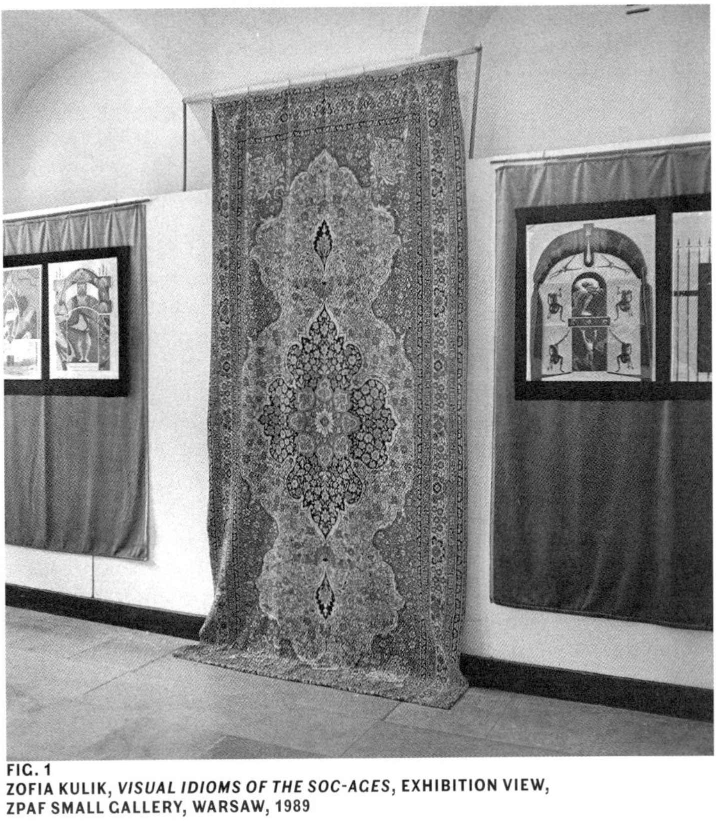

FIG. 1
ZOFIA KULIK, *VISUAL IDIOMS OF THE SOC-AGES*, EXHIBITION VIEW, ZPAF SMALL GALLERY, WARSAW, 1989

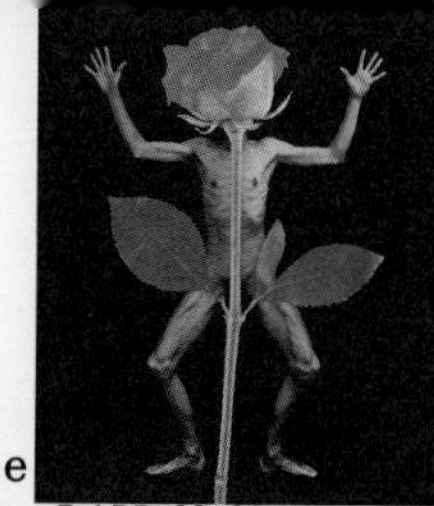

B / PP. 38–40

In comparison to works created in the 1990s, *Patterns* can seem banal. They are simpler—a segment composed of several motifs is repeated and covers a whole surface. They lack elements that have a direct political meaning, elements that could easily be related to communist and postcommunist conditions, which had been characteristic of Kulik's art. Their uncomplicated title offers no clue as to any deeper meaning of the work. They are accompanied by a text that links *Patterns* to the realm of design enterprise.[5] In it, the work is described as a set of samples offered to clients to view and to choose the design they want to buy in the quantity they wish. Yet, as I will try to demonstrate, *Patterns* are not anomalous in Kulik's art (although they bear many untypical features) but they mark an important moment in her career, when she reoriented her activities. The artist's focus moved from sociopolitical reality and an individual immersed in it, to what surrounded her in the direct environment—her garden, her family, and her archive. She still, however, remained loyal to the premises of her artistic practice, collecting and arranging, precisely and passionately.[6]

It was not in 2007—when the *Patterns* were exhibited for the first time—that Kulik's art changed: I perceive 2004 as marking a significant shift in her art, or at least in what she presented during exhibitions. That year at the Zachęta National Gallery of Art she showed the full version of *From Siberia to Cyberia*.[7] The work takes the form of a rectangle (21 meters long and 2.4 meters high) made up of 18,000 small photographs—TV screenshots of shows and films that the artist watched. The exhibition was accompanied by the release of a book supplementing the work, which contained

5 "Zofia Kulik—Patterns."

6 Tomasz Załuski, in his text published in this volume, also notices the important shift in Kulik's art after 2000, but he considers this in relation to a double artistic biography of Kulik: her work in the duo KwieKulik and her solo career. He writes that, after 2000, "the artist began to work on the massive documentation generated by KwieKulik," "using certain modes of practice from [her] individual career," and "brought her two biographies into a closer and more manifest dialogue with each other."

7 The first, smaller version was displayed during Kulik's solo exhibition at the National Museum in Poznań in 1999.

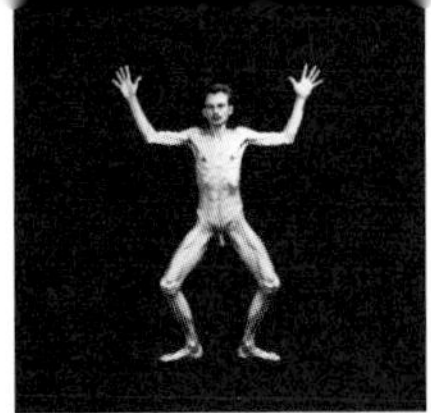

C / P. 20

descriptions of each frame.[8] Kulik had another show that year, also in Warsaw, at Galeria Le Guern, titled *Self-Portraits and the Garden*. While the former exhibition offered a continuation of threads that were already known to spectators, the latter presented Kulik's art from a new perspective. It did not necessarily show new elements in her art, but rather elements that had been present but somehow overlooked. One of them was self-representation—a series of self-portraits were shown (*Self-Portrait with a Flag* [1989], *The Splendor of Myself III* [1997], *Light Rose* [2000], *Land-escape* [2001]). Another element was the importance of floral motifs and the natural environment around the artist's house as a source of materials and also inspiration. For the first time, spectators could see the series **GARDEN (LIBERA AND FLOWERS)** B (1996–2004), consisting of eleven color (a rare exception in Kulik's art) plates, where the figure of the naked Libera—an element well-known from Kulik's critical works (**ARCHIVE OF GESTURES** C [1987–91])—was juxtaposed with a flower from her garden. In an interview published in the exhibition catalog, Kulik stressed the role of floral elements in her art by saying: "The floral-herbal elements built my works as much as the motifs of a naked body, architectural forms and TV images. The same thing happens in my self-portraits: my garment seems to be woven from various images, the majority of which are plants."[9]

One could think of these two completely different exhibitions organized by Kulik in the same year as separating two different periods of her work. *From Siberia to Cyberia*, which was in itself the culmination of a long process (Kulik began creating the piece in

8 Bożena Czubak and Zofia Kulik, eds., *Zofia Kulik: Od Syberii do Cyberii* (Warsaw: Zachęta National Gallery of Art, 2004). The exhibition traveled to the Bunkier Sztuki Gallery in Kraków.

9 "Self-Portrait: I Am, However, Myself, Not Somebody Else; Bożena Czubak Interviews Zofia Kulik," in *Zofia Kulik: Self-Portraits and the Garden*, ed. Bożena Czubak (Warsaw: Galeria Le Guern, 2004), 56.

1998), would close the more political and critical period in her art. *Self-Portraits* and *Garden* would indicate the opening of a new, more introverted period—private, rather than publicly oriented.[10]

In the abovementioned interview the artist says: "In 'Land-escape' this is a little like the state of transcendence and a little of absence. The motif of landscape over which my face is floating. And, certainly, the play of words in the title: scenery, ground, escape…."[11] Although the year 2004 is an important one in the history of postcommunist Poland—when the country joined the European Union—we can trace no reference to this or any other political event in the works Kulik exhibited at Galeria Le Guern and in the catalog accompanying the show; neither were any present in the exhibition of *From Siberia to Cyberia* organized during the same year. Direct references to particular events had never been present in Kulik's art, but what I mean here is that she seemed to have lost interest in politics and stopped accompanying the Polish transformation with her critical pieces; rather, she demonstrated her escapist (in a sense) attitude.

It is worth recalling that changes in Kulik's art have always resonated not only with political events but also with turbulence in her private life. As Angela Dimitrakaki rightly observes, writing about the beginning of Kulik's solo career: "this was happening in the late 1980s, when Kulik's world had accelerated: her personal reorientation, following the dissolution of KwieKulik, was matched by that of Poland and the upturn of the premises on which her art-life nexus had so far been built."[12] This can lead to the assumption that the changes around 2004 may also have had some personal causes. What might have been important for the artist was, for exam-

10 This encourages us to look at *From Siberia to Cyberia* from a more personal perspective, and to recall that she used images of TV screens shot in her kitchen while preparing meals. Kulik talks about this in "The Rebellion of a Neo-Avant-Garde Artist: An Interview with Zofia Kulik Conducted by Joanna Turowicz," *Kulik-KwieKulik Foundation*, accessed February 12, 2019, http://kulikzofia.pl/en/archiwum/bunt-neoawangardowej-artystki/. Originally published as "Bunt neoawangardowej artystki," *Artmix*, no. 9 (March 2005).

11 "Self-Portrait: I Am, However, Myself, Not Somebody Else," 50.

12 Angela Dimitrakaki, "The Struggle for Non-Alienation: Zofia Kulik's Work in Terms of Labor," in this volume.

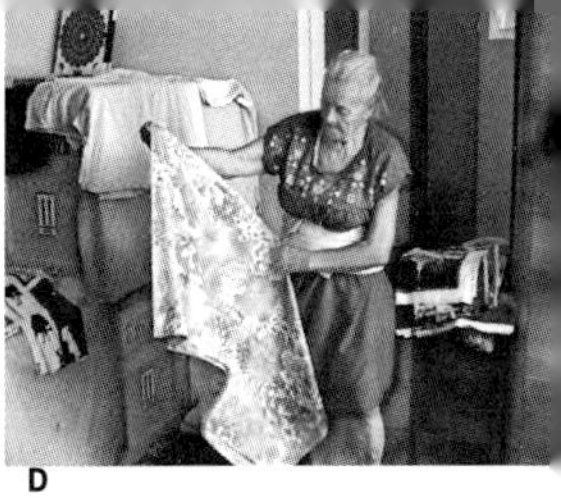
D

ple, the fact that in December 2003 her mother came back from the US, where she had lived for twenty-three years, and moved into the artist's house. She came with her collection of fabrics and her working habits. The tasks that Kulik's mother performed as a seamstress have always been important to the artist; in an interview, Kulik explains her interest in ornamental textiles, saying "As a girl, I would observe my mother, constantly bending over some fabric. She labored over patterns, adjusting models. I helped her a little."[13] And, speaking on the occasion of *Patterns*' premiere: "Since I can remember, pattern, ornament has always been present not only in my work, but also in my life."[14] Her mother's (and her collection's) return and constant presence in Kulik's house may have renewed the artist's interest in this legacy and encouraged the rethinking of its significance for her artistic practice. This was probably one of crucial inspirations for *Patterns*.

The *Patterns* exist in three formats now. One is the artist's book, published in 2007 by Dominik Art Edition. It consists of nine pages in a square format, each presenting one pattern. The publication makes one think of a sample book offered to the clients of upholstery, wallpaper, and carpet shops, corresponding in the best way with the idea behind the work presented above. It also resembles, more than Kulik's earlier works, her mother's collection. We can see the latter in one of the films made by the artist that form the series *Cultivating the Archive*, in **A SUM OF RAGS AND AN ARCHIVE NEXT DOOR** D (2017) (subtitled *Or, in Other Words, the Kingdom of Helena Kulik, Zofia's Mother, in Which the Archivist Grew Up*).[15] What the artist presents here is her mother Helena, in her room, examining various textiles—small pieces of fabric—lying on the floor, and discussing them with

13 "The Rebellion of a Neo-Avant-Garde Artist."

14 "Bzik kulturalny: Zofia Kulik" (2011), *Culture.pl*, accessed February 12, 2019, http://culture.pl/pl/wideo/bzik-kulturalny-zofia-kulik-wideo.

15 The film is dated 2017, but the artist used film materials shot in different periods.

her daughter, who stands behind the camera. Kulik asks Helena to present the samples one after another, in order to demonstrate that "there are many different ones."[16]

Kulik also made a larger version of the sample book, which extends from book format onto a wall, as each page/sample is 120×120 centimeters. She also created oblong pieces to be hung vertically, which are designed to resemble the samples found in shops that sell window dressings. As mentioned above, the artist imagined that she could make different versions of the work to order, to the design and size chosen by a client. To this day, no such order has been executed. When asked about it, the artist answered that "probably for practical reasons I did not go in this direction, because otherwise I would have to create a production workshop, which would be boring and depressing."[17] It is worth noticing that this practical reasoning, fully understandable, protects Kulik from losing control of the piece. One could imagine orders for dozens of square meters of particular designs, which would then be used to cover different walls or floors.[18] The *Patterns* are unusual in Kulik's œuvre, as the majority of the works previously created by the artist were based on closed structures with clearly defined centers and borders. Here we are dealing with an ornament that can be repeated an infinite number of times,[19] yet the versions of the work that exist are, conversely, finished works of art, where the composition is cut "suddenly" but still under control.

16 Another aspect present in these films is the relationship between how Kulik and her mother work. For more on this, see Agata Jakubowska, "Egzystencjalne i ekonomiczne wymiary 'czynnościowania' Zofii Kulik i jej matki Heleny," *Miejsce: Studia nad sztuką i architekturą polską XX i XXI wieku*, no. 4 (2018): 12–24.

17 Kulik, e-mail to the author, December 7, 2018.

18 In this version, the work would have chance to affect the viewer in the way Kulik imagined when she said: "My desire is for the viewer to feel, when looking at the *Patterns*, as if they were visual melodies that are supposed to reach him or her on the basis of certain associations, on the basis of a little gaze at the surface of the lake or sea, so that s/he can feel this immensity," "Bzik kulturalny."

19 Such an open form is also characteristic of *From Siberia to Cyberia*, although here we do not have a repeated element. What they have in common in the possibility inscribed in the structure of these works to extend them endlessly.

Whatever size and format of *Patterns* we deal with, a double look is inscribed into the viewing process: from a distance—when you see a pattern itself, and at close range—to identify what it is built from. It is one of the features typical for compositions made by Kulik, who fills ornamental schemas with surprising content that is not visible from afar. In the interview mentioned at the beginning of this text, both the artist and the interviewer agree that, in the case of *Patterns*, this content is less political and critical in comparison with Kulik's earlier works. In fact, it is not related directly to the postcommunist condition, which the artist had concentrated on before, because elements from the iconosphere of the communist and other regimes are barely present. Yet a closer look at what constitutes the patterns makes us aware that the content here is also far from soothing.

A human motif has been present in Kulik's art from the beginning of her solo career, and in *Patterns* it also functions as a primary element of the compositions. Most of the human figures come from the collection created at the end of the 1980s, when Kulik photographed Zbigniew Libera in multiple poses.[20] This creates a clear relationship between *Patterns* and other works in which she used elements from this part of her archive. Kulik's art from the 1990s, featuring the multiplied figure of a naked man who was closed—as if trapped—in ornamental structures, has been interpreted as dealing with the problem of subordination. It has been considered as referring to the relationship between the power of totalitarian regimes and the individual. As Ewa Lajer-Burcharth wrote: "Kulik's male protagonists [...] represent the idea of the communist subject as the function of a *system*—neither an anonymous state apparatus nor a mere ideological abstraction, but rather a system of cultural signification defined as a repertory of specific signs and poses."[21] Yet this interpretation, as much as it is correct, appears to be inadequate, or too narrow in the case of *Patterns*. Kulik often repeats that she is interested in subordination, but she also usually expresses

20 The figure of a naked woman is also used in the *Patterns* sometimes.

21 Ewa Lajer-Burcharth, "Old Histories: Zofia Kulik's Ironic Recollections," in *New Histories*, ex. cat. (Boston: Institute of Contemporary Art, 1996), 124. Reprinted in this volume.

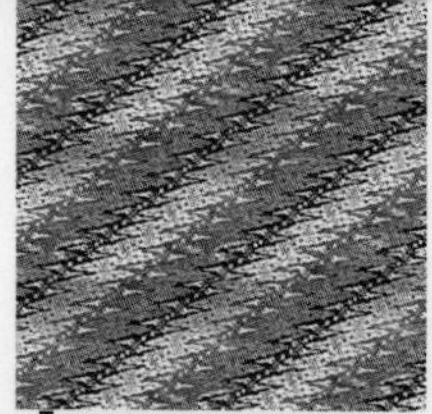

E

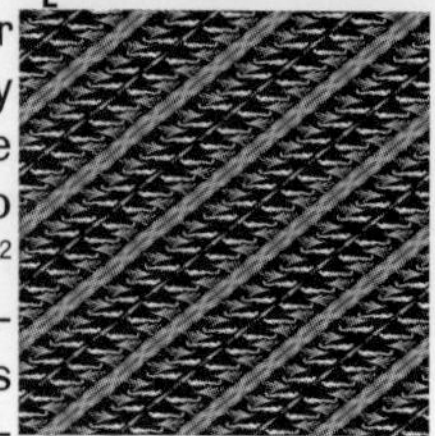

F

her uncertainty as to who or what subordinates her (or to what and whom she subordinates herself). Already in 1989 she asked: "But in front of whom is one to be humiliated nowadays? There is no god, there is no leader, there is no mystery. So whom is one to serve?"[22] This uncertainty has often been ignored by interpreters but cannot be disregarded in the case of *Patterns*, as here we are not offered an easy explanation. Some elements that had clear meanings in her earlier works even lose them here.

In *Pattern 3*, subtitled *Batik-Home*, Kulik uses the figure of a naked man, laying straight, shot in profile. The figure is placed alternately with a small plant, ripped out including the roots. Strips consisting of the man and the plant are separated with lines made of spears (the same photo, repeated the required number of times) and—alternately—an enigmatic wider strip.[23]

This pattern seems of special importance, as it is based on a fabric that appeared in Kulik's early work—in *Human Motif* a reproduction of the original was placed as if at the base of the Palace of Culture and Science in Warsaw. Kulik used this—a piece of **FABRIC** E (NO DATE) with a floral design—to imitate a photo of a crowd standing in front of the Palace. In **PATTERN 3** F (2007) we see this "photo" as if enlarged in such a way that we can distinguish the separate elements it consists of. Yet it is also deprived of the relation to the Palace, and as such becomes a statement that is related not so much to the particular geohistorical circumstances, but bears a more universal meaning.

Another pattern—*Pattern 4*—based on a floral design taken from the Chinese tradition (the artist did not pay much attention to the particular sources in most cases) is also built from human and floral motifs, and photographs of things. Once again we see a naked male figure, this time leaning forward as if in a fistfight, but

22 Kulik, "Self-Commentary," 1989. This text was published in the catalog of the *Idioms of the Soc-Ages* exhibition, organized at Galeria Labirynt in Lublin, Poland, in 1990.

23 According to the artist these are photographs of clouds. E-mail to the author, February 7, 2019.

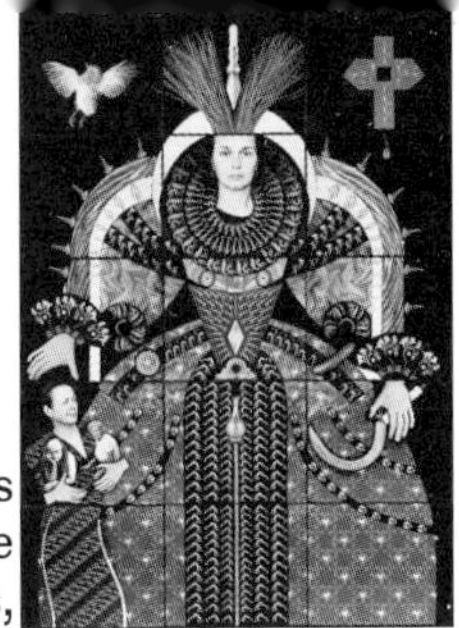

G

there are also dried thistle leaves and a sickle. It is worth paying attention to the sickle, as it had become one of the important elements in Kulik's compositions, whose semantic reallocations are meaningful for the changes in Kulik's art. The most significant shift took place in the self-portrait created in 2007, titled **THE SPLENDOR OF MYSELF V** [G (2007)]. This was the fifth version of the self-portrait in which Kulik presented herself as a queen on a throne, wearing a splendid dress that resembled the robes worn at royal courts, and confronted the viewer with her majestic presence.[24] This fifth version is the one that introduces major changes: Kulik changed the design of her dress—I will come to this shortly—and her attributes. In the first four versions, instead of the royal insignia, she has in her hands a cucumber and a weed (the "puff-ball" head of a dandelion). In the fifth version the puff ball was replaced by a composition consisting of three figures: she holds her mother and her ex-partner (Kwiek) in her arms[25] and a sickle takes the place of the cucumber. In the earlier versions the sickle was placed to the left of the artist's head. This looks like an emblem on a wall, probably taken from the communist symbol of worker-peasant alliance (the hammer and sickle). In *The Splendor of Myself V*, instead of the sickle there is a dead bird to the left of the artist's head, and the sickle now sits in the artist's left hand. This becomes a dangerous object in the hands of a proud queen—a tool in the hands of a woman who is presented not as being subjugated to the sickle, but being able to utilize it. The translocation of this element strengthens the image of Kulik as a woman in power. We could read it as the taking over of a political weapon, but now—in 2017—it seems to lose its political dimension. The artist explains that the sickle was "bought in a garden shop," yet had "never been used in a garden,"[26] but to use this as an argument would be false, as many elements from her

24 *The Splendor of Myself I–III* in 1997, *The Splendor of Myself IV* in 2005.

25 Both Helena Kulik, who came back from the US after retirement, and Przemysław Kwiek lived at the time in the house owned by Kulik. This portrait also replaced the figure of the naked man present in each of the first three versions.

26 *The Splendor of Myself V (Mother, Daughter, Partner)*, ex. cat. (Berlin: ŻAK BRANICKA, 2008).

immediate, private surroundings acquire political meaning in her works. The change rests more in the confrontation, in the work, of the sickle and a "family portrait," which may suggest battles other than political ones.

The Splendor of Myself V is worth recalling in a relation to *Patterns* not only because of a role the sickle plays in the composition. The dresses in all five versions of the work are composed of (or "sewn" from) a large number of elements that came from Kulik's photo archive. Yet, where in the case of versions one to four, Kulik created her dress using multiple-exposure technique, here she utilized her *Patterns*, ready-to-use ornaments.

When Kulik began her solo career she experimented with the technique of photomontage. Some of her first works were traditional collages in which she cut and glued fragments of different photos. Yet she also elaborated a new, cleaner technique of photocollage, which was used to make most of her pieces. The basis for each work was a precise drawing, transformed into a stencil by dividing it into smaller fields that could be opened and closed, one after another. In the darkroom Kulik put photo paper under the stencil, uncovered a small field, and exposed an image designated for the particular field (from the appropriate negative). After exposing the details one by one, she put the paper into a developer. For the *Patterns* she changed her technique—she decided to use a computer instead of the traditional photographic method. The negatives were scanned, and the ornaments were created using a computer program. This enabled the repetition of each segment numerous, unlimited times, in a simple way, without the necessity to make each ornament separately, which would have been necessary with the old technique.

What lies behind this change of Kulik's technique is the decision to use new, more accessible means that make her work easier and the results more accurate. As the artist explained: "I used templates and I exposed onto photo paper many times, but it was not possible to achieve precision there, i.e. the approximation of one image to another in such a way that they almost touch each other, and at the same time not to make certain mistakes. Not to mention the fact that it would be backbreaking work to duplicate segments in such a large number."[27] Yet this decision gains additional meaning when perceived in the context of the development of Kulik's career. She reached for the new technique at a time when it was no longer the creation of new works that mattered most, but "cultivating the archive," to use the title of Kulik's film series mentioned above.

In another text I analyzed *The Splendor of Myself*, paying attention to the fact that Kulik's dress is designed in such a way as to turn attention from herself onto the wealth of images and the mastery of composition.[28] She presents herself as a self-reliant woman artist—increasingly so with each version of the work—who is in possession of this wealth, capable of mastering it, but also—which is of great importance—responsible for it. The *Patterns* seem to be entertaining in comparison to the earlier pieces, yet they were created at the moment when she decided to devote her time and energy to working on archives—her own and that of KwieKulik. The *Patterns* mark some kind of release from the "necessity" to visualize the postcommunist condition, and offer the possibility of elaborating other aspects of her life and work. Simultaneously, they reveal that what Zofia Kulik wrote in 1989 remains in force: "Ordering and submission constitute compulsion, so strong for me, to behave and work in so-called life and so-called art."[29]

27 "Bzik kulturalny."
28 Jakubowska, "The Splendor of Myself," *View: Theories and Practices of Visual Culture*, no. 23 (2019): http://www.pismowidok.org/en/archive/power-of-women/zofia-kulik.-the-splendor-of-myself.
29 Kulik, "1989," in *Zofia Kulik: Idioms of the Soc-Ages*, ex. cat. (Lublin: Galeria Labirynt, 1989).

ZOFIA KULIK

COATLICUE
1961, plaster sculpture, 62×26×19 cm. **P.168**

INSTEAD OF SCULPTURE (ZAMIAST RZEŹBY)
1968–71 (digitized 2015), slide show sequence, 31:55. **P.13, P.169, P. 296**

COMBINATORIAL DRAWINGS (RYSUNKI KOMBINATORYCZNE)
1969–70, ink drawing on tracing paper, 18×13 cm each. **P.55**

LONDON, FROM THE SERIES INTERVENTIONS IN PHOTOGRAPHS (LONDYN, Z SERII: INTERWENCJE W FOTOGRAFIE)
1969–71, activities on black-and-white photographs, ink, plasticine, watercolor, slides. **P.275**

RAG DUPLICATE OF A MARBLE COPY OF MICHELANGELO'S MOSES (SZMACIANY DUPLIKAT MARMUROWEJ KOPII RZEŹBY MOJŻESZA MICHAŁA ANIOŁA)
1971 (reconstructed 2002), *rag-mâché*: textile, bone glue, resin, 260×120×110 cm. **P.14, P.169**

LETTER FROM MILAN (LIST Z MEDIOLANU)
1972, diapositives. **PP.15–17, P.83, P.194**

MAY DAY PARADE (POCHÓD PIERWSZOMAJOWY)
1972, diapositive. **P.88, P.194**

ALICE'S ADVENTURES IN FUCKED WONDERLAND (PRZYGODY ALICJI W PIERDOLONEJ KRAINIE CZARÓW)
1977, pencil, ink, paint, photograph on paper, own technique, 56×40 cm. **P.18**

ZOFIA KULIK'S BEGGING FOR FORGIVENESS (ZOFII KULIK BŁAGANIE O PRZEBACZENIE)
1978, performance, Dziekanka Gallery, Warsaw. **P.19, P.130**

Exterior view of Zofia Kulik's house
1982, Łomianki, Poland. **P.123**

BLACK TULLE, FROM THE SERIES GATES (CZARNY TIUL, Z SERII: BRAMY)
1987–89, collage: gelatin silver print, tulle, 60×50 cm. **P.21**

ARCHIVE OF GESTURES (ARCHIWUM GESTÓW)
1987–91, gelatin silver prints, variable dimensions. **P.20, P.250, P.297, P.311**

DRAWINGS, STUDIES OF GESTURES (RYSUNKI, STUDIUM GESTÓW)
1987–onwards, pencil and ink on paper, variable dimensions. **P.254**

HUMAN MOTIF I (MOTYW LUDZKI I)
1989, 48 gelatin silver prints, 252×480 cm. **P.22, P.23**

MASTER-BUILDER, FROM THE SERIES MEDALS (BUDOWNICZY, Z CYKLU: MEDALE)
1989, collage: gelatin silver print, transparent plastic sheet, 60×40cm. **P.24**

MONUMENT I (POMNIK I)
1989, collage: gelatin silver print, transparent plastic sheet, 90×25 cm. **P.25**

SELF-PORTRAIT WITH A FLAG (AUTOPORTRET Z FLAGĄ)
1989, collage: gelatin silver print, transparent plastic sheet, 50×50 cm. **COVER, P.26**

VISUAL IDIOMS OF THE SOC-AGES (IDIOMY SOCWIECZA)
1989, exhibition view, ZPAF Small Gallery, Warsaw. **P.309**

INTER-NATIONAL GOTHIC II (GOTYK MIĘDZY-NARODOWY II)
1990, 48 gelatin silver prints, 240×150 cm. **P.27**

THE GUARDIANS OF THE SPIRE (STRAŻNICY IGLICY)
1990, 12 gelatin silver prints, 240×150 cm. **P.28**

SELF-PORTRAIT WITH THE PALACE (MANDORLA) (AUTOPORTRET Z PAŁACEM [MANDORLA])
1990, collage: gelatin silver print, transparent plastic sheet, 60×50 cm. **P.29**

LIBERA–CHRISTMAS TREE (LIBERA–BOŻONARODZENIOWA CHOINKA)
1990, 9 gelatin silver prints, 180×150 cm. **P.30**

MAY DAY MASS (MSZA PIERWSZOMAJOWA)
1990, 12 gelatin silver prints, 240×150 cm. **P.31**

MARCH, MARCH, MARCH (MARSZ, MARSZ, MARSZ)
1990, 18 gelatin silver prints, 240×150 cm. **P.214**

FAVORITE BALANCE II (ULUBIONA RÓWNOWAGA II)
1991, 75 gelatin silver prints, 750×300 cm. **P.32**

ALL THINGS CONVERGE IN TIME AND SPACE; TO DISPERSE, TO CONVERGE, TO DISPERSE, AND SO ON I (WSZYSTKO SIĘ ZBIEGA W CZASIE I PRZESTRZENI, ABY SIĘ ROZPROSZYĆ, ABY SIĘ ZBIEC, ABY SIĘ ROZPROSZYĆ. NO I TAK DALEJ I)
1992, 5 gelatin silver prints, 150×150 cm. **P.33**

MYSELF, POPPIES, AND THE JOKE (JA, MAKI I ŻART)
1992, gelatin silver print, 50×50 cm. **P.201**

ALL THE MISSILES ARE ONE MISSILE (WSZYSTKIE POCISKI SĄ JEDNYM POCISKIEM)
1993, 85 gelatin silver prints, 300×850 cm. **PP.34–35**

KURGANS OF FAME AND INFAMY (KURHANY SŁAWY I NIESŁAWY)
1993, illuminated Plexiglas, variable dimensions. **P.36, P.201**

TWO DRAPERIES (DWIE DRAPERIE)
1993, installation: nylon and stretch velvet textiles, 120×160 cm. **P.279**

FACADE OF 500 EXPOSURES (FASADA 500 NAŚWIETLEŃ)
1995, 55 gelatin silver prints, 300×550 cm. **P.153**

MONSTRANCE I, FROM THE SERIES COLUMNS (MONSTRANCJA I, Z CYKLU: KOLUMNY)
1995, 3 gelatin silver prints, 150×50 cm. **P.37**

MOON-SKULL, FROM THE SERIES COLUMNS (KSIĘŻYCOWA CZASZKA, Z CYKLU: KOLUMNY)
1995, 3 gelatin silver prints, 150×50 cm. **P.37**

GARDEN (LIBERA AND FLOWERS) (OGRÓD [LIBERA I KWIATY])
1996–2004, archival inkjet print, variable dimensions. **PP.38–40, P.288, P.310**

THE SPLENDOR OF MYSELF III (WSPANIAŁOŚĆ SIEBIE III)
1997, 9 gelatin silver prints, 180×150 cm. **P.41**

ETHNIC WARS. LARGE VANITAS STILL LIFE (WOJNY ETNICZNE. LARGE VANITAS STILL LIFE)
1997–2017, archival inkjet prints, variable dimensions. **P.44, P.211**

FROM SIBERIA TO CYBERIA (OD SYBERII DO CYBERII)
1998–2004, multiple-exposure black-and-white photographs, 240×2100 cm. **PP.42–43, P.181, PP.262–65**

AUTOBIOGRAPHICAL AGGREGATE (AGREGAT AUTOBIOGRAFICZNY)
2000, installation, 240×1400×105 cm. **P.73**

LAND-ESCAPE
2001, 9 gelatin silver prints, 180×150 cm. **P.45**

FROM THE KWIEKULIK ARCHIVE (DETAIL 2) (Z ARCHIWUM KWIEKULIK [DETAL 2])
2005, photocopies, collage, 140×100 cm. **P.46**

AMBASSADORS OF THE PAST (MADE IN GDR, USSR, CZECHOSLOVAKIA, AND POLAND) (AMBASADOROWIE PRZESZŁOŚCI [MADE IN GDR, USSR, CZECHOSLOVAKIA, AND POLAND])
2006, archival inkjet print, 210×243 cm. **P.47**

THE SPLENDOR OF MYSELF V (WSPANIAŁOŚĆ SIEBIE V)
2007, 15 gelatin silver prints, 250×180 cm. **P.317**

PATTERN 5 (MORRIS 22), FROM THE SERIES PATTERNS (DESENIE 5 [MORRIS 22], Z SERII DESENIE)
2007, archival inkjet print, variable dimensions. Reproduced in the unique publication

Patterns 1-2-3-4-5-7-8-9 (edition of 35), published by Dominik Art Edition, Kraków **P.48**

PATTERN 8 (MORRIS 16–1), FROM THE SERIES PATTERNS (DESENIE 8 [MORRIS 16–1], Z SERII DESENIE)

2007, archival inkjet print, variable dimensions. **P.307**

PATTERN 3 (BATIK-HOME), FROM THE SERIES PATTERNS (DESENIE 3 [BATIK-HOME), Z SERII DESENIE]

2007, archival inkjet print, variable dimensions. **P.316**

KYOTO: HOW KULIK, WITHOUT LEAVING HOME, EXPLAINS HER WORK TO AN AUDIENCE THOUSANDS OF MILES AWAY AND SEEKS OUT A RELATIONSHIP WITH A JAPANESE ARTIST (KIOTO: JAK KULIK OBJAŚNIA SWOJĄ TWÓRCZOŚĆ PUBLICZNOŚCI ODDALONEJ O TYSIĄCE KILOMETRÓW I SZUKA ZWIĄZKÓW Z JAPOŃSKĄ ARTYSTKĄ NIE RUSZAJĄC SIĘ Z DOMU)

2016, film, 16:14. **P.118**

CULTIVATING THE ARCHIVE, OR, IN OTHER WORDS, A PERFORMATIVE WORK (KULTYWOWANIE ARCHIWUM, CZYLI ROBOTA PERFORMATY-WNA)

2016, film, 15:38. **P.75, P.134, COVER**

A SUM OF RAGS AND AN ARCHIVE NEXT DOOR: THE KINGDOM OF HELENA KULIK, ZOFIA'S MOTHER, IN WHICH THE ARCHIVIST GREW UP (SUMA SZMAT I ARCHIWUM ZA ŚCIANĄ, CZYLI KRÓLESTWO HELENY KULIK, MATKI ZOFII, W KTÓRYM DORASTAŁA ARCHIWISTKA)

2017, film, 7:40. **P.139, P.313**

THE LOST SCULPTURE AND RETURN TO SCULPTING, OR, IN OTHER WORDS, WET CLAY IN THE HANDS OF THE ARCHIVIST (UTRACONA RZEŹBA I POW-RÓT DO RZEŹBIENIA, CZYLI MOKRA GLINA W RĘKACH ARCHIWISTKI)

2017, film, 16:55. **P.273**

OTHER ARTISTS

G.D. Alekseev

CALLING LEADER (PRIZYVAYUSHCHIY VOZHD')

1924, reproduction from R. J. Abolina, *Lenin in Russian Visual Art*, Moscow, 1987. **P.155**

Oskar Hansen

A DREAM OF WARSAW (SEN WARSZAWY)

2005, exhibition view, Foksal Gallery Foundation, photograph by Jan Smaga, courtesy Foksal Gallery Foundation. **P.193**

Katarzyna Kozyra

KARASKI

1992, black-and-white photography series, variable dimensions, courtesy Katarzyna Kozyra Foundation. **P.303**

KwieKulik

ACTIVITIES WITH DOBROMIERZ (DZIAŁANIA Z DOBROMIERZEM)

1972–74 (digitized 2008), 48 gelatin silver prints, packing paper, courtesy Zofia Kulik and Kulik-KwieKulik Foundation. **P.61, P.170**

KWIEKULIK CIRCLE (KOŁO KWIEKULIK),

1976, 8 gelatin silver prints, typewriter text on paper, 48×25 cm, courtesy Zofia Kulik and Kulik-KwieKulik Foundation. **P.70**

THE MONUMENT WITHOUT A PASSPORT (POMNIK BEZ PASZPORTU)

1978, archival inkjet print, variable dimensions, courtesy Zofia Kulik and Kulik-KwieKulik Foundation. **P.161**

SUPERMARKET

1981, Stuttgart, video, 7:37, courtesy Zofia Kulik and Kulik-KwieKulik Foundation. **P.217**

POLISH DUO (POLSKI DUET)

1984, performance, Dziekanka Gallery, Warsaw, courtesy Zofia Kulik and Kulik-KwieKulik Foundation. **P.174**

AK KINGA PLAQUE—EARNING AND CREATING (PŁYTA AK KINGA—ZARABIANIE I TWORZENIE)

1974, PDDiU and PSP Atelier on Findlandzka Street, Warsaw, archival inkjet print, courtesy Zofia Kulik and Kulik-KwieKulik Foundation. **P.107**

ACTIVITY FOR THE HEAD: THREE ACTS (DZIAŁANIE NA GŁOWĘ: TRZY ODSŁONY)

1978, *Performance and Body*, Labrynt Gallery, Lublin, photograph by Andrzej Polakowski, courtesy Zofia Kulik and Kulik-KwieKulik Foundation. **P.136**

ARTISTS' BOOKS, POSTERS, PRINTS, AND CATALOGS

1985, exhibition view, *Contemporary Art from Poland*, Walter Philips Gallery, Banff, courtesy Zofia Kulik and Kulik-KwieKulik Foundation. **P.242**

Dóra Maurer

PRIVATE MAY DAY DEMONSTRATION IN AN ARTIFICIAL FIELD (V. MÁJUS 1-JEI FELVONULÁSA MESTERSÉGES TALAJON)

1971, paper, glued on fiberboard, photo, paint (in pulverized form), docubrom, newspaper, 69×88 cm, Hungarian National Gallery Collection, courtesy the artist. **P.87**

Tomasz Sikorski

1978, dispatches for *La Post/Avanguardia* by Przemysław Kwiek, left, and by Zofia Kulik, right, Mospan Gallery, Warsaw, courtesy Zofia Kulik and Kulik-KwieKulik Foundation. **P.113**

1978, Andrzej Partum putting a pebble in his mouth, Mospan Gallery, Warsaw, courtesy Zofia Kulik and Kulik-KwieKulik Foundation. **P.113**

Bálint Szombathy

LENIN IN BUDAPEST (LENIN BUDAPESTEN)

1972, silver gelatin print on barited paper, Ludwig Múzeum Collection, courtesy the artist. **P.89**

Anastazy B. Wiśniewski

1971, catalog entry for Zofia Kulik, the Dreamers' Congress, courtesy Zofia Kulik and Kulik-KwieKulik Foundation. **P.110**

ZOFIA KULIK: METHODOLOGY, MY LOVE

Editor
Agata Jakubowska
Series Editor
Katarzyna Szotkowska-Beylin
Managing Editor
Meagan Down
Translations
Marcin Wawrzyńczak (texts by Anna Kałuża, Dorota Łuczak, Wiktoria Szczupacka)
Ewa Kanigowska-Gedroyć (text by Luiza Nader)
Copyedited by
Darren Durham
Proofread by
Alan Lockwood
Design concept and layout
Ludovic Balland Typography Cabinet, Basel
Typesetting
Marcin Klinger, Studio Temperówka, Warsaw
Prepress
Krzysztof Krzysztofiak
Typeface
Ludwig Pro
Printed by
EPEdruk Sp. z.o.o.
Konwiktorska 9
00–216 Warsaw
Cover photographs
Front cover: *Self-Portrait with a Flag*, 1989
Back cover: *Cultivating the Archive, or, in Other Words, a Performative Work*, 2016
Insert
Detail of Zofia Kulik's archive, 2019, photograph by the artist
Acknowledgements
The editor would like to express special gratitude to the Kulik-KwieKulik Foundation for their invitation to work on this publication; and to the authors for their insightful readings of Zofia Kulik's work.

The Kulik-KwieKulik Foundation warmly acknowledges Weronika Bachman-Bogusz and Asia Żak Persons; additional special thanks are extended to Katarzyna Kulczyk, for her generous support during the initial stage of this project.

The Museum of Modern Art in Warsaw gratefully acknowledges permission to reprint the following texts: "Zofia Kulik: From Warsaw to Cyberia" by Sarah G. Wilson, first published in *Centropa* 1, no. 3 (September 2001); "Old Histories: Zofia Kulik's Ironic Recollections" by Ewa Lajer-Burcharth, first published in *New Histories*, ex. cat. (Boston: Institute of Contemporary Art, 1996); "What Do Archives Forget? Memory and Histories, *From the Archive of KwieKulik*" by Luiza Nader, first published in *A Story Differently Told*, ex. cat. (Gdańsk: Łaźnia Centre for Contemporary Art, 2008); and "Zofia Kulik's Performed Archives" by Katarzyna Ruchel-Stockmans, first published in *Images Performing History: Photography and Representations of the Past in European Art after 1989* (Leuven: Leuven University Press, 2015).

Publisher
Museum of Modern Art in Warsaw
Pańska 3
00-124 Warsaw
www.artmuseum.pl
ISBN: 978-83-64177-59-0

Distributed by
The University of Chicago Press
www.press.uchicago.edu

The Museum of Modern Art in Warsaw is funded by the Ministry of Culture and National Heritage:

Ministry of Culture and National Heritage of the Republic of Poland.

The premises and selected projects are funded by the City of Warsaw:

fall in love with warsaw

Patron of the Museum and the collection:

EY

Strategic partner of the Museum:

ERGO HESTIA Najwyższy standard ochrony

ARTYSTYCZNA PODRÓŻ HESTII

Legal advisor:

IDZP more than law

Kulik
KwieKulik
Foundation

The Kulik-KwieKulik Foundation was established to preserve the artistic accomplishments of Zofia Kulik and KwieKulik, and to open up new channels of cooperation between the Foundation and museums, collections, and other archives.

Operating on a national and international level, the Foundation has two main objectives: to manage the artist's estate and studio space, and to facilitate research into the work of Kulik and KwieKulik in light of current perspectives.

www.kulik-kwiekulik.com

BOOKS

THE MUSEUM UNDER CONSTRUCTION BOOK SERIES

No. 1 **1968–1989: POLITICAL UPHEAVAL AND ARTISTIC CHANGE**
Edited by Claire Bishop & Marta Dziewańska
Museum of Modern Art in Warsaw, 2009

The texts assembled in this reader are a selective record of presentations from the "1968–1989" seminar, held as a comparative reflection on the artistic significance of 1968, the political transformation of 1989, and methods of communication in art.

ISBN 978-83-92404-40-8

No. 2 **ION GRIGORESCU: IN THE BODY OF THE VICTIM**
Edited by Marta Dziewańska
Museum of Modern Art in Warsaw, 2010

This book is an attempt to read the work of one of the most charismatic and original artists from the former Eastern Bloc, who worked in relative isolation until 1989, and whose art can be viewed in relation to similar positions artists have taken in other parts of the world.

ISBN 978-83-92404-41-5

No. 3 **WARSZAWA W BUDOWIE 2009**
[Warsaw Under Construction 2009]
Edited by Marcel Andino-Velez
Museum of Modern Art in Warsaw, 2010

This book is a record of events that took place as part of the "Warsaw Under Construction" festival's first edition, focused on design, architecture, and town planning, and attempting to capture the spirit and creative energy that had then begun taking over the city. Book in Polish language.

ISBN 978-83-92404-42-2

No. 4 **AS SOON AS I OPEN MY EYES I SEE A FILM: EXPERIMENT IN THE ART OF YUGOSLAVIA IN THE 1960s AND 1970s**
Edited by Ana Janevski
Museum of Modern Art in Warsaw, 2010

This book is inspired by the first exhibition organized by the museum. It is a journey to a country that has ceased to exist, but which gave rise to the most important art myth in our part of Europe: the myth of radical art.

ISBN 978-83-92404-43-9

No. 5 **ALINA SZAPOCZNIKOW: AWKWARD OBJECTS**
Edited by Agata Jakubowska
Museum of Modern Art in Warsaw, 2011

Seen as a great artist in Poland, elsewhere Alina Szapocznikow (1926–73) has remained relatively unknown. Today she enjoys the status of a discovery, her sculpture entering museum collections worldwide. An artist who always put herself in the difficult position of pioneer heading towards the new and unknown, in 1972, near the end of her life, she confessed: "As for me, I produce awkward objects." Here that life and work is addressed by Griselda Pollock, Sarah Wilson, and Ernst van Alphen, among others.

ISBN 978-83-92404-46-0

No. 6 **LOVELY, HUMAN, TRUE, HEARTFELT: THE LETTERS OF ALINA SZAPOCZNIKOW AND RYSZARD STANISŁAWSKI 1948–1971**
Edited by Agata Jakubowska & Katarzyna Szotkowska-Beylin
Translated by Jennifer Croft
Museum of Modern Art in Warsaw, 2012

The previously unpublished correspondence between Alina Szapocznikow and Ryszard Stanisławski, a woman of increasing importance in twentieth-century art and a man who was an eminent critic and museum director.

ISBN 978-83-93381-86-9

No. 7 **POST-POST-SOVIET? ART, POLITICS & SOCIETY IN RUSSIA AT THE TURN OF THE DECADE**
Edited by Marta Dziewańska, Ekaterina Degot & Ilya Budraitskis
Museum of Modern Art in Warsaw, 2013

By placing emerging artists in their political and social contexts, this book attempts to confront the activist scene that has arisen in today's art world in Russia. Includes criticism by writers and scholars, and an extensive timeline of the artistic and sociopolitical context.

ISBN 978-83-93381-84-5

No. 8 **OSKAR HANSEN: OPENING MODERNISM**
Edited by Aleksandra Kędziorek & Łukasz Ronduda
Museum of Modern Art in Warsaw, 2014

This book analyzes diverse aspects of the architectural, theoretical, and didactical œuvre of Oskar Hansen (1922–2005), a Polish member of Team 10, and chronicles the impact of his theory of Open Form on architecture, urban planning, experimental film, and the visual arts in postwar Poland.

ISBN 978-83-64177-05-7

No. 9 **TEAM 10 EAST: REVISIONIST ARCHITECTURE IN REAL EXISTING MODERNISM**
Edited by Łukasz Stanek
Museum of Modern Art in Warsaw, 2014

Team 10 East never existed. This volume develops that term as a conceptual tool to discuss the work of Team 10 members and fellow travelers from socialist countries—such as Oskar Hansen of Poland and Charles Polónyi of Hungary, along with a number of architects from Czechoslovakia and Yugoslavia.

ISBN 978-83-64177-03-3

No. 10 **ANDRZEJ WRÓBLEWSKI: RECTO/VERSO**
Edited by Éric de Chassey & Marta Dziewańska
Museum of Modern Art in Warsaw, 2015

One of Poland's preeminent postwar artists, Andrzej Wróblewski (1927–57) created a highly individual and prolific form of abstract and figurative painting. His output reflects the original solutions he devised to address the personal and public issues of his time, in ways that are very relevant today and that continue to inspire artists.

ISBN 978-83-64177-16-3

No. 11 **MARIA BARTUSZOVÁ: PROVISIONAL FORMS**
Edited by Marta Dziewańska
Museum of Modern Art in Warsaw, 2015

Working alone behind the Iron Curtain, Maria Bartuszová (1936–96) was one of a number of female artists who not only experimented formally and embarked intuitively on new themes, but who, because of a position at odds with mainstream modernist trends, remained in isolation or in marginalized positions. This book deftly reveals how Bartuszová experimented with materials, never hesitating to treat tradition, accepted norms, and trusted techniques as simply transitory and provisional.

ISBN 978-83-64177-26-2

No. 12 **POINTS OF CONVERGENCE: ALTERNATIVE VIEWS ON PERFORMANCE**
Edited by Marta Dziewańska & André Lepecki
Museum of Modern Art in Warsaw, 2017

Always happening in the here and now, and yet implicating past and future, performance is a practice open to the unknown, constantly questioning its own subjects, materials, and languages. This book explores these ideas, potentials, and capacities of performance, stimulating new discussion between theorists and practitioners on the genealogies of performance, on unexpected lines of influence, and on off-center historiographies.

ISBN 978-83-64177-38-5

No. 13 **OBJECT LESSONS: ZOFIA RYDET'S SOCIOLOGICAL RECORD**
Edited by Krzysztof Pijarski
Museum of Modern Art in Warsaw, 2017

In 1978, Zofia Rydet (1911–97) began work on a monumental project that would come to be known as *Sociological Record:* photographing the people of Poland at their homes, she produced an extraordinary archive of around 27,000 negatives. The images include faces, interiors, furnishings, and more. *Object Lessons* aims to dispel the myths that have formed around the project in recent years. The essays here contextualize and interpret the *Record* from different perspectives, opening up the work to further inquiry as both an object of interpretation and a subject of theoretical interest. A celebration of Rydet's work, this book reminds us of photography's incredible power to provide a visual way of thinking and a provocative method for archiving the world.

ISBN 978-83-64177-37-8

No. 14 **THE OTHER TRANS-ATLANTIC: KINETIC AND OP ART IN EASTERN EUROPE AND LATIN AMERICA**
Edited by Marta Dziewańska, Dieter Roelstraete & Abigail Winograd
Museum of Modern Art in Warsaw, 2017

The Other Trans-Atlantic is attuned to the brief but historically significant period between 1950 and 1970, when the trajectories of the Eastern European and Latin American art scenes converged in a shared enthusiasm for kinetic and Op art. As the established axis of Paris, London, and New York became increasingly dominated by a succession of ideological monocultures—such as the master concepts of gesture and expression, Pop, or minimalism—another web of ideas was being spun, linking Warsaw, Moscow, and Zagreb, with Buenos Aires, Caracas, and São Paulo. These artistic practices were dedicated to a different set of aesthetic concerns: philosophies of art and culture dominated by notions of progress and science, the machine and engineering, construction and perception.

ISBN 978-83-64177-42-2

No. 15 **PAST DISQUIET: ARTISTS, INTERNATIONAL SOLIDARITY, AND MUSEUMS-IN-EXILE**
Edited by Kristine Khouri & Rasha Salti
Museum of Modern Art in Warsaw, 2018

The 1970s saw artists, curators, and militants gathering international collections of art, donated by artists, that traveled to established museums, galleries, and community spaces. These museums-in-exile were intended to incarnate the solidarity of artists with political causes and mobilize a wider public. *Past Disquiet* explores the histories of three such museums, plumbing the networks of artists who worked together to make them a reality. Starting with the forgotten International Art Exhibition for Palestine, the authors' research uncovered a global map of artists protesting the Pinochet dictatorship in Chile and the apartheid regime in South Africa, and supporting liberation struggles including that of the Palestinian people and the Sandinista revolution.

ISBN 978-83-64177-44-6

BOOKS

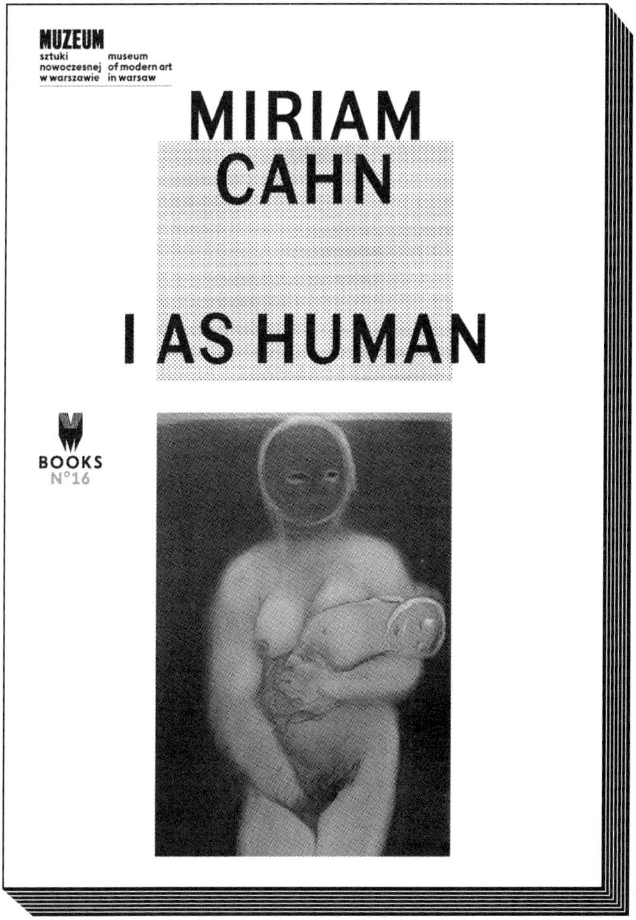

No. 16 **MIRIAM CAHN: I AS HUMAN**
Edited by Marta Dziewańska
Museum of Modern Art in Warsaw, 2019

A rebel and feminist, Swiss artist Miriam Cahn is one of the major artists of her generation. Known for her drawings and paintings, she also experiments with photography, moving images, and sculptures. Cahn's diverse body of work is disturbing and dreamlike, filled with striking human figures pulsing with an energy both passionate and violent. *MIRIAM CAHN: I AS HUMAN* looks at the artist's prolific and troubling œuvre from a variety of vantage points. It is an attempt to bring words and images together—an attentive contemplation of work that is heterogeneous, restless, and full of extreme emotions that coincide with our everyday lives: us, as humans.

ISBN 978-83-64177-55-2